God Give Us Christian Homes

Edited By Mike Willis

Truth Magazine Annual Lectures
June 26-29, 2006

truth
BOOKS
www.CEIbooks.com

Guardian of Truth Foundation
C E I Bookstore
220 S. Marion St. •Athens, AL 35611
1-855-49-BOOKS or 1-855-492-6657

ISBN 10: 1-58427-148-5

ISBN: 978-1-58427-148-2

truth
BOOKS
www.CEIbooks.com

Guardian of Truth Foundation
C E I Bookstore
220 S. Marion St. • Athens, AL 35611
1-855-49-BOOKS or 1-855-492-6657

Table of Contents

Foreword .... *v*

Part One — The Evening Lectures
Foundations of Family (Genesis 2), Steve Reeves 11
The Dangers of Marriage to Non-Christians, Lewis Willis 24
Godly Families in the Church, Chris Reeves 34
The Blessing of Godly Parents, Larry Hafley 61

Part Two — The Day Lectures
The Threat of Materialism to the Home, Randy Blackaby 83
Using the Family to Serve, Royce DeBerry 105
The Death of a Child, Tom Roberts 123
Things That Shouldn't End After Marriage, Morris Hafley 132
Dealing With Delinquent Children, Wayne Thurman 146
Choosing a Mate For Life, Frank Himmel 163
Teenagers and Sex, John Smith 179
Dealing With the Loss of a Parent, Jesse Flowers 202
Causes of Divorce, Stan Adams 222
Working With Young Adults, Kurt Jones 250
Evidences: The Historical Accuracy of the Bible, David Dann 266
Serving God in My Senior Years, Don Willis 285
Dealing With the Loss of a Spouse, Connie W. Adams 304
The Pain of Divorce, Art Adams 311
Overcoming the Ungodly Home, Ron Halbrook 333

Morning Classes
The Headship of Man, Steve Curtis 351
The Pain of a Wayward Child/Prodigal Son and Prodigal's Father,
    Melvin Curry 368
Teenagers For Christ, Steve Deaton 386

Open Forum:

Drawing the Young to Christ
    Jason Hardin.. 403
    Daniel Ruegg 419
    Steve Deaton 428

Ladies Classses

Winning My Children For Christ, Elma Monts 437
The Subjection of Women, Sandra Nite... 448
Overcoming An Abusive Parent, Sandy Willis 464

Foreword

We have chosen the theme "God Give Us Christian Homes" for the 2006 Truth Magazine Lecture series. We believe that a stable home is essential for the proper environment for rearing children, for a strong church, and for a strong nation. When the home crumbles its effects echo throughout the society. We believe that American homes are under attack and show ample evidence of serious problems for our society.

One can see the decay in the modern American family by looking at some relevant statistics. William J. Bennett, edited *The Index of Leading Cultural Indicators: American Society at the End of the Twentieth Century* (1999). Here are some of the interesting statistics:

- Between 1990 and 1997, the percentage of births that are out of wedlock increased 16 percent. Between 1960 and 1997, the percentage increased 511 percent (47).

- The percentage of births that are out of wedlock among blacks increased 200 percent between 1960 and 1997. Currently, more than two-thirds of all black children are born out of wedlock (48). In 1960, 5.3 percent of all births were out of wedlock. By 1997, the number had increased to 32.4 percent. Among whites, the percentage of out-of-wedlock births increased from 2.3 percent to 25.8 percent. Among blacks, the number increased from 23 percent to 69.2 percent (50).

- In 1994, for the first time in American history, more than half of all firstborn children were conceived or born out of wedlock (53).

- Between 1990 and 1998, the percentage of families that are headed by a single parent increased 13 percent. Between 1960 and 1998, the percentage of single-parent families more than tripled (57). Among industrialized nations, American has the largest percentage of single-parent familes (58).

- More than one-third (36 percent) of American children in 1990 were living apart from their biological fathers, an increase from 17.5 percent in 1960.

- Today, only about 50 percent of children will spend their entire childhood in an intact family (58).

- Nearly 80 percent of black women will be the head of the family at some point in their childbearing years (59).

- About 40 percent of the children who live in fatherless households have not seen their fathers in at least a year (60).

- Seventy-two percent of America's adolescent murderers, 70 percent of long-term prison inmates, and 60 percent of rapists come from fatherless homes (61).

- Daughters of single parents are 164 percent more likely to have a premarital birth of their own, 111 percent more likely to give birth as teenagers, and 92 percent more likely to divorce than daughters of married parents (62).

- The number of cohabiting couples increased from 439,000 in 1960 to 4.24 million in 1998—an almost tenfold increase.

- Virtually all research has concluded that the chances of divorce are significantly greater for couples who cohabit before marriage than for those who do not. Indeed, couples who cohabitate before marriage are almost twice as likely to divorce as those who do not (67).

- Today, forty out of every one hundred first marriages end in divorce, compared to sixteen out of every one hundred first marriages in 1960 (69).

- America has the highest divorce rate of Western nations (69).

- Children whose parents are divorced are more likely to exhibit conduct problems, psychological maladjustment, and lower academic achievement. They are more likely to drop out of school, engage in premarital sex, and become pregnant outside of marriage, compared to children in intact families (72).

- Almost 60 percent of chldren under 6 living in families with only a mother had an income below the poverty level, more than five times as many as children under 6 in married-couple familes (10.6 percent) (74).

These statistics demonstrate the need for preaching about the family. The American family is in trouble and America's attitudes toward marriage and family are shaping the attitudes of some Christians. Children of God face the same problem of every other generation of living in the world without becoming like the world (Rom. 12:1-2).

This series of lectures is designed to address the needs of American families. There are several lectures affirming the proper roles that the different family members have in the home: the headship of man, the subjection of women. There are several lectures which address particular items threatening the family: materialism, divorce. There are lectures by brothers and sisters who have overcome unhappy circumstances in their home life to be faithful to the Lord: overcoming an abusive parent, overcoming the ungodly home. There are lectures by those who have experienced some of life's sorrows giving guidance to others who must walk in the same path: dealing with the loss of a child, dealing with delinquent children, dealing with the loss of a parent, dealing with the loss of a spouse, the pain of divorce. We are going to experience a wide range of emotions as we hear these Christians discuss their personal struggles to overcome the scars brought on them by the breakdown of the home.

There also is a section designed to help us to reach out to win the young for Christ. Our open forum discusses that subject as does a lecture on "Teenagers for Christ" and "Teenagers and Sex." Parents will be glad that their teenaged children have opportunity to hear these lessons.

The Guardian of Truth Foundation is happy to present this material to you. I have not read other works on the family that so open the hearts of those who have experienced some of life's tragedies as are included in this series of lectures. I think you will not only want to read this yourself, but also to provide others copies of the material for their own benefit.

Mike Willis
May 2006

Part One —
The Evening Lectures

Foundations of the Family

Genesis 2

Steve Reeves

That our modern culture is attacking the family should be obvious to all. The daily news makes us aware of the sad state of the confused, chaotic, and dysfunctional family. This sad state is present in our nation for the simple reason that God is being pushed out of the daily lives of men, women, and children. What is left is human wisdom in conflict with divine wisdom which always brings destructive results. Man seeks wisdom from himself and attempts to guide himself by it (Jer. 10:23). However, man left to himself degenerates (Rom. 1:20-23). Given over to his own lusts, he knows only what "I want," what "I feel," and "What is in it for me?" His personal "comfort zone" is what dominates his thinking. This drive for immediate self-satisfaction breeds immorality, destroys the home and eats away at society as a whole. Eventually, the nation will crumble. It happened to Israel, it happened to Rome, and it will happen to America if repentance is not forthcoming.

Simply examining the statistics and bemoaning the sad state of family life today will not affect the change that is needed. There must be a return to the original institution of marriage as God designed it, not a mere reformation

---

Stephen (Steve) Reeves was born in McAllen, Texas, March 8, 1954, the son of Bill and Twilah Reeves. He and his wife Susan (Kovats) have been married for thirty years this August and are the parents of three children, Bonnie (Forrest), Stephanie, and Robert. Steve took studies at Florida College and has preached at churches in Austintown, Ohio, Columbus, Ohio, and Murfreesboro, Tennessee. Since 2001 he has been working with the brethren at the Oak Avenue congregation in Dickson, Tennessee. Recently he has been involved in preaching in the Philippines.

of the status quo. When Martin Luther saw the corrupt state of the Roman Catholic Church, he sought to affect a reformation. However, Luther's reformation did not change the apostate church. After time, other men such as Alexander Campbell and Barton W. Stone realized that restoration, rather than reformation was the answer to apostasy. Their call was the call to go back to the Scriptures to restore the New Testament church.

Jesus in his day called men back to the Scriptures when he said, "Have ye not read?" (Matt. 19:4). Paul also called men back to the Scriptures when he wrote, "What saith the Scriptures?" (Rom. 4:3). In the same way, the problems of the home today need more than a little reformation. The broken home needs to be restored to the standard of its Maker. The call to go back to the Bible to cure the ailing home is not just a quaint or novel idea. It is a must!

The family was under attack in Jesus' day. Some of the Jews considered easy divorce to be the solution to family problems. The Pharisees asked Jesus, "Is it lawful for a man to put away his wife for every cause?" (Matt. 19:3). Jesus told them that divorce was not the solution. Jesus' response took them back to the beginning, to the will of God who made man and woman and instituted marriage for them. Only God, the creator of all things, has the answer for broken homes, weak and sickly families, and marriages on the brink of disaster.

In this lesson, we will first study several characteristics of God that pertain to the home and family found in Genesis 1. Like the wise man who "digged and went deep, and laid a foundation upon the rock" (Luke 6:48), we will go to Genesis to dig deep and lay the foundation that God laid for the family from the beginning. The restoration of a rundown house starts with the foundation, just as the construction of a new house starts with the foundation. In the same way, one must start with the foundation when dealing with a broken family, just as one must start with the foundation when constructing a new family. After we study God's character from Genesis 1, then we will examine several texts in Genesis 2 to see the foundation God laid for the first home and family.

The Creation Account Reveals Characteristics of God (Genesis 1)
"In the beginning God created the heavens and the earth" (Gen. 1:1). With these words the Holy Spirit revealed to Moses how it all began. The first two chapters of Genesis reveal to us how the heavens and the earth were created and how man and woman were created, the first family.

God Is a God of Order

In Genesis 1, the Scriptures reads: "And the earth was waste and void and darkness was upon the face of the deep. And the spirit of God moved up on the face of the waters and God said let there be light and there was light" (vv. 2-3). The rest of the chapter describes how the God of order took the condition of waste and disorder and began to create an orderly heavens and earth. He created light and divided it from the darkness. He gathered the waters together into one place and caused the dry land to appear. Then he put living plants upon that dry land. In day four he made the solar system and said, "Let them be for signs and for seasons, and for days and years" (1:14). Much of the plant and animal life today depend upon these seasons and their order to continue to live and reproduce. Next, God filled the seas with living creatures and the skies with birds. On the sixth day, God made living creatures, cattle and beasts of the earth after their kind. Then God made man in his own image. God has always been a God of order, and we see this orderliness in the creation. In chapter 2, God made the family and that family unit is also orderly. Today, the family founded on God's order will be blessed. The apostle Paul wrote to the Corinthian church and instructed them to have orderly worship (1 Cor. 14). The reason that worship should be orderly is because God is not a God of confusion, but a God of peace (v. 33). Therefore, Paul wrote in verse 40, "Let all things be done decently and in order."

Man introduces disorder, chaos, and confusion. God takes chaos and confusion and brings to it order through his will and through his design. The earth and universe function well today as a result of God's order. God also designed the family unit, and the family unit that follows God's order will also function well and have peace.

God Has All Power and Authority

All things were created by the power of God's word. Each day of creation began with the phrase, "and God said" (1:3, 6, 9; etc.). God spoke plants and animals into existence. The creation of man was also the result of God's expressed will. God said, "Let us make man in our image and after our likeness" (1:26). Mankind did not evolve, but man was *made* in God's image. God *created* him (2:3).

God also said, "It is not good that the man should be alone" (2:18). So, God made for him woman. Made from the rib of Adam, this woman was to be a help meet (suitable, comparable) for him. God made them male and female and in his image (1:27). The man and woman possessed innocence (2:25), intelligence (2:19), moral capacity (2:16, 17), will power (3:17), and emotion (2:23). Because they were made in God's image, they represented an order of existence higher than the animal order. They had the ability to control their appetites and passions of the flesh; they had self control. They could understand the will of the Lord and obey him.

God is a God of Wisdom

True wisdom is seen in the creation. The psalmist wrote, "The heavens declare the glory of God; And the firmament showeth his handiwork. Day unto day uttereth speech, And night unto night showeth knowledge" (Ps. 19:1, 2). He also revealed that wisdom is found in the commandments of God when he wrote, "The law of Jehovah is perfect, restoring the soul: The testimony of Jehovah is sure, making wise the simple. The precepts of Jehovah are right, rejoicing the heart: The commandment of Jehovah is pure, enlightening the eyes" (Ps. 19:7, 8). Only the family whose foundation rests upon the wisdom of God's word will be blessed and will declare the glory of God as well.

God created man, the woman for him and the institution of marriage. Genesis 2:24 states, "Therefore shall a man leave his father and his mother, and shall cleave unto his wife: and they shall be one flesh." The passage does not state, "and he shall cleave unto a woman," but unto his woman, "his wife." Man and woman were to be one flesh in marriage. The family today that is ordered after the family which God created in the beginning reflects the wisdom of God.

God Has a Pattern

There is a pattern to the movement of the heavenly bodies (1:14-19). Therefore, the order of the seasons is predictable. God gave early man a pattern in worship (Gen. 4:1-8). When the pattern was followed, Abel was blessed (4:4). When the pattern was ignored by Cain, God did not accept Cain's worship (v. 5). The statement, "If thou doest well, shall it (Cain's countenance, SER) not be lifted up?" (4:7) implies that Cain knew what to do to please God. He chose not to follow God's way.

Later, "Moses is warned of God when he is about to make the tabernacle: for, See, saith he, that thou make all things according to the pattern that was showed thee in the mount" (Heb. 8:5). The Law of Moses was to be a schoolmaster to lead the Jews to Christ. It contained a copy or shadow of the heavenly things. Therefore, it was important for Moses to follow the pattern. Under the New Testament, Paul instructed Timothy to, "Hold the pattern of sound words which thou hast heard from me, in faith and love which is in Christ Jesus" (2 Tim. 1:13). God has always had a pattern and he has a pattern for marriage, home, and family. This pattern which lays down the foundation of the family is found in Genesis 2.

Examining the Texts That Lay the Foundation of the Family (Genesis 2)

Genesis 2:7-17—And Jehovah God formed man. . . .

Man was made first which explains why the wife is to be in subjection to her husband. Paul wrote, "Let a woman learn in silence with all submission. And I do not permit a woman to teach or to have authority over a man, but to be in silence. For Adam was formed first, then Eve. And Adam was not deceived, but the woman being deceived, fell into transgression. Nevertheless she will be saved in childbearing if they continue in faith, love, and holiness, with self-control" (1 Tim. 2:11-15). The words, "in childbearing," speak of the role of the wife in the family. To the Corinthians Paul wrote, "But I want you to know that the head of every man is Christ, the head of woman is man, and the head of Christ is God. . . . For man is not from woman, but woman from man. Nor was man created for the woman, but woman for the man" (1 Cor. 11:3, 8, 9). God exhorts wives to "be in subjection unto your own husbands, as unto the Lord. For the husband is the head of the wife, and Christ also is the head of the church, being himself the savior of the body. But as the church is subject to Christ, so let the wives also be to their husbands in everything" (Eph. 5:22-24). The home as God designed it will have a husband who takes responsibility as the head, and a wife who is in subjection to her husband and a help to him.

Genesis 2:18-22—It is not good that man should be alone. . . .

God gave mankind dominion over every living creature (1:28), and man gave the living creatures names (2:20). But, the Scriptures tell us that there was not found a help meet (suitable) for him (2:18). So, God caused a deep sleep to fall upon the man. As he slept, God took one of his ribs and closed up the flesh in its place. From the rib of Adam, God made woman and brought her to him. The woman was a gift from God to Adam. She was God's creation, not the creation of man. She was and is to be treated like all blessings from God, with thanksgiving.

Genesis 2:23—This is now bone of my bones. . . .

Adam was joyful and thankful (2:23)! Adam, together with his wife, was now complete. No other man or animal could provide what God provided in Eve. Adam called this female, "woman," because she was taken out of man. She was different from all other creatures, she was special, and she was a part of him. She was not made from a bone of his head that she might rule over him, or from his foot that she might be a slave to him. She was made from his side to be his companion, a helper and one to be protected. Paul referred to this relationship when he wrote, "Husbands, love your wives, even as Christ also loved the church, and gave himself up for it; . . . Even so ought husbands also to love their own wives as their own bodies. He that loveth his own wife loveth himself: for no man ever hated his own flesh; but nourisheth and cherisheth it, even as Christ also the church; because we are members of his body. For this cause shall a man leave his father and mother, and shall cleave to his wife; and the two shall become one flesh" (Eph. 5:25, 28-31). Paul's teaching here parallels the events of Genesis 2! Adam loved his wife; she was part of his body. Christ loved the church, gave himself for it and continues to nourish and cherish it even today because it is his body.

Husbands today should love their wives as though God had literally taken one of their own ribs and formed her! Homes are often destroyed because the command to love the wife as one's own body is ignored. What man today goes about beating and bruising his ribs when he is angry? Yet, he will beat his wife! What man looks in the mirror and insults himself? Yet, he belittles his wife whom he vowed to "love, cherish and adore"! Husbands, love your wives as you love your own body. Love your wives as Christ loved his body, the church.

The woman that God made from man brought him true companionship. She had the ability to communicate with and complement him. Together, they could share in the blessings, duties, and responsibilities of life before God.

Genesis 2:24—For this cause shall a man leave father and mother. . . .
The union of the man and woman in marriage was to be exclusive. This union excluded the oversight that their parents previously had exercised and the submission to their parents. "And they shall be one flesh" (2:24), leaves no room in this new relationship for the control of parents and/or in-laws. While the parent/child relationship is a special one (Prov. 4:1-4), this new relationship of marriage takes precedence over the former one. It is not wrong to seek advice from parents, but a married couple should not

depend on dad and mom like they did as a child. Newlyweds must "cut the apron strings" so-to-speak, and work on forming their new partnership with each other. Parents should be careful not to interfere after their child marries for this could lead the child to be co-dependent and irresponsible. Parents should encourage their child to work out his own problems with his new mate. If the parents of a spouse continue to interfere with the marriage, the husband must take the lead to remedy the situation. The husband should avoid trying to offend the parents, but ultimately he must take control to insure the strength and stability of his new home and family. His allegiance is now to his wife and her allegiance is to him. He is no longer under his parents' control. He is no longer single. He is a husband with a wife.

Genesis 2:24—And shall cleave unto his wife. . . .

This phrase, together with the previous one, constitutes the divine arrangement of marriage. Note that the man did not leave his father and mother and cleave unto a *woman* in order to fulfill the lusts of the flesh. He was joined unto a *wife*. God's arrangement for marriage is not the same as what we find often today. Many people today just "live together" with their "marital partners" in order to have a "meaningful relationship." Such modern expressions only describe the act of fornication in the eyes of God.

The Hebrew word *dabaq* translated "cleave" in Genesis 2:24 means to "cling, cleave, keep close . . . fig. of loyalty, affection, etc., sometimes with the idea of physical proximity retained" (Brown 179); "adhere" (Strong 30). The same word is found in 2 Samuel 23:10 where we are told that Eleazar's hand "clave" ("stuck," NKJ; "froze," NIV) to the sword. In the New Testament, Jesus quoted from Genesis 2:24. The Greek word Jesus used for "cleave" is *kollao* (from *kolla*, "glue"), meaning to "join fast together, to glue, cement" (Vine 104). Therefore, God established the permanency of marriage from the very beginning

In Deuteronomy 24:1-4, God gave a temporary concession to man's stubbornness in view of the shameful treatment of women in Moses' day. Jesus said divorce was allowed in Moses' day because of the hardness of their hearts, but "from the beginning it was not so" (Matt. 19:8). God has always hated divorce (Mal. 2:14-16). There is no place in God's design for so-called "trial marriages."

The principle of permanency in marriage is reflected in the New Testament as well. In Romans 7:1-4, Paul gave an illustration of marriage based on the pattern of Genesis 2:24. He said that marriage is for life. Paul wrote that God's law applies while men live (v. 1). God's marriage law applies while the husband and wife are still alive (v. 2). If, while the husband is living, the wife marries another, she will be committing adultery (v. 3). However, if the husband dies, she may marry another man and not be guilty of adultery (v. 3). This truth about marriage illustrated how the Jews who were once joined to the Law of Moses (now dead), could now be joined to Christ and not be guilty of spiritual adultery (v. 4). Simply put, marriage is the union of one man and one woman for life.

In Matthew 19:3-12, Jesus taught this same principle. When asked if a man could put away his wife "for any cause" (NRSV), Jesus directed the attention of the Pharisees to Genesis 2:24! They would not be asking this question if they were in agreement with the passage! Jesus said, "Have ye not read, that he who made them from the beginning made them male and female, and said, For this cause shall a man leave his father and mother, and shall cleave to his wife; and the two shall become one flesh? So that they are no more two, but one flesh. What therefore God hath joined together, let not man put asunder" (vv. 4-6). Man does not have authority over God's marriage law! Man can obey God's law or man can violate God's law, but he cannot change, modify or overrule it! Jesus went on to say, "Whosoever shall put away his wife, except it be for fornication, and shall marry another, committeth adultery: and whoso marrieth her which is put away doth commit adultery" (v. 9). The rule of Jesus concerning putting-away and remarriage is this: if one puts away his spouse for any cause (v. 3), and marries another, he is not joined by God to that second mate. His bed will be a bed of adultery, not the undefiled bed of marriage (Heb. 13:4). Jesus made one exception to this rule: the faithful mate who puts away his spouse "for fornication" and marries another will be joined by God to that second mate and not be guilty of adultery. If this sounds too strict for one today, then he should not marry.

The act of "cleaving" in marriage involves more than just permanency. It involves the closeness of a husband and wife. The marriage bond carries with it a responsibility for the husband to provide for the wife's well-being, to protect her and to share in her joy and sorrow. The husband and wife are to develop a strong and deep relationship with each other in marriage. Spouses are to cleave to each other, not to old friends, habits, hobbies, interests, or careers. The foundation of many homes never solidifies because the closeness of marriage is not cultivated. Mates need to take time for each other, take time to communicate, go places with each other, and develop mutual interests. Some husbands have allowed hobbies, sports, or other interests outside the home to make "widows" of their wives. Some husbands and wives have pursued the success of their careers to the detriment of their marriage. Their lives take separate paths and one day they wake up to a mate that they do not really know. Such behavior is against God's design for marriage and those who ignore his design will suffer for it. God always brings upon man the fruit of his thoughts and of his doings (Jer. 6:19; 17:10).

Genesis 2:24—And they shall be one flesh. . . .
The two lives of a man and woman are beautifully blended together in marriage. In marriage, a husband and wife come together in a tender, intimate, and loving sexual union. The physical needs of a man and woman are met in a legitimate way in the marriage union.

God created mankind with physical needs. He also created the proper avenue to fulfill these needs. In the beginning, man's appetite for food was to be fulfilled in "tending the garden" (Gen. 2:15) and later by tilling the ground (3:18, 19). Paul wrote to the Thessalonians, "Even when we were with you, we commanded you this: If anyone will not work, neither shall he eat. For we hear that there are some who walk among you in a disorderly manner, not working at all, but are busybodies. Now those who are such we command and exhort through our Lord Jesus Christ that they work in quietness and eat their own bread" (2 Thess. 3:10-12). While it is not a sin to be hungry, it is a sin to steal food to satisfy that hunger. The legitimate means to satisfy hunger is to work for food and "eat our own bread" and not the bread of another.

In the same way, man's appetite for sexual fulfillment comes from God and in the beginning he provided the right way to satisfy it. Sexual satisfaction was to be found in the "wife" that God brought to Adam. The woman would also find her satisfaction in her husband. To the Corinthians Paul wrote, "But, because of fornications, let each man have his own wife, and let each woman have her own husband. Let the husband render unto the wife her due: and likewise also the wife unto the husband. The wife hath not power over her own body, but the husband: and likewise also the husband hath not power over his own body, but the wife. Defraud ye not one the other, except it be by consent for a season, that ye may give yourselves unto prayer, and may be together again, that Satan tempt you not because of your incontinency" (1 Cor. 7:2-5).

This Scripture informs us that fornication (any kind of sex outside of marriage) is forbidden by God. Fornication is a work of the flesh that will keep one out of heaven (Gal. 5:19-21). Paul argued in 1 Corinthians 6:12-20 that the sexual appetite can be controlled until one marries. Paul also exhorted everyone to "flee fornication." Adultery (sex with anyone other than one's own mate) is also a forbidden means to fulfill the sexual appetite (Exod. 20:14, 17; Prov. 6:22-33). Just as one is to "eat his own bread," he is to find sexual satisfaction in his own mate (1 Cor. 7:2; Prov. 5:15-20).

The words "one flesh" in Genesis 2:24 point to more than just sexual fulfillment. These words contain a deeper meaning. "One flesh" is symbolic of the closest of all earthly relationships. The proper setting for the sexual union between husband and wife is one of unselfish love, companionship, and mutual giving that goes beyond the sex act itself. This unselfish love should permeate all aspects of marriage. Sexual fulfillment is one blessing of marriage, but it is not the sole purpose of marriage. Our evil and wicked culture has developed fantasies and expectations for people that are harmful and destructive to true love. The pursuit of unreasonable and selfish demands, instant gratification, and sexual perversions, frustrate a marriage and starve it of true love. It is no wonder that many modern-day vows expressed at weddings contain such phrases as: "as long as love shall last" (not "as long as I live"). Such people today vow to stay married as long as *they feel* that *their needs* are being met. Such selfishness was never a part of God's design for the home. God is a God of love!

Happiness in marriage comes when both mates strive to understand the feelings and needs of each other (Phil. 2:4). With love and patience, one should seek to fulfill the needs of his mate first, instead of demanding that his needs be met first. Additionally, the oneness of the marriage union does not change should the Lord bless that marriage with children. The *two* become *one* flesh before the child comes home, while the child is at home and after the child leaves home. Some spouses destroy their union by allowing themselves to be drawn closer to their children than to their mate. The children "become their life" as the parents forget their first love. The wife becomes a slave to the children, or the husband becomes a mere provider for the children. Children are not to be the center of the universe, or the family either! God gave children to parents so that the parents might nurture them in the chastening and admonition of the Lord (Eph. 6:4). Children need to see dad and mom in a loving relationship which will in turn train them to be good husbands/fathers and wives/mothers in the future.

Finally, the phrase "the two become one flesh" in Genesis 2:24 teaches that God's design for the home excludes all forms of sexual immorality. God intended *one* man for *one* woman for life. God's design for the home excludes and condemns . . .

- Communal living: two men for two women. "Wife swapping" and "open marriages" also fit into this same sinful category.

- Polygamy and polyandry (plural mates in marriage): two men for one woman or vice versa.

- Child molesting. Adults having sex with a child is an abomination before the Lord. Pornography has encouraged this scourge upon our society.

- Incest: a father with his daughter, a mother with her son, or a brother with his sister (Lev. 18:6-18). The incestuous relationship in Leviticus 20:12 is called "confusion" (ASV, KJV). Incest is "confusion" because it is out of place with God's order.

- Homosexuality: a man with a man or a woman with a woman. God saw that it was not good for the man to be alone, so he created a woman for Adam, not another man. He created a woman for man (1 Cor. 11:9), not for another woman. In Leviticus 18:13 the Lord said, "If a man also lie with mankind, as he lieth with a woman, both of them have committed an abomination. . . ." Jude defined homosexual fornication as men "going after strange flesh" (Jude 7). When people deny the Creator of the universe, they deny the order of his creation as well. This denial of God results in sexual perversion. Paul described those who refused to acknowledge God as Creator as having been given over to "vile passions." He wrote, "For even their women exchanged the natural use for what is against nature. Likewise also the men, leaving the natural use of the woman, burned in their lust for one another, men with men committing what is shameful, and receiving in themselves the penalty of their error which was due" (Rom. 1:26, 27).

- Bestiality. In Genesis 2:19-20, God caused the animals to come before Adam. Adam named the animals, but there was not found a help meet for him among the animals. Since God did not create animals for

21

man's sexual needs, God condemned bestiality when he said, "Thou shalt not lie with any beast to defile thyself therewith; neither shall any woman stand before a beast, to lie down thereto: it is confusion" (Lev. 18:22).

The institution of marriage ordained by God in Genesis 2:18-25 is a lifelong relationship with mutual responsibilities. The man is to lead and the woman is to help. Each one is to leave his father and mother and cleave to each other. In this loving relationship, they will seek to fulfill the needs of each other, they will become one flesh and they will reflect the wisdom and love of God their Creator.

What Then Are the Foundations of the Family?

1. The most important family foundation is God himself. If God's will for marriage and the home is not followed, then the family cannot prosper or prevail. Marriage founded by man always fails.

2. A lifelong relationship with mutual responsibilities must undergird the family.

3. The respect for the roles of the husband and the wife in marriage, as God ordained them, is a necessary foundation for the family. The rejection or confusion of these roles eventually results in chaos and unhappiness in the family.

4. The happy, lasting family is the family that is founded on the principles of leaving father and mother and cleaving to each other. A godly husband and wife will cleave to each other rather than use their father and mother as a "safety net" or allow them to enter the one-flesh relationship as co-directors.

5. The loving relationship in which each mate seeks to fulfill the needs of the other is another part of the foundation of the happy, enduring family.

6. The godly family is also founded on the wisdom and love of God, the Creator. God created man, he created woman and he instituted marriage.

Happy is the one who seeks the biblical foundations of the family as he seeks marriage. Herein lies true happiness, peace and fulfillment.

Bibliography

Brown, Francis. *The New Brown-Driver-Briggs-Gesenius Hebrew and English Lexicon.* Peabody: Hendrickson Publishers, 1979.

Strong, James. *New Strong's Concise Dictionary of Words in the Hebrew Bible.* Nashville: Thomas Nelson Publishers, 1995.

Vine, W.E. *Vine's Complete Expository Dictionary of Old and New Testament Words.* Nashville: Thomas Nelson Publishers, 1985.

The Dangers of Marriage to Non-Christians
Lewis Willis

Happy homes are essential to happy, useful, and successful lives. Proper homes are essential if the Lord's church is to grow and prosper. Strong congregations cannot be built out of homes filled with discord, torn by strife, or broken by divorce. To secure the future of the church, we must fortify our homes.

Through the ages, the influence of the home has been powerful and lasting. Here character is molded; personality is formed. To speak of the home is to touch the tender cords of the heart. Talk to the criminal in his cell, or the beggar on the street. They speak of their home life either fondly or bitterly.

Lewis Willis is one of four brothers in the flesh who became preachers of the gospel: Cecil, Donald, and Mike are well-known for their work in the Lord. Lewis has worked with churches in Missouri (Macon and Kirkwood), Kentucky (Valley Station), Texas (Nacogdoches, Amarillo, and Irving), and Brown Street church in Akron Ohio. In total, he is now in his forty-sixth year of local work. Since he is not presently working with a local church as its full-time evangelist, he is available for meetings.

Lewis married Frankie Flanagin, of Farmington, New Mexico when they finished college in 1958. They were the parents of three children, Andrea (Middleton), Scott, and Angela (Turnbow). In 1988, after a short five and one-half month illness, Frankie died of cancer. Almost a year and a half later, Lewis married Joyce Feist, of Moundsville, West Virginia. Joyce is a professor at Youngstown State University, in Youngstown, Ohio. They have eight grandchildren.

Home is the place of refuge and rest for the weary. After being tossed upon the turbulent ocean of our daily lives, with many problems of our day, it is wonderful to return to a happy home. There we seek peace, comfort, understanding, and solace with our families. A happy home makes our burdens lighter, our journeys shorter! Such adds meaning and zest to life. We all need to find these blessings in our homes and families.

Unfortunately, fewer and fewer people—even Christians—experience the blessings of a happy home. One reason for this sad result is, we choose the wrong companion for our marriage. Personally, I wish God had said, "Christian, marry a Christian!" This instruction would have simplified marriage for many. Imagine all the trouble which such a law would have solved.

On second thought, perhaps a law prohibiting Christians marrying non-Christians would not be so desirable. Numbers of marriage partners have been converted by their mates. They now have hope of eternal life in heaven, because their mate led them to the truth. Probably some of you in this audience are Christians today because you married a Christian.

So, perhaps God knew what he was doing after all. Facts demand, however, that we acknowledge that not all such marriages end with such hope. Several years ago, I saw statistical results compiled by Alvin Jennings from forty-nine marriages involving Christians and non-Christians.

- Twenty-eight of the Christians became unfaithful—55%.
- Twenty-one remained faithful—45%.
- Of those who remained faithful, twelve never converted their mates.
- Only nine converted their mates—18% — 82% failed to do so.
- Thus, where forty-nine were serving the Lord, now there are only thirty, including the converted mates.
- Those are old figures; I rather suspect that today the percentages would be even worse.

1 Corinthians 7:39

"The wife is bound by the law as long as her husband liveth; but if her husband be dead, she is at liberty to be married to whom she will; *only in the Lord.*" Consider some views advocated on *"only in the Lord"* in this passage.

- Albert Barnes concludes that marriages of Christians and non-Christians "are a violation of the New Testament" (*1 Corinthians* 133).

- David Lipscomb and J.W. Shepherd, in the *Gospel Advocate* commentary, conclude "that the spirit and teaching of the Bible is against Christians marrying those not members of the body of Christ, *and yet there is no direct and specific prohibition of it*, other than for widows" (*First Corinthians* 115-116, my emp., LW).

- Mike Willis says, "The limitation put upon the widow in remarrying is that she marry one who is in Christ, i.e., another Christian," but he added: "The limitation . . . must be considered in light of the present distress," when Christians were being persecuted (*A Commentary on First Corinthians* 213-214). Willis noted that "treating this as a universal law" introduces the problem of "determining how one repents of the 'sin' once it is committed."

Two other passages are frequently introduced in this connection.

1. "Be ye not unequally yoked together with unbelievers: for what fellowship hath righteousness with unrighteousness? And what communion hath light with darkness? And what concord hath Christ with Belial? or what part hath he that believeth with an infidel? And what agreement hath the temple of God with idols? For ye are the temple of the living God; as God hath said, I will dwell in them, and walk in them; and I will be their God, and they shall be my people. Wherefore come out from among them, and be ye separate, saith the Lord, and touch not the unclean thing; and I will receive you" (2 Cor. 6:14-17). There are obvious reasons why the union of a Christian and a non-Christian would introduce problems; we shall discuss some of these momentarily. But, the demand "come out from among them, and be ye separate" if applied to such marriages, would require leaving those marriages—divorces?— and being separate. Are we ready to affirm those divorces?

2. "Children, obey your parents *in the Lord*: for this is right" (Eph. 6:1). Should children obey their parents who are Christians? Absolutely! But, what if their parents are not "in the Lord"? Can they disobey them at will? Hardly! Colly Caldwell wrote that Paul's statement, "in the Lord," required obedience "because it is right before God to obey and honor" parents. . . . When children obey their parents, they obey the Lord. When they disobey them, they disobey the Lord" (*Truth Commentaries: Ephesians* 286-288).

Thus, I conclude that "in the Lord" signifies "in harmony with the will and teaching of the Lord."

Personally, I am of the view that the "only in the Lord" requirement is limited by the "distress" then being experienced by first century Christians. I find it difficult to explain why such a restriction, if it exists, is not stated to the young, instead of just to older Christians. For these reasons it seems evident to me that this expression in 1 Corinthians 7:39 does not preclude marriages between Christians and non-Christians.

But There Are Specific Problems Introduced by Such Marriages
Please understand, not every non-Christian will embrace the things I am about to discuss. Some are basically good folks; they just have not or will not obey the Gospel. Unfortunately, these "good folks" are the exception, rather than the case.

1. Worship attendance. Hebrews 10:25 and Acts 20:7 are still commands. Non-Christian mates do not share the Christian's conviction about obedience to this command. The Christian ends up attending *alone!* What happens when children arrive in the home? They are pulled between two opposing views. One parent wants to go to worship; the other wants to go fishing. Which will interest children the most? Parents arguing about the issue will only make the matter worse. Complaint: "We can never do anything. You have to go to worship." He wants to go to the ballgame, golfing, visiting, the car show, etc. "Why can't we go just once?" Once you make that compromise, you surrender the spiritual ground you once held. Your mate just learned it is not all that important to you after all.

2. Contribution. Giving is also a command of the Lord (1 Cor. 16:2; 2 Cor. 9:6-7). The non-Christian mate wants to use the money for something else: a new car, house, riding lawn mower, vacation, etc. Every Lord's day, the issue is explosive. Your children hear this debate! What do they prefer the money be used for?

3. Some mates are financially irresponsible. They don't pay their bills. Because of unwise decisions, they frequently can't pay them. Note the teaching of Scripture regarding this problem.

> Owe no man any thing, but to love one another: for he that loveth another hath fulfilled the law (Rom. 13:8).

Let him that stole steal no more: but rather let him labour, working with his hands the thing which is good, that he may have to give to him that needeth (Eph. 4:28).

And that ye study to be quiet, and to do your own business, and to work with your own hands, as we commanded you; That ye may walk honestly toward them that are without, and that ye may have lack of nothing (1 Thess. 4:11-12).

For even when we were with you, this we commanded you, that if any would not work, neither should he eat (2 Thess. 3:10).

You will not be happy living with a deadbeat. Such mates spend money on frivolous things, instead of the house payment. They often have plenty of beer on hand, even if the phone is ringing every day, with someone asking for payment of the electric bill.

4. What about alcohol? Many see nothing wrong with social drinking. Consider what law enforcement agencies think of social drinking. You are "drunk" if driving with .08% or .10% blood-alcohol content, depending on the state in which you live. You reach this level after two 12 oz. beers, if you weigh 150 lbs. (See your state driver's handbook.) As a Christian your non-drinking view is Scripture based.

And be not drunk with wine, wherein is excess; but be filled with the Spirit (Eph. 5:18).

God has always recognized alcohol as a problem.

Wine is a mocker, strong drink is raging: and whosoever is deceived thereby is not wise (Prov. 20:1).

Who hath woe? Who hath sorrow? Who hath contentions? Who hath babbling? Who hath wounds without cause? Who hath redness of eyes? They that tarry long at the wine; they that go to seek mixed wine. Look not thou upon the wine when it is red, when it giveth his colour in the cup, when it moveth itself aright. At the last it biteth like a serpent, and stingeth like an adder. Thine eyes shall behold strange women, and thine heart shall utter perverse things. Yea, thou shalt be as he that lieth down in the midst of the sea, or as he that lieth upon the top of a mast. They have stricken me, shalt thou say, and I was not sick; they have beaten me, and I felt it not: when shall I awake? I will seek it yet again (Prov. 23:29-35).

Now the works of the flesh are manifest, which are these; Adultery, fornication, uncleanness, lasciviousness, idolatry, witchcraft, hatred, variance, emulations, wrath, strife, seditions, heresies, envyings, murders, drunkenness, revellings, and such like: of the which I tell you before, as I have also told you in time past, that they which do such things shall not inherit the kingdom of God (Gal. 5:19-21).

Will the unconverted share your conviction about alcohol? Alcoholism is one of America's greatest public, social problems. There are millions of alcoholics in this country. You do not want to marry one of them! "Alcoholism is the most devilish destroyer of home-love and home-happiness and honored womanhood ever known to the human race. Ever since human history has been recorded, alcohol has always and everywhere degraded womanhood, wrecked childhood, turned husbands and parents into beasts, and converted happy homes into hells on earth" (Henry Louis Smith, President of Washington and Lee University).

Different Values Often Cause Major Troubles
Christians base decisions and actions on Scripture; non-Christians are often antagonistic toward those views and approaches. Let's consider some of these differences.

1. Raising children. There is an implied difference between the mother and father of Timothy (Acts 16:1-3). He had been led to faith in Christ by his mother, Eunice, and his grandmother, Lois (2 Tim. 1:5). However, his father was a Greek or Gentile, and Timothy had not been circumcised according to the law. Thus, Paul circumcised Timothy before taking him into the work. Obviously, his parents had not been able to come to a decision about Timothy's circumcision. Such problems as spiritual activity and responsibility are often occasions of difference and confusion when one mate is not a child of God. Trouble comes in deciding what the children can and cannot do (drinking; immodest dress; dancing; etc.).

A major cause of difference is in the matter of discipline. A relatively modern theory of educational psychology has swept our country. It says children should not be restrained or inhibited; they should be allowed to freely express themselves however they wish. The Bible teaches that they should be raised with "the rod of correction," or raised "in the nurture (chastening) and admonition of the Lord." Discipline is vital for the good of the child and the success of the home. God has emphatically spoken on the question.

He that spareth his rod hateth his son: but he that loveth him chasteneth him betimes (Prov. 13:24).

Foolishness is bound in the heart of a child; but the rod of correction shall drive it far from him (Prov. 22:15).

Withhold not correction from the child: for if thou beatest him with the rod, he shall not die. Thou shalt beat him with the rod, and shalt deliver his soul from hell (Prov. 22:15),

The rod and reproof give wisdom: but a child left to himself bringeth his mother to shame (Prov. 29:15).

Correct thy son, and he shall give thee rest; yea, he shall give delight unto thy soul (Prov. 29:17).

The problem is obvious if the non-Christian mate rejects this teaching. How are children to learn what to do when mom and dad do not agree on this most basic biblical truth?

2. Kindness. Note Bible teaching here. "The desire of a man is his kindness: and a poor man is better than a liar" (Prov. 19:22). Of the worthy woman it is said, "She openeth her mouth with wisdom; and in her tongue is the law of kindness" (Prov. 31:26). A footnote on "law" gives "teaching."

And be ye kind one to another, tenderhearted, forgiving one another, even as God for Christ's sake hath forgiven you (Eph. 4:32).

Parents should be kind, and teach kindness to their children, by word and example. Unless they "are on the same page," they will send a mixed message.

3. The Golden Rule. "Therefore all things whatsoever ye would that men should do to you, do ye even so to them: for this is the law and the prophets" (Matt. 7:12). This must be taught and lived in a happy home. Will it be, if one mate rejects the truth?

4. Confession of faults. Christians should readily do this. "Confess your faults one to another, and pray one for another, that ye may be healed. The effectual fervent prayer of a righteous man availeth much" (Jas. 5:16). Children must see both parents living by this rule; otherwise, they are confused.

5. Forgiving. "And be ye kind one to another, tenderhearted, forgiving one another, even as God for Christ's sake hath forgiven you" (Eph. 4:32). An unforgiving heart creates confusion anywhere. What happens if a non-Christian mate scoffs at this command?

6. Love must abound. Love is the "bond of perfectness." "And above all these things put on charity, which is the bond of perfectness" (Col. 3:14). Love is the foundation of a happy home. It is the tie that is to bind husband and wife, father and mother, parents and children. Loveless marriages are unfortunate and tragic. Such is evidenced by nagging, fussing, feuding, and fighting. This is the very atmosphere that reigns in many homes where one mate is not a Christian, living the truth. Too many children have been raised who truly wonder if their parents love each other. *This sad situation is also true of some homes where both parents are Christians!*

Fundamental Principles of Christianity

Importance of spiritual things. There is a place for a balanced amount of wholesome recreation: baseball, football, TV, and movies, etc. However, emphasis should not be placed on recreation. Children should be taught to put spiritual things first. "But seek ye first the kingdom of God, and his righteousness; and all these things shall be added unto you" (Matt. 6:33). "If ye then be risen with Christ, seek those things which are above, where Christ sitteth on the right hand of God. Set your affection on things above, not on things on the earth" (Col. 3:1-2). This message can hardly be taught if parents disagree about it.

Importance of respect. There must be respect for God, Christ, the word, and the church, adults (especially the aged), parents, authority, and the rights, wishes, and property of others.

Responsibility. "For every man shall bear his own burden" (Gal. 6:5).

Humility. "Humble yourselves therefore under the mighty hand of God, that he may exalt you in due time" (1 Pet. 5:6).

Fairness and **impartiality**. "I charge thee before God, and the Lord Jesus Christ, and the elect angels, that thou observe these things without preferring one before another, doing nothing by partiality" (1 Tim. 5:21).

Conclusion

If I have made my point, it is evident that marrying a Christian will enhance the prospects of a happy and successful life. When you marry, choose someone who will help you and your children go to heaven one day. If scriptural truths and principles are lived in your lives, you will assure that your marriage will not end in divorce, as so many do.

Marriage counselors recognize four principle causes for divorce: sexual incompatibility, financial irresponsibility, alcoholism, and religious differences. My aim has not been to deal with sociological and psychological considerations; I am neither a sociologist nor a psychologist. These professions emphasize personality, education, hereditary factors, manners, friendliness, etc., as a basis for a good marriage. I do not discount these either.

My conviction is, if you both are faithful Christians, you will avoid the four major causes of divorce:

1. You will adjust to your mate sexually. "Now concerning the things whereof ye wrote unto me: It is good for a man not to touch a woman. Nevertheless, to avoid fornication, let every man have his own wife, and let every woman have her own husband. Let the husband render unto the wife due benevolence: and likewise also the wife unto the husband. The wife hath not power of her own body, but the husband: and likewise also the husband hath not power of his own body, but the wife. Defraud ye not one the other, except it be with consent for a time, that ye may give yourselves to fasting and prayer; and come together again, that Satan tempt you not for your incontinency" (1 Cor. 7:1-5).

2. You both will live financially responsible lives. "And that ye study to be quiet, and to do your own business, and to work with your own hands, as we commanded you; That ye may walk honestly toward them that are without, and that ye may have lack of nothing" (1 Thess. 4:11-12).

3. You will eliminate the possibility of alcohol becoming a problem. "And be not drunk with wine, wherein is excess; but be filled with the Spirit" (Eph. 5:18).

4. You will remove the danger of a spiritual problem if both of you are faithful Christians. "Fear none of those things which thou shalt suffer: behold, the devil shall cast some of you into prison, that ye may be tried;

and ye shall have tribulation ten days: be thou faithful unto death, and I will give thee a crown of life" (Rev. 2:10).

Just marrying someone who is called a Christian is not enough (for example, a mate who was "baptized" just to please you). You want to marry a converted, convicted child of God. If you choose otherwise, you will have trouble with your spiritual father-in-law! *Your marriage is a binding contract before God, to be broken only by death or adultery. Be careful in choosing the mate with whom you will live "till death do you part."*

Godly Families in the Local Church

Chris Reeves

Our theme for this series of lectures is: "God Give Us Christian Homes." Yet, when I look around for Christian homes I ask, "Where have all the godly families gone?" They are disappearing rapidly.

This lecture will focus on two main points: family closeness and family faithfulness in the local church. First, the factors leading to family dissolution today will be discussed. Second, the ancient Bible family and modern family will be compared and contrasted. Third, God's plan in the Bible for family unity will be reviewed. Fourth, Bible examples of family activity together will be taken from both the Old and New Testaments. Fifth, family

---

Chris Reeves was born October 20, 1965 in San Antonio, Texas to Bill and Twilah Reeves. He is the last of eight children. His parents have been married 59 years and his father has faithfully preached the gospel in English and Spanish for over 60 years. Three of his brothers, Steve, Tim, and Mark are all faithful gospel preachers. Chris attended Florida College from 1984 to 1988 and received a Bible Certificate. He was awarded a B.A. in Biblical Studies from Florida College in 2000. Chris began preaching regularly in 1984 and worked full time with the McRae Road church of Christ in Camden, South Carolina (1988-1990) and the Highway 9 church of Christ in Corpus Christi, Texas (1991-1995). He is currently working with the Memorial Blvd. church of Christ in Springfield, Tennessee (1995 to present). He has also done preaching work outside the country in Mexico, Spain and the Philippines. Chris married Cheri Goodall (daughter of Charles and Vernita Goodall) in 1988 and they have four children, Jessica, Jacob, Mason, and Carlin. He writes articles regularly for *Truth Magazine* and was added to its staff in 2001. Chris is currently working on manuscripts for *Micah* in the Truth Commentary series and *Ephesians* in the Bible Text Books series.

activities in the local church will be suggested. Sixth, attitudes necessary for family unity will be reviewed. Finally, the local church planning for family involvement will be outlined.

Family Dissolution Today

Families are disappearing from society due to the high rate of divorce, "dead-beat" dads, child abuse (emotional, physical, and sexual), runaway children, juvenile delinquency, casual "live-in" relationships, illegitimacy, single parents, unwed mothers, "blended" families (step-parents with step-children), homosexual marriages, children having children, drug addictions, both parents employed outside the home, and "latch-key kids." The concept of "family" has also been redefined. We have all kinds of "family" arrangements in our society, from the one parent "Murphy Brown family," to the homosexual "Barney Frank family," to the unfaithful "Bob Packwood family" (Acuff 9-18). The modern family is unquestionably fragmented.

Consider just how bad it has become in our nation. The following statistics are taken from a recent work by Bridget Maher called, *The Family Portrait: A Compilation of Data, Research and Public Opinion on the Family* (2004):

- "The marriage rate has dropped by 50 percent since 1950" (2).
- "In 1960, 87.7 percent of children under 18 lived with married parents. By 1995, that percentage had dropped to 68.7 percent" (18).
- "Between 1960 and 2002, the birthrate among married women decreased by 45 percent" (18).
- "One percent of children in America live with an adoptive mother and father" (30).
- "In 2001, a majority of women with children under age six were employed part time or not at all; 42 percent were employed full time" (42).
- "In 1992, 25 percent of men and 15 percent of women reported that they had committed adultery" (67).
- "In a 2003 poll, 58 percent of adults said sex between an unmarried man and woman is morally acceptable" (71).
- "In 2002, one of every three babies was born outside of marriage" (74).
- "In 1970, just over a half a million couples cohabited; by 2002, 4.9 million unmarried couples were living together" (88).
- "More than half of all first marriages are preceded by cohabitation" (88).

- "The annual divorce rate has almost doubled since 1960, but has declined since the 1980s" (102).
- "One fifth of all adults have been divorced" (104).
- "In 1970, 8.2 million children lived in a single-parent family, compared to 19.8 million in 2002" (122).
- "One out of four children lives with a single parent" (123).
- "In 2000, 4.4 million children under 18 lived in a stepfamily" (136).

Modern society, termed "modernity," clearly has a negative impact on families. Jack Balswick documents four general negative effects (332-346). First, the consciousness of family members today is relative and subjective. Each family produces its own value system and standard of authority. Second, family communication is difficult or non-existent. Family members find themselves spending time together but not talking to each other in an understanding way. The so-called "generation gap" between parent and child is largely a communication gap. Third, family and church community have become fragmented and replaced by governmental agencies. Individual family members turn to government or economic institutions rather than other family members or church members when they need help with raising children, caring for the elderly, etc. Finally, commodities (careerism—making money, and consumerism—spending money) are at the center of family life today. Families gauge their success and self-worth by how much money they make and spend. Many families are obsessed with material things. It is naively believed by many that "the family that consumes together blooms together" (Balswick 345).

Godly families are disappearing from local churches of Christ. There are more and more parents attending by themselves without one or more of the children. When you ask a parent why his child is not present at the worship service, he offers up some excuse as to why he could not come. There are more and more disinterested teenagers staying at home or going out with their friends instead of attending a local church service. Grandparents bring grandkids because one parent or both parents have left the church. There are more single parents and divorcees in the Lord's church today. Even when you find a family still living under one roof, it is rare to see them doing good works together as a family.

The faithful, family unit is slowly becoming a thing of the past. Today, families with their busy schedules find themselves living separate lives and doing less and less together. They have two or more jobs, two or more cars going in different directions, and various electronic gadgets laying around the house that occupy their attention (TVs, cell phones, DVD players, X-box games, computers, Internet, instant messaging, iPods, etc.). Rarely do families eat together, talk together, read the Bible together, worship together, attend a gospel meeting together, visit together, or do good works together. Many today are also ignorant concerning the home and family as God would have them to be. Many just do not know what their home and family is to be. For some, the home is where they work the hardest but are appreciated the least. Others view their home like a filling station or rest stop where they drop by to eat and sleep before going on their way to work, school, or play (Buchanon 219).

Unfortunately, many families do not see that they are in trouble. They feel that as long as they are living under the same roof that everything is fine. Bob Buchanon writes, "Some brethren are ignorant enough to believe that our marriage is only a failure if it ends in divorce. 'Not divorcing' is not God's goal! Just to have the same residence does not constitute a God-pleasing home. I believe a marriage fails when it fails to be what God would have it to be even if it doesn't end in divorce" (221).

There are several factors that have led to the dissolution of the average family today. Consider the following: lack of Bible knowledge and lack of commitment to God's word, selfishness, individualism, unconverted church members, false philosophies (atheism, humanism, feminism, evolution, and situation ethics), false doctrines on divorce and remarriage, the sexual revolution, rebellion and disrespect for authority, promiscuity, homosexuality, pornography, divorce, abortion, euthanasia, permissiveness and lack of discipline, physical abuse, and the liberal media.

Lack of homemaking. God attaches great importance to homemaking (Prov. 31:10-31; 1 Tim. 5:14; Tit. 2:5). Today, however, homemaking is not considered important nor is it respected by many. Roland Lewis wrote, "Mothers with children should choose caring for their children instead of working if possible. (This does not apply to those who must work to provide necessities.) It does apply to those who want more material wealth or the things it can buy. It also applies to those who find working challenging, invigorating, and satisfying while homemaking and child care are drudgery" (U-2).

Materialism and Worldliness. Much of what separates and fragments the modern family involves our material possessions and modern conveniences. Buchanon mentions six threats to the modern family (222-223). First, entertainment takes people out of the home. Second, modern communication keeps us from having to visit a family member. Third, modern transportation allows us to leave family easily. Fourth, urbanization ("big city life") causes family to be too busy for one another. Fifth, social programs take away responsibilities from family members to care for their own. Sixth, materialism ("things") excites people more today than family time together. Buchanon believes that the threats to the home today can be grouped into three major areas (223-224). First, a radical change in basic values (from godly values to humanistic values). Second, a radical change in environment (from static to nomadic, from country life to urbanization). Third, a radical change in communications (from family communications to worldly communications). The Devil has used materialism and worldliness for centuries to attack the home. Take a look again at Matthew 13:22; Mark 4:19; and Luke 8:14. The Devil continues to use cares, riches, pleasures of this life and lust for things to pressure families to point of breaking (Adams 191-195).

Lack of Parenting Skills. Some parents just do not know how to parent. Either they were not raised right themselves or they reject the proper way to parent. They cause breakups in the home due to parental inconsistencies, disagreements, injustices, indulgence, indifference and stupidity (Cope 7).

Neglect. Family decay may also come about by simple neglect. J.D. Tant reminds us that neglect can be just as dangerous to the family as active abuse. He wrote, "And we need not actively abuse the family in order to undermine and destroy it, for we can simply let it die through neglect. It is as with a house that is not lived in. In time the house will decay and rot through neglect. A house needs to be lived in, and a family needs to live and be together" (166).

Liberal Agendas. The slow dissolution of the family is not just the result of neglect. There are active forces working to tear down the family. There are political groups that exalt the individual and devalue the family in order for individuals to experience a kind of no-fault freedom of life—free to choose and do as one wishes. Liberal social and political policy makers in America and around the world actively work to tear down the family (Santorum 14-16). Other groups, like the American Civil Liberties Union

(ACLU), actively promote an agenda that is harmful to marriage, parents, and children (Sears and Osten, *The ACLU vs. America* 34-98). Likewise, pro-homosexual groups actively attack family values (Sears and Osten, *The Homosexual Agenda* 89-116). Just as long as liberals dominate academic colleges and universities, Hollywood, the mainstream media, national labor unions, and political parties, the attack on the family will continue.

Families in Ancient and Modern Society

Our English word "family" comes from the Latin *familia*, meaning "household." A "household" is a family of persons living in a house. There are many houses being built today, but fewer "households" being built upon the principles of God's word (Ps. 137:1; Matt. 7:24-27; Luke 6:47-49). The common Hebrew word for "family" in the Old Testament means "household." The nation of Israel was basically divided into three levels: (1) tribe, (2) clan/family and (3) household. A "tribe" (Heb. *sebet*) was made up of "clans" or "families" (Heb. *mispaha*) and "families" were made up of "households" (Heb. *bayit* or *bet'ab*; lit. "father's house"). An example of this kinship structure is found in Joshua 7:14-18 and Judges 18:19. The Greek word *oikos* or *oikia*, meaning "house" (Matt. 13:57; Mark 6:4; John 4:53), and the word *patria*, meaning "lineage" (Luke 2:4; Acts 3:25; Eph. 3:15) were used by New Testament writers for "family."

In Bible times, and the Ancient Near East in particular, the family relationship was like a series of concentric circles. The husband and wife formed the nucleus of the circle, the children formed the inner circle, and the extended family of grandparents, aunts, uncles, cousins, and in-laws formed the outward circle. "Family" included both the immediate family and extended family as in the case of Rahab in Joshua 2:12, 18 and 6:23 (Tsumura 60). Families were in a close knit "circle." Solidarity (unity) was a marked characteristic of families in Old Testament times (Mitchell 371). Family life was father-centered and was governed by the father's authority (Hunt 281). Family members also protected each other. Each family member was "obligated to protect the entire family by the uprightness and correctness of his own conduct" (Baab 240).

Families in Old Testament times commonly lived in an agricultural and tribal setting which brought the family together through their work and social activities. In Patriarchal times, a family member saw himself as a member of his father's house, not as a free-floating individual. Families lived together in one house and extended family members lived in nearby homes often surrounding a common courtyard (Wenham 21). As families and extended families grew, there may have been anywhere from fifty to one hundred fifty people living in an area from a half-acre to an acre (Sánchez 36). Families often ate, slept, worked, worshiped, and lived together. M. Daniel Carroll Rodas writes:

> Gender and age-group roles in large measure were determined by the interdependent responsibilities that each member of the household had to contribute individually and corporately to help ensure survival. This kind of extended family structure, with all its interconnected commitments and values, clearly differs from the nuclear family (whether of the two biological parents, single parents, blended families, and the like) and the concept of isolated individual rights that define so much of North American society. The routines of daily life of ancient Israel also were radically dissimilar in all sorts of ways from what most of us in modern North America are familiar with. Can that family world reflected in the Biblical text, which seems so foreign to our experience today, inform the life of Christians and the church? I would say, "Yes it can. Indeed, it must, as our holy Scripture." Even though that world is very different from ours, there are some significant enduring lessons to be drawn from that ancient and far-off context (106).

Recent, conservative studies of ancient Bible families have been made and we can profit from these studies. The following works are offered for your consideration: *God, Marriage and Family: Rebuilding the Biblical Foundation* (Kostenberger, 2004); *Family in the Bible* (Hess and Rodas, 2003); *Marriage and Family in the Biblical World* (Campbell, 2003); *Families in the New Testament World: Households and House Churches* (Osiek and Balch, 1997); and *God's People in God's Land* (Wright, 1990). The main point of these studies is that families today are in decay and they must return to biblical principles in order to survive. History demonstrates that families were closer together in ancient Bible times than they are today. We must recover this closeness before our family, and ultimately our nation, collapses.

God's Plan For Family Unity
Husbands and Wives Together. God's goal for the family is that each family member care for the other and live in harmony together with the other. The oldest institution in the world is the family and a godly family begins with a godly man and a godly woman joined together (Gen. 1:27-28). C. Caverno writes, "The Bible is the world's great teacher of monogamy—the

union for life of one man and one woman in marriage as the basis of the family" (1094). Unfortunately, class is not in session in our society today and "the world's great teacher" is not being heard. Many today just will not listen to the Bible on the subject of marriage and the family.

God's plan is for the husband and wife to remain together. This plan has been in place from the very beginning of time. God intended for Adam and Eve and all married couples to be bound together for life (Gen. 2:18-25; 3:16). God said, "It is not good that man should be alone" (Gen. 2:18). (All Scripture quotations in this lecture are taken from the American Standard Version, 1901.) God created Eve to be Adam's wife so that Adam could be together with someone and not be alone. Eve's creation was special. She came from Adam, therefore, she was inseparable to him. "And the man said, This is now bone of my bones, and flesh of my flesh: she shall be called Woman, because she was taken out of Man" (Gen. 2:23). The man/ husband was called *'ish*, and the woman/wife was called *'ishsheh*. Because Adam and Eve were one, they were to love no other. David T. Tsumura reminds us that "exclusiveness is the nature of love between husband and wife" (68). Marriage is designed by God to be monogamous, meaning literally, "one" (*mono*) marriage (*gamous*)," or "one mate." God joins "a man" and "his wife" together and they are to be "one" (Gen. 2:24). Marriage was instituted by God from the beginning to be a life-long relationship of companionship and mutual support. There was harmony and happiness in this first marriage until sin entered the picture in Genesis 3. When sin entered, harmony was replaced with shame, blame, and discord (Gen. 3:7-13).

Other Old Testament Scriptures praise the monogamous relationship that God had made at the beginning (Prov. 5:15-19; 31:10-31). When a woman left her husband for another man, she was described as forsaking "the friend of her youth" and forgetting "the covenant of her God" (Prov. 2:17). Adultery is always wrong. It breaks up the marriage and the family. Proverbs teaches that a man is to love the right woman by means of five instructions (Longman III, 91-95). A godly husband should (1) avoid the immoral woman (Prov. 2:16-22; 3:13-18; 4:4-9; 5:1-23; 6:20-35; 7:1-27; 22:14), (2) cultivate a strong relationship with his wife (Prov. 5:15-20), (3) appreciate the joys of a good wife (Prov. 18:22; 31:10, 30-31), (4) be aware of the agony of choosing a bad wife (Prov. 11:22; 12:4; 21:9,19; 25:24; 27:15-16), and (5) choose a wise wife over an unwise woman (Prov. 9:1-6,13-18; 24:3).

Prophets like Isaiah, Jeremiah, and Ezekiel spoke of the relationship between Israel and God in terms of a monogamous, marital devotion (Isa. 50:1; 54:5-8; 62:4-5; Jer. 2:2; 3:14, 20; 31:32; Ezek. 16:1ff; 23:1ff; Hos. 2:4ff). On the other hand, Israel's idolatry was like committing adultery against God (Hos. 2:2-7; 3:1). The Old Testament closes the way it began by reminding the Israelites that the marriage covenant and marriage companionship are permanent. A husband and wife are to remain "one" for life. No putting away! Malachi writes:

> Yet ye say, Wherefore? Because Jehovah hath been witness between thee and the wife of thy youth, against whom thou hast dealt treacherously, though she is thy companion, and the wife of thy covenant. And did he not make one, although he had the residue of the Spirit? And wherefore one? He sought a godly seed. Therefore take heed to your spirit, and let none deal treacherously against the wife of his youth. For I hate putting away, saith Jehovah, the God of Israel, and him that covereth his garment with violence, saith Jehovah of hosts: therefore take heed to your spirit, that ye deal not treacherously (2:14-15).

When we turn to the New Testament gospels, we find that Jesus reiterated God's plan for the husband and wife. When asked if a man could put away his wife for any cause, Jesus said that a husband and wife are "one" and they are "joined together" (Matt. 19:5-6; see also Matt. 5:32; Mark 10:1-12; Luke 16:18). Jesus taught that a husband and wife are to stay "together" and not put each other away for any cause. He taught that marriage is permanent and indissoluble and his message was understood (Matt. 19:10). Marriage is for this life only, but it is to be life-long (Matt. 22:30). Even John the Baptist preached the permanency of marriage. When he preached to Herod and Herodias who were married but were not so joined by God, he rebuked them and said, "It is not lawful for thee to have thy brother's wife" (Mark 6:17-18; Luke 3:19).

Paul taught in the New Testament epistles the same thing Jesus taught in the gospels. Writing to married couples, he told them to stay together. He wrote that, if married couples are having troubles, they are to get them worked out that they "may be together again" (1 Cor. 7:5). He told the wife that she should "not depart from her husband" and "the husband leave not his wife" (1 Cor. 7:10-11). If the wife were to ignore Paul's instructions and depart, she should "remain unmarried, or else be reconciled to her husband" (1 Cor. 7:10). After departing, reconciliation is prescribed so that the married couple can stay together. Concerning a Christian married to an unbeliever, Paul goes on to write, "let him not leave her" and "let her not leave her husband" (1 Cor. 7:12, 14). Later in the chapter Paul writes, "Art thou bound unto a wife? Seek not to be loosed" (1 Cor. 7:27). Finally, he closes by writing, "A wife is bound for so long time as her husband liveth" (1 Cor. 7:39). Clearly, Paul desired that married couples stay together. Paul believed that marriage is a life-long commitment. He wrote, "For the woman that hath a husband is bound by law to the husband while he liveth; but if the husband die, she is discharged from the law of the husband. So then if, while the husband liveth, she be joined to another man, she shall be called an adulteress: but if the husband die, she is free from the law, so that she is no adulteress, though she be joined to another man" (Rom. 7:2-3).

Peter taught the same thing as Jesus and Paul. He wrote to married couples: "Ye husbands, in like manner, dwell with your wives according to knowledge, giving honor unto the woman, as unto the weaker vessel, as being also joint-heirs of the grace of life; to the end that your prayers be not hindered" (1 Pet. 3:7). Peter's words "dwell" and "joint-heirs" point to the closeness and unity of marriage. A "joint-heir" (Gr. *sunkleronomos*) is a "co-inheritor" (Vine 300). A "joint" is a place where two things come together. Remove the letter "t" from "joint" and you have "join." Peter is saying that Christian husbands and wives share the same spiritual blessing as they are united in Christ, and husbands should treat their wives properly in order to maintain these blessings. They share blessings in Christ together and they share the blessings of a married life together. They are "joint-heirs." Husbands and wives are joined together by God in marriage, they are joined together by Christ in conversion and they should remain that way for life.

However, not all people have been content with God's plan. Lamech is the first man recorded in the Bible to deviate from God's ideal when he "took unto him two wives" (Gen. 4:19). Others followed Lamech's example of bigamy which led to sorrow (Gen. 29:32-34; 30:18-20; 1 Sam. 1:5-8). Bigamy (two wives) and polygamy (many wives) became popular among many ancient peoples through the centuries. Solomon, for example, was destroyed when his one man-one woman relationship was destroyed (1 Kings 11:1-8; Neh. 13:26). Other men simply chose a casual relationship like prostitution over monogamy (Gen. 38:14). There came a time in Israel's history when the creation-ideal and the Mosaic precepts concerning marriage were completely ignored by many. What once was the rule (one man, one woman, joined together in one bond) slowly became the exception. So, in our culture today there is a complete disregard for the unity of marriage among many.

Husbands and wives together is God's wisdom for all mankind and we must all be content to follow God's wisdom instead of the wisdom of the world. The world says break up and separate the marriage as soon as possible. God says to the husband and wife, you are "one," so stay "together" until death. The lifelong marriage relationship that is designed by God for us here on earth anticipates the eternity long relationship that God has designed for the church (the bride) and the Lamb in heaven (Rev. 19:7; 21:9). W. White, Jr. writes, "Regardless of all evolutionary and psycho-analytic theories of explanation, the monogamous, lifelong relationship is that which is the nature of man and the creation" (497).

After hearing from God's word that husbands and wives should stay together for life, the following question is usually raised: "Is there any cause at all for which one spouse may put away his spouse?" The answer is "Yes." Jesus said there is one, and only one cause. He said a faithful spouse may put away his spouse who has committed fornication and marry another without committing adultery (Matt. 19:9). While a faithful, innocent spouse may have the right or cause to put away his mate guilty of fornication, this does not mean he has to immediately exercise his right. Nowhere in Scripture are God's people counseled to immediately put away a spouse guilty of fornication. The only time in Scripture when God's people were counseled to put away a spouse was when the marriage was unlawful to start with (Ezra 10:2-3, 10-11, 19, 44; see also Neh. 13:23-27). A faithful spouse needs to know about his right contained in Matthew 19:9, but he should also know what God's word says about forgiveness (Luke 17:3; Eph. 4:32). We should be willing to grant an innocent mate time to forgive his guilty spouse and allow time for them to be reconciled (1 Cor. 7:10-11). A faithful spouse, seeking to stay together with his mate as God would have him to do (Matt. 19:6), can encourage his mate to come back. Like God, a faithful spouse can be longsuffering (1 Pet. 3:9), giving a guilty mate time to repent (Rev. 2:21; see also Hosea). A faithful, innocent spouse has two choices when their mate commits fornication: (1) put away their mate for fornication; or (2) forgive their repentant mate. When a faithful, innocent mate needs to know which choice to make, and when to make it, he should turn to prayer, Bible study, and the wise counsel of godly Christians.

Parents and Children Together. The first recorded command given to mankind was: "Be fruitful and multiply" (Gen. 1:28). Children are viewed positively in Scripture from the very beginning. The Bible does not begin with individuals only, but with family! The family was, and still is, the foundation of all society. However, just as sin entered the first marriage (Gen. 3), sin also entered the family. Sin affected and infected family members (Gen. 4:8; 9:22; 19:30-38). All families were soon affected by sin (Gen. 6:5-13). However, just as family members were torn apart by sin, so family members could be brought back together again through forgiveness and reconciliation (Gen. 33:4; 50:15-21; Luke 15:11-32). The act of family reconciliation and restoration in the Bible is a good example for families today. Remember, the things written aforetime were written for our learning (Rom. 15:4).

God's plan for the unity of the family was protected and reinforced in the Law of Moses (Exod. 20:12, 14, 17; 21:1-11, 15-17; Lev. 18:6-18; 20:10-21; 24:14-21; Deut. 5:16, 18; 15:1-18; 21:10-13, 18-21; 22:22; 27:16; Num. 5:13-29). Three of the Ten Commandments (fifth, seventh, tenth) deal specifically with the family. Various other laws and regulations for the family are found in the Pentateuch. There are laws related to family property (Lev. 25:25-28; Num. 36:7-9), the well-being of the household (Lev. 18, 20; Deut. 16:9-14; 14:28-29; 22:13-24; 24:1-4, 19-21; 26:12) and functions within the family (Exod. 21:15, 17; Deut. 21:18-21; 27:16) (Sánchez 36-41). The "levirate marriage" law is a good example of God's concern for family solidarity (Lev. 25:25; Deut. 25:5-6; Ruth 4:5-6; Jer. 32:6-15; Matt. 22:24).

The importance of family unity is also seen in the Wisdom Literature. Families are not to be divided (Prov. 11:29). Families are to be a safe haven for one another (Prov. 14:1; 27:8). Godly instruction is to take place in a familial setting (Prov. 1:8; 4:3-4; 6:20; 10:1; 13:1; 15:5, 20; 17:21, 25; 19:26; 28:7, 24; 29:3; 31:1) and children must respect this teaching (Prov. 30:11-14, 17). The preface to the book of Proverbs makes it clear that young people should begin at home to learn how to live right in life (Prov. 1:2-7). Discipline (both instruction and corporal punishment) begins in the home (Prov. 13:24; 19:18; 22:6, 15; 23:13-14; 29:15; Heb. 12:7-11). Godly behavior is also to be modeled by parents in front of their children (Prov. 11:21; 17:6; 20:7). When you survey the Wisdom Literature you find that, "The ideal is strong, cohesive families in which parents, children, husbands, and wives support each other in the midst of a chaotic world" (Longman III, 99).

Parents and children should also enjoy life together. The husband is to enjoy his wife (Prov. 5:18; 12:4; 18:22; 31:11, 28; Eccl. 9:9) and parents are to be happy about their children (Pss. 127:3-5; 128:3). Parents and children need to spend more time doing wholesome things together and enjoying life together. Plan activities on a regular basis that involve the entire family. Wholesome secular activities and spiritual activities should be enjoyed together by all.

The state of the family is not so bright during the period of Prophetic Literature. Individual families "modernized," "secularized" and "urbanized" after they came into Canaan. Over a period of a few hundred years, they declined in their structure, welfare, and morality. The rise of Israel's monarchy negatively impacted the social welfare and family life of Israel. In short, families were "Canaanized" then, just like families today are "Americanized." Families did not take care for each other and worship God together as they once did. They turned to idolatry (Hos. 4:13-14; Amos 2:7-8; Mal. 2:13-14; Zeph. 1:5; Jer. 19:12-13; 32:29), child sacrifice (Isa. 57:3-13; Jer. 7:30-32; 19:4-6; 32:35; Ezek. 16:21; 20:31; 23:39) and unethical and unjust practices (Isa. 1:17, 23; 3:16-4:1; 5:8; 10:1-2; Jer. 5:26-29; 22:3; Zech. 7:10; Mal. 2:10-3:15; Amos 2:6; 4:1; 8:6; Jer. 34:8-22; Mic. 2:1-2; 6:6-8; Hos. 6:4-6) (Carroll Rodas 108-114).

In the New Testament gospels, Jesus cared about families. Some of his miracles were concerned with family sorrows and relationships (Matt. 8:1-13; 9:18-26; etc.). Jesus also strengthened the family through his teaching. He valued children (Matt. 18:1-5; 19:13-15; Mark 9:33-37; Luke 9:46-48; 18:15-17), reinforced the command to honor parents (Mark 7:9-13), encouraged fidelity in marriage (Matt. 5:27-28) and he discouraged divorce (Matt. 5:31-32; 19:1-9; Mark 10:1-12; Luke 16:18). Jesus taught the importance of family "nurture, personal responsibility, inside-out faithfulness, and commitment" (Westfall 134). We all need to follow Jesus' example and have the same concern for families today.

Jesus not only strengthened the family, but he also taught about family priorities. He taught that kingdom relationships take priority over family relationships. For example, he taught that the Lord is more important than family (Matt. 10:34-37; Luke 14:26), that God's kingdom is more important than family (Mark 3:20-21, 31-35; Luke 11:27-28), and that secular and domestic duties must be kept secondary (Matt. 8:19-22; Mark 1:16-20; 10:28-30; Luke 9:59-62). Jesus practiced what he preached by putting God's will above that of his own family (John 7:1-9).

Bible lessons that are taught in the local church. Parents, talk with your children each week about the sermon or the Bible class and how it can be applied in life.

Work and Serve Together. Families can contribute together to do the work of the local church (Eph. 4:16). They can volunteer together for work in and around the church building (Tit. 2:14; 3:1, 8, 14). They can come together to encourage brethren (1 Thess. 5:12-14). They can contact visitors together (1 Cor. 14:23). They can be benevolent together toward needy saints (Acts 11:29). Like Priscilla and Aquila, married couples can teach together (Acts 18:26). Be a married couple that works together to do what is right in the local church, not a married couple like Ananias and Sapphira who worked together to do evil (Acts 5:1-11). Fathers and sons can learn together to take an active role in leading singing, leading prayers, making announcements, waiting on the Lord's table, and delivering a Bible lesson. Fathers and older sons can teach a Bible class together. Mothers and older daughters can do the same. Many local churches lack teachers (Heb. 5:12). What are you doing as a family to solve this problem? Parents, there is plenty to do in the Lord's kingdom. Do it together with the whole family! Pick one day a week and do one activity together in the Lord's work.

James Cope set forth some good questions years ago concerning the young Christian's activity in the local church. Parents today would do well to ask these same questions of their own families. Brother Cope asked,

> As one pledged to Christ, does a young Christian have any obligation to reach non-Christians? Is his responsibility different toward sinners than that of an older Christian? Does youth have opportunities to reach their friends as do older persons? . . . Does a young Christian frequently have opportunity to teach Bible classes to small children or younger teenagers? Should they take advantage of the opportunity? Shall one beg off when requested even though he or she finds time to participate in various social and school activities and perhaps hold a money-making job? May one improve his spiritual maturity by meeting this challenge? Shall a young Christian man refuse any opportunity to better equip himself for greater usefulness publicly? When asked to lead prayer, read the Scriptures, make a talk, teach a class, serve or preside at the Lord's table, lead singing or perform any other service, should he not do it? Does God require less interest and effort of the younger than the older? (25).

Be Hospitable Together. Godly families together can visit the needy and offer to give to the needy (Jas. 1:27; 2:15-16). Parents, do you want

Balance. We are in the world, but not of the world (John 17:14-16). There are many worldly activities that compete for our family attention. We must balance worldly activities that are good in themselves, with putting the kingdom of God first (Luke 10:38-42). When faced with the choice between a worldly activity and doing some spiritual activity together with your spouse and family, choose the latter. You cannot engage in all kinds of worldly activities by yourself (clubs, work, entertainment, hobbies, etc.) and expect to keep your family together.

Genuine Love and Respect. When husbands have a sacrificial love for their wives as Christ loved the church, when wives respectfully submit to the headship of their husbands and love their husbands and children, and when children honor and obey their parents, families will stay together (Prov. 1:6; 6:20; 31:10-31; 1 Cor. 11:3; Eph. 5:22-6:4; Col. 3:18-21; 1 Tim. 2:8-15; Tit. 2:1-5; 1 Pet. 3:1-7). When each family member truly loves the Lord wholeheartedly, they will stay together as a family (Matt. 22:37). Also, love includes discipline to keep the family together and living the right way (Rev. 3:19).

Care and Concern. Even though Paul was not married and did not have children, we know from Scripture what kind of parent he would have been. Consider his "parenting skills" found in 1 Thessalonians 2:7-12. Paul's great care and concern for the Thessalonians is a model for families today. For example, parents need to be gentle and cherishing toward their children (v. 7). Parents should show kind affection and wholehearted devotion to their children (v. 8). Parents need to be an example of hard work (v. 9). Parents need to set a holy and righteous example for their children (v. 10). Parents need to be available and present in the lives of their children to exhort, encourage, and warn them on a daily basis (v. 11). Parents need to make sure that each family member is walking worthily before God (v. 12). We need more child caring, following childbearing (1 Tim. 2:15).

Purity and Honor. Husbands and wives must remain pure, devoted and loyal to one another. They must not mar their marriage with the sin of adultery. They must keep their marriage honorable and pure (Heb. 13:4; 1 Thess. 4:3-7). Purity and honor bind the family together.

Local Church Planning For Family Involvement
Local Churches. One educational slogan that is often heard today is "No Child Left Behind." We need to apply this slogan to the Lord's church. We

The Blessing of a Godly Home

Larry Ray Hafley

This is one of the sweetest, yet one of the most difficult assignments I have ever been given, for it has caused me to recall the blessed and blissful days of my childhood, growing up in the home of my dear and devoted parents, Cecil and Marie Hafley. They are both gone to the home of the soul, and I miss them every day. By the grace of God, and with faith in the Lord and his word, their lives epitomized the character and quality of a godly home. "Above five hundred brethren at once" yet remain who could testify to that effect. How much more so one of their children?

As much as I would like to take the time to remind you of their goodness and godliness, I know I must, as my mother would be quick to remind me, "get on with preachin' and stop messin' around." (At this point, Dad would be smiling his kind, gentle smile, and mother would be listening intently to see if she was "gonna hear the Bible preached.")

I have great and continuing sorrow in my heart for those who, unlike myself, were not privileged to be raised in a godly home. What a favored

---

Larry Ray Hafley was born on July 18, 1943 in Peoria, Illinois. He is the son of Cecil and Marie Hafley. He and his two brothers (Morris and Douglas) preach. He and his wife, Marilyn, were married on June 11, 1966 and he has two sons, Shawn and Curtis, and three grandchildren. Larry taught school for two years and began full-time work in June 1967. He has had a number of debates. He has preached full-time at Plano, Illinois; Washington Avenue in Russellville, Alabama; Pekin, Illinois; East Memphis, Tennessee; and from 1992 to the present he has worked at the Pruett and Lobit Streets church in Baytown, Texas. He holds many meetings each year.

3. Compare Mrs. Job—"curse God and die," and the beautiful Abigail (Job 2:9; 1 Sam. 25:3, 14-35).

4. Contrast Hannah's humble motherhood and Eli's negligent fatherhood (1 Sam. 1-3). One gave her son "unto the Lord all the days of his life," while the other's sons "made themselves vile, and he restrained them not."

Each narrative contains the outcome of eternity within its borders and boundaries. How much more so in our day? Are we exempt and immune? No, though the stories vary in their sometimes sordid and assorted details, their affects and results are, in principle, the same. Apostasy has its root in the soil of ungodly homes.

Psalm 78 calls for attention to the word of God, "which we have heard and known, and our fathers have told us. We will not hide them from their children, showing to the generation to come the praises of the Lord, and his strength, and his wonderful works that he hath done. For he established a testimony in Jacob, and appointed a law in Israel, which he commanded our fathers, *that they should make them known to their children:* That the generation to come might know them, even the children which should be born; who should arise and declare them to their children: *That they might* set their hope in God, and *not forget the works of God*, but keep his commandments: And might not be as their fathers, a stubborn and rebellious generation; a generation that set not their heart aright, and whose spirit was not steadfast with God" (vv. 3-8). Our homes must not be the source of "a stubborn and rebellious generation," whose heart is not right before God and whose spirit is not set in God. They will be, though, if we obscure the word of God and do not teach it unto our children.

Why are the nations of the world suffering societal breakdowns, lawlessness, and rebellion? (Remember the riots and destruction of large segments of Paris, France, in November of 2005?)

Why are communities faced with crime, dissension, and disruption? Why are drugs and drug lords reigning supreme over many sections of our major cities? The chief cause is the breakdown of the home and family unit. A nation does not suffer internal disarray until its society is under pressure. A society does not have pressure threatening its survival until its communities become centers of "ungodliness and worldly lusts." A community does not become a wasteland of burglary and bars on windows until the home ceases

God's plan for the unity of the family also calls for children and grand-children to take care of their "own family." This plan involves taking care of elderly parents (1 Tim. 5:4-16; Prov. 23:22-25).

Bible Examples of Family Activity Together

Old Testament Examples. In Bible times there were godly families who stayed together and served God together. We certainly need families like this today! For example, there were families in the days of Nehemiah who worked together and worshiped together. There is a family mentioned in Nehemiah 3:12, Shallum and his daughters, who worked together in rebuild-ing a portion of the wall. Some parents today cannot (or will not) get their children to help them do the Lord's work in the local church. The children are too into worldly activities to get involved in spiritual things. But this does not have to be. There is room in the kingdom for family members to do their part. Families are also mentioned in Nehemiah 8:2-3 who came together to worship God and hear and understand the reading of God's word. These families stayed from early morning until midday and were attentive at the same time. Can you imagine such a thing? Some families today do well just to sit together through a one or two hour service.

New Testament Examples. When we come to the New Testament, we find Bible families in the days of Paul who supported gospel preachers together. Luke tells us in Acts 21:4-6 that Christian men came together with their wives and children to pray with Paul and bid him farewell to Jerusalem. These families showed up together in order to encourage Paul and hold up the hands of a gospel preacher. No doubt, this meant much to Paul. All families today can be more sacrificial in getting out, leaving their comfortable surroundings and busy schedules and doing something together to encourage gospel preachers and other brethren in their service to God. Later in Acts 21:8-9, Luke records that Paul stayed in the home of Philip the evangelist who had four virgin daughters who prophesied. We do not have the gift of prophecy today. But, how encouraging it would be to see more fathers whose daughters or sons are faithful Christians and who would open their homes and be more hospitable to brethren.

Families Activities in the Local Church?

When we speak of families doing things together in the local church, we have in mind of course things that are authorized by the New Testament. For years, denominational churches have provided all kinds of unnecessary and unauthorized practices for their families. A flyer was recently mailed out advertising the "Nashville Kats Church and Family Night." The Nashville Kats (arena football) hosted a game, a post-game concert and "testimony from one of Nashville's most popular professional athletes" all in the name of religion. This is unauthorized

In the past forty years or so, some churches of Christ have done the same. Some brethren have formed "Church of Christ" ball teams for the adults, "Church of Christ" youth camps for kids, "Church of Christ" retreats for married couples, etc. One local church nearby offers a "Mother's Day Out" program which is a baby sitting service. Some local churches build gymnasiums so family members can have a place to play, or multi-purpose rooms for various "fellowship" activities. Other churches of Christ buy tickets for their young people to theme parks like Six Flags. Some churches provide "Church of Christ" buses to transport the elderly to various senior citizen social activities. There are also "Church of Christ" schools and colleges to educate the young, "Church of Christ" orphan homes to care for the fatherless, and "Church of Christ" retirement facilities for the elderly. More could be said, but the point has been made. There is no Bible authority for local churches to be providing things that should be provided by the home. When godly families stay active together in the local church, they are supposed to be doing only those things that local churches are authorized by God's word to do.

One other area of caution concerns the over emphasis of family in the local church. You can drive down the road and see signs that read "Family Bible Church," "Family Community Church," "Family Fellowship Church," etc. Some churches have a "Family Life Center." In the words of Cynthia Long Westfall, "One sometimes senses the conviction that the church exists to serve the family and to maintain the family's well-being" (146). We must remember that the Lord's church belongs to the Lord, not to families. He purchased it with his blood, not the blood of families (Acts 20:28). We are a church "of Christ" (Rom. 16:16), not a "Family Church." We exist to do the Lord's will, not to do what families want. Consider now some things that families can do together in the local church.

Be Converted Together. Families need to be Christians together. Both the husband and wife need to be Christians (1 Pet. 3:1-2). All the children of accountable age need to be Christians. Like the families of Cornelius, Lydia, the Philippian Jailor, and Crispus, there needs to be families today where the entire "household" is converted to the Lord (Acts 11:14; 16:15,

34; 18:8; see also 1 Cor. 16:15). Even in a religiously mixed family like the family of Timothy (Acts 16:1-2), one believing parent can raise children to become Christians. The local church will grow numerically through conversions. Make sure your children are among the conversions. Irven Lee wrote: "The church would grow from the inside if all the members could save their own children. Too often they take for granted that their children will be faithful, but there must be constant watching and teaching" (122).

Worship Together. Children need to grow up not just knowing God, but worshiping God (Bunting 128). Godly families can worship God together and attend a local church service together (Heb. 10:25). The church pew should be the "family pew" where every family member has his place. It is unfortunate the many families stay home or attend only when it is convenient. Other families might not miss a service, but because of the parents' hypocritical lifestyle, the children do not grow up to be faithful Christians. This should not be so in the Lord's church. Families should sing, pray, and study the Bible together. They can prepare their Bible class lessons together (1 Tim. 4:13). Spend a portion of one night each week doing your lessons together. Parents, make sure all of your children (who are old enough and able) open their songbooks during the service and sing out, open their Bibles and read along, take notes and bow in prayer when it is time to do so. Like Abraham's family (Gen. 18:19), families today can make sure that each family member learns God's word. Like Cornelius' family (Acts 10:24), families today can assemble together to hear God's word proclaimed. Families can attend gospel meetings together. Sometimes a Christian (including gospel preachers) will attend a gospel meeting without the spouse or children. Why is this? Why leave your family at home? Attending a gospel meeting is even a good opportunity for your children to meet young Christians their age. Families can also lay by in store together (1 Cor. 16:1-2). Do your children get an allowance? If so, teach them to contribute cheerfully together with you (2 Cor. 9:6-7).

Private worship in the home is important also. Families can and should come together at home to "bless Jehovah at all times" (Ps. 34:1). Families can sing together when they are by themselves at home (Acts 16:25; Heb. 13:15). Singing at home is a good time to explain to small children what the words of a song mean. Married couples can find some private time alone to pray together (1 Pet. 3:7) and families can also pray together (Acts 21:5). Families worshiping God together at home is a good time for families to put the family back in the "family room" (Diestelkamp 82-83). Do you have a "family room" in your house? Use it with the entire family. Do you have a "living room"? Spend some time actually living together in it with your entire family. Private worship at home should never be substituted for the regular worship assemblies of the local church, but neither should private worship be neglected. Family worship can be structured to set aside time each day or each week to sing, pray, and read God's word together. If you find yourself saying, "I do not have time for all that." Ask yourself, "How badly do I want to do it?" and "How important is it to me?" We all do what is important to us.

God has always desired that worship be a family affair. Consider Deuteronomy 16:11: "and thou shalt rejoice before Jehovah thy God, thou, and thy son, and thy daughter." Parents, do you include your family in worship? Edith Deen writes, "From the first altars to the tabernacles, temples and religious festivals, we see Israel's families united together. . . . These primitive people bear a striking contrast to many of today's families, who have not time for worship together, and consequently walk toward many dangers" (155).

Read and Study Together. Families need to read God's word together. Christianity is a taught religion, not a bought, fought, or caught religion. Parents must raise their children to know and follow God's word (Gen. 18:19; Deut. 6:4-9; 11:19; Josh. 4:6,21; Judg. 2:10; Prov. 22:6; Eph. 6:4; 2 Tim. 1:5; 3:14-15). Do not allow a child to make his own way in life (Prov. 29:15; Jer. 10:23). Parents can read the Bible at home and they can let the children read also. Parents and children need to read and study the Bible together on days other than Sunday and Wednesday night. And they also need to read and study the Bible together in places other than the church building. Bible reading at home is also a good time for families to work on Bible memory verses (Josh. 1:8; Ps. 119:11). Turn off the TV and computer, put away the games, put down the magazines and read God's word together. Sit around the kitchen table with your Bible and prepare your Bible class lessons together. It takes work sometimes to read, teach, and apply God's word to the family regularly, but it is worth it. Delton Porter wrote, "Immorality can break the heart; therefore, moral teaching in the home is worth all the effort it takes to accomplish it" (153). In addition to Bible reading, families can read good Bible related materials produced by sound brethren (1 Tim. 4:13; 2 Tim. 4:13). There are a number of good church bulletins and religious journals that can be placed in the home along side the Bible. Families also need to spend more time together putting into practice the your children to practice "pure and undefiled religion" just as you do? If so, include them in your visitation. Take them with you. Teach them to help others and speak to others. Do not leave them at home in front of the TV, on the computer, or on the phone. It will do your children more good to get out and visit the needy. Parents, let your children see your zeal to help the needy (Gal. 2:20). Like Lydia (Acts 16:14-15,40), families today can also offer hospitality together (Acts 2:46; Rom. 12:13; Heb. 13:2,16; 1 Pet. 4:9). Hospitality teaches kindness (Luke 10:33-37) and it teaches sharing (Heb. 13:16). Parents, include your children in your hospitality. Tell them to do some things around the house to get ready for company or go to a home of a shut-in together and serve them. They will grow up to be giving people, not selfish and self-centered. The home can be an attractive gathering place for old and young. Your home can be opened up to other Christians in order for your children to have positive, godly associations instead of worldly associations (1 Cor. 15:33). Like Mary and Mark (Acts 12:12), your home can be opened up to brethren for worship as well. Also when church members want to be hospitable and invite you and your family to come be with them, make time to do so. Allow your family time to be with godly Christians and benefit from their positive influences.

Evangelize Together. Families can do evangelism together (Acts 8:4). They can all sit in together on a home Bible study or host a Bible study together. They can pass out flyers together around the church building before a gospel meeting. They can work together to invite their neighbors to hear a Bible lesson. Fathers and mothers can also encourage their sons to be faithful gospel preachers.

Edify Together. Families can work together to build up other Christians (1 Thess. 5:14-15). Families can visit other Christians. Families can write cards or emails to preachers supported, wayward members, or the sick.

Grow Together. Families need to grow together. We are to mature as Christians the older we get (1 Pet. 2:2; 2 Pet. 1:5ff; 3:18). Christians are not to remain babes (1 Cor. 3:1-3; Heb. 5:12-14). Growth will benefit us, our family and others in the local church.

Lead Together. Godly families can also work together to qualify men for godly leadership and service. The Lord's church greatly needs elders and deacons today (Acts 14:23; Phil. 1:1). A part of the requirement for a godly elder and deacon involves the family (1 Tim. 3:2, 4-5, 11-12; Tit.

1:6). Fathers, make becoming an elder or a deacon a goal in your life and work toward it. Bring your family together and talk with them about this important place in the local church and then work together with your family to qualify yourself to fill these roles. Read the verses above and see what you have to do to with your family so that your family requirement is met. You will then be on your way to being qualified for this great work. Wives can support their husbands, and children can support their fathers to be qualified leaders and servants in the local church. Fathers and mothers can also encourage their sons to be elders and deacons.

Be Respectful Together. The home should be the place where young people learn great respect for the Lord's church and never despise the church (1 Cor. 11:22). Our children need to hear us talk about the importance of the Lord's church (Eph. 3:21). They need to see us set the right example of respect also. The home should be the place where young people learn great respect for worshiping God and faithful attendance at every church service should be practiced. The home should be the place where young people learn great respect for the soul-saving work of the Lord's church (1 Tim. 4:15). Parents can also raise up children who know God's word and are committed to it. This will enable them to become great pillars in the Lord's church. We all know of past influential men and women in the Lord's church who got their start in a godly home. Our children do not need to hear us unjustly criticizing anything about the Lord's church. They do not need to hear us disrespect the preacher, the elders, the deacons, the Bible class teachers, or any other member of the Lord's church. Parents must not gossip about church members or cut them down. Parents, teach your children by word and by example to love and respect the Lord's church.

Be Loyal Together. Finally, families need to be loyal to the local church. We live in a society of consumerism where everyone asks, "What's in it for me?" Unfortunately, this attitude exists in the local church, too. Many families think that if the local church is not "meeting my needs," then they will leave to find a "church home" somewhere else. Families instead need to be saying, "What are we giving to the local church?" Families do not need to be bouncing from church to church like church shoppers looking for the best deal that suits them. Families need to be loyal to the local church in their love (Rom. 12:10), their attendance (Heb. 10:24-25), their work and service (1 Cor. 15:58), their edification (Heb. 3:13), and their good works (Tit. 3:1, 8, 14). Families can show their loyalty by putting the local church first in their lives over all others things like sports, recreation, school, or work (Matt. 6:33).

When Jesus was in his own home he demonstrated spiritual priorities (Luke 2:49-52) and when he was in someone else's home he taught spiritual priorities as well (Luke 10:38-42). Sometimes a Christian even has to choose between loyalty to the local church and another family member (Matt. 10:37; 19:29; Mark 10:29-30; Luke 18:29-30). Just as a wife is to be joined to a husband with loyalty for life, so the bride of Christ (the church) should be joined to Christ with loyalty for life (Rom. 7:4; 2 Cor. 11:2; Rev. 19:7-9; 21:2).

When families move or go on vacation they should consider the local church. When young people go off to college they should do the same. Will there be a faithful group of Christians to work and worship with where you are going? Families need to adopt the motto of former President Kennedy and apply it to the local church: "Ask not what your local church can do for you—ask what you can do for your local church." We need more parents today like Hannah of old. We need parents who will give their children back to God in the local church all the days of their lives (1 Sam. 1:11).

Looking back over the list of what you and your family can do together in the local church, ask yourself: "How much and how often do I and my family do these things together?" You may want to make some kind of "Family Progress Chart" and post it so you can keep track of how much or how little you do together (Tant 165). List conversion, worship, reading the Bible, good works, hospitality, evangelism, edification, growth, leadership, respect, and loyalty; then, keep track of your weekly progress. Get serious and change your schedule to make family time together for these things. You may need to stop the clock and hang a "Do Not Disturb" sign on the door in order to make time together for these important spiritual activities (Diestelkamp 23-25). Spend some time each week going out together and staying in together (Diestelkamp 84).

Attitudes Necessary For Family Unity
Self-Examination. Spouses must be willing to examine their marriage. Parents must be willing to examine their parenting skills. We will not change until we realize we need to change. A good question to ask today is this: "Is it well with thee? Is it well with thy husband? Is it well with the child?" (2 Kings 4:26). After you ask this question, then go to God's word for the answer.

True Knowledge. Families need to know God's will for their lives (Eph. 5:17). Many families today are ignorant of what God wants for them.

Families need to know what the Bible teaches about marriage and family. In our world of cultural relativism, there are fewer absolutes today concerning family relationships. We need to get back to the "old paths" of the Bible concerning marriage and the family (Jer. 6:16).

Strong Commitment. After families have examined themselves and know what is expected of them by God, they all must be devoted and committed to doing God's will. Take control of your family (Sellers 111-113). Spouses and parents need more fortitude today. They need to stop being wimps and pushovers. When the Duke of Windsor visited America he was asked what impressed him the most. He said, "The way American parents obey their children." There is much truth to this. Parents need to take control of their families and make it what God wants it to be. Quit making excuses for a poor marriage or a broken family.

Parents need to take control of their children and raise them the way God wants them to be raised. Quit making excuses for uncontrolled children. Like Eli (1 Sam. 2:17ff; 3:13), Samuel (1 Sam. 8:1-3), or David (1 Kings 1:6), many parents today just do not take control of their children. Concerning King David's permissive approach toward Adonijah in 1 Kings 1:6, Tsumura writes, "David might have had hesitation about disciplining his son firmly because he feared that he might lose another son . . . David's indeterminate attitudes caused these unnecessary tragedies in this family" (77). Parents need a strong commitment to family. They need to take control of their work, their weekly schedule, and their world around them and bring themselves and their families back to God.

Great Resolve. Fathers need to be like Joshua and take the lead in the family to serve God. Joshua said, "but as for me and my house, we will serve Jehovah" (Josh. 24:15). More families need a "we will" resolve in themselves to do what is right together. Like Enoch (Gen. 5:22), walk with God together with your family.

Godly Jealousy. Paul wrote, "For I am jealous over you with a godly jealousy: for I espoused you to one husband, that I might present you as a pure virgin to Christ" (2 Cor. 11:2). We need the same type of zeal in the family today that Paul had for Christ and his bride (the church). Married couples must be zealous to stay together. Parents and children must be zealous to stay together.

55

need to be saying, "No soul left behind." Do you want your spouse to be left behind? How about your children? We can certainly have godly families in the local church who get involved together. But, we have to make it happen. All brethren in local churches (even singles and married couples without children) can work together to promote family unity. Families should be the focus in a local church program as well as individuals. Families can serve other families. Families can teach and evangelize other families (Tit. 2:1-7). Like Noah, who saved his entire family (Gen. 6; Heb. 11:7; 1 Pet. 3:20), families today can make sure that each member of the family is serving God and is saved in the Lord's church.

Local churches should provide opportunities for entire families to be active together. Often local churches will offer activities for select groups like a ladies' Bible class, a men's training class, or a youth Bible drill. These classes are good. But, what about planning activities for the entire family? For example, a work group plan could be put in place to encourage the whole family to stay active. A Bible class arrangement could set up at the building to include the entire family. Or, families could be encouraged to pass out flyers together around the church building for an upcoming gospel meeting.

Preachers. Godly preachers in the local church can help. Preachers need to preach on the important topic of the home and family. It may not be popular to address certain family problems or marriage issues, but it is greatly needed. From the pulpit, regularly address the subject of the family. This subject is a part of preaching "the sound doctrine" (Tit. 2:1, 15). Preachers need to offer sound direction to families from God's word. Preachers can work with parents to reinforce from the pulpit what godly parents are trying to teach their children at home. Preachers must not let a generation go by without hearing sound Bible teaching on the home and family. Make your sermons specific and practical to the family and teach on the sin of divorce.

A preacher can also help families in the local church by setting the right example with his own family. Like Philip the evangelist's family (Acts 21:8-9), preachers need to make sure that their children are right with God and get them involved in the Lord's work together. Some of the biggest offenders in the Lord's church are preachers and their families. There are preachers' children who are unruly, immodest, and worldly. There are preachers and preachers' wives who are ungodly and selfish. Preachers need to set the right example before the entire congregation (1 Tim. 4:12, 16). All preachers are encouraged to read the chapter on "The Preacher's Home" in Irven Lee's book, *Good Homes in a Wicked World* (159-167).

Elders. Godly elders in the local church can help. Men who serve as elders in the local church need to be vigilant over the families in their flock. They need to know what is going on in the home and address any problems that may be found therein. They can also make sure that families are getting a steady diet of God's word concerning the family. Elders can also make sure the entire family is evangelized. Home Bible studies should be set up with non-Christian spouses and children who need to obey the gospel. Do not assume that each family member who is of accountable age has heard the gospel. Elders, guide families in the right way with all your might. Watch over all the families in the local church (Heb. 13:17). Do not be spineless to correct any marriage or family problems. Elders, if you are truly qualified, then you know how to take care of your family and other families as well (1 Tim. 3:3-5). Today is the day to do just that.

Bible Class Teachers. Godly Bible class teachers in the local church can help. Local churches should arrange their Bible class curriculum to include a study of marriage and the family. Good Bible class workbooks on these topics are available to study on a regular basis; workbooks like, *The Family Circle* by Leslie Diestelkamp; *Family Life: A Biblical Perspective* by L.A. Stauffer; *Harmony in the Home* by Mike Willis, and *God's Plan for Parenting* edited by Kevin Maxey. Many religions today (including some churches of Christ) are so focused on entertainment in the pulpit and recreation outside the building, they are losing their families to the Devil through a lack of sound Bible teaching on marriage and family.

Conclusion

God gives us Christian homes. God is more than happy to give us Christian homes, but we must be willing to follow his word to that end. God is the divine author and architect of the family and the local church. May both the family and the local church work together to bring glory to God. Jesus said, "Suffer the little children, and forbid them not, to come unto me" (Matt. 19:14). Let us do all we can to make sure every family member has access together to Jesus in the local church. Jesus also said, "And if a house be divided against itself, that house will not be able to stand" (Mark 3:26). Let us do all we can to make sure every home is unified together and not divided in the local church. We want our families and local churches to stand, not fall.

A Personal Note: I learn from Luke 16:23-27 that we are all conscious after death. I will know if my spouse and my four children are with me in comfort or in torment after I die. When I die, I do not want to look across the "great gulf fixed" and see my wife, Cheri, or any one of my four children, Jessica, Jacob, Mason, and Carlin, "afar off" in torment while I am in comfort. And I do not want to see my wife or any one of my four children "afar off" in comfort while I am in torment. I want all of us to be together and be ready to hear, "Well done, good and faithful servant . . . enter thou into the joy of thy Lord." And I hope you will hear the same with your entire family.

Bibliography

Acuff, Larry. "Contemporary Trends in the Family." *Family, Church and Society Restoration and Renewal.* Freed-Hardeman University Lectureship. David L. Lipe, Editor. Henderson: Freed-Hardeman University, 1995.

Adams, James W. "Contagion: Social Pressures Upon the Family." *The Godly Family in a Sick Society.* Florida College Annual Lectures. Second Edition. Melvin D. Curry, Editor. Las Vegas: Nevada Publications, 1983.

Baab, O.J. "Family" in *The Interpreter's Dictionary of the Bible.* Volume 2. G.A. Buttrick, Editor. Nashville: Abingdon, 1962.

Balswick, Jack O. and Judith K. Balswick. *The Family: A Christian Perspective on the Contemporary Home.* Grand Rapids: Baker Books, 1999.

Buchanon, Bob. "Recovery of Family Life." *Humanism: Devotion to Man.* Florida College Annual Lectures. Melvin D. Curry, Editor. Tampa: Florida College Bookstore, 1985.

Bunting, Tom. "Worship in the Family." *The Godly Family in a Sick Society.* Florida College Annual Lectures. Second Edition. Melvin D. Curry, Editor. Las Vegas: Nevada Publications, 1983.

Caverno, C. "Family." *The International Standard Bible Encyclopedia.* Volume 2. Reprinted. James Orr, Editor. Grand Rapids: William B. Eerdmans Publishing Co., 1974.

Cope, James R. *Solving Family Problems.* Revised. Temple Terrace: James R. Cope, 1971.

Deen, Edith. *Family Living in the Bible.* New York: Pyramid Books, 1963.

Diestelkamp, Leslie. *The Family Circle.* Bowling Green: Guardian of Truth Foundation, 1987.

Hunt, L. "Family" in *The International Standard Bible Encyclopedia.* Revised Edition. Volume 2. Geoffrey W. Bromiley, Editor. Grand Rapids: William B. Eerdmans Publishing Co., 1982.

Lee, Irven. *Good Homes in a Wicked World.* Hartselle: Irven Lee, 1976.

Lewis, Roland H. "Dissolution in the Family." *Ancient Faith and Modern Thought.* Florida Christian College Annual Lectures. James R. Cope, Editor. Tampa: Florida Christian College, 1961.

Longman III, Tremper. "Family in the Wisdom Literature." *Family in the Bible: Exploring Customs, Culture, and Context.* Richard S. Hess and M. Daniel Carrol, Editors. Grand Rapids: Baker Academic, 2003.

Maher, Bridget. *The Family Portrait: A Compilation of Data, Research and Public Opinion on the Family.* Washington, DC: Family Research Council, 2004.

Mitchell, T.C. "Family" in *The New Bible Dictionary.* Second Edition. J.D. Douglas, Editor. Wheaton: Tyndale House Publishers, 1982.

Porter, Delton. "Moral Teaching in the Family." *The Godly Family in a Sick Society.* Florida College Annual Lectures. Second Edition. Melvin D. Curry, Editor. Las Vegas: Nevada Publications, 1983.

Rodas, Carrol and M. Daniel. "Family in the Prophetic Literature." *Family in the Bible: Exploring Customs, Culture, and Context.* Richard S. Hess and M. Daniel Carrol, Editors. Grand Rapids: Baker Academic, 2003.

Sánchez, Edesio. "Family in the Non-narrative Sections of the Pentateuch." *Family in the Bible: Exploring Customs, Culture, and Context.* Richard S. Hess and M. Daniel Carrol, Editors. Grand Rapids: Baker Academic, 2003.

Santorum, Rick. *It Takes a Family: Conservatism and the Common Good.* Wilmington: ISI Books, 2005.

Sears, Alan and Craig Osten. *The ACLU vs. America.* Nashville: Broadman & Holman Publishers, 2005.

Sears and Osten. *The Homosexual Agenda.* Nashville, Broadman and Holman, Publishers, 1963.

Sellers, Boyd. "What I Would Say to Parents." *If I Had One Opportunity: Urgent Messages For Today.* Florida College Annual Lectures. Daniel W. Petty, Editor. Temple Terrace: Florida College Bookstore, 2004.

Tant, David. "Family Together Activities." *The Godly Family in a Sick Society.* Florida College Annual Lectures. Second Edition. Melvin D. Curry, Editor. Las Vegas: Nevada Publication, 1983.

Tsumura, David T. "Family in the Historical Books." *Family in the Bible: Exploring Customs, Culture, and Context.* Richard S. Hess and M. Daniel Carrol, Editors. Grand Rapids: Baker Academic, 2003.

Vine, W.E. Vine's *Complete Expository Dictionary of Old and New Testament Words.* Nashville: Thomas Nelson Publishers, 1985.

Wenham, Gordon J. "Family in the Pentateuch." *Family in the Bible: Exploring Customs, Culture, and Context.* Richard S. Hess and M. Daniel Carrol, Editors. Grand Rapids: Baker Academic, 2003.

Westfall, Cynthia Long. "Family in the Gospels and Acts." *Family in the Bible: Exploring Customs, Culture, and Context.* Richard S. Hess and M. Daniel Carrol, Editors. Grand Rapids: Baker Academic, 2003.

White, W. Jr. "Family." *The Zondervan Pictorial Encyclopedia of the Bible.* Volume 2. Merrill C. Tenney, General Editor. Grand Rapids: Zondervan Publishing House, 1976.

life they miss who are not nurtured and nourished in a home centered in serving the Savior. I thank God and my dear mom and dad that I was not so deprived.

Preliminary Perspectives

First, the Bible is the standard, the measuring stick, of what constitutes a godly home (Isa. 8:20). It provides this pattern by "instructing in righteousness" the duties of husbands, wives, and children (Prov. 31:10-31; Eph. 5:22-6:4; Col. 3:18-20; Tit. 2:3-5; 1 Pet. 3:1-7).

Second, the blessing of a godly home cannot be measured by any standard of man. Likewise, the curse of an ungodly home is equally incalculable (2 Chron. 22:3). The length of the reach of each will abound and resound throughout eternity.

Third, the blessing of a godly home will not save all its progeny. The blight of a godless one will not condemn all its issue. One will be carnal Cain. The other will be righteous Abel. Some defy the odds and some deny their benefits.

Fourth, all the ingredients of a holy home cannot be compiled in one address. "And what shall I more say, for the time (and my own limited knowledge) would fail me to tell" all the factors involved in a family of faith.

Fifth, while certain principles will characterize all godly homes, the application and imprint of them will vary from one family to another. What characterized your godly home may not have played a large part in mine, and *vice versa*, though the larger, spiritual elements will typify both.

Home: The Primary School of Godliness

And these words, which I command thee this day, shall be in thine heart: And thou shalt *teach them diligently unto thy children*, and shalt talk of them when thou sittest in thine house, and when thou walkest by the way, and when thou liest down, and when thou risest up. And thou shalt bind them for a sign upon thine hand, and they shall be as frontlets between thine eyes (Deut. 6:6-8).

The home and family unit is to be the basic source of a child's teaching and instruction in the way and word of righteousness. Many, though, have turned over this work to school teachers, Boy and Girl Scout organizations, and various other social clubs and institutions. If our children need to be taught "morals and values," let them become Boy or Girl Scouts. Do they need to interact in recreational activities with those of their own age? Let them join a YMCA program or a ball team at school. These are the answers and solutions of our day. However, baseball and the Bible, football and the faith are best learned at home. Certainly coaches and counselors from various walks of life may be part of a child's life, but let the home be the initial center of all schooling and learning, especially regarding those "things that pertain to life and godliness."

It never seems to occur to many that the home and family relationship is the cornerstone of a child's education and development. Whether we are discussing physical or social skills, or moral and spiritual ones, the home is the essential element for a child's growth and maturation. "And he went down with them, and came to Nazareth, and was subject unto them: but his mother kept all these sayings in her heart. And Jesus increased in wisdom (mentally) and stature (physically), and in favor with God (spiritually) and man (socially)" (Luke 2:51, 52). Jesus was subject to Joseph and Mary and their godly influence. They were faithful to keep the Passover "every year" (Luke 2:41). They were not casual attendees, but were there "every year." This was a great example for the young child, Jesus. As every home should be, his home was part of his education and edification.

The worthy woman of Proverbs 31 also proves this. Her preparation and provision for her children were not limited to physical, material things. She also opened "her mouth with wisdom" (Prov. 31:26). "Her children arise up, and call her blessed," in part, no doubt, because they treasured memories of how they were raised in the home. How, though, did the children have a thankful disposition toward their mother? Where did they develop the character of heart that would cause them to "arise up and call her blessed"? They learned this sweet spirit from their mother and father. (Remember, her husband praised her, too, v. 28.) By example and training—"strength and honor" were her clothing—they were shown how to be gracious and grateful. They err greatly who place their children's growth and maturation into the hands of strangers.

"And, ye fathers, provoke not your children to wrath: but bring them up in the nurture and admonition of the Lord" (Eph. 6:4). Note who it is that is to "bring them up in the nurture (training) and admonition (instruction) of the

Lord"—"ye fathers," that is, ye parents. "I will therefore that the younger women marry, bear children, guide (manage) the house, give none occasion to the adversary to speak reproachfully" (1 Tim. 5:14). Both mother and father are to teach and direct their children in the way of truth and righteousness. The home is the citadel of a child's nurturing and nourishment in the word of God. In all things, whether physical or material, whether mental or moral, the home must be the school of the soul.

A spiritual home exemplifies the life that does not give occasion and opportunity for the devil to defile and revile godly garments of grace. By principle and precept, it shows the value of virtue. It espouses holiness and exposes heinous actions, words, and deeds. When that home teaches the child how to distinguish good from evil, it sets the tone and tenor of what is to be seen as normal and natural in the midst of a crooked and perverse generation.

It eschews every form of evil (1 Thess. 5:22). It shrinks back in shame from people and things that are unholy and impure. "Enter not into the path of the wicked, and go not in the way of evil men" (Prov. 4:14). "Let not thine heart envy sinners: but be thou in the fear of the Lord all the day long" (Prov. 23:17). "Be not thou envious against evil men, neither desire to be with them" (Prov. 24:1). "Be not deceived: evil communications corrupt good manners" (1 Cor. 15:33).

Equally important, the godly home teaches the child with whom to associate. Such a home is known by the company it keeps. Its quality is seen by those who are welcomed into it. Neither a home nor an individual should bring a poisonous snake into its bosom. David said, "I am a companion of all them that fear thee, and of them that keep thy precepts" (Ps. 119:63). Children must be schooled in the home concerning those items and individuals with whom they may associate.

Right and proper thoughts must reside in the home and heart that would be godly. They must direct them in paths of righteousness. "Keep thy heart with all diligence; for out of it are the issues of life" (Prov. 4:23). "Finally, brethren, whatsoever things are true, whatsoever things are honest, whatsoever things are just, whatsoever things are pure, whatsoever things are lovely, whatsoever things are of good report; if there be any virtue, and if there be any praise, think on these things" (Phil. 4:8). Filthy movies and magazines and uncensored viewing of the Internet and television have corrupted millions of homes and hearts. The home is where purity of heart and life must be learned and lived.

It is sometimes said, "Let the church be the church." That is, let it fulfill its divinely authorized duties and let it not enter into the works of the world. Likewise, let the home be the home. Let the home be more than a relationship which provides a dwelling place wherein all reside. Let it be the school of virtue and the training institution of every grace which leads to godly living (2 Pet 1:5-11).

Home: The Primary Source of Apostasy

We previously have alluded to the curse of an ungodly home. The home, like a religious debate, is a two-edged sword. In a debate, the truth has the greatest opportunity to succeed. It also, in debate, as James P. Needham told me many years ago, has the greatest opportunity to suffer. The same is true of the home. It can be the foundation of faith and fidelity. It also can be the foundation of the flesh and infidelity. "But there was none like unto Ahab, which did sell himself to work wickedness in the sight of the Lord, *whom Jezebel his wife stirred up*" (1 Kings 21:25). "Jehoram . . . walked in the way of the kings of Israel, like as did the house of Ahab: *for he had the daughter of Ahab to wife*: and he wrought that which was evil in the eyes of the Lord" (2 Chron. 21:5, 6). "(Ahaziah) also walked in the ways of the house of Ahab: *for his mother was his counselor to do wickedly*" (2 Chron. 22:6).

Observe the influence of ungodliness in the home in the cases cited above. Imagine how different would have been the outcome of the ages if the women mentioned had been "daughters" of Sarah (1 Pet. 3:6)! What would have been the result of the souls and the centuries if the women had been "of a meek and quiet spirit . . . being in subjection to their own husbands"? Do we dare to wonder?

1. What would have been the story had Mrs. Haman soothed her husband and encouraged him to get over his fit of pique against Mordecai, rather than stirring him to build gallows of bitterness (Esth. 5:12-14)?

2. Suppose Sapphira had told her husband, "Now, you can tell the apostles and brethren whatever you want to tell them, but I am going to tell them the truth about the price of the land and our contribution to the needy saints" (Acts 5:1-10). Would Ananias have told his lie? Perhaps not (cf. 1 Pet. 3:1).

to function as God would have it to do. It behooves us, therefore, whether we are speaking of life in this world or in that to come, to seek and to secure the blessings of a godly home.

The Blessings of a Godly Home
1. In a godly home one learns that he is a creature of God for eternity. The earliest memories of a child's learning ought to be that "God made the sun, the moon, the stars, the seas, the rocks, the hills, and the trees." Burned and imprinted deep in the heart and soul of our precious children, from the first days of their ability to comprehend anything, ought to be inscribed the words, "Lord, thou art God, which hast made heaven, and earth, and the sea, and all that in them is" (Acts 4:24). I am so blessed to have been raised in a home where there was never any doubt about who our Creator was.

Children must learn that they are as much a creative part of God as are the trees. This sense must be implanted in their little hearts. God often reminds his people that he is their Originator and Creator, the Giver of life, and the Creator of all things (Gen. 1:1; Pss. 19:1; 97:6, 7). "I will praise thee; for I am fearfully and wonderfully made: marvelous are thy works; and that my soul knoweth right well" (Ps. 139:140). The psalmist praised God, honored him as God, because he recognized that God was his marvelous Designer and Creator. In his patient humility, Job said, "Naked came I out of my mother's womb, and naked shall I return thither: the Lord gave, and the Lord hath taken away; blessed be the name of the Lord" (Job 1:21). Without that knowledge, devoid of any concept of it, the world becomes worse and worse, deceiving and being deceived. With it, man humbly praises, worships, and serves the Lord who made him.

Many hearts are fully set to engage eagerly in all forms of impurity and iniquity because they have no concept of God and no understanding that they are his creatures. That there is such an august, Divine Being is not in their mind. Because (to them) hell is an adjective and not a literal place of fire and brimstone, the thought that they must someday give account to him is the punch line of a ribald joke.

2. In a godly home, one learns to fear God. My mother would be embarrassed if you knew how limited was her public education, but she was one of the wisest women who ever lived. She not only had "good common sense" in abundance, she also had the fear of God embedded in her reverent, sweet heart. She taught that fear to her children and spoke of it to everyone. "Behold, the fear of the Lord, that is wisdom; and to depart from evil is understanding" (Job 28:28). "The fear of the Lord is the beginning of knowledge: but fools despise wisdom and instruction" (Prov. 1:7). "In the fear of the Lord is strong confidence: and his children shall have a place of refuge. The fear of the Lord is a fountain of life, to depart from the snares of death" (Prov. 14:26, 27).

There is no fear of God in the eyes of the wicked. That is why they are able to carry out their wicked ways with impunity (Ps. 36:1-4).

> There is none that understandeth, there is none that seeketh after God. They are all gone out of the way, they are together become unprofitable; there is none that doeth good, no, not one. Their throat is an open sepulchre; with their tongues they have used deceit; the poison of asps is under their lips: Whose mouth is full of cursing and bitterness: Their feet are swift to shed blood: Destruction and misery are in their ways: And the way of peace have they not known: There is no fear of God before their eyes (Rom. 3:11-18).

And why is this so? In part, it is because men have cast God out of the equation of life. God has been dismissed as a myth or as the absurd hope of a dying man who is grasping futilely for deliverance (cf. Rom. 1:18f). Thus, "there is no fear of God before their eyes."

One of the most riveting and powerful things ever uttered was the statement of the Lord Jesus, "And fear not them which kill the body, but are not able to kill the soul: but rather fear him which is able to destroy both soul and body in hell" (Matt. 10:28). Consider the serious implications of those striking words! Eternity in heaven or in hell is determined by whether or not one fears the Lord. A godly home is a blessing because it possesses this fear and imparts it to its children. Each member is exhorted to live in the fear of the Lord all the day long (Prov. 23:17).

3. In a godly home, one learns the relevance, significance, and importance of the orders and ordinances of God. Since "whatsoever things were written aforetime were written for our learning," we go to the book of Exodus and see the establishment of this principle. Regarding the Passover, God said:

> And ye shall observe this thing for an ordinance to thee and to thy sons for ever. And it shall come to pass, when ye be come to the land which

the Lord will give you, according as he hath promised, that ye shall keep this service. And it shall come to pass, *when your children shall say unto you, What mean ye by this service?* That ye shall say, It is the sacrifice of the Lord's passover, who passed over the houses of the children of Israel in Egypt, when he smote the Egyptians, and delivered our houses. And the people bowed the head and worshipped.

And the children of Israel went away, and did as the Lord had commanded Moses and Aaron, so did they. . . . And *thou shalt show thy son in that day, saying, This is done because of that which the Lord did unto me when I came forth out of Egypt. . . . And it shall be when thy son asketh thee in time to come, saying, What is this? that thou shalt say unto him, By strength of hand the Lord brought us out from Egypt, from the house of bondage* (Exod. 12:24-28; 13:8, 14).

Consider the penalty for violation of God's ordained order for work and worship in the Old Testament.

First, Nadab and Abihu used fire to burn incense which God had not authorized (Lev. 10:1, 2). They were not worshiping idols or burning incense unto a false God. They were acting in the role God assigned to them. What, then, was their error? They used fire from an alternate source, from a place God had not sanctioned. Fire to burn the incense was to come from the coals of the altar (Lev. 6:12, 13; 16:12; cf. Num. 16:46). They used foreign or strange fire, fire which the Lord had not approved. Result? They were incinerated on the spot! These things were written for our admonition (1 Cor. 10:6, 11). Let us therefore fear and be certain that we are serving the Lord on his terms and not on our own.

Second, despite the fact that he was trying to do a good work, Uzzah lost his life because he touched that which God said should not be touched (1 Chron. 13:2-10; 15:2, 13-15). The ark of the covenant, a small wooden box, overlaid with gold, contained a pot of manna, Aaron's rod which had miraculously budded in Numbers 17, and a copy of the Ten Commandments. "Don't touch it lest ye die," was God's command and warning. It was to be carried by the Levites. Poles were inserted in rings on the sides of the ark of the covenant. Those poles were not to be removed (Exod. 25:14, 15). Perhaps, if they had never been moved, the ark of the covenant may not have been carried in an ox cart to begin with and Uzzah would not have lost his life. Because they did not operate as God would have them to do in the transportation of the ark of the covenant, Uzzah died.

Third, Saul was told to "utterly destroy" Amalek (1 Sam. 15:3). He and the people spared Agag, the king of Amalek, and the best of the flocks to do sacrifice unto the Lord (1 Sam. 15:8, 9, 15). Observe that they did not save the best of the flocks to enrich their own, but to do sacrifice unto Jehovah. That sounds like a "good work," and in the worldly mind of man it is accepted. However, God rejected every bit of it. He would rather have our complete obedience than for us to offer worship which he has not authorized by his word. "And Samuel said, Hath the Lord as great delight in burnt offerings and sacrifices, as in obeying the voice of the Lord? Behold, to obey is better than sacrifice, and to hearken than the fat of rams" (1 Sam. 15:22). Does the Lord prefer that we offer sacrifices which he has not appointed, or would he rather that we obey his word and do what he has commanded? It is better to obey God than to offer sacrifices, no matter how well intentioned they may be. It is better to listen to the word of God than to offer the choicest offerings which God has not ordained.

Godly homes teach these principles and burn them indelibly into the hearts of their children (Ps. 78:3-8). I can still hear my mother's voice and see her animated features as she told them to us.

One of the greatest failures in the homes of our day is that our children are not being taught "the way of God more accurately." Oh, they may know certain, general facts—"Noah and the ark; Jonah and the whale"—but often they are not being taught to understand the deeper things of the purposes and promises of God. Assuredly, surface facts are essential. Hebrews 11 shows this. Hebrews 11 also instructs us in some of the underlying, ultimate details.

A. Children love to listen and learn the basis facts about Noah. Such stories fascinate them. Godly parents in godly homes speak of Noah's total obedience to the plan and pattern of God for the ark (Gen. 6:14-16, 22). They impress on the absorbing minds and precious souls of their children the necessity of obedience to God in all things. The ark had to be built as God directed. Noah would have been lost if he had not built the ark as God said to build it. Remember the old Bible school song, "Good old Noah built the ark, *like God told him to"*? Applications are made to God's pattern of work and worship for the church today. Young, thirsty hearts soak up these principles. Only later, perhaps, will the importance of them strike and stir their hearts, but the groundwork of the gospel and the foundation of the faith has been laid. Such are the benefits of a godly home.

believe that broad smiles, laughter, a quickened pulse, a heightened sense of friendship, acceptance by their peers, and joyful feelings are equivalent to "growth in the grace and Spirit of God." It is a lie. It is carnal, worldly. It is not spiritual. While such reactions may accompany one who is steeped in the grace of Christ, they are not the essence of what it means to be devoted to Christ. Great swelling words of vanity, uttered by vain men with pompous hearts, induce and seduce young hearts. They are enraptured and taken captive by an emotional atmosphere of pseudo spirituality.

Children raised in a godly home are not as likely to be deceived. They know better. They are joyful, happy, and well adjusted. They, too, have fun. They live joyfully. They enjoy the pleasures of their youth, as God exhorts and encourages them to do (Eccl. 11:9). However, they know the difference between social, sensual appeals to the flesh and true worship.

The Lord's supper is not simply "a pinch of bread and a sip of juice." No, it is the communion of the body and blood of the Lord (1 Cor. 10:16, 17). It shows the Lord's death (1 Cor. 11:26). Godly parents set the pattern for respect and reverence as they examine themselves and discern the Lord's body. With eyes closed (as was the constant practice of my parents), they concentrate on the Lord's death and remember him. Every child raised in a godly home has that blessed image of his mother and father burned into his mind. That precious memory serves as a lesson for reverence for the true things of God.

Because the appointments of God are going to be kept, attendance at worship services of the church is never a question. As Joseph and Mary kept the ordinances of God "every year," so godly homes attend to the statutes of the Spirit "upon the first day of the week" (Acts 2:42; 20:7; 1 Cor. 16:2; Heb. 10:23-25). Meetings in central Illinois where I was raised were not as common as in other parts of the country. There were fewer churches. So, when a meeting was two hours away, it was not a problem. We packed up and went. After services, Dad would talk until the last person left the building. We would drive back home after midnight. Sleepy little boys were undressed and put to bed. Still, at 7:00 A.M. the next morning, it was time to get up and go to school. And, so we did. How sweet is the memory of a godly home!

During our meetings at home, Mom and Dad nearly always kept the preacher. Every night, after services a house full of people were invited over. Getting to bed after midnight was not uncommon, even though Mom had to get up at 4:30 every morning. Still, in the afternoon, she took food to others and visited the hospital with my dad. They never thought of it as a sacrifice, or as a hardship. It was the love of God in the hearts of loving parents, his representatives in the home (Matt. 25:34-45). Thank you, Mom and Dad, for the blessing of a godly home.

4. In a godly home, the traditions of men are clearly marked, abhorred, and avoided. Early in life, youngsters in a godly home are taught that Easter and Christmas, like infant baptism and instrumental music, are human, man-made traditions. As soon as their little hearts are able, they are instructed in the differences between what constitutes divine religion and human religion.

In Psalms 78, 105, 106, in 1 Corinthians 10, and the book of Hebrews, there are reminders of the judgment of God on those who reject the ordinances of the Lord for the traditions of men. "Thus they became unclean in their practices, And played the harlot in their deeds" (Ps. 106:39). Truly, as the old adage says, those who do not learn from the errors of the past are destined to repeat them. It is no less true in the church today. The godly home, therefore, must be where children learn that the Lord will accept neither amendments, substitutes, nor additions to his will, his way, and his word.

In how many homes among us is this being done today? In every godly home, it is being done for sure. How about yours?

In Matthew 15 and Mark 7, the Lord exposed a human tradition that made void the word of God.

> And he said unto them, Full well ye reject the commandment of God, that ye may keep your own tradition. For Moses said, Honor thy father and thy mother; and, Whoso curseth father or mother, let him die the death: But ye say, If a man shall say to his father or mother, It is Corban, that is to say, a gift, by whatsoever thou mightest be profited by me; he shall be free. And ye suffer him no more to do ought for his father or his mother; Making the word of God of none effect through your tradition, which ye have delivered: and many such like things do ye (Mark 7:9-13).

Thus, if one kept their tradition, he could no longer honor his father and his mother. In effect, the commandment of God would be cancelled by their tradition. The same is true today with respect to any number of denominational traditions which are widely accepted by men. Note some examples:

A. If infant baptism were universally practiced, there would be no baptism of adult, penitent believers, as the Bible requires (Mark 16:16; Acts 2:38; 8:12, 35, 36, 37). Ask a Catholic who was "baptized" when he was an oblivious infant if he needs to be baptized. He will say, "No." In that way, does the human tradition make void the divine teaching.

B. Closely related to this is the practice of sprinkling for baptism. Baptism is immersion (Matt. 3:16; John 3:23; Acts 8:35-39; Rom. 6:4; Col. 2:12). However, where the practice of sprinkling or pouring of water is accepted, the scriptural action rarely is seen, "making the word of God of none effect through (their) tradition."

C. Where the modern day one man "Pastor" system is a part of congregational organization, the New Testament pattern of a plurality of men ruling and shepherding the flock is generally unknown (Acts 14:23; 20:28; 1 Tim. 3; Tit. 1; 1 Pet. 5:2). "Ye see, then, how that" a tradition of men nullifies the arrangement of God.

D. When churches rely on pancake breakfasts, pie suppers, rummage sales, and sales of tapes to raise money, the need for each member to give as he has purposed and prospered is diminished. Why should we give our money when we can participate in a fish fry and a sale of pecans to raise it? Again, man's way to raise money supercedes and displaces God's way (1 Cor. 16:2).

E. Churches that celebrate so-called holy days with their plays, pageants, parades, and "praise teams" give very little time for preaching (cf. Acts 20:7). Mother's Day, Father's Day, and a host of other humanly devised events on the "Church Calender," along with their choruses, musicals, and children's skits have crowded out any appreciable time for gospel preaching. (For some of these social-religious organizations, the less preaching they do, the less harm they can do! So, perhaps it is a blessing that they have little time for preaching.) These trappings of men "choke the word" and do away with the traditions of Scripture.

In a godly home, these things are pointed out. The children learn, not only the value of God's way, but also the destructive nature of the things that are ordained by men.

5. In a godly home, one learns to pray. As with every aspect of what it means to be a child of God, Jesus is the greatest example of prayer. He prayed often and taught his disciples to do the same (Rom. 12:12; 1 Thess. 5:17). He prayed for long periods of time, even "all night" (Luke 6:12). He instructed his disciples how to pray a brief prayer (Matt. 6:9-13). He prayed privately, making sure he was alone (Mark 1:35). He prayed openly before others (Luke 9:28; John 11:41, 42).

In the godly home, the young children do not see Jesus praying, but they can see and hear "Daddy and Mommy" praying. Such sights will be in their little hearts and minds all the days of their lives. Many times have I come in the kitchen and seen my mother either reading the Bible or bent over it at the table praying. How I would love to hear my dad lead another prayer. So, I can say, with the voice of the Spirit of God and with an example that will never leave me, that prayers in the home are so very vital and important.

Children should never come to the table to eat nor go to bed at night without a prayer. Never! When such practices are begun at birth, the child never knows anything else. When the law demanded seat belts and car seats for children, I wondered how "the poor, little things" would be able to endure it. Our children had been allowed to play in the back seat with their toys in the space above the back window. So, I thought it would be impossible to "strap them down" like that. Well, now, of course, a child comes home from the hospital in a car seat. They never know any different. Small children take it for granted that getting in the car means they will be in a car seat. Perhaps that is a poor illustration, but prayer in the home needs to be an inherent part of daily life. In a way, it needs to be "taken for granted." It is a natural, normal part of life. It is a "given"; we pray before meals and before we go to bed. That being done, with training, other prayers will follow as the children grow in life and in the Lord.

I pity the parents who have missed those special sweet times. We always held the hands of our boys and prayed with them. What a blessed, blessed memory that is. But, more than the memory is the knowledge that such prayers were a benefit to them and to the circumstances of their lives. Only eternity can reveal the good that has been done through fervent prayer. How much the more so with our precious children!

6. In a godly home, children learn the attributes of character that will shape their spiritual, social, and secular relationships. Honesty,

B. Yes, Abraham obeyed God, "and he went out, not knowing whither he went." He left his clan, his kin, and his country, but why? "For he looked for a city which hath foundations, whose builder and maker is God" (Heb. 11:10; cf. vv. 13-16). He was looking for a "better . . . heavenly" country. To attain this goal, he had to do some things and go to some places that he did not choose. He went, not because that is where he wanted to go, but because it was where God wanted him to go. Children in godly homes learn that the way to heaven is not always the easiest. It is a strait and narrow way, one which will not always please my desires. Difficult choices will have to be made. Do I do what I want to do, or do I, like Abraham, go where God directs?

They see the example of their godly parents. Like Abraham and the Lord, they see them make tough choices. They watch them make decisions that may mean less income, but which will enhance and increase their ability to serve the Lord. They hear them speak of doing some things and of refusing other things "because it's what God wants us to do." In a godly home, Abraham's faith is lived every day.

C. Thrill children with the story of Moses, but let them also know why he endured and suffered and served as he did. "By faith Moses, when he was come to years, refused to be called the son of Pharaoh's daughter; Choosing rather to suffer affliction with the people of God, than to enjoy the pleasures of sin for a season; *Esteeming the reproach of Christ greater riches than the treasures in Egypt: for he had respect unto the recompence of the reward.* By faith he forsook Egypt, not fearing the wrath of the king: *for he endured, as seeing him who is invisible"* (Heb. 11:24-27). Let our children learn the facts, but let them also know why. When they do, the future—theirs and that of the church—is secure.

Children in a godly home are instructed to know what it means to worship "in spirit and in truth" (John 4:24). Singing is not simply an emotional, happy release of energy, designed to "raise the roof." It is more. It is "teaching and admonishing one another"; it is "singing with grace in your hearts unto the Lord"; it is singing praise unto the Lord (Rom. 15:9; Eph. 5:19; Col. 3:16; Heb. 2:12). God, and glorifying him, is the focus of everything (1 Cor. 10:31).

Fleshly appeals often are made to young people. As though excitement, enthusiasm, and inspiration are ends in themselves, many young people fairness, sharing, unselfishness, self control, sacrifice for others—these and a number of other attributes are products of a home that is centered in God, Christ, and the Bible. These traits are installed by example and instruction. "Show me thy ways, O Lord; teach me thy paths" (Ps. 25:4).

A. Parents must know how important their behavior is before their children, for they are being watched by hearts that will emulate and imitate them. It will be difficult, though not impossible, for a child to live better than the example he has had set before him. In view of this, every mother and father should "greatly fear and tremble" before the solemn duty that is theirs to display the truth in love before their priceless progeny.

Compare the principle of 1 Timothy 4:12—"Be thou an example of the believers, in word, in conversation, in charity, in spirit, in faith, in purity." Of course, our Lord Jesus is the paramount pattern—"For even hereunto were ye called: because Christ also suffered for us, leaving us an example, that ye should follow his steps" (1 Pet. 2:21). That is what we, as parents, must do. We must *be* an example; that is, our character must be reflected in our conduct before our children. Our interaction in day to day living, especially in the home, must display integrity, honor, patience, and the willingness to sacrifice for those whom we love. Ephesians 5:25, "Husbands, love your wives, even as Christ also loved the church, and gave himself for it." See the power of the pattern of the Lord's unselfish love ("even as") in that text? As the husband is what he ought to be by being conformed to the Lord's example, so must we be in the home before our children. We, too, must *leave* an example, a trail, as it were, across the plains of life, that others may follow and not be led astray.

B. Holiness of the heart must be taught (Eph. 6:4). "I will instruct you and teach you in the way which you should go; I will counsel you with My eye upon you" (Ps. 32:8, NASB).

Patience and persistent, consistent training is essential. Each age and stage of children's lives requires different types and styles of teaching, but nothing can take the place of kindly warnings and reminders and faithful admonition and adherence to the rules of truth and righteousness. Remember the intense diligence of instruction stressed in Deuteronomy 6:7. "And thou shalt *teach them diligently unto thy children,* and shalt talk of them *when thou sittest* in thine house, and *when thou walkest* by the way, and *when thou liest down,* and *when thou risest up."* In other words, all the time! It takes time, energy, and patience, but the fruit of such labor in the vineyard of a child's spirit will produce an hundredfold more here (thy children shall arise up and call you blessed), and in the world to come, eternal life.

To stamp the hearts of our offspring with the virtues of life, wise, thoughtful parents will speak and plan of such determinations even before they are married. They will cherish and treasure in their hearts the content of the character they wish to implant. They will pledge to help and encourage one another and pray for the wisdom necessary to implement their godly goal to raise up seed unto God and heaven after awhile.

7. Godly homes teach little boys how to be good husbands and fathers and little girls how to be good wives and mothers. Though it is a negative illustration, such influence is noted, in principle, in the word of God. Concerning King Ahaziah, it is said, "He also walked in the ways of the house of Ahab: for his mother was his counselor to do wickedly" (2 Chron. 22:3). She could as well have been his counselor to do well.

It has often been said that a young man likely will treat his wife as his father treated his mother, and that a young woman will treat her husband the way her mother treated her dad. This witness is true. Thus, the home must be the very essence of love, kindness, courtesy, compassion, and consideration.

A. One of the most memorable and noteworthy things said about the worthy woman of Proverbs 31 is that, "Strength and honor are her clothing; she shall rejoice in time to come. She opens her mouth with wisdom, and on her tongue is the law of kindness" (vv. 25, 26). Her clothing is that inner apparel of a "meek and quiet spirit, which is in the sight of God of great price (1 Pet. 3:4). This is the loom upon which her strength and honor are woven. Her husband never lacks anything he needs to perform his tasks as a leading man (Prov. 31:11). He is admired and esteemed because he can attend to his work without distraction. His wife is the foundation of his success, yea, "the wind beneath his wings," as a popular song attests.

A little girl hears her mother's tongue send forth endearing words of compassion, tenderness, and gentleness. Her tongue is ruled by kindness. She learns that this is the way a woman is to speak. It is how she is to present herself unto her husband, her children, and her community.

Consider the opposite. What if the woman is belligerent and antagonistic? What if she is slow to hear, swift to speak, and quick to anger (cf. Jas. 1:19)? Suppose she is argumentative, turning every little disagreement into World War III. Suppose she is taunting and derisive of her marriage and her husband, always complaining and never satisfied. Imagine how that will impact and influence the children. What kind of future wife and mother is such a woman rearing?

B. Some of the most challenging passages for a man are Ephesians 5:25, 28, and 1 Peter 3:7. "Husbands, love your wives, even as Christ also loved the church, and gave himself for it. . . . So ought men to love their wives as their own bodies. He that loveth his wife loveth himself." "Likewise, ye husbands, dwell with them according to knowledge, giving honor unto the wife, as unto the weaker vessel, and as being heirs together of the grace of life; that your prayers be not hindered" (1 Pet. 3:7).

Every young boy deserves to see the unselfish devotion of a dedicated husband through the life of his father. How is the man to love his wife? Unselfishly, as Christ loved the church, a man must deny himself for the good of his wife. That is what Christ did. A boy needs to learn that a father is one who will do without for the sake of all. He will give himself for the good of his family. Often without regard for his own welfare, he will work long and hard hours so that his family can be supported and comforted. Such a man honors his wife by being considerate of her wants and needs as a woman and by being kind and compassionate when she needs strength to face the challenges of being a keeper at home.

Such a man is not given to "strong drink." He is not wasteful. He does not squander money with foolish habits or hobbies. His wife will get a new dress before he gets a new suit. His little ones learn duty and responsibility in the home. They will learn how to share and how to "bear their own burden" by tending to household chores. His children will learn the value of saving for the future. They will be taught how to handle money so that all may prosper, and for the proverbial "rainy day" (Eph. 4:28).

A godly man does not lead through intimidation. This is the rule of beasts and brutes. Rather, he leads through love for his family and for God who gave them to him. That is how Christ heads the church. Likewise, a man nourishes and cherishes his wife and family by leading them in the paths of righteousness. He leads by his word and his way, both of which are taken from principles of duty and honor found in the Bible.

Yes, it is true that the grace and virtues of both the husband and the wife co-mingle, like the rain and sunshine, to produce their harvest. Both boys and girls learn from their mother and their father. It is not as one-sided as it may appear above. Each grows in the grace and knowledge of the Lord by absorbing the godly influence and example of a home ruled by the will and word of God.

Conclusion and Thanksgiving
As stated in the introduction, this material has been prepared with bittersweet tears. My mother and father, Cecil and Marie Hafley, were not perfect people, but they were a model of godly parents. For this, I thank God. To them, I owe everything in whatever understanding and knowledge I may have of God and his divine word. From them, I learned respect for God and the Bible. Wherein my life has failed to honor and respect God, it is not because of their teaching and example, but, rather, despite their best efforts. Cecil Hafley was honest and totally unselfish. He always considered others before himself (Phil. 2:3). My dad was the kindest man I have ever known. He was firm, strong, but always kind. He was kind to everyone he met and that without exception. (See my tribute to him in *Truth Magazine,* "Cecil S. Hafley, The Kindest Man," February 1999.)

My mother's faith and trust in God were indomitable. Her confidence in his word was total and absolute. She spoke of going to heaven to all who would listen. The last time she came to visit us, at the age of 80, she related that she sat beside a Baptist preacher on the plane. She said she asked him why he was a member of the Baptist Church and not the Lord's church and tried to study with him. (Does anyone who knew my mother doubt that?!) She told him her son was a preacher and that she would like for him to talk with me when they got off the plane. To the end, that was my mom.

Mother Always
Larry Ray Hafley

Beauty in youth;
Grace in her ways;
Seeking eternal truth;
Blushing at praise.
Virtue in her deeds,
Always lending self
To other's needs;

Clearing her shelf
To squelch hunger
In a strange face;
A godly wonder,
An angel misplaced.

In the reverie of my mind, with confidence in the word of God, I believe Cecil and Marie Hafley are now basking in the bosom of Abraham and that they soon will be taken to enjoy the blessing of God's eternal home.

Part 2 —
The Day Lectures

The Threat of Materialism to the Home

Randy Blackaby

In the early days of my preaching, when I was about twenty-one or twenty-two years old and traveling to different congregations each week, I was invited by a Christian man to come home with him for dinner and learn of a way to make money without working. I guessed what he had in mind and told him I'd be glad to come to dinner, but that I didn't have time to sell soap. When we arrived at his home, it was only a basement. The upper level had not been built. This didn't dismay me, but puzzled me that the man living here was going to tell me how to make money without working. His wife fixed an excellent meal and we all enjoyed it, including his three or four children.

As the dishes were cleared, he got out his flip chart and made me the presentation other "brethren" had made to me before. But I explained to this brother that with a full time job as a newspaper reporter, helping my father

---

Randy Blackaby serves as a preacher and elder of the New Carlisle Church of Christ, not far from where he was born and raised in Xenia, Ohio. He has preached "full-time" for about eighteen years in Indiana and Ohio. Previously, he was employed as a newspaper reporter and managing editor for seventeen years and preached regularly during that time by appointment in a 100-mile radius of his home. He has written two workbooks for the Guardian of Truth Foundation, one in the *Bible Textbook Series* on *Galatians,* and another in the *Great Bible Characters* series on *Moses.* He currently is writing another on what the Bible teaches about *Money.* He became a staff writer for *Truth Magazine* in 2005. He and his wife, Karen, have four sons, Joshua, Josiah, Ezra, and Amos. He was involved in efforts to evangelize Eastern Europe, making five trips to Lithuania from 1994 to 2000.

evenings and Saturdays, preparing for and preaching each week, and dating the woman who is now my wife, I just didn't have time to sell anything.

Undeterred, this brother asked me, "Don't you ever have Bible studies with people?" When I answered affirmatively, he said, "Well, while you're teaching them the Bible, you can tell them about this great opportunity." When I asked him if he didn't think they might get confused as to my purpose for coming, this brother just looked perplexed. He couldn't see a problem. He couldn't see this approach as a misuse of trust. His focus just wasn't on the spiritual.

In the years that followed I had only occasional contact with this family. His wife had several emotional crises. I talked with her at length one year while holding a gospel meeting, and she told me of her husband's continued focus on making a lot of money. After several more years their marriage ended in divorce, I heard. One of their children died of a drug overdose far from home and another was tortured and apparently ritually murdered not far from where I lived at the time.

I have not heard of the family now for several years, but the last time I did hear, this brother was still chasing a variety of get rich quick schemes. This man had a beautiful family once. No amount of money can ever replace what he has lost and especially what he will lose in the future, if he doesn't repent. The sad outcome illustrates well the high price of materialism.

Affluenza
Writer Randy Alcorn has coined the term "affluenza" to describe materialism as it afflicts modern American life. Here's how he defines the disease. "Affluenza is a strange malady that affects the children of well-to-do parents. Though having everything money can buy, the children show all the symptoms of abject poverty—depression, anxiety, loss of meaning, and despair for the future. Affluenza accounts for an escape into alcohol, drugs, shoplifting, and suicide among children of the wealthy. It is most often found where parents are absent from the house and try to buy their children's love."[1]

All but the poorest of us have seen affluenza up close and personal at Christmas time. Children deluged with toys and clothes, grabbing for the next present in a big pile. And instead of being thankful, they are crabby and wanting more, in spite of the fact that they already have discarded gifts already opened. They are an embarrassment to everyone—and precisely because they've been given too much.

Alcorn suggests, quite accurately, that parents who "spoil" their children under the guise of "love" are actually committing acts of child abuse.[2] These children will grow up expecting every whim to be fulfilled. They will be lousy employees, poor parents, unable to manage money or credit. They will be irresponsible members of society and the church.

The Great Scourge of Modern Life

Materialism menaces modern families like no other sin. It lurks just below the surface of daily life. A majority is vaguely aware of its existence, but ignorant of its true potential. It operates like cancer. A small appearance raises minor concerns but most remain unaware that it is metastasizing.

The cancer analogy serves us well as we seek to define materialism. Ask one hundred people to define the term, and don't be surprised if you get one hundred variant answers. This isn't because materialism is difficult to characterize but because it is so immense in scope. Like the array of cancers that attack the human body, materialism is a multi-faceted monster of spiritual diseases that consumes human souls and casts them into the abyss of eternal hell.

"Vast numbers of us have been seduced into believing that having more wealth and material possessions is essential to a good life. We have swallowed the idea that, to be well, one first must be well off. And many of us, consciously or unconsciously, have learned to evaluate our own well being and accomplishment not by looking inward at our spirit or integrity, but by looking outward at what we have and what we can buy," writes Tim Kasser, associate professor of psychology at Knox College.[3]

Yet most families don't see the tentacles of this per-

Defining Materialism

- Belief that physical matter is the only or the primary reality and that everything can be explained by material phenomena.
- Concept that life's highest value is to be achieved in material well being and progress.
- A preoccupation or stress upon the material, rather than the intellectual or spiritual.

---

nicious deviancy enwrapping their hearts. Deceived, more see materialism as the answer to life's dilemmas, rather than the cause of those problems and afflictions. Kasser writes, ". . . selfishness and materialism are no longer seen as moral problems, but as cardinal goals in life."[4]

This ignorance comes in spite of the fact that the Bible speaks voluminously about materialism. Jesus made materialism one of his regular "talking points" almost everywhere he preached. The Bible says more about money and possessions than heaven and hell combined. There is something about material wealth and poverty in every major segment of the Bible from Genesis to Revelation. One denominational preacher contends that fully one fifth of all that Jesus is recorded to have said was about money and possessions.[5] Others suggest fifteen to 33 percent, depending on what is included in the calculation. Another writer's research shows 2,350 verses in the Bible dealing with money. That is about twice as many as there are on faith and prayer combined. The only subject Jesus spoke more about was the kingdom of God itself.[6]

Materialism's Fruit Conspicuously Evident

The evidence of materialism's assault on families, the nation and even the church is all about us, though it often isn't recognized as such.

- **Growth of gambling:** The United States now has 5.5 million pathologically addicted gamblers; 1.1 million of whom are teenagers. The average American gambles $1,174 annually.[7] And our greedy state governments have enthusiastically switched from policing the "numbers rackets" to operating them as state lotteries. It is estimated that more than $500 billion is wagered legally every year in the U.S. and perhaps $1 trillion annually when illegal betting is included.[8]

- **Upsurge in bankruptcies:** Millions of Americans file for bankruptcy each year, including a fair number of Christians. Many of these bankruptcies are caused by misuse of credit and greedy materialism.

- **Divorce crisis:** It is estimated that 56 percent of all divorces are the result of financial problems or disagreements about money in the home.[9] And when both spouses focus primarily on making money, there is little time to give to one another. Few marriages can survive inattention.

- **Infidelity:** Studies show that among both men and women the incidence of marital infidelity rises in conjunction with an increase in income."[10]

- **Epidemic of sleep disorders:** Money is so powerful that one third of all adults say financial worries prevent them from sleeping or relaxing.[11]

- **Pitiful giving patterns:** While it is impossible to accurately document what Christians give in their Lord's day offerings, Internal Revenue Service analysis shows that of Americans who itemize their deductions, the average American gives less than three percent to church and charity combined. This is generally confirmed by polling done among professed Christians by The Barna Group. They find that giving to churches amounts to about 2.2 percent of income.[12]

- **Engrossed by the grossly material:** "Psychologists tell us that people think about money more than they do about sex," says Gary Moore.[13]

- **Creation of a new class of orphans:** Millions of "latchkey" children come home from school every day to empty homes. Others are shuffled off to day care centers, where they live life much like orphans because both parents are so busy working to provide the family the "things" they want.

- **Murder of unborn babies:** Yes, abortion is largely a fruit of materialism. A baby is viewed as an inconvenience, an economic hardship, an impediment to job advancement, or a lifestyle spoiler.

- **Euthanasia:** There is a growing disposition to help older people die, once their ability to care for themselves is gone. When they are just an economic hardship, they are viewed as expendable.

- **Pandemic of depression and other unaccounted for illness:** Studies show that the more materialistic people are the more anxiety, stress, and depression they suffer. This general unhappiness causes a host of health problems, ranging from sleeplessness to headaches, backaches, sore muscles, and sore throats.

- **Hectic hysteria:** Despite the constantly multiplying number of time and labor saving devices, Americans constantly are talking about their frantic lives.

- **Social isolation:** More and more people either live alone or as families live in isolation from neighbors and community. Interpersonal relationships are declining as people become more absorbed in television, computers and the like. But close relationships are one foundation of psychological health and high quality of life. Conversely, isolation weakens the fibers that bind couples, friends, families, and communities. And we might add—churches.

- **Upsurge in compulsive buying:** Inability to control one's appetite for buying things has become the newest addiction to require treatment in the twenty-first century. This is "a psychopathology characterized by intense impulses to purchase things even when people know that they do not need the items."[14]

- **The Disneyland gospel:** This is the health and wealth doctrine popularized by TV evangelists like Jim Bakker, Oral Roberts, Benny Hinn and Kenneth and Gloria Copeland. It argues God wants us all to be physically rich. Wealth is equated with spirituality. Taken to its logical conclusion, if a person is poor or only of moderate means, he or she must be spiritually weak or sinful. It "syncretizes Christianity with selfish individualism and the materialism of our age."[15]

Few See Themselves as Materialistic

Virtually everyone knows something about materialism, but almost no one sees himself as materialistic, unless it is the pornographic, obscene pop singer Madonna, who sang, "Cause we are living in a material world, and I'm a material girl" or the late billionaire Armand Hammer, who is quoted as saying, "Money is my first, last and only love."[16]

The most visible manifestations of materialism—conspicuous consumption, gross selfishness, insatiable cravings for more and better, and frantic lifestyles—are oft-addressed issues in the secular press.

But the root of materialism lies in a philosophy that has swept Europe and now besieges America. Often termed secularization, this life rationale begins with the elimination of God and proceeds to eradicate the spiritual element from human life. When the math is completed, the remainder is only the material.

Randy Alcorn has written, "Materialism will inevitably produce the kind of society increasingly evident in America—a society of individualism, where people live parallel lives, not meaningfully intersecting with others. A society where independence is the only absolute, where self-interest is the only creed, where convenience and expediency and profitability are the only values. A society where people know the price of everything, but the value of nothing—where people have a great deal to live on, but very little to live for."[17]

While many focus on excessive, if not obscene, consumption and on teenagers' demands to have the latest jeans, shoes, and "looks," materialism has a far more deadly legacy for our families. John West of the Seattle-based Discovery Institute[18] suggests our culture is now dominated by materialism's most deadly legacies:

- Rejection of reason and objective truth.
- Rejection of objective morality.
- Rejection of personal responsibility.

And this makes the assault of materialism on the home all the more pernicious. We are so affected by materialism that we don't even seem capable of recognizing it. When objective truth and morality (as defined in God's word) are set aside, who will take personal responsibility and admit, "I'm materialistic"? The typical person, even the average Christian, doesn't seem to know materialism when he sees it—at least in his own life. Is materialism having a lot of stuff? Is it an attitude? Do you have to be rich to be materialistic, or can poor people be such? For the majority, materialism is a problem or sin of someone else.

We tend to ignore materialism for the very reason that we are materialistic. To know you are materialistic requires you to examine the spiritual component of your life, where your heart is focused. Materialism denies the importance or existence of such a spiritual factor.

Jesus on Materialism

The absolute foolishness of focusing only on the material part of life was Jesus' point when he told the parable of the rich fool. "The ground of a certain rich man yielded plentifully. And he thought within himself, saying, 'What shall I do, since I have no room to store my crops?' So he said, ' I will do this: I will pull down my barns and build greater, and there I will store all my crops and my goods. And I will say to my soul, Soul, you have many goods laid up for many years, take your ease; eat drink, and be merry.' But God said to him, 'Fool! This night your soul will be required of you; then whose will those things be which you have provided?'" (Luke 12:16-20).

This parable clearly describes a materialist. All of the rich man's confidence and sense of security was invested in what he owned. He had more than he could use, yet selfishly failed to consider those less fortunate. He only thought of his own ease and pleasure. But God called this man a fool, for he gave no consideration to what would become of his soul when material life ended.

Jesus essentially called materialists fools—people bereft of a fundamental knowledge of the truth. Fools, we are told elsewhere, declare there is no God (Ps. 14:1).

Our Lord demonstrated the end of such fools also when he told of the rich man and Lazarus (Luke 16:19-31). This rich materialist found his material blessings didn't follow him beyond the grave. In torment, he agonized for just a drop of water and desired to send word of his folly and warning to family members still living. It is worth noting that Jesus didn't accuse this rich man of getting his wealth by stealing or other sinful means. He simply made them the primary focus of his life.

In his kingdom manifesto, preached from a mountainside, Jesus made clear that materialistic attitudes and behavior are incompatible with discipleship and citizenship in the kingdom of heaven. "Do not lay up for yourselves treasures on earth, where moth and rust destroy and where thieves break in and steal; but lay up for yourselves treasures in heaven, where neither moth nor rust destroys and where thieves do not break in and steal. For where your treasure is, there your heart will be also" (Matt. 6:19-21). The Lord went to the "heart" of the issue. What a person places as the priority or treasure of his life defines who and what he is. You are a materialist and a lover of this world if money and physical things are your priority. You are a disciple of Jesus and a lover of God if the spiritual and the kingdom of God have priority in your thinking and behavior.

Can we be a little bit materialistic and also be spiritual? Jesus answers emphatically in the negative. "No one can serve two masters; for either he will hate the one and love the other, or else he will be loyal to the one and despise the other. You cannot serve God and mammon" (Matt. 6:24). This also was illustrated in Jesus' exchange with a rich young man who came to learn what he needed to do to obtain eternal life. Jesus told him to keep God's commandments. The young man replied he had done so since his youth. So, the Lord told him to sell all he had and give it to the poor. The young man couldn't bring himself to do this and left sorrowfully (Matt. 19:16-22). Jesus knew the young man had divided loyalties. He wanted to be a materialist and inherit eternal life. Jesus nixed that idea.

Yet the material heart retorts, "But I have to make a living!" And Jesus answers again. "Therefore I say to you, do not worry about your life, what you will eat or what you will drink; nor about your body, what you will put on. Is not life more than food, and the body more than clothing?" (Matt. 6:25). One of the symptoms of a materialistic heart is worry or anxiety. That is because the materialist sees himself as self-dependent.

Jesus proceeded to attack the mythology of self-dependence by pointing to the natural world and God's superintending providence. "Look at the birds of the air," he said, "for they neither sow nor reap nor gather into barns; yet your heavenly Father feeds them. Are you not of much more value than they? Which of you by worrying can add one cubit to his stature? So why do you worry about clothing? Consider the lilies of the field, how they grow: they neither toil nor spin; and yet I say to you that even Solomon in all his glory was not arrayed like one of these. Now if God so clothes the grass of the field, which today is, and tomorrow is thrown into the oven, will He not much more clothe you, O you of little faith?" (Matt. 6:26-30).

Materialism, remember, seeks to make the material world all there is and to leave God out of the equation. This is the myth of materialism. And Jesus demonstrated the fallacy of the myth by focusing on God's provision for lesser forms of life than human beings. Those grasses and animals are provided for in superb ways without the anxiety and energies the materialist expends. And if God does that for soul-less birds and flowers, what will he do for those created in his own image?

Jesus then urged his disciples to focus primarily on the spiritual aspect of life, putting God's kingdom, Christ's rule and obedience to the divine pattern at the center of life. And the Lord said God would then provide for our material and physical needs in due course. "But seek first the kingdom of God and His righteousness, and all these things will be added to you. Therefore, do not worry about tomorrow, for tomorrow will worry about its own things. Sufficient for the day is its own trouble" (Matt. 6:33-34). The Lord's conclusion here is remarkably similar to Solomon's conclusion in Ecclesiastes 12:13, "Let us hear the conclusion of the whole matter: Fear God and keep his commandments, for this is man's all" (NKJV).

Spirituality does not preclude thought and work designed to provide for ourselves materially. The man who won't work to provide for his family is deemed "worse than an infidel" (1 Tim. 5:8). And Jesus rebuked any effort to justify such failure with some sort of fake spirituality. "All too well you reject the commandment of God, that you may keep your tradition. For Moses said, Honor your father and your mother; and He who curses father or mother, let him be put to death. But you say, If a man says to his father or mother, Whatever profit you might have received from me is Corban—(that is, a gift to God), then you no longer let him do anything for his father or mother, making the word of God of no effect through your tradition which you have handed down. And many such things you do" (Mark 7:9-13).

The number of neglected parents in America suggests that the materialism that underlies such spiritual tomfoolery remains quite alive in the twenty-first century.

The example of our Lord is again instructive. If ever a man might be justified in neglecting his family, it would be our impoverished Lord, the day all his work and mission culminated in his death for our sins. But, despite the agony of scourging and crucifixion, and regardless of the emotional and spiritual wretchedness he bore in shouldering the sins of mankind, he arranged from the cross for the care of his mother (John 19:25-27).

Materialism, Like All Sin, Delivers the
Opposite of What it Promises

One of the allures of materialism is its promise of freedom. But as many find out too late, it actually diminishes freedom. Husbands working such exorbitantly long hours to pay huge debts for "toys" that there is no time left to use or enjoy often get the point too late. Wives joining the workforce are committed to paying the same debts, with the same results. Both come home from work exhausted but still facing the chores of keeping up the home. Where's the freedom?

The enticing promise of prosperity is a less stressful, more relaxed life. The boat and recreational vehicles and mountain cabin are supposed to usher in "the life." But instead they create a demanding rat race to meet the payments, pay for maintenance, insurance, and more taxes.

Solomon discovered this truth centuries ago, and God inspired him to write his discoveries in Ecclesiastes, part of the wisdom literature of the Old Testament.

The third king of Israel is a worthwhile case study in the vanity (uselessness) of a materialistic pursuit of happiness and meaning in life. Solomon found that every earthly pursuit, if the spiritual guidance of the Almighty is lacking, brings no real reward. For most of us, consideration of what life would be like if we were billionaires and able to demand anything we wanted is mere speculation. But Solomon had the wealth and kingly governmental power to explore every materialistic avenue to its extremity.

Here are the things with which he experimented. Compare them to our own materialistic pursuits today.

1. Mirth, pleasure and laughter (2:1-2).
2. Fine dining (2:3).
3. Beautiful houses with pools, gardens, orchards and vineyards (2:4-5).
4. Numerous servants to do work for him (2:7).
5. Cattle and livestock ranches—businesses producing income (2:7).
6. Bank accounts of silver and gold (2:8).
7. Vast stores of valuable "collectibles" (2:8).
8. Musical entertainment (2:8).
9. Power, position and prestige (2:9).

Solomon said, "Whatever my eyes desired I did not keep from them. I did not withhold my heart from any pleasure. . . . Then I looked on all the works that my hands had done and on the labor in which I had toiled; and indeed all was vanity and grasping at the wind" (2:10-11).

Ever tried to "grasp the wind"? It's impossible. And so is finding freedom, security, happiness, and sense of well being in materialistic pursuits. Solomon said he didn't refrain from any effort to find pleasure—but still found it all vanity. In addition to all the things mentioned in Ecclesiastes, we know Solomon also surrounded himself with 700 wives and 300 concubines.

Beautiful women constantly on his arm and sexual pleasures most abundant were his, yet instead of serving him well they drew him away from God and into a materialistic religious experience that had him building temples to and worshiping gods of wood, stone, and metal (1 Kings 11:1-8).

Solomon found that many possessions don't deliver happiness. Rather they create new and difficult problems:

1. "When goods increase, they increase who eat them; so what profit have the owners except to see them with their eyes?" (Eccl. 5:11). He refers to all the servants he had to feed, clothe, and shelter to maintain and manage his possessions. The modern equivalent might be accountants, tax consultants, investment advisors, repairmen, and other hired help.

2. "The sleep of a laboring man is sweet, whether he eats little or much; but the abundance of the rich will not permit him to sleep" (Eccl. 5:12).

3. "Then I hated all my labor in which I had toiled under the sun, because I must leave it to the man who will come after me. And who knows whether he will be wise or a fool?" (Eccl. 2:18-19). The rich man has to worry about whether his wealth will bless or ruin his children.

Materialism Functions Like Addiction
Someone addicted to alcohol, drugs, pornography, or gambling discovers rather quickly that it takes more and more of the substance or habit to satisfy the craving or to just make life seem tolerable. The pursuit of material things operates exactly the same.

Most of us have experienced the truth of this. When we were young and just starting out in life on our own, we thought a nice little tract house and a decent used car would make us happy. And it did, briefly. Then, when we saw others with bigger and better houses and cars, we thought we'd be happier if we could get those things, too.

What happened was that our imagined baseline of happiness moved. If we managed to achieve the new baseline, it moved again.

Again, this isn't some new discovery. Solomon wrote nearly 3000 years ago, "Yet there is no end to his labors, nor is his eye satisfied with riches" (Eccl. 4:8). And, again, "He who loves silver will not be satisfied with silver; nor he who loves abundance, with increase. This also is vanity" (Eccl. 5:10).

The Role of Television

Television may be the single greatest purveyor of materialism. From its programming to its advertising most of what appears on TV is predominantly materialistic. Movies, talk shows, situation comedies, soap operas, and weekly dramas all emphasize and glamorize the carnal and the worldly. Even the news is largely devoid of any focus on the spiritual.

Drinking, gambling, and sexual deviancy are presented as "normal" on television. There are even shows where women try to "sell" themselves for marriage to a millionaire. Others emphasize the importance of an external "make-over" to feel good or have a good self-image. Nice cars, beautiful houses, manicured lawns, leisure time around the pool, and prestigious jobs are the backdrop to many shows.

And then comes the advertising, sometimes overtly and other times covertly, selling you dissatisfaction with everything about your life and touting all sorts of promises if you just buy this product or that.

More and more our children are becoming the primary targets of this advertising. Madison Avenue is using child psychologists to hone their skills at hooking children on materialism, according to Dr. Allen Kanner, a clinical child psychiatrist.[19] Kanner says he has studies demonstrating that three year olds recognize 100 brand logos. Television is the main tool in this accomplishment—or crime—depending on the way you look at it.

So, it is no wonder that many parents have a bunch of little whiners and beggars on their hands, always demanding this new toy or that brand of new clothing. And many of these parents, totally materialistic in their thinking, assume they have to fulfill these demands or their children will hate them, grow up deprived, warped and ruined.

The result, however, in spite of closets bursting with unused clothing and rooms so full of toys you can't walk about, is a generation of some of the brattiest children the world has ever produced. You can guess what kind of adults these youngsters will be, when they grow up.

95

And if all that weren't bad enough, Kasser writes, "People with a strong materialistic orientation were likely to watch a lot of television, compare themselves unfavorably with people they saw on television, be dissatisfied with their standard of living, and have low life satisfaction."[20]

Materialism Has Invaded the Church

It is an oft-repeated truism that whatever troubles the world and denominationalism will one day trouble the Lord's church. This is certainly true regarding carnality and materialism.

Awe-inspiring buildings, performance and entertainment in the place of true worship, the social and health and wealth gospels and, most recently, the super Walmart-style mega-churches with their latte bars, gymnasiums, finance seminars, and politically correct, all-inclusive and inoffensive messages simply ooze the message of materialism.

J.I. Packer has called the phenomenon "hot tub religion." Packer went on to say, ". . . it struck me that the hot tub is the perfect symbol of the modern route of religion. The hot tub experience is sensuous, relaxing, floppy, laid-back; not in any way demanding, whether intellectually or otherwise. . . . Many today want Christianity to be like that and labor to make it so. The ultimate step, of course, would be to clear church auditoriums of seats and install hot tubs in their place; then there would never be any attendance problems."[21]

This author continued, "Symptoms of hot tub religion today include a skyrocketing divorce and remarriage rate among Christians; widespread indulgence of sexual aberrations; an overheated supernaturalism that seeks signs, wonders, visions, prophecies and miracles; constant soothing syrup from electronic preachers and the liberal pulpit; anti-intellectual sentimentalism and emotional 'highs' deliberately cultivated, the Christian equivalent of cannabis and coca; and an easy, thoughtless acceptance of luxury in everyday living."[22]

Packer's premises pinpoint the problems and peculiarities of carnality and materialism in the denominational church. But look carefully at the Lord's church and what we often define as liberalism and you see seeds, sprouts, and symptoms of the very same things.

Materialism Changes How We Look at People

When money and things rule our thinking they also define how we measure and value other people. Many in the business world today look at people merely as "consumers," economic units that can buy products and cause a profit. Things are marketed and advertised to these people without regard to the fact that they may become addicted, lose their livelihoods, become sick, obese, and diseased—or even die.

A materialist judges the value and importance of people on such criteria as their job, position, wealth, looks or secular level of education. Rather than assessing people on the basis of spiritual factors, like their love, goodness, kindness, self-control, and faithfulness, they are judged for their power, their ability to help us materially or the honors their association brings us.

This is not only singularly wrong on its face; it undermines the very purpose of our lives and the mission of the Lord's church. James put it this way, "My brethren, do not hold the faith of our Lord Jesus Christ, the Lord of glory, with partiality. For if there should come into your assembly a man with gold rings, in fine apparel, and there should also come in a poor man in filthy clothes, and you pay attention to the one wearing the fine clothes and say to him, 'You sit here in a good place,' and say to the poor man, 'You stand there,' or 'Sit here at my footstool,' have you not shown partiality among yourselves, and become judges with evil thoughts?" (Jas. 2:1-4). Then, in verse 9 he declares, "but if you show partiality you commit sin."

Our purpose is to be lights in a dark world and salt in an unsavory society (Matt. 5:13-16). Our mission as the church of Christ is to "Go into all the world and preach the gospel to *every creature*" (Mark 16:15) and to "make disciples of *all the nations*" (Matt. 28:19). All of this is impossible when we measure men carnally, rather than spiritually.

God's love of all men is evidenced in the cross (John 3:16). Our Lord is "longsuffering toward us, not willing that any should perish but that all should come to repentance" (2 Pet. 3:9). He values the souls of all men and shows no partiality with regard to a man's possessions, earthly position, or power.

If the missionary zeal of the Lord's church is today stymied, could it be because materialistic value systems have devalued the souls of sinners in our eyes and left us willing to evangelize only those we deem similar to ourselves?

Families Ignore Bible Warnings at Own Peril

The Bible has a number of illustrations of rich men who pleased God. Among them were Job, Abraham, David, Solomon (for a time), and Joseph of Arimethea. But the successful mixing of wealth and spirituality is the exception, not the rule. Jesus made that clear when he said, "Assuredly I say to you that it is hard for a rich man to enter the kingdom of heaven. And again I say to you, it is easier for a camel to go through the eye of a needle than for a rich man to enter the kingdom of God" (Matt. 19:23-24). His disciples were amazed and asked who then would be able to enter the kingdom. Jesus' answer was, "With men this is impossible, but with God all things are possible" (Matt. 19:26). Only through careful obedience to the principles of God's word can anyone, particularly the rich, enter God's kingdom. Just remember, when it comes to spiritual things, it is the rich who are disadvantaged.

The Apostle Paul reiterated and expanded upon the Lord's teaching when he wrote, "And having food and clothing, with these we shall be content. But those who desire to be rich fall into temptation and a snare, and into many foolish and harmful lusts, which drown men in destruction and perdition. For the love of money is the root of all kinds of evil, for which some have strayed from the faith in their greediness, and pierced themselves through with many sorrows" (1 Tim. 6:8-10).

Let us recognize that while the rich have great difficulty entering God's kingdom, the poor and the merely comfortable face disaster also if their hearts are set on the "desire to be rich." Poor people can be every bit as materialistic as rich ones.

The apostle urged contentment with what we have, whether little or much. In writing to the Philippians he said, "I have learned in whatever state I am to be content. I know how to be abased, and I know how to abound. Everywhere and in all things I have learned both to be full and to be hungry, both to abound and to suffer need" (4:11-12).

Again, he didn't say being rich was the problem, necessarily. He said the "desire" to be rich is what propels people into all sorts of temptations and traps. That desire evolves into foolish and harmful lusts that lead men to destruction.

Money isn't the problem. But the "love of money" is the sub-surface root of all kinds of evil. We looked at some of those evils earlier in our discussion. And greed leads men to forsake their faith and then suffer all sorts of sorrows as materialism serves up the opposite of every promise it makes.

Greed is another term that helps us understand materialism. Greed has two components:

1. Possessiveness: Our attitude regarding what we already possess.
2. Covetousness: An ungodly desire for what we don't possess.

The answer is self-denial, particularly denial of the fleshly urge to satisfy every carnal urging. Remember Jesus' words. "If anyone desires to come after me, let him deny himself, and take up his cross daily, and follow me" (Luke 9:23). John wrote, "Do not love the world or the things in the world. If anyone loves the world, the love of the Father is not in him. For all that is in the world—the lust of the flesh, the lust of the eyes, and the pride of life—is not of the Father but is of the world" (1 John 2:15-16).

So, How Do We Avoid the Trap of Materialism?

Jesus told us to seek the kingdom of heaven first and our material needs will be met. Few people have enough faith in God's promise to trust that approach to life. And others misunderstand it if they fail to work. The Apostle Paul said if a man won't work, he shouldn't eat, and brethren shouldn't give him a handout (2 Thess. 3:6-14).

Jesus wasn't teaching us to sit and wait for manna from heaven, but to make the focus, the priority and the mission of our lives serving God and doing his will. This is spiritual living.

Many seem to think that if they spend their lives in worship, teaching others, helping the needy, comforting the sick and being diligent to mature into a person approved by God, that they won't have any time or money for physical necessities. But they are wrong. Jesus said so.

Actually, when the heart is focused on God's kingdom and righteousness, several things are eliminated that actually strip a man of wealth and happiness. These include covetousness, selfishness, and greed. Many a faithful Christian has seen his prosperity soar and his ability to meet his family's needs surpassed so that he has extra with which he can help others. And when a man does what he knows is right, he feels good about it and about himself. And the result is contentment and happiness. So, as we noted the Apostle Paul said, a man who is doing right can be content and happy whether he has much or little.

Ultimately, what every person in this world craves most is contentment and happiness. Materialism promises such, but delivers the opposite. The spiritually dominated and focused life in Christ actually produces the well-being we all desire.

In his letter to the church at Rome, the Apostle Paul contrasted two approaches to life. One was a "walk according to the flesh." The other was a walk "according to the Spirit." He said, "For those who live according to the flesh set their minds on the things of the flesh, but those who live according to the Spirit, the things of the Spirit. For to be carnally minded is death, but to be spiritually minded is life and peace" (8:1-6). The apostle's point in this passage is broader than our application here, but certainly includes our point.

When all this is summarized, the emphasis is on living a God-directed life. That is what spirituality is all about. When we fail to inculcate the spiritual into the lives of our families, we rob our children and ourselves of the best of God's gifts and we bring upon ourselves the curses of disobedience. We've clearly demonstrated that materialism is disobedience. It is sin.

The challenge today is to teach our children about money and possessions. The oft-quoted proverb is never truer than in this context. "Train up a child in the way he should go, and when he is old he will not depart from it" (Prov. 22:6). Teach your children to give and show them "it is more blessed to give than to receive" (Acts 20:35).

Alcorn made another suggestion for a teaching experience I thought impressive. "Try taking them to a junkyard or a dump. It can actually be a great family event. Show them all the piles of 'treasures' that were formerly Christmas and birthday presents. Point out things that cost hundreds of dollars, that children quarreled about, friendships were lost over, honesty sacrificed for, and marriages broken up over. Show them the miscellaneous arms and legs and remnants of battered dolls, rusted robots, and electronic gadgets that now lie useless after their brief life span. Point out to them that most of what your family owns will one day be in a junkyard like this. Read 2 Peter 3:10-14, which tells us everything will be consumed by fire. Then ask this telling question, 'When all that we owned lies abandoned, broken, and useless, what will we have done that will last for eternity?'"[23]

Am I Materialistic?

None of us escapes totally the traps of materialism. Materialism, like selfishness, is so inherently a part of what produces and is sin that whenever we commit sin we likely are guilty of the fleshly focus Paul spoke to the Romans about.

So, the question, "Am I materialistic?" is a bit like the question, "Am I a sinner?" If by either question we mean, do I ever act in accordance with fleshly desires or do I ever sin, the answer to both questions is "yes."

But if the questions pertain to whether my general habit of life is to be a materialist or a sinner, a closer self-examination is needed.

If you are seriously interested in answering this question, look at two things: your checkbook and your daily planner or calendar. Look carefully at what you spend your money on and how you spend your time. Once you have a good mental picture of your habits, just compare them to what the Lord and his spokesmen set before us as spiritual living. Remember that our Lord said, "Blessed are those who hunger and thirst for righteousness, for they shall be filled" (Matt. 5:6). For what do you hunger and thirst?

You'll be able to assess yourself adequately, if you're honest. And virtually none of us will be able to do this assessment without recognizing, at minimum, a need for improvement. Some of us may find a need for a total overhaul of our lives.

What's at Stake For My Family and Me?

What is at stake for you and your family is literally life or death, heaven or hell, salvation or damnation. Materialism, with its temptation to see money and things as the real power instead of God, will wring spirituality out of your life. If you set the example of materialistic living before your spouse and children, the likelihood is that they'll imitate your example and become as spiritually dry as you—or maybe more so.

And before the ultimate judgment of Christ occurs, there will be a long series of lesser, earthly judgments as a result of your materialism. You can expect one or more of the curses of materialism cited earlier, whether it be constant discontent, a divorce, an addiction or children so spoiled they are a misery to watch.

Jesus is ultimately to be our judge. If there is any doubt about his attitude regarding materialism, it is erased when we remember the anger it evoked in him when he found moneychangers and livestock dealers making his father's house a "den of thieves." He made a whip and drove them from the temple (John 2:13-17; Mark 11:15-17).

Materialism is decadence. Decadence speaks of decline or falling away from morality or spiritual righteousness. Jesus said, "God is Spirit, and those who worship him must worship in spirit and in truth" (John 4:24). God created man in his own image, thus as a spiritual being (Gen. 1:26-27). Adam and Eve's sin involved materialism, craving to eat a physical fruit when God had commanded them to abstain. Materialism and sin always move us further from God, not nearer.

We all want to live "the good life." The question really is, which route will we travel to obtain it. Jesus said, "I have come that they may have life, and that they may have it more abundantly" (John 10:10). Materialism makes a similar promise. You and your family must decide which promise is true and which only holds out false hope.

Jesus put the whole matter into perfect perspective when he asked the penetrating pair of questions, "For what profit is it to a man if he gains the whole world, and loses his own soul? Or what will a man give in exchange for his soul?" (Matt. 16:26) Thus, as Alcorn has written, "materialism is not simply wrong. It is stupid."[24]

Judas betrayed the Son of God for thirty pieces of silver. Some today sell him out for much less, others for much more. But all who put money, things, and physical pleasure ahead of Christ and his righteousness are materialists. The Apostle Paul's admonition must resonate with those of us who are Christians, living in the richest nation on earth. He told Timothy, "Command those who are rich in this present age not to be haughty, nor to trust in uncertain riches but in the living God, who gives us richly all things to enjoy. Let them do good, that they be rich in good works, ready to give, willing to share, storing up for themselves a good foundation for the time to come, that they may lay hold of eternal life" (1 Tim. 6:17-19).

If we learn anything from our study of the Scriptures and our observations of materialism, let it be that the greatest needs of our husbands and wives, our children and grandchildren isn't more possessions—their deepest needs are spiritual and emotional.

Footnotes

1. Alcorn, Randy. *Money, Possessions and Eternity,* Revised edition (Tyndale House Publishers, Wheaton, IL, 2003), 382.
2. *Ibid.* 383.
3. Kasser, Tim. *The High Price of Materialism* (A Bradford Book, the MIT Press, Cambridge, MA and London, 2002), from the Introduction, ix-x.
4. *Ibid.* ix.
5. Billy Graham is quoted giving this estimate in the introduction to the *Westminster Collection of Christian Quotations,* compiled by Martin H. Manser, Westminster Knox Press, Louisville, KY, 2001.
6. Alcorn, Randy. *Money, Possessions and Eternity,* Revised edition (Tyndale House Publishers, Wheaton, IL, 2003), 3-4.
7. Getz, Gene. *Rich in Everyway: Everything God Says About Money and Possessions* (Howard Publishing Co., West Monroe, LA), 2004, in the Introduction, xiii-xiv.
8. John MacArthur, "Gambling: The Seductive Fantasy," http://www.biblebb. com/files/MAC/90-164.HTM.
9. Getz, Gene. *Rich in Everyway: Everything God Says About Money and Possessions* (Howard Publishing Co., West Monroe, LA), 2004, in the Introduction, xiii.
10. Alcorn, Randy. *Money, Possessions and Eternity,* Revised edition, (Tyndale House Publishers, Wheaton, IL, 2003), 3.
11. *USA Today*, May 15, 1996.
12. Barna Group, April 13, 2004, *Giving to Churches Rose Substantially in 2003,* http://www.barna.org.
13. Moore, Gary. *Faithful Finances 101* (Templeton Foundation Press, Philadelphia and London, 2003) 39.
14. Kasser, Tim. *The High Price of Materialism* (A Bradford Book, the MIT Press, Cambridge, MA and London, 2002), 85.
15. Moore, Gary. *Faithful Finances 101* (Templeton Foundation Press, Philadelphia and London, 2003) 12.
16. Kasser, Tim. *The High Price of Materialism* (A Bradford Book, the MIT Press, Cambridge, MA and London, 2002), 61.
17. Randy Alcorn, *Materialism, Man and Morality,* www.epm.org/articles/materialism2.html.
18. F.R. Duplantier quotes John West in an article entitled *The Deadly Legacies of Materialism,* www.americasfuture.net/1996/dec96/96-1222b.html.
19. Miriam H. Zoll quotes Dr. Allen Kanner, *The Progress Report: Youngsters Taught to be Materialistic;* www.progress.org/archive/ethics01.htm.
20. Kasser, Tim. *The High Price of Materialism* (A Bradford Book, the MIT Press,

Cambridge, MA and London, 2002), 55.

[21] J.I Packer, *Hot Tub Religion* (Tyndale House Publishers, Wheaton, IL, 1987, 67-69.

[22] *Ibid.* 85.

[23] Alcorn, Randy. *Money, Possessions and Eternity,* Revised edition (Tyndale House Publishers, Wheaton, IL, 2003), 390-391.

[24] *Ibid.* 15.

Using the Family to Serve
Royce U. Deberry

As a Christian, we are to be disciples, following Jesus. We are to be priests, worshiping and offering sacrifices. We are to be servants, serving God and others. Jesus, in Matthew 20:26-28, says, "but whoever desires to become great among you, let him be your servant. And whoever desires to be first among you, let him be your slave—just as the Son of Man did not come to be served, but to serve, and to give His life a ransom for many." Can

---

Royce U. DeBerry was born November 8, 1953 in Jackson, Tennessee to L. Parvin and Pauline DeBerry. He was moved to Aurora, Illinois at ten months of age where he was reared and graduated from high school. He obeyed the gospel on August 11, 1971 at the Westside congregation in Aurora. Royce married Cynthia McCann on January 8, 1972. This union has been blessed with nine daughters and one son. The five grown children and their spouses are all faithful Christians working with the Eastside congregation. Two sons-in-law serve the congregation as deacons. They have also been blessed with twenty-one grandchildren. Royce started working as a full-time evangelist in Pekin, Illinois in September 1975. He moved to Indiana in February 1976 and worked with the congregation in DeMotte, Indiana until June 1982. Then he started working with the Emerson Avenue congregation in Indianapolis, Indiana (June 1982-January 1986) and has been working with the Eastside church for twenty years. He has also served as an elder there since 1990. He has held gospel meetings in Illinois, Indiana, Georgia, Florida, Tennessee, Iowa, Ohio, Maine, and Kentucky.

Royce and Cindy were licensed as foster parents in March 1986 for the state of Indiana. They then became a special medical needs foster home from March 1987 until March 2004. Royce taught Fosterparentscope classes for the state of Indiana for several years. This is a class required by the state of Indiana for any family wishing to license to foster care or adopt children. His daughters, Amanda and Alicia, are now teaching the class for the state.

we be a faithful Christian if we are not following Jesus? We would readily answer "no." Can we be a faithful Christian if we are not worshiping and offering those spiritual sacrifices demanded by God? Again, we would all say "no." Can we be a faithful Christian if we are not *serving* as God has directed? An honest person would have to answer "no."

How has God directed us to serve? According to the words of Jesus in Matthew 23:11, we must become a servant to be great among our brethren. In Colossians 3:22-24 Paul states, "Bondservants, obey in all things your masters according to the flesh, not with eye service, as men pleasers, but in sincerity of heart, fearing God. And whatever you do, do it heartily, as to the Lord and not to men, knowing that from the Lord you will receive the reward of the inheritance; for you serve the Lord Christ." It's not just a good idea to be a servant, the Lord demands that we do so from the heart.

An enemy of righteousness is *selfishness.* An enemy of the church is *selfishness.* An enemy of the individual is *selfishness.* An enemy of the home is *selfishness.* An enemy of service is *selfishness.* Beyond the selfishness in our society, we also have sophistication. Webster's *New World Dictionary Basic School Edition* defines "sophistication" as "1. Not simple, natural, or innocent; wise in the ways of the world. 2. Very complicated and based on the latest ideas, techniques, etc." We are striving in our society to be sophisticated. This is contrary to God's plan. God's plan is simple and natural. We have given up God's plan for a more sophisticated one. An obstacle to service may be education. We send our children to college so that they can get a great job, one making a lot of money for the use of their brain instead of their brawn. There is nothing wrong with this, but here's the problem. In some of our minds, when we are educated, we have gone beyond manual labor. This may be true on our job site, but we still have a duty to serve as God directed. God has a plan bigger than this world. We have to guard against forgetting this.

Attributes in Serving
1. We must be taught to serve. Serving is not an inherited or bestowed attribute. An individual must be taught to *serve.* Therefore, as parents, we must teach our children, by word and example to *serve.* As children we should want to learn to *serve.* Without this *knowledge* and *understanding*, we cannot serve God as he directs.

2. In order to serve we must be humble. We cannot think of ourselves as being bigger, better, more important than others (see Rom. 12:3). If we do that we will sound the death knell of our serving. Look at all the great servants in the Bible: Jesus, Moses, John the baptizer, Paul—just to name a few—they were *humble*. On the other hand, look at King Saul of Israel, he ceased to serve God, his family, his nation, and himself, when he lost his humility.

3. Another part of serving is compassion. This is the ability to look at others, see their plight and needs, and then desire to help them. Jesus, on several occasions in his earthly ministry, looked on people, was moved with compassion, and sought to aid and help them (see Matt. 9:36; 14:14; 15:32; 20:34). The apostle Paul says, "Therefore, as the elect of God, holy and beloved, put on tender mercies, kindness, humility, meekness, longsuffering" (Col. 3:12).

4. We must be determined to serve. If we are determined, it means that we have a fixed purpose. Our fixed purpose should be to serve as God has directed in his word. Determination does not just happen or appear. It is what transforms our thoughts into action. Serving is a part of "man's all"; if we do not have the fixed purpose of serving him and others, we have not feared God and kept his commandments as we should (Eccl. 12:13).

5. We must be focused. What I mean by "focus" is not to become sidetracked. If we are to *serve*, we cannot be distracted by the temptations and wiles of the devil. We must concentrate upon putting God first (Matt. 6:33; 22:37-38) and doing good to all men (Gal. 6:10).

6. We must spend time in serving. If we fill up our days with me and mine, there will not be any *time* left for serving others. If we do not make serving a priority, the devil will make sure we find enough to fill all our time with ourselves. Time is a precious commodity, but without it there can be no serving.

7. We must expend energy to serve. Thinking or contemplating about all the good deeds available for us to do, will not accomplish one deed. We must expend energy. Is it possible for us to produce "good works" without working? Remember in several of the parables of Jesus, Christians were illustrated by his use of *laborers*. Do laborers work and expend energy? What about Christians? Can we serve without laboring?

Serving With the Family

So now that we have established that we as Christians are to serve, how does that apply in our home life? A family is composed of individuals. In order for the family to be what God would have it to be, each member of the family must fulfill his individual duty. We have all heard the saying that a chain is only as strong as its weakest link. That is very true in families. We all have our duties and obligations within the home, but when one does not fulfill this, then the family chain is weakened by that weak link. In 1 Corinthians 12:12-27 we have the example given by Paul of our bodies. Different organs provide different needs but all are necessary. This is explaining how the church can work efficiently as one unit with many members. In the same way, mom, dad, and children all have different roles, but all are necessary for everything to get done.

The Bible example in the Old Testament of families is multi-generational. Genesis 11:31 and Acts 7:4 show us that there was more than one generation involved in Abraham's family. Abraham had important work to do, as God had directed him. Our example shows the journey halted and did not continue on until after his father died. Today, more often than not, we would put Dad in a nursing home so that we could continue our important work. We have no Bible example for this. We also see in Ruth 4:16 that there was more than one generation involved in Ruth's family. Naomi became her grandson's nurse. That is an active role, not a passive one.

The American culture has chopped up the family, dividing each generation from the other. We put our oldest, wisest generation in a nursing home. We don't have time to mess with them. We have jobs and important things to accomplish. The kids have ball games and lessons which keep us from having time. The second generation is the busiest with responsibilities to generations above and below. Their careers are often the most important thing on their mind. Our kids are left to raise themselves. Grandparents are in a nursing home, safe, where they won't bother anyone. Parents are working many hours and need time for the fitness center, professional clubs, and their own interests. We have school to come to the rescue. Now we can drop off the children early and they can eat breakfast at school. After school, there is after school care until they are old enough to give them a key. We have all kinds of convenience foods so they can make their own dinner. They don't have to eat alone; they can get on-line and chat with anyone. The devil has a lot to smile about. He has succeeded in dividing us and no one can accomplish much of anything. It's every man for himself.

However, if we keep all our generations working together as one unit, we can accomplish so much! Taking care of our old people teaches our youngest generation respect, compassion, unselfishness, and responsibility. Plus, they benefit from the life experiences, wisdom, and love. These connections will ground them.

Families Must Serve God

As a family we are to serve God. Abraham, our father of faith (Gal. 3:7), taught us by his life and example. "For I have known him, in order that he may command his children and his household after him, that they keep the way of the Lord, to do righteousness and justice, that the Lord may bring to Abraham what He has spoken to him" (Gen. 18:19). Another great man of faith, Joshua, spoke these words, "Choose for yourselves this day whom you will serve, . . . as for me and my house, we will serve the Lord" (Josh. 24:13). This should be the foundation ideal for each family here. Are we putting God first? We must if we want to be great in the kingdom. Matthew 6:33 says, "But seek first the kingdom of God and His righteousness, and all these things shall be added to you." Parents, we need to bring up our children in the nurture and admonition of the Lord (Eph. 6:4). We need to teach our children to fear the God of heaven. By our teaching and example, they need to understand the importance of obeying the gospel and becoming a child of God. Then, by our godly and faithful life, they can be influenced to faithfully serve the Lord.

As families, how excited do we get about serving God? We sometimes sit out in the cold night air for hours cheering for our favorite football team. The benches are hard, our fingers are frozen. All the way home, we relive the exciting plays over and over, relishing the event. And, if the game goes into overtime with our team winning at the end, it's all the more exciting. The next morning we go to worship God. We are in a building with air conditioning and heat. We have pews to sit on. Sunday after services, do we relive the exciting gems we read from the word of God? Or, do we complain about how cold the building was today, how long the preacher spoke, or how hard the pews were on our backs? Our precious children are listening to us. We are forming opinions in their little minds, even when we don't realize it.

Serving God is not a chore. It is the greatest privilege we have. It is our reason to get up. Do we as families serve God? We can host Bible studies in our homes. These will be varied from home to home. They can involve the single family living in one house, or we can invite neighbors, friends, Christians, etc. for various studies. If we are not comfortable leading a study with others, we can ask an older Christian to come and lead. They will be excited to have the opportunity! How prepared are we for the worship services? Do we plan ahead to get to services without feeling rushed and harried? Do we get enough sleep the night before so that we can worship clear headed, or do we have trouble staying awake and concentrating? We will spend money for tickets to a show or concert and expend much effort setting our house in order so nothing interferes with our plans. God deserves more of ourselves than a concert or show does. Do we prepare for our Bible studies ahead of time or just read it as we go that day? Do we spend more time with school work than Bible study? Serving God through worship is one of our family's highest services.

Has your family ever cleaned the church building? What a privilege to excite our children with the honor of doing this great thing for God. If your attitude is one that is taking pride in doing this for the Lord, your children will know it and adopt this same attitude. Do we want God's house to shine? Haggai 1:4 states, "Is it time for you yourselves to dwell in your paneled houses, and this temple to lie in ruins?" Our attitude will determine how we and our children view this. Chore or privilege, that is the question. What about preparing the Lord's supper? Mothers, can you think of a recipe more important or exciting to teach your daughters and sons? What about the area around the building? Pulling the weeds, planting flowers, chore or privilege, that is the question. Our little children will be excited to serve God, if we are. Families, we need to be serving the God of heaven, every day and every hour. It is our greatest privilege. Let's involve our children and let the families serve God together.

Families Must Serve Each Other

As a family we are to serve each other. In Colossians 3:17-21 Paul states, "And whatever you do in word or deed, do all in the name of the Lord Jesus, giving thanks to God, the Father through Him. Wives, submit to your own husbands, as is fitting in the Lord. Husbands, love your wives, and do not be bitter toward them. Children, obey your parents in all things, for this is well pleasing to the Lord. Fathers, do not provoke your children, lest they become discouraged." For our family units to be healthy and working as God expects, we must serve each other. This passage shows us that each part of the family has certain roles to fulfill in the service. We cannot serve each other by switching roles. We could readily understand this in other areas. Would a teacher allow the student to serve her by fulfilling her role as teacher? We can see how ridiculous this sounds. Brethren, when we reverse the roles God has given us, it is just as ridiculous to God. We need to serve each other in our own family units by fulfilling the roles God has given us.

In America, we have individual freedoms. Sometimes this confuses us, and we feel we need to look out for number one. No one is going to get in our way. The problem is, we are not number one as society teaches. God is number one and, according to the Bible, we need to serve others to be what God wants us to be. Jesus is our example and he did serve others. Notice what is said about Jesus in Philippians 2:5-8: "Let this mind be in you which was also in Christ Jesus, who, being in the form of God, did not consider it robbery to be equal with God, but made himself of no reputation, taking the form of a bondservant, and coming in the likeness of men. And being found in appearance as a man, He humbled Himself and became obedient to the point of death, even the death of the cross." Jesus came to this earth not to be served, but to serve.

Unfortunately, we have lost the service ideal in a lot of our families. Dad is gone working, exercising, socializing, etc. Mom is gone working, exercising, socializing, etc. Children are gone to school, exercising, socializing, etc. It's every person for himself. Anyone who stumbles in throws something in the microwave and turns on the TV. This is not the family serving one another. God gave us a plan because it works. Dad is to provide for the family. He is also instructed to teach the children. The father is to be the head of the home. If Dad is leading as God commanded, there won't be a family in chaos. Dad is commanded to love Mom. If Dad truly loves Mom, her happiness will be necessary for him to be happy. Mom is charged with being in subjection to Dad. 1 Timothy 2:11-15 states why. "Adam was not deceived, but the woman being deceived, fell into transgression." We might say what does that have to do with me? It's God's word and his decision. Physically, if a body has two heads, are we happy about that? What do we do? We call it Siamese twins and we surgically separate them because we have an unhealthy situation. It's the same in our families. If we have two heads, there will be problems. Someone has to make decisions. Again, we readily understand this in a football game. The coach is the head. The players do not decide to go their own direction. One might say, they are the ones that may get hurt on the play. They have a right to decide which play they want to perform. All eyes will be on them during the game. They also

111

might be smarter than the coach, This doesn't matter. The players follow the leader. God decides who the leader is in our family.

We have to put our families back together. I believe it is important if we want America to be allowed to remain a great power. If you study the Roman Empire you can see that the fall of this great power had a lot to do with the deterioration of the family unit. We have become so sophisticated that our goals do not include all of our family generations. Our oldest generation belongs with their families (see Matt. 15:4-6; 1 Tim. 5:4, 8, 16). I understand that there will be situations that call for a nursing home. But if that is the case, the family should not abandon grandma, grandpa, mom, dad, aunt, or uncle but should be there around the clock, in and out, as each family member can be there, fulfilling their responsibilities. Just because we can't meet all of their needs doesn't mean we don't have a responsibility to meet the ones we can. On top of the good it will do our loved one, our example here might lead a worker from the nursing home to the Lord. If possible, think of all the good that can come from having those precious loved ones home where they belong!

We have worked with our various relatives in differing ways to meet the needs in our family. We have gone to other states to help for a week or two at a time when a loved one was terminally ill. My aunt had a stroke a few years back. The doctors said she could not go back home. It was determined by the family to move her in with us. Did it help my aunt? Yes, but it helped our family more. Our children got to know her as well as I already did and hear all the old stories. Entertaining, yes, but much more than that, our children became more grounded on who they are by hearing where our loved ones have been. My children know more about what our older generation did and thought. They belong to something bigger than themselves. It helped their self esteem. We have a seven-year-old who only drinks water because that was all Aunt Jean drank. The habit stuck and Aunt Jean's been gone four years. Even though Aunt Jean needed help to accomplish even the basics, she did not "retire." She was still serving God by serving our little ones. How compassionate children become when they are worried about their older relative's comfort level on a daily basis. Their priorities change when they are trying to meet the needs of someone who needs them. How important a child feels when an adult is depending on him. Our children always knew whose turn it was to get Aunt Jean's wheelchair and escort her to the dinner table. When a family bands together to meet the needs of one of their own, it changes who they are on the inside. You don't have regrets because you tried to the best of your ability.

In 1993 Cindy's pop passed away. He died in his own home with his wife, Cindy and me, and one of the elders at his congregation. That was his wish. I promised him that I would take care of Cindy's mom. She had had two strokes and he was worried about what she would do. He relaxed when I made this promise. That was his concern in his final hours. She moved in with us and still lives with us to this day. She stays busy helping in any way she can. Has it helped her? Yes, but it has helped our children more. Grandmas have more time. Time to read books. Time to talk. Time to ground the children in their values, self esteem, and priorities. Those conversations are the ones that help our little ones grow into what God wants them to be. Time to make desserts. If you want to see an excited child, just make them a little dessert in their own fancy dish. Priceless gifts.

My father passed away in 2001. He collapsed suddenly and never regained consciousness. He died in a hospital room with his wife, two sons and their wives, and several of his grandchildren present. We could not meet all his needs. He had to remain in the hospital. That however, did not nullify our responsibilities. We still fulfilled all we could for him, taking turns around the clock. We served him as completely as possible. Mother remained in their home until the fall of 2005 when she moved in with us because of her health. Has it helped her? Yes, but it has helped us more.

I am saddened today when I hear older Christians say something like this: "I've raised my kids, I'm done." Dear brethren, as Christians we are never done while there is breath in our bodies. Jesus is our example here. Shame on us when we feel we don't need to serve our family members anymore. We do not want our family chopped up. We have much to give each other (going both directions). We can all accomplish more when we work together. When we give our older generation the respect due them, our children are watching and learning. What a great education!

Husbands and wives need to serve each other. When we fulfill the responsibilities of the roles God gave us, we can accomplish so much! This relationship is like the hub of the family wheel. If the husband is loving the wife as Christ loved the church, he is making sure she has what she needs. He can't be happy unless she is happy. They are one; they have the same goals, same desires. Luke 2: 52 states, "And Jesus increased in wisdom and stature, and in favor with God and men." Humans have mental, physical, spiritual, and social needs. Husbands, we need to make sure our wife has what she needs in all these areas. Do you cherish her as Christ cherishes the church?

Wives, your husbands have needs that are your responsibility to fulfill. He needs a helper (Gen. 2:20-21). If you are filling all your hours in the day with your career, your friends, and your classes, how can you be a helper for your husband? The devil is very happy with our marriages going two directions. We are excited if we meet once or twice a week. Wives are told to be "homemakers" (Tit. 2:4). What does that mean? Does it mean she can't work? Proverbs 31 talks about the worthy wife and she was very busy working. She wasn't working for her own goals though, but for her husband's. Wives can be as busy as their own husband wants. Remember the husband and wife are one. Wives should be in tune with the needs of her husband to keep him going. Wives should be the wind beneath their own husband's wings. There are houses all over town that are not homes. Wives need to make their home a haven—a place for dad and children to come for recharging. Many homes today are more like a pit stop for everyone. Our football team example works here too. How many ball teams can win championships without spending many, many hours together. They listen to the coach and drill, drill, drill. Then they practice, practice, practice. We want our families to win championships. This means we must all be working together, serving one another.

Now we come to our youngest generation. Our precious children. We love our children, right? We love ours. We have ten. Yes, I said ten, We have nine daughters and one son. He is number four out of ten. Don't feel sorry for him. He's spoiled rotten! Alicia is thirty-three. Angela is thirty-two. Amanda is thirty. Royce Michael is twenty-nine. Melissa and Vanessa are both eighteen. Kassandra is seven. Savanna, Brianna Jo, and Aurora are each five. We really have three different families of children. When the baby of the first four turned eleven, we started over and adopted two more. When they turned eleven, you guessed it, we started over and adopted four more. We don't think we will start family number four when these girls turn eleven! We have responsibilities given to us by God to serve these precious gifts. Deuteronomy 6:5-9 states,

> You shall love the Lord your God with all your heart, with all your soul, and with all your strength. And these words which I command you today shall be in your heart. You shall teach them diligently to your children, and shall talk of them when you sit in your house, when you walk by the way, when you lie down, and when you rise up. You shall bind them as a sign on your hand, and they shall be as frontlets between your eyes. You shall write them on the doorposts of your house and on your gates.

Can you think of a time or place not covered? Brethren, this is a tall order, Basically, we can't play at religion. We need to use every opportunity to teach or reinforce God's word with our children. We must teach our children that our lives are to be spent in *service*. God put children in families with a mom and dad. Children need their mom and dad. When our children spend their days watching TV, playing video games, practicing and playing sports or instruments, who are they serving?

Our family did foster care from 1986 until 2004. We have had dozens of children in our home for anywhere from a few days to years. They would be with us because their own family could not meet their needs for various reasons. When we were doing foster care, we had Christians ask us if we were sure we weren't "cheating" our own children. We thought about the question. We discussed the question. We couldn't figure out how we could be cheating our own children. Our children may not have been allowed to go to the movies as often as others. They might have missed out on some physical "stuff." But our children learned so much serving these children who were missing the most basic needs. The compassion, love, responsibility, and selflessness involved taught our children what is important in this world.

I remember one year our son had to write an essay for a PTA project. It was to finish this sentence: "If I had one wish it would be." Michael was eleven. Think for a moment of the choices an eleven-year old might make. I wish I could be a famous ballplayer. . . . I wish I could be a brain surgeon. . . . I wish I was rich. . . . Michael's essay and his wish was about a tiny baby girl that was born drug addicted. We would hold her close while she had tremors as her body went through withdrawal of the drugs. Michael's wish was for Missy's happiness. When Missy left us we all cried for days. Cindy was done with foster care. She said she could not handle it when the baby left. Our son responded, "But mom, if we can help for a little while, shouldn't we?" I don't think foster care "cheated" our children.

Through the years our children helped with children who couldn't breathe without the assistance of machines, children who could not swallow so we fed them directly into their little tummies. We helped one sweet baby get through chemotherapy for cancer. We helped one little fella as long as we could. His heart just couldn't pump anymore at three months old. He passed away and we helped bury him. We had children come to us with lice, one celebrated her first birthday with us because mom was in jail. She was caught shoplifting presents for the baby. I think she needed her mom more than presents. We have had children with broken legs, broken ribs, broken collar bones, broken arms, a broken sternum, and fractured skulls because of the anger of adults in their life. We had a little guy that was a vegetable from being shaken. He could not control his own vital signs. They called it storming. His body would go rigid, his temperature would go up to 104F, his pulse would go over 230 beats per minute, his respiration would go above 80 per minute. We would have to work with medications to help him relax. We had a little girl who was left a vegetable from spinal meningitis. She would have seizures that would cause her to scream out. We didn't know if she was in pain because she could not tell us. We had her from the time she was five until she was eleven. We attended her funeral when she was fifteen. She had been in that condition since she was three months old. We had children with third degree burns. We had many drug addicted babies. Their little bodies would tremor as they came down off the drugs that were in their bodies. I could go on and on. The point is yes, we helped these children, but, the children helped us more. They reminded us of priorities. They helped us be part of the solution instead of part of the problem. Our children have grown up to be loving, caring Christians and I believe they have these children to thank. Instead of leaving our children to be raised by others, we need to serve our children. We need to make sure we meet all their needs.

Our family has many handicapped children. We have mental handicaps and physical ones. We have a mute child, several hearing impaired children, two severe enough for bilateral hearing aids, a legally blind child, one with autism, one with Down syndrome, a child with dwarfism, a child with cerebral palsy, two with fetal alcohol syndrome, one with hydrocephalus, and some with developmental delays. Luke 2:52 tells us that our children need mental, physical, spiritual, and social guidance. We have a physical therapist, an occupational therapist, and a speech therapist in the compound several hours every week trying to help the children be all they can be. Again, we have helped the children with handicaps, but they have helped us in so many ways. You can't help someone else without them affecting who you are. It will change who you are. We need to show our children how to make wise choices. Social functions should never come first. God needs this position. When our children see us by example never putting our social functions before God and his work, they become grounded.

Our five oldest children are grown now. They all live around us. We have fenced in the perimeters of the backyards together. We have twenty-one grandchildren. They can be seen running back and forth playing in the compound. Our three oldest children have all done foster care. We are blessed with ten adopted grandchildren. We can accomplish so much more because we live so close and can be available for whatever happens. Our children all benefit from having all the generations of their family in their lives. We work together and accomplish more.

As we work together with generations intertwined, every one is a winner. Our families are falling apart because we have chopped them up! It's every man for himself. Thankfully, Jesus did not have this attitude. If we are Christians, which means Christlike, we cannot have this attitude.

Families Must Serve Other Christians

As families, we must serve other Christians. In Acts 2:44-45 it says, "Now all who believed were together, and had all things in common, and sold their possessions and goods, and divided them among all, as anyone had need." Wow, these brethren were serving one another. Today, we seem to be in competition to accumulate the most "stuff." Then we also don't know enough about our brethren to know what they need. This is wrong. We must serve each other. Back in 1978, Cindy and I went to the lectures in Temple Terrace, Florida. We had a huge blizzard and could not get back to northern Indiana. After a few days, we called our next door neighbor (an unbeliever) to see if the roads were open yet for us to get home. He told us they were. We told him we were coming home in the morning. He then called an acquaintance he knew to be a member of our congregation. He told the member that we were coming home the next day and asked if some of the "folks" could come help him shovel our 120 foot driveway. We had four children ages four and under and he wanted us to be able to get them in the house. The member at our congregation explained to this dear seventy-year old neighbor that we don't treat our preachers special. They shovel their own driveways. The neighbor shoveled our driveway alone, and we never could interest him in a Bible study. He wanted no part of a religion that didn't help one another. He thought he was doing a better job on his own.

When we serve one another in the simple ways, sometimes it can have a big impact. This is true in the reverse. When we fail to serve one another in the simple ways, sometimes it can have a big impact for the negative. In 1 Timothy 5:1-2 it states, "Do not rebuke an older man, but exhort him as a father, younger men as brothers, older women as sisters, with all purity."

117

We need to interact with one another in the day in, day out simple ways. Without that foundation our brethren will not feel they can come to us. Our congregations are like our families, all chopped up. We socialize with those of like precious age group, education status, or recreation interests. It is great to find those we can relate to, but we must go outside our comfort zone and get to know everyone. Then older women can help the new moms with parenting advice.

The wife of one of our elder's has the young girls over twice a year to bake cookies. Some are now young adults and they still get so excited when it's cookie time. While they are baking they chat and get to know one another. Who do you think the young girls will turn to if they need advice? The young teens can help the older people with yard work or inside tasks, like washing windows. The time they spend together will help the older one yes, but the younger one will gain so much from the conversations with the older wise Christian. The older men can help the new husbands figure out how to be the leader God wants. He can show him by example how to love his wife as Christ loved the church. The young men can work with the teenagers so that they will have a relationship when the teenager hits hard places. Then that teenager will turn to the older Christian instead of unbelievers for advice.

We had a dear sister in Indianapolis who was very poor. She had five little children. They would spend their Saturdays out collecting cans. They would take them in for payment. Then they would buy as many cards and stamps as that would purchase to send to our sick or shut-in brethren. What a beautiful example of serving one another! This sister has left this earth, but her daughter visited our congregation's last gospel meeting. She is still serving God and others.

We had a member in Indianapolis who had a situation which ended with her children being put in foster care. Christians in that locale did not want these three children in unbelievers' homes. We felt they should be with Christians. We and two other families licensed with the state so that we could keep the children with Christians. That was what led us into foster care. If we had not gotten involved, we would not have been blessed with our six daughters and ten grandchildren.

Stepping up for our brethren has bonuses for us we cannot even imagine. Cindy's father had cancer. He wanted to be home. For this to be accomplished his three sisters (all lived in Tennessee) took turns going to Aurora, Illinois and helping. The local congregation signed up for shifts. Seven nights a week, someone came from 10 p.m. until 2 a.m.; they would then be relieved by another member of the congregation who stayed from 2 a.m. until 6 a.m. He was a full-time patient and this allowed Cindy's mom a proper night's sleep to keep going. This went on for fifteen months. There was never an unattended time! I know of a member of the church whose house payment was made for the entire year he was terminally ill by another member of the congregation. Do we serve each other? I believe these examples prove that we do. But there is even more that we can do.

God wants us to serve each other and have all things in common as each has need. Where does this lead? Another responsibility that we have in serving others is to rebuke them when we see them sinning. If we have all been busy serving each other, how will we react to this rebuke? When our first child was born, we were very busy being good parents. We missed two Sunday morning Bible classes because it was hard to get everything together on time. One of the dear elders at our congregation approached us. He simply said he had noticed we had missed two Bible classes and wondered what we needed or how he could help. Wow, that woke us up. Bob had already established long before that he loved us. When he rebuked us we knew his motive. We have never missed a Sunday morning Bible study since for rushed timing. What about when we are rebuked by a brother who has never established a relationship with us? We might question their motive because they have not shown us they love us with actions.

We can serve one another through our Bible classes. Sometimes, it is hard for us to get brethren to teach. We don't want to be tied down to being at the class. We don't want to put the time into preparation. We don't want to mess with the kids. Think about the example it would be to these souls to hear the truth from not only their parents but other adults who are interested in their souls? We prefer the more important adult class. If we are older, we skip the Bible classes on raising children because we don't need that. What about being the example to those at that stage? Who is going to teach the young parents? We should not have the attitude of let them figure it out themselves. We feel we have done "our time" when our child was young but we are "retired." Have you ever thought about what these excuses will sound like on the day of judgment? We need to serve our youngest charges.

There are many other ways we can serve each other. I offer these to help us think about the different ways we can serve one another. We had Christians with needs because of the hurricanes last year. They received so much assistance they returned the extra. Their need was abundantly met. We are very good with the big needs, while tripping over the little needs. Let's intertwine our members at our local congregations. We can accomplish so much more!

Families Must Serve the World

We need to serve the world. Matthew 5:13-16 states, "You are the salt of the earth; but if the salt loses its flavor, how shall it be seasoned? It is then good for nothing but to be thrown out and trampled underfoot by men, You are the light of the world. A city that is set on a hill cannot be hidden. Nor do they light a lamp and put it under a basket, but on a lamp stand, and it gives light to all who are in the house. Let your light so shine before men, that they may see your good works and glorify your father in heaven." Our little ones learn the song "This little light of mine" before their first birthday. They can hold up their little finger so proudly. That should be our attitude. We need to be enthusiastic about life and others. This attitude will help others see what God has to offer. We sing the song, "The World's Bible." It says,

> Christ has no hands but our hands to do His work today,
> He has no feet but our feet to lead men in His way;
> He has no tongue but our tongues to tell men how He died,
> He has no help but our help to bring them to His side.
>
> We are the only Bible the careless world will read,
> We are the sinner's gospel, we are the scoffers' creed;
> We are the Lord's last message given in deed and word,
> What if the type is crooked? What if the print is blurred?
>
> What if our hands are busy with other things than His?
> What if our feet are walking where sin's allurement is?
> What if our tongues are speaking of things His life would spurn,
> How can we hope to help Him and welcome His return?

Wow, that song really sums it up!

We are all out in the world in various ways. We work, go to school, go to club functions, belong to a fitness center, have neighbors, and go shopping to name a few. Romans 12:2 states, "And do not be conformed to this world, but be transformed by the renewing of your mind, that you may prove what is that good and acceptable and perfect will of God." We are being watched at times by the people in the world. They know that we are Christians. They wonder what that means. They look to see if they can see a difference. Our neighbor who shoveled our driveway looked. He didn't think we had anything to teach him. We can't let that happen, brethren. We need to use our opportunities. Our neighbors know if we attend services regularly or if we go only when nothing else is happening. We want the world to look at us and think, "Wow, I want what they have." We will all have different opportunities and that gets the whole world covered. We have had opportunities out in the world dealing with the foster children. One of the little children we had visits our assembly from time to time. His mother, grandmother, siblings, and an aunt have all come several times. The apostle Paul in 1 Corinthians 3:6 states, "I planted, Apollos watered, but God gave the increase." We need to be planting and watering. If we have taken the time to help people physically, they will know we care. Then when we try to teach them God's word, they will know we care and be more likely to listen. Have you ever been talking to someone and the conversation go something like this: "The church of Christ . . . oh, I know so and so who attends there . . . if so and so goes there I have no desire to come." What do you say to that? We need to be serving people. We are much less likely to have this problem if we are trying to serve others. At the work place, do we work diligently or do we half-heartedly do our job? Our co-workers are paying attention. Whenever we are out in public, we are ambassadors for the Lord. What kind of example are we setting? We are all blessed by God with different talents. If everyone is busy, accomplishing all they can for the Lord with the talents they have been given, just think about what will get done!

Conclusion

Some of us have no problems serving others. Some of us however, have problems letting others serve us. It is as important to receive as it is to give. Yes, I wrote that correctly. Think about it for a moment. We need to depend on our family members, our fellow Christians, and even people in the world if we want to have the type of relationships that can grow. This point was brought home to me several years ago. One of my dear brothers at the congregation inherited some money. He was very excited and wanted to take me shopping. He bought me two new suits and a pair of shoes. I must confess I did need those items, but I was a little embarrassed. Two days later I received a thank you card in the mail. They were thanking me for letting them buy me those things! Can you imagine? I was shocked. Then, it hit me. This precious soul was ahead of me in wisdom. Give and take, working together, gets the job done.

Jesus is to be our example in everything we do. To set us free from the bondage of sin and that we might have eternal life, Jesus gave his physical life for us. Let us be busy and give our physical lives to help our families, the church, our brethren, and even the world. We have a dear friend and sister in Christ in Illinois who refers to serving as "putting ribbons on our packages." Remember that some day "we must all appear before the judgment seat of Christ, that each one may receive the things done in the body, according to what he has done, whether good or bad" (2 Cor. 5:10). Brethren, *what have we done?*

The Death of A Child

Tom M. Roberts

The death of a child is an intensely personal and painful experience. It is futile to compare such a loss with the loss of a parent, spouse, sibling, or other close relative or friend as though one death exceeds another in grief. Though many have said that the death of a child is the worst event one can experience, all death is painful and carries its own personal and tragic loss. Thus, I would never argue whether the death of a child exceeds the pain of one who loses a husband, wife, or parent. It is enough to realize that each person must come face to face with this reality in due season. We all share in common the fact that "it is appointed for men to die once, but after this the judgment" (Heb. 9:27). Perhaps the uniqueness of a death "out of due season," *before its time*, carries an additional weight in consideration. Par-

Tom Roberts was born in Gladewater (northeast), Texas on February 8, 1935. He married Pauline Kelley the year he graduated and attended Florida College during the 1954-55 school year. Together, they had three children, Curtis (1956), Tommy, Jr. (1957) and Paula (1964). Tommy was accidently killed in a motorcycle accident in 1981 at 23 years of age. Tom and Pauline have been married over fifty years (1953-). They currently reside in Tampa, Florida, working with the Forest Hills congregation.

He began preaching full time in 1956 in south Texas and has preached continually since then, having lived in North Carolina (twice), Texas, and Florida. He has been a staff writer for *Truth Magazine*, co-editor for *Watchman Magazine* and co-author and editor of *Neo-Calvinism in the Church of Christ*. He has preached in gospel meetings across the nation, preached on radio and television and helped start congregations in Sherman, Texas, Morehead City, N.C. and Fort Worth, Texas. Current plans include a move back to Texas in July where he will work with the Northside church in Mansfield, in the Dallas-Fort Worth metroplex area.

ents expect to outlive their children. When death interrupts this "natural" progression, it sets in motion an extreme series of emotions. Grief, pain, horror, anger, confusion, denial and guilt often struggle within the parents for an answer. It is not "normal" to lose a child as it is with aged parents. We know that our parents are going to age and pass from this life, but not our children. This incredulity attaches to the loss of a child. Yet it is enough to admit that all such loss results in nearly insurmountable grief.

Because the death of a child is intensely personal and painful, it is difficult to speak about it. Unless the audience clearly understands the purpose of such a lecture, it is possible that such a discussion could be misconstrued as a maudlin appeal for sympathy. It is never appropriate to leverage sympathy for an advantage, real or imagined. Yet, in the telling of personal triumphs and tragedies, one's personal experiences may be able to temper and modify another's grief. I understand this to be the purpose of these lectures: to focus on the family, to strengthen what may become weak, to uplift those who might be discouraged, to point each one to the wisdom of God's word to help us meet the stress of life and death. It is in this vein that I speak of something so personal and terrible that I often shrink from even thinking about it.

Yet the Bible exposes us to others who have had tragedy in their lives and opens up their experiences to teach valuable lessons. What would you think of having the shameful experience of Hosea with Gomer only to have it become public knowledge? Not only was he commanded to take a wife of "whoredom" (Hos. 1:2), but to take her back after she abandoned him and returned to her promiscuous lifestyle. Through the exposure of Hosea and his family problems, we learn of the depth of God's love for sinful human-ity. Through Joseph, we learn of hateful brothers who sold him into slavery and how to react nobly and spiritually to such treachery. Through David, we learn of lust so deep and so controlling that it caused the Psalmist to commit adultery and murder. Through David, we also learn of the treachery of a beloved son and the grief at his death. Few statements of Scripture are more filled with sadness than the tears of David, who loved more deeply than wisely, as he went to the chamber over the gate, weeping: "O my son Absalom—my son, my son Absalom—if only I had died in your place! O Absalom my son, my son!" (2 Sam. 18:33). As others have had sadness and tragedy in their lives and such things have been used by the providence of God to teach lessons to others, perhaps we can find some direction in coping with the death of a child. Perhaps something we learned will comfort those in similar circumstances or help in facing the reality of death.

The Brief Life of Our Son

My wife and I have had three children, two boys and a girl. Our middle child, Tommy, Jr., died in 1981 at the age of twenty-three in a motorcycle accident. It is always awkward for us how to reply to the question, "How many children do you have?" If we answer, "two," we feel guilty in omitting Tommy as though he had never lived. We will certainly never forget him. If we say "three," it sometimes becomes necessary to explain why only two remain, and that becomes awkward as well. Such quandaries often arise at the most unexpected of times. After twenty-five years, a song used at his funeral, a memory, a picture, a remembered event can swiftly bring tears to our eyes and an emptiness in our heart. There is still an unreal quality to the fact that death claimed one of our children.

We never wanted our sons to ride motorcycles because of the inherent danger imposed by them. However, after he married, Tommy finally decided to have his dream come true and purchased his own motorcycle. Late in October of 1981, just before Halloween, he collided with a truck and was comatose, having massive head and body injuries, totally unresponsive for three and one-half weeks in intensive care. We were with him daily, talking to him since the doctor had informed us that hearing is the last physical sense to leave a person. We also prayed with him since he had not been living faithfully in the last years of his life. To this day, we hope that he was able to hear us and make the necessary change of heart that repentance can bring. Believe me when I say that there is something worse than the physical death of a child. There is no comparison to the dread that one's child may not be right with God as his life drifts beyond our reach. Truly, there are some feelings for which the human voice has found no words to describe. But we are able to bear this burden, knowing that the Great Jehovah is a merciful God who will judge righteously and I bow to his wisdom, knowing that "He doeth all things well." My wife and I are content to leave such matters in the hand of God and to know that the Lord loves him even more than we do and we will accept whatever fate God righteously administers.

There are many untold moments about Tommy's death that we leave unsaid. He was buried the day after Thanksgiving and this has always changed our view of holidays. While the knowledge of his passing is always with us, time has worked its way and it is not as sharp and constant as at the moment he breathed his last. The sweet memories of his early life remain, the joy he brought us, the life we shared. We hope to have him with us in eternity, as with all our children, but we must bow to God's will and trust him for all things beyond our control.

There are a number of things that have helped us cope with this loss. We would like to pass them along to you as they have served to strengthen our faith in God and to look forward to heaven. It is our prayer that the pain and agony we went through may help you in case you ever have to walk this mournful road.

First of all, I have learned that there are some things that must be experienced. They cannot be evaded, avoided, or ignored. There are times when human beings have to suffer and there is no surcease. Suffering Job learned this, and so did we. No one could remove the reality that our son was dead, gone from our reach, and beyond human control. I once saw a cow standing in a sleet storm in a pasture in Texas, without a tree or shed for shelter. All that poor creature could do during that storm was to hump its back and take the sleet until the sun came out. And so it is with us humans: it is our lot to suffer at times. Life is not all roses. Life can be exceedingly cruel. This is not God's will, but the devil's intrusion into the affairs of man, with the usual consequences of pain and torment (Rev. 12:12). In such times all we can do is stiffen our resolve and pass through to the other side. As the song says, "The sun will come out tomorrow." And it always does, if we will allow our faith to remain constant.

We learned also that God often works his grace through other Christians. During the interminable days when Tommy was in the hospital, and following the funeral, the good brethren at the Westside church in Fort Worth were by our side, both at the hospital and in our home. They prayed with us and for us. Brethren preached in my place when I couldn't. Ladies brought food to the house when we were too distraught to think of normal things. Brethren from across the country found time to let us know of their prayers. In such times, there is a tendency to withdraw into yourself, to isolate yourself, to be totally alone in your pain and grief. But God helped us mightily through our brethren. I cannot number the times when I have been in the house of grief with others, but it is different when it is your house. We had to learn to receive, rather than to give, condolences. If such a time comes to you, please open your heart to your brethren in the Lord. Such brethren are God's messengers to alleviate and ease the pain and hurt that you are having.

We learned to distinguish clearly between acts of God and the devil. It is easy for some to blame God for tragedy, being ignorant of God's infinite mercy. Unable to comprehend why evil has to exist, men blame God for everything bad that happens to them. Again, a good study of the book of Job would help us understand human suffering. We must learn that God allows free will to operate and with that fact, man can choose either good or evil. When Adam and Eve chose evil in the Garden of Eden (Gen. 3), they were not forced to do what they did, nor did God create them inherently evil. The risk of free moral agency is that man often chooses evil over good and this has brought evil into the good world that God created (Rom. 8). Evil is in the world because all have sinned (Rom. 3:23) and we die because of sin (Rom. 6:23). While our other two children had a great deal of confusion over the loss of their brother, and it affected their faith deeply and adversely, there was never a moment when we doubted God or questioned his wisdom in the events. In fact, one of the things that got us through Tommy's death was our complete and final trust in God's will. At the same time, we learned that the devil is merciless. There is no time when he will say, "I have dealt them enough misery for now. I will let them alone for a time." During the time of Tommy's injury and subsequent death, we also had to prepare for major surgery for Pauline (her doctor mistakenly diagnosed her with cancer) and my third back surgery. We were denied access to Tommy's six-month old daughter for many years through in-law interference. In actual fact, there was a period of ten years when the devil unremittingly haunted us with one thing after another. Yes, we have learned who our true enemy really is. During that bleak time, when it seemed that there was no let-up from our tribulations, faith in God led us through that dark valley into the sunlight of God's care. With God, all things are possible (Rom. 8:31-39).

One of the things we had to learn through personal experience was that each person connected to Tommy in the family had to grieve in his own way. Both parents and siblings approach their loss in separate ways and must be permitted time and space to express grief as they are able. About a year after Tommy's death, close friends of ours lost their son and it drove them finally to divorce and total loss of faith. The mother of that boy was hysterical in her grief while the husband suffered silently, inwardly. Finally, the distraught mother accused the father of not loving the son, of not understanding her grief and they drove each other apart. While being supportive of each other, each parent must allow the other their own manner of grief. The danger of the situation is that being submerged in grief, we become oblivious to the needs of others in the family.

There is certainly a place in the suffering time for professional help. The family just alluded to sought professional grief counseling but their loss of faith overwhelmed any help they might have received. My wife and I did not seek professional counseling, while others might well do so. There is a wonderful self-help group called "Compassionate Friends" that has chapters in most major cities (www.compassionatefriends.org). These are people who have banded together because each of them has lost a child, and they extend help to others (without cost) because they know what others are experiencing. Their mission statement reads: "The mission of The Compassionate Friends is to assist families toward resolution of grief following the death of a child of any age and to provide information to help others be supportive." Likewise, with careful screening, competent professional counselors can be found who can guide family members through the grieving time. Thankfully, there are a few Christians who are counselors, such as brother Art Adams, who can help or put you in touch with those who can help.

The Grieving Process

I do not want to be clinical in the process of this lesson, but there are professional efforts which have been made to analyze and describe what is called the "grieving process." This pre-supposes that grief will have a "closing," that there is "resolution," and that it follows a predictable course. Those who are in the midst of such a process may be anything but analytical or expect there ever to be a closing to their suffering. But, to one degree or another, some steps of healing take place, either consciously or subconsciously. There is quite a lot of debate among professionals about this process: what are the steps of grieving, in what order do they occur, how long does each step take, etc. Because I believe there is some value to be received from knowing that grief does, indeed, follow through a series of steps from its inception to a point in time where it becomes, at least, bearable, I would like to share some information about this process.

Elisabeth Kubler-Ross wrote *On Death and Dying* (Macmillan Publishing Company, 1969) in an early study of those who were approaching death. In her study, she introduced the now-popular (but debated) "steps of dying," which included: Denial, Anger, Bargaining, Depression, Acceptance. Not only those dying, but their survivors, she felt, experienced these reactions. Additionally, she felt that any great change of life might lead to the same steps: divorce, bankruptcy, criminal sentencing, etc.

I believe there is some profit for us in understanding the range of human emotions that are somewhat forced upon us during dramatic and eventful times. Look at these steps individually:

- **Denial** (This can't be happening to me! Such things happen to others.)
- **Anger** (Why is this happening to me? What did I do to deserve this?)
- **Bargaining** (I promise to change my life if this doesn't happen. I will go to church more, read my Bible more, be a better person.)
- **Depression** (I just don't care what happens to me. I am resigned to the worst. My life is out of control and things can only get worse.)
- **Acceptance** (I'm ready for death. I am resigned to whatever happens. Let come what may.)

Personally, I do not believe that emotional behaviors are scripted in such detail. While there may be stages of grief, there is no set pattern that follows logically in every instance for every stage has its own peculiarities. But who has not felt denial at an unexpected and dramatic event in his life. And which one has not railed in anger against death? Depression is an ever-present danger in times of turmoil and may, itself, be lengthy and a separate medical problem aside from the death of a loved one. Acceptance, in the face of the inevitable, may be a blessing.

Another study worth mentioning is *Life With An Empty Chair — a guide through grief*, by Dr. Roberta Temes. Rather than five steps, she describes three types of behavior: numbness (mechanical functioning), disorganization (inability to function; feelings of loss), reorganization (re-entry into a more "normal" social life). We can likewise identify with such behavior.

The good part of all these studies is that some are trying to make sense of helping those who suffer, to help them reach a place in life *beyond* the tragedy. And if we are to be productive in our family circle or in life as a Christian, we must move into a more "normal" social life. There is no disrespect to the dead for the living to continue to live. One cannot assume a state of perpetual grief and be productive as a child of God.

While there is no contradiction between faith and professional medical help in times of crisis, some might perceive seeking medical help as a lack of faith. On the contrary, Luke was a physician (Col. 4:14) and Jesus is nothing if not the Great Physician. Healing, today, is not miraculous (as in the apostolic age), but providential, through natural means and the grace of God. Do not hesitate to seek appropriate medical help. But realize, at the same time, that medicine is not a substitute for faith. Anti-depressants and other prescriptive medicines can, in themselves, become a major addictive problem. Do not rely on medicine alone or underestimate the power of God's word which is able to supply tremendous aid to suffering saints. The Psalms of David have counseled many people in times of grief and anxiety. The message of Scripture is that God is in control even when the world is in disarray and we can rely on him for "he cares for us" (1 Pet. 5:7). It is comfort indeed to know that God is aware of how many sparrows are alive in the world and that the hairs on my head are numbered (Matt. 10:29-31). But Jesus has said that we are "of more value than many sparrows" and he is aware of the needs of our life. Do not fail to turn to the Bible to buttress your spirit and lift up your heart in the dark days.

Practical Advice to Relatives and Friends

There is a great deal of awkwardness connected to the loss of a loved one as close relatives and friends struggle to comfort those who are left behind. What are we to say or do? Will I inadvertently say the wrong thing? Will I add to their grief? Perhaps some practical suggestions will be helpful.

- Do not avoid emotions or separate yourself from those who grieve. There are no magic words to take away the pain, but there is healing power in the touch of those who care and who shed a sympathizing tear. "I am so sorry," offers real comfort.
- Do not feel the need to talk at length to those bereaved. But be ready to listen if they want to talk. Providing a sympathetic shoulder for one to cry on has therapeutic value beyond psychiatry. You might ask, "Do you want to tell me about it?"
- Bereaved people are often disconnected from the ability to handle everyday chores. This realization has led to the custom of friends or Christians bringing in food and doing laundry or house cleaning. You may quietly schedule this good work with others to avoid overwhelming the family with visitors.
- During the bereavement period, survivors are often dazed by their loss and unable to remember that you visited or when. They may or may not realize that you were at the funeral. They may have questions to ask of you later about some of the events and you can comfort them by retelling what they missed.

- Give special attention to surviving children or siblings. Brothers and sisters are often confused and overwhelmed by death and their needs must not be overlooked. Grief has different dimensions to different family members and surviving parents may be overwhelmed themselves and unable to think clearly.
- Continue to remember the family in the weeks that follow interment. Their loss will be fresh for weeks and they do not want the one who has passed away to be forgotten. Do not hesitate to mention the name of the deceased or make comments about his/her memory.
- Send cards and notes of condolence. You may be assured that these are treasured and often re-read as time passes. It is good that others say, "I am just thinking about you. . . ."
- Avoid saying, "I know how you feel." All loss is not the same and, as deeply as you felt your loss, it is not the same. The loss of a child is more puzzling and enigmatic than that of a parent or older person, though all death is tragic.
- Be constant in your prayers for all those affected by death. "The effective, fervent prayer of a righteous man avails much" (Jas. 5:16). Believe in prayer and go to God in prayer often. Lift up their names before the throne of grace. As the opportunity permits, let those in grief know that they are often in your prayers.

Even the preparation of this manuscript brought back many painful memories, but also joyful remembrances of the son that we had with us so briefly and lost so tragically. It is my fervent prayer that none of you has to face this kind of trial. If you do, we pray that you may find the "peace of God that passes understanding" (Phil. 4:7), and that the "God of peace" may be with you all (Rom. 15:33).

Things That Shouldn't End After Marriage

Morris Hafley

And these words, which I command thee this day, shall be in thine heart: And thou shalt teach them diligently unto thy children, and shalt talk of them when thou sittest in thine house, and when thou walkest by the way, and when thou liest down, and when thou risest up. And thou shalt bind them for a sign upon thine hand, and they shall be as frontlets between thine eyes. And thou shalt write them upon the posts of thy house, and on thy gates (Deut. 6:6-10).

Our nation is paying and will continue to pay for the sins of the parents. God knew that Abraham would teach his children. "For I know him, that he will command his children and his household after him, and they shall keep the way of the Lord, to do justice and judgment; that the Lord may bring upon Abraham that which he hath spoken of him" (Gen. 18:19). Many parents aren't walking worthy of their vocation (full-time work) because service to God has become their avocation (part-time work).

Morris Hafley was born in Danville, Kentucky on March 20, 1945. He is the middle son of Cecil and Marie Hafley. His brothers are Larry and Douglas. At age five his family moved to Peoria, Illinois. He met his future wife, Judy Warman, at Florida College in 1963. Morris and Judy have three children (Tina, Joe and Michael) and nine grandchildren. Morris began preaching in Danville, Indiana in 1972. He moved to Salem, Ohio in 1975, then to Greencastle, Indiana in 1982. They moved to the Lafayette Heights congregation in Indianapolis in 1988, then to the West Ave. congregation in San Antonio, Texas in 1994. In 1995 they moved to Paden City, West Virginia where they presently live. Morris serves also serves as an elder. He conducts a 30-minute radio program.

Whether it is in the church, the business world, or the home, any relationship that begins on the wrong foundation is in deep trouble (Matt.7:24ff). With television movies and sitcoms and their immoral, ungodly themes of the day, and the Soap's (what a misnomer) daily immorality, being the teacher and babysitter of many of our youth is it any wonder that marriage is in trouble? Many young people don't know how to treat one another while dating because sex is their reason for dating. Therefore, the marriage gets off on the wrong foot. The main reason is that parents and preachers are not doing their job as teachers. God's word not only helps us get to heaven but also shows us how to live with all the blessings and happiness possible on earth. Jesus said, "Blessed are the meek, for they shall inherit the earth" (Matt. 5:5). When our goal on earth is not to attain earthly wealth, but to reach heaven, then we truly "shall inherit the earth." Because the material things in life won't own us, we will own them (Matt. 6:19-21). Israel failed to follow God's instructions in the Old Testament and they paid dearly. Does God know this about you and your children/grandchildren? Yes he does. Listen to these passages: "Neither is there any creature that is not manifest in his sight: but all things are naked and opened unto the eyes of him with whom we have to do" (Heb. 4:13). "The eyes of the Lord *are* in every place, beholding the evil and the good" (Prov. 15:3).

One mother told me, and the father was just as guilty, that she just couldn't talk to her children about dating and sex. So it was no wonder that four of their six children's marriages were failures. Her boys had no clue about what makes a woman happy. Obviously their wives knew as little as their husbands about dating and marriage or they would never have married them. You talk about a pooling of ignorance. When we build our marriage on the sand don't be surprised when the winds and rains come that the house will collapse (Matt. 7:26-27). Whatever happened to, "Train up a child in the way he should go: and when he is old, he will not depart from it" (Prov. 22:6)? Whatever happened to "children, obey your parents in the Lord: for this is right" (Eph. 6:1), and whatever happened to, ". . . bring them up in the nurture and admonition of the Lord" (Eph. 6:4)?

"The Runaway Bride"
A few years ago a movie was made called "The Runaway Bride." It is better to runaway, yes, even on the wedding day, than to wish you had the day after the wedding. Marriage is serious and not too many parents let their children know just how serious. More time is spent on getting a place for the wedding, who's going to preach the ceremony, the bride's dress, the

groom's tux, who's going to stand up with them, who's going to be invited, and on and on it goes. How much time is spent warning the bride and groom of the pitfalls of a marriage when the two are not compatible, when they have nothing in common, and when they fight like tigers while dating?

Why do we spend so much time when we buy a car or a house or a new suit? When buying a car we give it a test drive, we check the engine, the tires, the mileage, the paint job, the interior etc. When buying a house we check the location, we go through every room, we have it inspected by an electrician and for termites, we talk to neighbors, and we ask a myriad of questions to educate ourselves about this material object. However, when it comes to getting married, we are not too concerned about the important aspects of this lifelong commitment.

One lady described her marriage when she said, "Wedlock is a padlock that leads to a deadlock." This is a description of a marriage where somebody quit doing the right things, if they ever did them. One must know that dating is not marriage. When you are angry with each other after marriage, you don't just take her home, you are home. If you can't work out problems before marriage, please don't think it will get better after you slip rings on fingers and say, "I do."

Where the Blame Belongs

God will not only blame the parents but also the elders for not feeding the flock and preachers today for not doing more preaching on this subject. God blamed the priests and prophets in the Old Testament for not doing their job.

> Again the word of the Lord came unto me, saying, Son of man, speak to the children of thy people, and say unto them, When I bring the sword upon a land, if the people of the land take a man of their coasts, and set him for their watchman: If when he seeth the sword come upon the land, he blow the trumpet, and warn the people; Then whosoever heareth the sound of the trumpet, and taketh not warning; if the sword come, and take him away, his blood shall be upon his own head. He heard the sound of the trumpet, and took not warning; his blood shall be upon him. But he that taketh warning shall deliver his soul. But if the watchman see the sword come, and blow not the trumpet, and the people be not warned; if the sword come, and take any person from among them, he is taken away in his iniquity; but his blood will I require at the watchman's hand. So thou, O son of man, I have set thee a watchman unto the house of Israel;

therefore thou shalt hear the word at my mouth, and warn them from me. When I say unto the wicked, O wicked *man*, thou shalt surely die; if thou dost not speak to warn the wicked from his way, that wicked *man* shall die in his iniquity; but his blood will I require at thine hand (Ezek. 33:1-8).

Isaiah warns, "His watchmen are blind: they are all ignorant, they are all dumb dogs, they cannot bark; sleeping, lying down, loving to slumber. Yea, they are greedy dogs which can never have enough, and they are shepherds that cannot understand: they all look to their own way, every one for his gain, from his quarter. Come ye, say they, I will fetch wine, and we will fill ourselves with strong drink; and to morrow shall be as this day, and much more abundant" (56:10-12). As the home continues to be destroyed by works of the flesh in our generation, are we blind, ignorant, dumb, sleeping dogs too? We will be held accountable.

Teach your children that, just because he's handsome or she's beautiful, it doesn't mean the "hidden man of the heart" is (1 Pet. 3:1-7; 1 Sam. 16:7). Teach them that "living together" comes after the marriage. Teach them what love is and what it isn't (1 Cor. 13:1-8).

The failure in marriage today is not God's fault. When God finished his creation in six days he said it was "very good" (Gen. 1:31). He doesn't make mistakes, so we need to step up and admit where the failure lies and the blame belongs.

Some Things to "Put Off"
The Bible tells us there are many things we need to "put off" or to put away from our lives. It means to lock them up and throw away the key. For example,

That ye put off concerning the former conversation the old man, which is corrupt according to the deceitful lusts; And be renewed in the spirit of your mind; And that ye put on the new man, which after God is created in righteousness and true holiness. Wherefore putting away lying, speak every man truth with his neighbour: for we are members one of another. Be ye angry, and sin not: let not the sun go down upon your wrath: Neither give place to the devil. Let him that stole steal no more: but rather let him labour, working with his hands the thing which is good, that he may have to give to him that needeth. Let no corrupt communication proceed out of your mouth, but that which is good to the use of edifying, that it may minister grace unto the hearers. And grieve not the holy Spirit of God, whereby ye are sealed unto the day of redemption. Let all bitterness, and wrath, and anger, and clamour, and evil speaking, be put away from you, with all malice: And be ye kind one to another, tenderhearted, forgiving one another, even as God for Christ's sake hath forgiven you" (Eph. 4:22-32).

Do we wait to put these things off until we become a Christian? Shouldn't we be taught such from our youth? Would not a young person with this kind of knowledge have a head start on the world? Wouldn't his character already be developing into what he ought to be? See also Colossians 3:5-4:6 in this connection.

If we put these things on again we are like the dog returning to his own vomit again, and the sow that was washed to her wallowing in the mire (2 Pet. 2:22).

Now we have to be aware of teenage violence on dates because we are living in "The Me Generation" of self-gratification. Many young people today have no restrictions. Parents have become their children's "buddies" and are not an authority figure to guide and direct them in helping them to make their daily decisions. Why do you think the phrase "What part of NO don't you understand?" came about? We learn in Genesis 19 that restraint from sexual immorality can cause a more severe sin. When Lot said "No" to the homosexuals of Sodom, listen to what they said, "Get out of our way," they replied. And they said, "This fellow came here an alien, and now he wants to play the judge! We will treat you worse than them!" (Gen. 19:4, NIV). We must put our children "on the alert" to any hint or sign of abuse. The physical abuse amounts to shoving, hitting, pushing, and the emotional abuse are lies, spreading rumors and such like. Then there is the sexual abuse of unwanted touching. These are only a few items of what could be listed as abuse. No kind of abuse should ever be tolerated or acceptable during dating. The teenager should be aware before dating, because many end up married to an abuser. To be forewarned is to be forearmed. Warning our children of such abuse will prevent them from continuing to date an abuser let alone marrying the creep. He/she, the abuser, will only "wax worse and worse." Many abusers, and don't forget the drinker who promises to quit "going out with the boys when we get hitched," won't quit. Then the blame will be placed on the innocent party for "driving him to drink" or whatever his choice of abuse is. Believe me, it isn't pretty.

It would be well if each couple would hear, know, and understand their wedding vows long before the wedding rather than when it is about over. Also be reminded they are making these vows to Almighty God and that he doesn't take lightly those who break their vows to him. "When you make a vow to God, do not delay in fulfilling it. He has no pleasure in fools; fulfill your vow. It is better not to vow than to make a vow and not fulfill it. Do not let your mouth lead you into sin. And do not protest to the temple messenger, 'My vow was a mistake.' Why should God be angry at what you say and destroy the work of your hands? Much dreaming and many words are meaningless. Therefore stand in awe of God" (Eccl. 5:4-6). "When thou shalt vow a vow unto the Lord thy God, thou shalt not slack to pay it: for the Lord thy God will surely require it of thee; and it would be sin in thee" (Deut. 23:21, NIV). "If a man vow a vow unto the Lord, or swear an oath to bind his soul with a bond; he shall not break his word, he shall do according to all that proceedeth out of his mouth" (Num. 30:2). While talking with a young couple before their wedding, we went over the vows and the young lady said, "Do you have to say that I will be in subjection?" I asked her why she would ask such a question. She replied, "My friends will laugh at me." This happened over thirty years ago.

Also, about thirty years ago, Dr. Joyce Brothers said that out of twelve marriages six end in divorce, four are endurance contests and two are what she calls happily married. Not a good ratio for the happily married. Thus the need for such a study as this. Many are buying books written by men to help their marriages. Seems like you and I are the only ones who haven't written a book on the subject. However, God has written much on the subject in his book, the Bible.

Many dating couples don't know each other. They spend an evening together but don't talk to each other. They don't ask questions or even know what questions to ask. This is one thing that should never stop after marriage. We must keep learning about each other, but it is best if we know many things before the wedding. Obviously if we talked to each other and asked questions many would never marry the person they wed. A few years ago a question was asked of several women. The question was, "If you had it to do all over again would you marry the same man?" Eight of ten said they would not. I'm guessing they didn't know each other when they said "I do" because a short time later they wished they had said "I don't." As a matter of fact, six months after I performed a wedding ceremony the bride came to me, and these are her words when she said, "Mo, do you remember when you talked with us, you said, 'I'm going to try to talk you out of this'?" I said, "Yes, I sure do remember." She then said tearfully, "I wish you had talked us out of it." Her husband was drinking, taking drugs, and what naturally follows that behavior is that he was abusive. Yes, he beat his new bride. Any wonder she wanted out of the mess she was in? Another young lady married a college "hunk," an athlete. He not only could hit a baseball, but he also hit his wife, he blackened her eye, and broke her arm. Do you wish that for your daughter/granddaughter? So what's holding you back from teaching her?

We had a coach who told us, "What you do in practice is what you will do in a game." The same is true in dating and marriage. As a matter of fact the bad habits will "wax worse and worse." If you think his bad habits irritate you while you are dating, they will drive you up a wall after marriage. You won't be able to tell him to, "Go home!" because he is already there and you made the vow until death do us part. If you think you will just overlook them you need to wake up to reality.

Today we hear people talking about "finding the right one." I think the answer is you "being" the right one. Remember the one you are dating is or ought to be taking a close look at you too. This is a two-way street.

We've all heard of the man who married Miss Right, but, he said, after he married her, that he didn't know her first name was "Always." It's too late after the ceremony to find out that "Houston, we have a problem!" You'd better be smart enough to be finding out the points you don't like about a person before the engagement and especially before the wedding.

Things That Should Continue After Marriage
To say that these must continue after marriage implies they were under-way before marriage. This is only a partial list, but these are things that will make for a good relationship before and after marriage. I don't know about you, but I like being happy. Solomon said, "A merry heart doeth good like a medicine, but a broken spirit drieth the bones" (Prov. 17:22).

Pray Together. "For he that will love life, and see good days, let him refrain his tongue from evil, and his lips that they speak no guile: Let him eschew evil, and do good; let him seek peace, and ensue it. For the eyes of the Lord are over the righteous, and his ears are open unto their prayers: but the face of the Lord is against them that do evil" (1 Pet. 3:10-12). Again, I like being happy and the Lord has given us a recipe that always works for our happiness. The condition given for prayer to be answered is for us to obey God's commands.

"The family that prays together stays together" is an old saying, and it is still true. Why not start praying together before marriage? If someone doesn't want to pray with you, why would you even consider marrying such a one? Pray with and for one another. By the time you are married it is a habit already in progress. Good habits, like the bad, are just as hard to break. Take the word "habit" for example. Remove the H and you still have ABIT, remove the A and you have the BIT, remove the B and you still have "IT." The old gospel song says, "Take time to be holy speak oft with thy Lord." Praying together will help keep you pure before marriage and it will keep the devil away after your marriage. Sometimes, before services, I will ask a brother to lead an opening prayer and he will say, "I'd rather not." Now, if he's sick I understand, but to say, "I'd rather not talk with God" something is wrong. Ladies, if a boy won't pray with you while dating, that habit will more than likely continue after your marriage. Do you want to marry one who doesn't like to pray to God?

Read God's Word Together.

> How shall the young secure their hearts?
> And guard their lives from sin?
> Thy word the choicest rules imparts
> To keep the conscience clean.
>
> Thy word is everlasting truth;
> How pure is every page!
> That holy book shall guide our youth,
> And well support our age.

While dating it may be a Bible class lesson that you work together to complete. One of you may be a class teacher. How awesome to have help from someone who knows and cares about spiritual matters. If your companion refuses or doesn't want to study with you, let that be a warning sign. That individual doesn't feel about God's word as David did. Listen to few quotes from Psalm 119.

Wherewithal shall a young man cleanse his way? by taking heed thereto according to thy word (v. 9).

Thy word have I hid in mine heart, that I might not sin against thee (v. 11).

O how love I thy law! it is my meditation all the day (v. 97).

Thy word is a lamp unto my feet, and a light unto my path. The entrance of thy words giveth light; it giveth understanding unto the simple (v. 105).

Why would one not want to study God's word with his date? Reading God's word together will be one of those "precious memories" as we grow older and recall that we had remembered our Creator in the days of our youth (Eccl. 12:1). Reading God's word together will help keep our hearts pure (1 Tim. 5:22; 1 Pet. 1:22; John 15:3).

Worship Together. Distance may slow this while dating, but nothing should hinder it after marriage. If he or she has a tendency to miss worship for frivolous excuses, it will not get better after marriage. You will hear, "I'm too tired," "I have to work tomorrow," "Today is my only day off," "Stay home with me, it won't matter if we miss just this once." Before a car quits, it starts missing. A young man told me that he wanted to marry a girl who was a good Bible student, one who would help him to be faithful in the church and to help him go to heaven. I told him that, if he found such a girl, she wouldn't want him because he missed so many services. I said she is not going to want to have to drag you out of bed every Sunday morning and beg you to go to Sunday and Wednesday night services. You may find her but when she sees you for what you are, if she is smart, she will kiss you goodbye because the church means nothing to you. She won't want to be saddled with the ball and chain you are bringing into that relationship.

Trust One Another. Don't learn this lesson the hard way. If you see the evil monster of jealousy roaming during your dating period, run as fast as you can to get away. If you are questioned whenever you talk to someone of the opposite sex or wave hello mark it down as a sign to "beware." After the wedding the suspicions will grow and fester and fill your marriage with heartache and corruption. If he comes home a minute or two late, don't automatically think he's being unfaithful or if she's gone a little longer to Wal-Mart don't give her the third degree, just take her Discover Card. Love won't allow jealousy to run rampant in your marriage (1 Cor. 13:5). Look what jealousy did to Joseph's brothers. "And when his brethren saw that their father loved him more than all his brethren, they hated him, and could not speak peaceably unto him" (Gen. 37:4). They would have killed him had it not been for Reuben (vv. 20-22).

David was Saul's best friend, but Saul couldn't see it for the jealousy that was eating him alive. Just look what it did to that relationship and to Saul's life and kingdom.

However, it is also a two-way street. Be considerate, when possible, because our communication system is too good not to let each other know, "I'll be later than I thought."

Be Faithful. While dating or while engaged some think it exciting to go out with another girl. After all, who's going to know? So what if she finds out what I did. If she does find out she'd better drop you like hot horseshoe. In marriage variety isn't the spice of life (Matt. 19:5-6). You don't want the consequences of infidelity. Here's what God says will happen to the "Playboy." "Can a man take fire in his bosom, and his clothes not be burned? Can one go upon hot coals, and his feet not be burned? So he that goeth in to his neighbour's wife; whosoever toucheth her shall not be innocent. Men do not despise a thief, if he steal to satisfy his soul when he is hungry; But if he be found, he shall restore sevenfold; he shall give all the substance of his house. But whoso committeth adultery with a woman lacketh understanding: he that doeth it destroyeth his own soul. A wound and dishonour shall he get; and his reproach shall not be wiped away. For jealousy is the rage of a man: therefore he will not spare in the day of vengeance. He will not regard any ransom; neither will he rest content, though thou givest many gifts" (Prov. 6:27-35).

Be Sensitive With the Feelings of Your Spouse. Don't exploit the faults of your spouse in front of friends. One man, while at party, was talking about his wife and said, right in front of her, that "She is so bucktoothed that she could eat corn off a cob through a picket fence." He was the only one that thought it was funny. How humiliating for his poor wife. She left the party in tears. He had obviously forgotten Matthew 7:12. "Therefore all things whatsoever ye would that men should do to you, do ye even so to them: for this is the law and the prophets." He certainly had forgotten Paul's statement in Ephesians 4:32; "And be ye kind one to another. . ." or was that only written to two Christians who are not related? Paul says, in 1 Corinthians 13:4-5 that "love is kind" and that "it is not rude." This man was certainly not "giving honor" unto his wife as the Lord commands in 1 Peter 3:7. Pride will cause a man to act like this. While trying to make himself "look big" he is heading for destruction and a fall (Prov. 16:18).

Do Things for Each Other. When you see she needs something at home get it for her or if something needs fixed, the garbage disposal, a burner on the stove, or if her car isn't running right, don't let centuries go by and have her "get by" without it. When one is taking care of the hands that take care of him, he is doing himself a favor. Didn't God say for husbands to love their wives as Christ loved the church and as we love our own bodies (Eph. 5:25, 28)? I do things for myself that make it easier for me and since she is part of me, the two become one (Matt. 19:6), then why wouldn't I want to do any and everything to help her? When I do that, I am not only taking care of her but part of myself as well. I know I love myself because I am careful with sharp instruments, I don't slam my fingers in doors, and when carrying heavy objects I am careful not to drop them on my toes. Likewise, it is hard for your spouse to hate the one who is constantly thinking of her. The love will be reciprocated and like Jesus said, "It is more blessed to give than receive" (Acts 20:35). Be selfless not selfish.

Do Things the Other One Likes. Does she have to go where he always wants to go? Give in, young man, be considerate and do the things she likes. Does he have to do whatever she wants to do? Give in, young lady, do things he likes. Love will do that. You may find out why he likes what he does when you do it with him. I'm not talking about "changing an engine" or "going skydiving." You will find out many things that you either do or don't have in common. It is not true that "opposites attract." That may be true with magnets, but it is not true with love. If you find that you are not alike at all then find someone else.

Spend Time Together. No, not in front of the television or at a movie! We don't talk to each other when the television is on or when we're at a movie. Take a walk, play games with just the two of you: Checkers, Dominoes, Scrabble, Uno, and Aggravation. You can learn much about an individual. You may learn that he/she is not for you because of their attitude, temper etc. You may learn that he is a poor loser or that he cheats. Better to get the divorce *before* the marriage. You may also learn that she is so kind, so sweet, so thoughtful, so patient, so understanding. You may learn that he is so kind, so sweet, so thoughtful, so patient, so understanding. You don't want that kind to get away. Spending time together will help you see these things.

Appearance. Did you try to look sloppy while dating? Need I say more? Did you begin to see the need for personal hygiene? Ladies, didn't you use some of your mom's best perfume, or guys, your dad's best cologne? Guys, didn't you shave, if you needed to, and bathe more than once a week? Why go around looking like an unmade bed after marriage or smelling like a garbage can? Do you think that is attractive? Do you say, "Well, I'm married now I don't have to be so careful with my appearance"? Some never outgrew the "Hippies" of the 1970s or the "Grunge" look of the 1990s. Some today look like Emmet Kelly the circus clown. All they would need is a big red rubber nose to finish their outfit. What's worse they come to worship God in the same attire. When you dress like that you are a reflection on your entire family. You bring shame and embarrassment upon them. We usually "put our best foot forward" while dating. Why should that stop when we marry?

Surprise Each Other with Little Things. "It's The Little Things That Make Me Love You So." It's not just a song title, it's the truth. You don't have to buy a mansion or a Lamborghini. If you are dating someone who expects only the most expensive items, kiss them goodbye. Any man or woman, who is worth his/her salt, will love the little things you do. If they don't appreciate the "little things" while dating, drop them like a hot horseshoe. Do you know what her favorite candy bar is? Do you know what his favorite meal is? Guys, you may not know what good a bouquet of flowers will do, and you may even think it "a waste," but get over it and see what good that little deed can do or even a card for no special occasion. Red Skelton left little notes all around the house for his wife. Those little notes made her day. She would find them under her pillow or breakfast plate, in the refrigerator and they would light up her life. When constantly giving to others, you will find part of the meaning to Paul's quote of Jesus' statement, "It is more blessed to give than receive" (Acts 20:35). My wife's dad got into the habit of bringing her mother flowers every week. After a few weeks the florist said, "OK, what have you done?" Why did it have to be a negative thought instead of a happy marriage? It is the exception and not the rule when we do those "little things."

Compliment Each Other. "Pleasant words are as an honeycomb, sweet to the soul, and health to the bones" (Prov. 16:24). You may have to search to find something, but do it. It will bring many happy returns. "Wow, you look beautiful!" "Thank you Sweetheart for fixing my favorite meal." "Thank you for taking me to Outback." "Thank you, Sweetheart, for keeping the house looking so good, for washing and ironing, for folding and putting away all those clothes and doing such a great job rearing our children."

"Thank you, Honey, for working so hard and giving us the necessary things of life, for caring about our souls, and loving us so much." Have you seen the bumper sticker that reads "Have you hugged your kids today?" We all need hugs and kind words of encouragement from time to time. Today they are too few and too far between.

As you begin to compliment your spouse, the list will grow and you will find it easier and you will see the result very quickly.

Teach Your Children the Truth
Hopefully you were taught in your youth, and you should continue that type training for your own children after you are married. We are to instruct and discipline our children in the way of the Lord so that when they are old they can say that they "Remembered their Creator in the days of their youth (Prov. 22:6; Eph. 6:4; Eccl. 12:1). Please don't say, "I don't have time with all that's going on in my life." NO! you are just not taking the time to teach them. I remember hearing sister Irven Lee say that her father had died when she was young and that she had several sisters and that her mother taught them all the word of God. Her mother did it during the Great Depression while taking in washing and ironing to survive. Someone asked, "When did she have the time to do all she had to do and on top of that teach her daughters the truth? Sister Lee said her mother taught them all while they sat on the floor as she was ironing or doing dishes. She said she couldn't remember a day that she didn't know about Saul, David, Solomon, Abraham and Sarah, Ruth and Boaz, Jacob and Joseph.

Loving your children is teaching them the "unfeigned faith that is in thee, which dwelt first in your" parents (2 Tim. 1:5). You must teach your children "the holy scriptures which are able to make them wise unto salvation though faith which is in Christ Jesus" (2 Tim. 3:15). By so doing you will make theirs and your lives, as in-laws, much happier. They will be happier because it is God's way they have chosen and not man's. They will be happier because they will have knowledge to choose the right person to be their lifetime companion. You will be happy because you won't be having to try to fix a marriage whose doors have already been blown off because you had no clue what was going on behind closed doors or step in the middle of a heated argument or listen to the pain your son or daughter has gotten themselves into. When they repeat their vows, "for better, for worse, for richer, for poorer; in sickness and in health; till death do us part" they will mean it and keep their vows to the Almighty. They will keep those vows

144

they made to each other and to God because someone took the time to teach them. Remember, you don't get "Do-overs" in rearing your children.

Finally brethren, these few remarks will not only help a young dating couple but will also help any marriage no matter how long you've been married. For the plan to work, you must work the plan.

Dealing With Delinquent Children

Wayne Thurman

For years I have taught or worked in other ways with children of all ages. I have worked as a teacher in public schools, a teacher of juveniles in a day treatment program, an elementary principal, and as the administrator for after school programs for children preschool through teens. I am currently helping migrant families who in most instances have children who are at very high risk of becoming delinquent. Hispanic families are becoming a large part of our minority population in Kentucky. Many of these children are at risk of becoming delinquent, even those who seem well adjusted and do well in school. One reason that many older immigrant children give up and become more delinquent as they get older is that they see their future as bleak. They cannot get scholarships, being non-citizens, so they often do not have the means to continue their education, etc.

During thirty-five plus years of working with children, I have encountered many children showing delinquent tendencies. Early intervention can help bring about changes in their behavior, but changing their attitudes and behavior patterns becomes more difficult as the child ages. Children

---

Wayne Thurman lives in Danville, Kentucky. He graduated from Morehead State University in 1968 and majored in math and Spanish. He trained teachers in the Dominican Republic in the Peace Corps. He has been teaching or in school administration for 36 years and although retired, continues to work three days a week with the Lincoln County Board of Education. He and his wife Kaye are members of the Danville Church of Christ. They are the parents of Mrs. Michael (Pippa) Hunt and Mrs. David (Polly) Hosay. They have three grandsons, Gabriel and Titus Hunt and Isaac Hosay.

form habits, attitudes, and perceptions early and these are reinforced by the community surrounding the child. The community includes all immediate family members, the extended family, the entire school population, the town, city, or rural area in which the child lives, the church he may or may not attend, the media the child accesses, and any other people with whom he has even the slightest contact. A child is molded early. We only have to watch a show like "The Nanny" to see that some children are taught or learn at a very early age to be abusive, cheats, thieves, chronic liars, disrespectful, aggressive, and many other delinquent behaviors. Some children are or become problematic due to chemical reasons or to a variety of syndromes. These children are not the ones being addressed today, although they are very much at risk of becoming delinquent in their behavior. They require medical intervention. Today our discussion will center on children who begin demonstrating delinquent behavior, usually at a fairly early age, but for whom there is hope that with intervention this behavior will at least be modified so they can be responsible, contributing adults.

When I worked with a Day Treatment Program for juveniles, a place where the students have treatment and educational programs during the day, but return home at night, I found that when children were initially brought into the program, they did not all react the same way. Some of them conformed to rules and routines quickly, while others tried to manipulate the staff and their peers to get what they wanted, instead of what they needed. In order for any change to take place with this group who were very intelligent, very capable of placing blame on others, and not quickly caught in a lie, the staff had to be constantly on guard and adept at being consistent and to work as a team. Unfortunately, because our program only worked with the students, but not with the parents and the schools to which they would return, many of these students reverted to their previous behavior shortly after being released from the Day Treatment Program. For years after teaching in that program, I saw the names of former students as they were arrested for offences and some of them were sentenced to prison.

Some students were successful, however, in changing many of their behaviors, or at least enough to make them responsible members of society. One boy, who was in my self-contained classroom, completed the Day Treatment Program and attended a local high school, played football, was popular among the teachers and peers. My wife Kaye and I ended up teaching at that high school while he was there. Recently he was featured in our local paper as an outstanding coach for Little League. His brother, on the other hand, had more and more problems after completing the program. Although they had the same family, other circumstances helped determine the outcome.

Definition

A delinquent child is not the child who, although he/she loves family, feels the need to rebel from time to time. That child might get a body part pierced and probably be sorry later, tell a fib and feel guilty, question authority to a degree, hide a tattoo, be argumentative and perhaps make more than a few bad decisions. Some rebellious behavior is natural for a child as he grows older and wants to be seen more as an adult than a child. But he still holds family in his heart and knows where home and help are.

A child who likes to blame parents, school, and society for his problems, who says he is not accountable or responsible for his actions, who surrounds himself with friends who are similar or friends that he can manipulate to get what he wants, is a delinquent. He may steal, cheat, and reject authority figures. He may become addicted to drugs, sex, and alcohol. At school, he may be considered "just plain mean." He is seeking thrills beyond what would be considered normal behavior for most children. He will drop out of activities he doesn't want to do. And if things at home don't go his way, he may run away from home or from the dilemma.

Juvenile delinquency is the legal term for any child whose behavior is such that, if he were an adult, the behavior would be judged criminal. One offence often displayed by juvenile delinquents, however, would not be considered criminal among adults, namely running away. Arriving at adulthood varies from state to state, but generally once a child is eighteen he is considered an adult by most states. The causes of the behavior juvenile delinquents display are complex involving psychological, social, and economic factors. No one can give a definitive reason because some children being raised under similar conditions grow to be responsible adults, while others show antisocial behavior. Clinical studies show persistent patterns of disorganized family units among many delinquents.[1] It is difficult to ascertain, however, whether these patterns came first and led to the behavior of the child, or if the antisocial antics of the child may have so stressed the family unit to the point that the structure falls apart.

In 1991 the following described the delinquent youths who were found in jail:

- The average age was 16.
- 93% were boys.
- 54% were white, 40% black.
- More than 70% came from homes with only one parent.
- Half had family members who had been locked up; 20% have two or more close relatives who have served time; almost 25% had fathers in jail or prison in the past year.
- Only 42% completed eighth grade, compared with 76% of other youth.
- Almost half had been taking drugs or drinking when they committed the crime for which they were arrested; almost 20% admitted taking drugs for the first time before age ten; two out of five used drugs regularly.
- About 40% were locked up for violent crimes such as murder and rape; 40% of this group had used a deadly weapon.[2]

These children may not sound like children who could possibly come from homes where the Bible is used and people go to church. But delinquency knows no boundaries. It occurs in homes that are totally dysfunctional, in ghettos, in middle class homes, and among the wealthiest. It occurs among the children of atheists as well as among children of Christians. It can be found in families that are permissive, extremely strict, or somewhere in between.

These statistics make it sound as if delinquency only occurs during the teens. That is not the case. Everyone who has had more than one child knows that every child seems to have his/her own personality at birth. Some babies are fussier than other babies; some seem to be always content, etc. Children often begin to show many of the same behaviors as a delinquent to a lesser degree at a much earlier age. Parents need to be aware of what is going on with their child. At the age of three and four or earlier, some children have learned to control their parents, and the parents are at a loss about what to do. A mother once told me that she had to let her six-year old son play with a gun and smoke cigarettes, because that's what he wanted to do and he would just keep fussing at her until he got his way. Another child at six and seven years of age would take her clothes off when the bus arrived at the house, so her mother couldn't take her out and physically put her on the bus. The mother did not know what she could do about this. These children ruled the roost. The boy is now in prison but not before fathering several children to be raised by his mother. The girl luckily had two interventions but not until middle school because that is when the mother finally agreed that there was a problem. The court system became involved with the mom and the school provided the mother with help in learning to parent and the child with a mentor/counselor. The child was made to come to an after school program by the courts. She became very involved with the role models she found there. Her grades and attendance improved immensely. The point is that delinquency doesn't wait to start until a child hits the teens. It usually is becoming full blown by that time.

Children's Needs

Every child has needs that if met hopefully will lead him to become a responsible member of society instead of delinquent.

- Attachment to parents on an ongoing basis. (If not parents, attachment to some individual who will be there for the child.)
- He needs to develop a sense of trust.
- He needs to be able to empathize with others.
- He needs to be able to share.
- He has to accept responsibilities.
- He needs his self-esteem validated.

Every child needs to be free of as many disruptions that raise his risks of becoming delinquent.

- Disruptions in attachments: divorce, separation, desertion, nonsupport, single parenting, foster care.
- Disruptions by adults such as physical or sexual abuse, severe verbal abuse, substance abuse, gambling, severe financial debt, unemployment (prolonged), social isolation of family.
- Disruptions outside the home with peers, school, teachers, classmates, etc.[3]

How Did He/She Become Delinquent?

Of course family is always the first to be blamed for a child's behavior. In the Old Testament, children were delinquent when they would not honor their mother and father. Provisions were made for these children to be eliminated from society by stoning. Stoning to death did not stop this type of behavior because we read about delinquent behavior with the children of David. We also have the example of the prodigal son, who squandered his inheritance doing many of the things that delinquent children do today.

Lack of a cohesive family unit seems to play a role in many a delinquent's decisions, especially those in which there is no father figure. The proportion of children living in single-parent homes more than doubled between 1970 and 2003. Over 32% of children live in single parent or nontraditional marriage homes. That is about three out of ten children. Most of the single parents are women, although the number of single men parents has increased from 9% to 17%. Many of these parents, 41%, have never married. Children living with both parents are less likely to live below the poverty level. Children living with only their mothers in 2003 lived in poverty more often than children living only with a father.[4]

Is it society's responsibility to do something to keep children from becoming delinquent? There are good programs that keep children busy. The Office of Juvenile Justice has offered grants to sponsor after school programs to keep children off the streets between the times they get out of school until six o'clock because statistics show that is when youth commit crimes. These programs offer role models and caring adults for those children.

Often the church is named as part of the reason for a child's rebellion. A child resents being forced to go to church and do something that he considers a waste of time. That is especially true if the child sees that the parent feels the same way but goes to church services because he/she feels it necessary to move up the ladder economically or socially, or for some other reason. Children catch on quickly and usually understand the intentions of the parents.

Our children are bombarded daily with messages that say, to be accepted, you need to be part of a crowd. This crowd is usually not very intelligent acting, drinks alcohol, and has little or no respect for authority.

To Be or Not to Be a Delinquent: What Are Parents to Do?

Wouldn't it be great if there really were an "Easy Button" for raising children? We could just push it every time a problem arose and the answer would be there. Unfortunately children do not come into this world with a manual on how to rear them successfully. I get manuals with my TV, lawnmower, refrigerator, and many other appliances, but sometimes I ignore those instructions and end up with a delinquent mower that won't start because the oil hasn't been changed, or some other maintenance has been ignored. No matter how I talk to it, encourage it, or kick it, it still won't start. Even with a manual, my TV and VCR remain mysterious and foreboding when I have to try to adjust something on them.

There is no easy button, so forget about looking for a quick fix. Parents must start before birth and work continually every day, being vigilant, consistent, and proactive to make sure they know their child, they know where their child is, and what he might be doing.

According to Kimberly A. Gordon Rouse, Ph. D., some rare children overcome even the most difficult circumstances and grow up to lead well adjusted competent lives, while others become delinquent living under similar circumstances. She feels that the key to this successful growth on the part of the former is a characteristic of the child called "resilience."

> Resilience is the ability to thrive, mature, and increase competence in the face of adverse circumstances. These circumstances may include biological abnormalities or environmental obstacles. Further, the adverse circumstances may be chronic and consistent or severe and infrequent. To thrive, mature, and increase competence a person must draw upon all of his or her resources: biological; psychological, and environmental.[5]

In a God-fearing "Christian" home, children should have all the opportunities they need to become resilient, to be able to master their world, to feel secure and safe, and to not worry about many of the disruptions that were mentioned earlier, such as divorce, desertion, or abuse. But "Christian" homes are at times dysfunctional and when that happens our children are put at risk.

What Does God Expect?

As Christ teaches in Matthew 19 that from the beginning God expected the family to consist of one man and one woman who were to take marriage seriously and not divorce for any reason other than adultery on the part of one or the other. In 1 Corinthians 7:11, we read, "That the wife should not separate from her husband (but if she does, let her remain single or else be reconciled to her husband) and that the husband should not divorce his wife."

God wants the family unit to be one, to be cohesive. An omniscient God understands what is needed in the way of family for the best conditions for rearing children. In the Bible, when a man took more than one wife, we find that the children and family had problems. Abraham was a fine man chosen by God to bring forth a mighty nation of people, but when Sara decided to help out by giving him Hagar, thus breaking God's rule, there were problems with the children and these problems continue today with nations descended from those children. Jacob worked hard to obtain two wives and two concubines who gave him twelve sons. We see delinquent behavior on the part of at least ten of these sons. Solomon and David took many wives and suffered for it. We see delinquent behavior such as not listening to good advice, following peers, raping, killing, stealing, etc., especially by the children of David. However, some children, such as Joseph, chose a totally different path. I am not saying that children have to become delinquent when a parent disobeys God in breaking the marriage bond, but it does raise the risk for the children involved. God expects there to be one man and one woman in a marriage.

One of the characteristics of many delinquent children is that they come from a home where there is a single parent, usually a mother, often deserted by the father. Look to Ephesians 5:21-6:4 for instruction on how God expects the marriage relationship to be and for some clue about why.

> Be subject to one another out of reverence for Christ. Wives, be subject to your husbands, as to the Lord. For the husband is the head of the wife as Christ is the head of the church, his body, and is himself its Savior. As the church is subject to Christ, so let wives also be subject in everything to their husbands. Husbands, love your wives, as Christ loved the church and gave himself up for her, that he might sanctify her, having cleansed her by the washing of water with the word, that he might present the church to himself in splendor, without spot or wrinkle or any such thing, that she might be holy and without blemish. Even so husbands should love their wives as their own bodies. He who loves his wife loves himself. For no man ever hates his own flesh, but nourishes and cherishes it, as Christ does the church, because we are members of his body. For this reason a man shall leave his father and mother and be joined to his wife, and the two shall become one flesh. This mystery is a profound one and I am saying that it refers to Christ and the church; however, let each one of you love his wife as himself, and let the wife see that she respects her husband. Children, obey your parents in the Lord, for this is right. Honor your father and mother (this is the first commandment with a promise), that it may be well with you and that you may live long on the earth. Fathers, do not provoke your children to anger, but bring them up in the discipline and instruction of the Lord.

No, we do not get a manual with the new child, and granted every child is special, different, and unique, but we do have a manual for marriage and if we follow that manual and stay together, work out problems, show love and respect for each other, and think of our partner as a part of us that we do not want to cause pain and anguish, our children will benefit and may choose to pattern their lives after two adults with whom they have a strong attachment, two adults they are able to love, trust, and respect.

The single parent has a more difficult road in rearing children, especially if he/she has a child who is willing to take advantage of every opportunity to further his/her own wants and desires, because there is no partner with whom to develop and enforce a plan of action. A single parent has less time, less energy, and often fewer resources to tackle the problems that such a child brings into the family. More than likely, that parent will have to work longer hours and the child may have more unsupervised time on hand than would be available in a two parent family. A child on the way to becoming delinquent, even while very young, will watch for weakness in the defenses of a single parent and strike when defenses are down. This child will know how to lay the blame squarely on the single parent for the child's behavior, laying a guilt trip on the parent which he/she does not deserve, but may accept, thereby allowing the delinquent child to win over and over again. This child will also play two parents who have divorced against each other. If there is divorce, both parents should still work together for the good of the children involved.

If we have children, or are going to have children and do not meet the criteria listed in Ephesians 5, we better make it right and reduce those disruptive risk factors from our child's life.

How Does God Expect Us to Deal with Our Children?
God gave us the Old Testament for our example (Rom. 15:4; 1 Cor. 10:6,11). God gave those examples for more than one reason. We have the Song of Songs to tell us how to love. We have the story of creation so that we have an answer to the question most people are still asking, "Where did it all begin?" We have stories of people who did right and people who did wrong so that we can learn from the good and the bad. We have the stories of Esther and of Ruth that let us know that, even without a family, if we have one person who is good to us, one person who is decent and of good moral character who takes an interest in us, one person to whom we are attached and can trust to always be there for us, then we will take the high road. We have the story of Hannah, mother of Samuel, who did not take him to serve God until she had formed a bond for life with him. Eli,

whose own sons were delinquent because he did not discipline them, gave instruction and care to Samuel so that he grew up to be just the opposite of his own children. The stories of Jacob and Esau show that favoritism for one child over the other by either parent caused distrust, dishonesty, and rebellion among the children. David, a man after God's own heart, apparently did not teach his children morals, filial love, and loyalty. The good mother who came to Solomon for judgment was willing to give up her child instead of seeing him cut in half. Moses who chose the beliefs of his parents over riches because of their teaching and ability to influence his life became the leader of Israel. Many Proverbs are addressed to parents as well as to the children with instructions on the rearing and training of children. In Deuteronomy 11:19, the Jews were to teach God's law to their children, talking of the laws when they were sitting in the house, walking by the way, when they laid down, and when they arose. And they were to be written upon the doorposts of their house and gates that their days and the days of their children might be multiplied in the land. In other words, God knew that, if the children were not taught his Law, the children would eventually stray from him and would lose the land.

These principles are many of the same things that research shows helps children to avoid becoming delinquent.

Caring attachments. Children need to develop a strong bond from birth. Babies who do not receive this attention languish, withdraw, and many of them die. Hopefully the child will have the extra benefit of a caring attachment with a loving two parent family, but if not, with a teacher, grandparent, social worker, family friend, someone whom he/she can trust to always be there, the child stands a better chance of being influenced for good and avoiding delinquent behavior. The child needs someone he can trust and confide in about his life. It would be a relationship not unlike the relationship that existed between Esther and her cousin Mordecai. When Esther's parents died, Mordecai took her under his wing. When she was taken into the royal harem and even after she became the most powerful woman in Persia, she continued to confide in and listen to the advice of her cousin. What a good relationship they must have had. Parents need to strive to have this kind of relationship with their children.

Trust. When a child asks his parents for something which he knows is out of reason, or to go somewhere that he shouldn't, or to buy something they cannot afford, he is testing them. If they say no, he may accuse them of not loving him, not trusting him, or berate them until eventually they give in because of guilt, or because his words make them wonder if the child really feels this way about them. By giving in to his demands, they are betraying his need to be able to trust them to do what is best for him. Consider Absalom and David in 2 Samuel 13:20. Although it had been two years since Absalom's sister had been raped by his half-brother Amnon, David should have known that Absalom had something up his sleeve when he asked that his half-brother Amnon be allowed to go up to the sheep sheering with him. David asked why, but the Scripture says that more than once Absalom pressed him on the matter until he gave him permission. Later, he gave in to pressure again and allowed Absalom to come back to Jerusalem after he had killed Amnon. Absalom, like any antisocial person, continued to take advantage of his father because he considered him weak and did not trust him. Children are looking for an authority figure that makes sense, not dictatorial, not mean and spiteful, but concerned for their well being and willing to take the time to explain what rules are, why they exist, and how they relate to the child, and someone who will consistently enforce those rules with love and with the child's best interest in mind.

Empathy. Children need to be able to consider the feelings of others. Even very small children will stop what they are doing if they see someone crying and may try to comfort them. The delinquent child does not feel the need to do that, because he has not learned this skill. If he hurts someone he does not worry about it unless he gets caught. He may say he is sorry, but he is not sorry that he hurt the person, only sorry that he was caught. His apology is not real and he may only give it as a last resort to get out of trouble or for the benefit of someone else who is there to bail him out, usually the parent. These children are labeled "just plain mean." In younger children it usually involves bullying and then claiming that the other child started it. By the time this child is a teen he might be involved in shooting someone just for kicks. It is a thrill.

Empathy needs to be learned early and reinforced. Talk to the child about the feelings of others. Help them to learn about empathy by example. Include them in your acts of kindness. Encourage them to be kind and to feel the pain and grief of others from a young age. Encourage them to associate with all children in their class. Often we try to shield our children from grief and pain, even of other people, but it may be an opportunity to teach.

Apparently, Rehoboam in1 Kings 12 did not learn much about empathy or about respect for his elders as a child. When he took over his father's throne, he did not listen to the advice of the elders nor did he feel the pain of the people. Because of that he lost most of the kingdom.

Esther, on the other hand, learned empathy for others. When she learned of the plot of Haman against the Jewish people, she could have kept quiet and possibly saved herself from death. Instead, we read in Esther 4:16 her reply to Mordecai: "Go, gather all the Jews who are present in Shushan and fast for me; neither eat nor drink for three days, night or day. My maids and I will fast likewise. And so I will go to the king, which is against the law, and if I perish, I perish!" Esther had to be encouraged by Mordecai, but it was obvious that she had learned empathy earlier in order to make a great decision.

Ability to share. Parents teach children to share their toys with other children. When children are small they are more into parallel play, playing near each other instead of with each other. But as parents or siblings encourage them they begin to actually play with others and play becomes a time of give and take, being fair, and learning to be a good loser or winner. Children who do not learn these things feel that they are owed something. They should win every time and they make their own rules to do so.

In the story of the lost son in Luke 15:11-32, there are two sons. One son seems delinquent through his behavior, leaving, wasting money, and lifestyle, but the other son also has lessons to learn. We see the father teaching, coaching, the son who stayed at home after this son realizes that the lost son has come home and is being treated well. In verses 28-32 we read,

> But he was angry and would not go in. Therefore, his father came out and pleaded with him. So he answered and said to his father, "Lo, these many years I have been serving you; I never transgressed your commandment at any time; and yet you never gave me a young goat that I might make merry with my friends. But as soon as this son of yours came, who has devoured your livelihood with harlots; you killed the fatted calf for him." And he said to him, "Son you are always with me and all that I have is yours. It was right that we should make merry and be glad, for your brother was dead and is alive again, and was lost and is found."

The second son did not want to share what he had with his brother. That does not mean that he had never learned to share, but under the circumstances he did not want to at that time. The father's speech was meant to reassure his son, something that every parent needs to do often with their children. Reassure our children that we love them by telling them and showing them, not with things, but with our time and devotion.

Accepting responsibility. Nothing is the delinquent child's fault, unless he has something to gain or being at fault makes him the winner. That is one of the reasons that school is such a problem. There are rules and work. If the child does not get the good grade he does not accept the responsibility for the grade. It becomes the teacher's fault for not giving fair tests or the dog's fault for eating the homework, but it is certainly not his fault. When school rules are broken by this child, he tells his parents or any adult who will listen to him a story that absolves him of any blame. If something is stolen, even though it may be found on his person, he did not do it and will find someone to blame. As a teacher and an elementary principal, I have sat through many explanations of how it was not a child's fault when I knew he was guilty. Often, the parent would come in the same or following day to let me know that I should be punishing the other party involved because their child did not do anything wrong. This action is called denial and many parents of delinquent children could be named as the song goes the "Queen of DeNial." David certainly continued in denial that Absalom was bad to the core. After Absalom led a revolt against his father, David ordered his soldiers to "deal gently with the young man Absalom for my sake" (2 Sam. 18:5).

Parents who continually deny that their child is in the wrong and bail him out of every problem the child is responsible for hurt the child by not teaching him to face the consequences of his actions and prepare him for accepting responsibility in the future.[6] Admitting that there is a problem and that your child is at fault is not admitting failure as a parent.[7] This admission may be the first step to help the child or find professional help that will give some guidance about what needs to be happening in the child's life to keep him from becoming more delinquent.

Self-esteem. Children need self-esteem. Parents are not depriving them of it by giving them discipline. God instructs us to discipline, not through physical abuse, but with consistency, instruction, and the rod if needed. Some children who are brought up in a totally permissive climate without discipline are insecure, feeling unloved and uncared for.[8] Proverbs teaches us that parents should give instruction and discipline to their children and that children should listen and follow.

Hear, my son, your father's instruction, and reject not your mother's teaching (Prov. 1:8).

My son, if you receive my words and treasure up my commandments with you, making your ear attentive to wisdom and inclining your heart to understanding (Prov. 2:1).

So you will walk in the way of good men, and keep to the paths of the righteous (Prov. 2:20).

So you will find favor and good repute in the sight of God and man (Prov. 3:4).

What more could you want in the way of self-esteem than to find favor with God and man. That would definitely validate your worth as a person.

Self-esteem is more than just feeling good about you. Self-esteem is being able to make mistakes and learn from them in a positive way. Self-esteem is being able to take another person's criticism and put it into perspective. Self-esteem is having goals and reaching to meet them, believing all the while that meeting them is possible. Self-esteem enables a person to give and receive love, admiration, honest praise. Self-esteem is empowering and allows the person to empower others without losing his own power.

Delinquents do not have this kind of esteem. Their esteem is temporary or fleeting. It often depends not on empowering, but on taking power or things away from others. How often have parents felt powerless when dealing with a delinquent child? Parents have to take that power back.

There were many more children beginning elementary school with me than the number that graduated with me. Even as a child, I began to notice that some children seemed to have advantages that seemed to help them rise to the top. Other children seemed doomed from the beginning. Some children, who seemed to have all the advantages, didn't seem to appreciate them. I had a difficult time understanding that until I became an adult. I realize now that their circumstances really were too much for them to overcome, even though many of them were bright and tried in school.

As a teacher and an administrator, I have met many others in my field and in other fields who cater to those who have and give them more, not even throwing scraps of encouragement to the children who are in need.

In fact, some of these individuals encourage delinquency by not having the same high expectations for all children, putting them down, or making them feel powerless.

On the other hand, I have met the caring, nurturing, individuals who attempt to make every child reach for success. One such individual was my sixth grade teacher, Jessie Bertram, who would sit on her porch steps and ask me questions and talk to me as if I were an adult when I would drop by her house after school or on Saturdays. I was probably a nuisance, but she never treated me like one. Nor did she treat any other student any differently. You knew where you stood with Mrs. Bertram. You worked for Mrs. Bertram because she expected it. When I began teaching she was there to encourage and explain what children needed. Years later when I was a principal and visited my former elementary school to make observations with some of my teaching staff, in walked Jessie Bertram, in her eighties, coming to volunteer and read aloud to the children who might not be receiving the help at home. She let my teachers know that I was special and wanted to know what I was doing to help children.

Mr. Jim Boyd, my high school principal, never let a student walk past, without having a kind word, or a pat on the back. He encouraged me, and later when I began teaching, I had the opportunity to return the favor to his son and his classmates.

Store keepers, policemen, restaurant owners and waiters, and my neighbors definitely influenced me to stay on the right path, by just showing an interest, by knowing my name, and at times by letting me know they were going to call my mother or my grandmother. At about age eight, I was the proud owner of a new coat. It was heavy, black and thick with big buttons. I used it at the corner drug store to slip candy up my sleeve to eat on my way home from school. I learned the trick from Paul and Silas, teenage brothers who sat by me in my third grade class. One day I noticed the clerk watching me, but by that time I thought I was slick enough to get the candy and leave without being caught. She stopped me on the way out the door and totally shamed me. "What would your Granny think?" she asked. She gave me two choices. Either I would swear to her that I would never steal anything again and she would be watching me, or she would call my house right then. Of course I chose the first option, but I knew that if she even suspected I was doing something like that again, that a call would go home. When I went back into the store after that event she treated me just as she had before and never again mentioned the theft. I didn't either. When I was fourteen, I started working in that same store.

We need to take an interest in the children in our community. After retiring, I took a job as a part-time math resource teacher at our alternative high school. One young man nineteen years of age, who looked to be thirty, with his full beard and large build, began coming to my room and immediately would try to go to sleep. I would go and sit with him and let him know that if he was coming to my room, that he would work. He grudgingly would do the math with me but all the time he would grumble and tell me he needed sleep. I soon found out that he was working at a fast food place and usually was getting off work at about 2:30 or later in the morning and then coming to school. One morning he came in and literally was so tired he could not function. I went to the principal and told him I was going to find this boy a place to sleep for several hours and that I would check on him. I found a cot and took him to an adjoining room. He slept about two hours and then came to work the rest of the day. At the end of the first semester, I was asked to take a job working with the Hispanic and migrant populations, so I made the change. Two days later, on a Sunday, as Kaye and I were coming out of a restaurant, a small car that was speeding by came to a screeching halt and this bearded head shot out the window and yelled. "Mr. Thurman, when are you coming back, I need help." It was my sleeper. I yelled back that I would come and see him. I visited him and his principal and worked out a time when he could come to my office which was in the same complex. He and another boy worked with me a couple of hours a week until graduation. Their work and attitude changed in all their classes. I was getting regular reports from their teachers. They both graduated and wanted me there to see the ceremony.

How we relate to children in our families, our neighborhoods, or our communities may make a difference. We are told to judge not, lest ye be judged (Matt. 7:1). Perhaps we need to be most careful about this matter with children. You may be the person who can so influence a child that he may take a turn that will lead him or her to become a responsible citizen instead of a drain on society.

Whatever tact you take in trying to help any child, remember to do the following: Be honest, be there, listen, but be slow to speak, care, be consistent, and pray. You may or may not be entirely successful, but at least you will have tried and it may pay off down the road for the child.

Footnotes

[1] The Columbia Electronic Encyclopedia, "Juvenile Delinquency," Columbia University Press.

[2] Susan S. Lang, *Teen Violence*. New York: Franklin Watts, 1994, p. 31, Youth in Jail, 1991.

[3] Raymond B. Flannery Jr., Ph.D., *Preventing Youth Violence*, Continuum, New York, 1999.

[4] Internet citation: OJJDP Statistical Briefing Book, Online. Available: http://ojjdp. ncjrs.org/ojstatbb/population/qa011201.asp?qaDate-20050531.May 31, 2005.

[5] Data Source: U.S. Bureau of the Census. Current Population Survey-Families and Living Arrangements, Historical Tables. Table CH-1: "Living arrangements of Children under 18 Years 1960 to Present." [Internet release date: September 15, 2004]. Web-based data files available at [www.census.gov/population/www/socdmo/hh-fam.html#history].

[6] Internet: Kimberly A. Gordon Rouse, Ph.D., "A Review of Research and Practice," *Human Development and Family Life Bulletin*, Vol. 4, Issue 1, Spring 1998.

[7] Stanton E. Samenow, Ph. D, *Before It's Too Late,* Times Books-Random House, New York, 1989, p.194.

[8] *Ibid.* 133.

[9] *Ibid.* 136.

Choosing a Mate for Life
Frank Himmel

The wise man observed, "He who finds a wife finds a good thing and obtains favor from the Lord" (Prov. 18:22). The Septuagint and other ancient translations say "a good wife." While the proverb is evidently extolling the virtue of marriage itself, obviously finding a good mate is essential to making the union all that God intended. Proverbs 12:4 soberly reminds us, "An excellent wife is the crown of her husband, but she who shames him is as rottenness in his bones."

How does one find a good mate, the kind that will be a crown, not a curse? The Bible does not specify a procedure. However, God has revealed "everything pertaining to life and godliness" (2 Pet. 1:3). As in all areas of life, the principles of God's word will guide us to success if we follow them. Bible history is also helpful: it records numerous examples of people choosing mates, some wisely and some unwisely. "Whatever was written . . . was written for our instruction" (Rom. 15:3).

Where Do I Begin?
Begin with a realization of what is involved. After the choice to serve God, selecting a husband or wife is the most important decision you will make in life. No one else will have greater impact on your life than your mate. No one will be with you more. No one will know you better. No one

Frank Himmel was born April 26, 1955 at Jacksonville, Florida. He is the son of Irvin and Doris Himmel. Frank preached five years at Metairie, Louisiana and fifteen years at Palmetto, Florida. For the past eight years he has been working with the Manslick Road church in Louisville, Kentucky. Frank and his wife, Sandy, have one daughter, Lisa Vernor, and two grandchildren.

has the potential to bring you more joy or sorrow. No one will be a greater influence on you. A wise choice will indeed prove to be a crown. An unwise choice will make happiness on earth elusive and may even contribute to eternal sorrow.

Because marriage is a lifelong relationship (Matt. 19:6), choosing a mate is often a once-in-a-lifetime decision. Of course, there are exceptions. In any case, it is an irrevocable decision, which makes it like few others. You cannot change your mind after the fact. Jesus' teaching on the permanence of marriage prompted his disciples to respond, "If the relationship of the man with his wife is like this, it is better not to marry" (Matt. 19:10). Doubtless many in today's society would agree. However, God designed the relationship this way, knowing how vital commitment is to its success. Appreciating the permanence of marriage will surely bring much needed gravity to the choice of a mate.

Marriage is the norm. Men and women are attracted to each other and need each other. However, there are worse things than not being married. One of them is being married to the wrong person. This is not said to discourage but to caution.

Begin with prayer. "House and wealth are an inheritance from fathers, but a prudent wife is from the Lord" (Prov. 19:14). The first step in obtaining any favor from the Lord is to ask him. If Jesus needed to pray all night before choosing the Twelve (Luke 6:12), how much more do we need to pray frequently and fervently regarding this choice! An interesting Bible example of choosing a mate is recorded in Genesis 24. Abraham charged his eldest servant with the task of finding a wife for Isaac. Prayer is a prominent part of that story, including thanksgiving when God granted the servant success.

Begin with a good look at yourself. Jesus taught us in the Sermon on the Mount that before we attempt to apply God's standard to another, we must first apply it to ourselves (Matt. 7:1-5). So, before I begin to discerningly look at a potential mate, I need to ask myself a few questions.

Am I ready to make a lifelong commitment? Most people marry at a relatively young age, when maturity is less than abundant. Perhaps that is why in some societies parents arrange the marriages. But even that system is not foolproof, as several Bible examples illustrate. King Saul, for example, tried to use the marriage of his daughters for his own selfish ends (1 Sam. 18). Some people are mature enough to make a good choice, but they may not be emotionally stable enough. Perhaps they have recently lost a mate through death or divorce. God made no rules governing how long one must wait to remarry, but obviously one needs to allow enough time to make a poised decision.

Am I ready to make adjustments and sacrifices? Marriage is two becoming one (Gen. 2:24). That does not happen without a few changes. It is selfish and unfair for anyone to expect his mate to do all the adapting. If I am not ready to give, I have no business taking a marriage partner.

Do I have the basic skills essential to daily living? Marriage is blissful, but there is more to it than sitting around gazing into each other's eyes, no matter how beautiful they may be! There are bills to pay. There are chores to be done. Young people who have spent most of their time playing video games or hanging out at the mall may be poorly equipped to take on life's responsibilities.

Boys, can you hold down a job? You must provide for your family (1 Tim. 5:8). Do you have enough self-discipline to get up and go to work every day? Can you manage money? Do you have any fix-it skills? Do you have any leadership ability? God says you are to be the leader in your home (Eph. 5:23-6:4).

Girls, do you know how to cook? Eating out all the time is not an affordable option for most. Can you clean? Do laundry? To be sure, Paul's instruction to be a "worker at home" (Tit. 2:5) is broader than this, yet these things are essential.

Until young people pay all the bills out of their own pockets, they do not appreciate how much things cost. Until they get out on their own, they do not fully realize how much has been done for them while they were growing up. Parents, while we do not want to rob our children of fleeting childhood, we do them a great disservice if we do not, somewhere along the line, train them to be functional members of society.

What do I have to offer? Perhaps this is the "bottom line" of these questions. Before we look too closely at what a potential mate has to offer, we ought to take a good look at ourselves. If I cannot hold up my end of the agreement, I have no business entering it. If I am not perfect, I have no right to expect perfection in a mate. This is not said to encourage people to settle for mediocrity; all of us surely want the best husband or wife we can find. The point is, we need to be realistic and approach marriage with a humble awareness of our own shortcomings.

Begin with Bible study. A successful house begins with builders who know what they are doing—at least, they know what they are supposed to do. A home is no different. And the blueprint for the home, for marriage, is found in God's word. He gave the relationship. He governs it. His way works. An obvious first step, then, is to open our Bibles and study what he says about marriage. I need to understand my role if I am to successfully fulfill it, and I need to understand my spouse's role if I am to successfully find someone to fill it. The failure of homes not patterned after God's will, whether that failure is seen in divorce or in ongoing strife and unhappiness, is a living testimony to the futility of ignoring God's instructions. The Lord's commands are for our good always (Deut. 6:24).

How Do I Go About It?

Look in the right places. Christians meet their mates in all sorts of different places and ways. Some marry a neighbor, perhaps their "childhood sweetheart." Some meet in the workplace. Many meet at school. Florida College has certainly produced its share of "MRS Degrees"! I know one couple who met via an online singles site. Others are introduced by mutual acquaintances.

What you are shopping for dictates where you shop. You won't find fine diamonds at a thrift store. Neither will you find a woman whose "worth is above jewels" or a corresponding man at a place which extols worldly values. If a man chooses a wife from among his associates, it stands to reason that he will find a quality wife only if he is associating with quality people. If he runs with a corrupt crowd, he has virtually no chance of finding a crown of a wife.

If you want a gem, the best place to look is at church. It may the local church where you are a member. It may be at the Crosstown church. It may be at a congregation in another community where you happen to be traveling or are away at school. While this is not the only or the best reason for doing so, meeting other Christians is one benefit that comes from attending gospel meetings. Our children have an abundance of worldly contacts from the neighborhood and public schools. Let's make sure they have some acquaintances from godly homes as well.

People you meet in secular circumstances may come to be good mates. Conversely, not everyone in every congregation is what he or she ought to be or is necessarily a good match for you. That leads us to some other considerations.

Look patiently. No decision of this magnitude should ever be made hastily. You must live with it the rest of your life! Unfortunately, for a variety of reasons, some act too quickly and suffer the consequences.

In some cases, young people living in tragic circumstances at home cannot wait to get out of that situation. Seeking the companionship and nurturing that was lacking from parents, perhaps even abusive parents, they readily take up with whomever is available. And as an old expression puts it, "they jump out of the frying pan into the fire." Similarly, some young people, especially girls, start feeling desperate as they see friend after friend marrying, but there seems to be no one for them. It is tempting in such circumstances to lower one's standards instead of patiently waiting for Mr. Right.

Young people are not the only ones in a hurry. I have seen several cases in which older people have lost a mate of twenty, thirty, forty, or more years. Loneliness quickly sets in, as is to be expected. Anxious to replace the companionship they so long enjoyed, some of these folks show less patience than the teens and make foolish choices! While I cannot and do not wish to appreciate from personal experience what they are going through, I can testify from watching their mistakes what a terrible mess can be created.

One other situation merits consideration. What does a couple do when the product of their fornication is pregnancy? Often they hurry up and marry. In some instances they had planned to do that anyway. In others, however, there was absolutely no thought of marriage prior to this development. It is admirable for people to want to be responsible for their actions. Every child, no matter how conceived, needs a good home, a father and a mother. However, being a party to fornication does not necessarily make one a good partner for life. This can be a case of reacting to one mistake by making another. It is a time for sober reflection, calm heads, and prayer, not a hasty trip to the justice of the peace.

Look objectively. The best time to study lessons like this is *before* you get emotionally involved with someone. The more physical desires and emotions stir, the more difficult it is to be objective. Is love blind? No, but lust certainly can be. Even when significant deficiencies are obvious, it finds a way to dismiss or minimize them. Some have even changed their position on what the Bible teaches about remarriage following divorce in order to justify themselves or a family member who is guided by the flesh instead of the spirit.

Anyone can put on a good front, at least for a while. First impressions may be deceiving. By observing someone in a variety of situations over a lengthy period of time, you have a much better chance of accurately assessing him or her. Watch how he or she acts and reacts to others, not just to you.

Talk openly and honestly. Talk about many different subjects. And listen. You have much to learn. If the two of you have trouble communicating now, what makes you think it will be any better once you marry? Effective communication is a vital component of any partnership, especially marriage.

Objectivity is hard in matters of the heart. It makes sense, then, to listen to others whom you trust who are not emotionally involved. What do your close friends say? How about your parents? Do they think you are making a mistake? They might be right! You may not always like what these advisors tell you, but consider that they may be seeing dangers you are ignoring. Remember the proverb: "Faithful are the wounds of a friend, but deceitful are the kisses of an enemy" (Prov. 27:6).

What Do I Look For?
Eligibility. The first question we ought to ask before doing anything is, Do I have God's permission? If the answer is "Yes," there are other factors to weigh, questions of judgment or expediency; it is not necessarily good to do all that we have God's permission to do (1 Cor. 6:12). If the answer is "No," that is the end of the matter. No amount of other considerations can possibly override this one. Violating God's law is sin, and "the wages of sin is death" (Rom. 6:23).

When we are seeking a marriage partner, therefore, we must begin with eligibility. Is this man or woman allowed by God to marry? Societal approval is not enough. Nor is legal eligibility. We must comply with civil law, but more is involved than mere legality. Neither can you rely on the fact that some preacher tells you it would be an acceptable relationship. Preachers are saying all kinds of things about this subject these days, much of it nonsense. For that matter, whether the person you are considering feels that he or she is eligible is not conclusive. The question is, What does God say in his word?

Keep it simple. We sound like a bunch of lawyers nowadays when we discuss marriage, divorce, and remarriage. It is not that complicated! The New Testament authorizes three categories of people to marry. First, those who have never married. They are the ones God had in view when he instituted marriage, saying, "For this cause a man shall leave his father and his mother, and shall cleave to his wife; and they shall become one flesh" (Gen. 2:24; Matt. 19:6). Second, those whose mates have died (Rom. 7:2-3; 1 Cor. 7:39). Not only are they allowed to marry, Paul urged younger widows to do so (1 Tim. 5:14). Third, those who have divorced a mate because of fornication (Matt. 19:9). It should be noted that this is the only verse in the New Testament that permits marriage to another after a divorce, it does so only by implication, and it does so only for the one who divorces a mate for fornication. (1 Corinthians 7:11 permits a husband and wife who have divorced to reconcile.)

If a prospect is not in one of these three categories, *stop right now!* There is nothing else to consider. Furthering the relationship in any way only invites the temptation to rationalize disobedience. You must look elsewhere for a mate.

Spirituality. Once eligibility has been established, the next thing to look for is spirituality. What could be more important to a spiritually minded person than for a marriage partner to share his or her faith in and commitment to God?

Some people argue that for a Christian, spirituality in a mate is a matter of eligibility. In other words, a Christian *must* marry another Christian. To do otherwise is to violate God's law. Several passages are suggested as establishing this requirement. A brief analysis of a few of them is in order.

2 Corinthians 6:14-16. This is the one most often cited. "Do not be unequally yoked together with unbelievers. For what fellowship has righteousness with lawlessness? And what communion has light with darkness?

And what accord has Christ with Belial? Or what part has a believer with an unbeliever? And what agreement has the temple of God with idols?" The marriage of a Christian and one who is not could certainly be described as an unequal yoke. However, for several reasons it is a mistake to apply this passage universally to such marriages.

First, it is not Paul's context. Marriage is mentioned only one time in this epistle, much later, and that by way of illustration (11:2-3). The context, both before and after these verses, points to association with various teachers as the subject. The Corinthians were too receptive to false ones and too restrained toward Paul.

Second, Paul's illustrations are of things that are mutually exclusive, things that cannot peacefully coexist: righteousness and lawlessness, light and darkness, Christ and Belial, etc. Any attempt to yoke such things is doomed because it requires the right element to compromise its rightness in order for a partnership to exist. That is not true of "mixed" marriages. Paul affirms in 1 Corinthians 7:12-16 that a Christian can successfully live in such a relationship.

Third, the text demands that believers end whatever relationship is in view. Look at it carefully. It does not say "do not become" unequally yoked, it says "do not be" unequally yoked. The phrase *do not be* always demands cessation of existing practice as well as prohibiting future practice (cf. Rom. 12:2, 16; Col. 3:19; etc.). Verse 17 confirms this as the proper response: "come out from their midst and be separate." Applying this passage to "mixed" marriages requires ending them, and that makes Paul contradict what he earlier wrote to this same church (1 Cor. 7:12-16).

1 Corinthians 9:5. "Do we not have a right to take along a believing wife, even as the rest of the apostles and the brothers of the Lord and Cephas?" The argument is, since the text specifies a believing wife, it disallows an unbelieving one. Yes, but what kind of *taking* is in view here? Paul's context is his rights as an apostle and a gospel preacher. He has the right to be financially supported in that work by his brethren, to refrain from secular work, to eat and drink at their expense. And he has the right for that support to be adequate to extend to a wife he takes along. A believing wife. The only thing this passage implies about an unbelieving wife is that a preacher who has one (have you ever known such a case?) has no right to church support for her.

1 Corinthians 7:39. "A wife is bound as long as her husband lives; but if her husband is dead, she is free to be married to whom she wishes, only in the Lord." If any verse establishes that a Christian must marry another Christian, this one is it. Yet we must be cautious about universally binding that conclusion from this one text.

The expression *in the Lord* means in relation to Christ. It may denote that relation itself (e.g., 1 Cor. 4:7, Timothy was Paul's child in the Lord), hence a Christian. Or, it may direct activity to be done in view of that relation (e.g., Rom. 16:2, the Romans were to receive Phoebe in the Lord). "Children, obey your parents in the Lord" (Eph. 6:1) says more than that children are to obey parents who are Christians, or that children who are Christians are to obey their parents, both of which are certainly true. The obedience is to be done in view of relation to the Lord: He requires it and he governs it. A child is not obeying in the Lord if he obeys a parental command to disobey God. Likewise, a widow marrying in the Lord is one who marries in view of her relation to him. That will govern her choice. Does that *require* that her new husband be a Christian? To so argue may be to assume the very point in question.

Beyond the precise import of the phrase *in the Lord,* there are other considerations. If the rule is that widows must marry Christians, does that automatically extend to singles as well? Why did Paul say nothing about this when discussing singles, which he had been doing in the verses leading up to this one? Finally, much of what Paul says in this chapter is "in view of the present distress" facing the Corinthians (v. 26). Verse 40 certainly is; Paul's advice there is opposite to what he recommended in 1 Timothy 5:14. That leaves open the very real possibility that, if such a rule were intended, it, too, was part of his inspired advice for the present distress.

Two New Testament passages specifically address the subject of Christians married to non-Christians: 1 Corinthians 7:12-16 and 1 Peter 3:1-2. Neither prohibits such a relationship. To the contrary, both indicate it is acceptable. These passages demonstrate that a "mixed marriage" is neither inherently sinful nor an insurmountable challenge to the Christian's faith.

Having said all that, I do not want to be viewed as trying to advocate or even defend the practice of a Christian marrying a non-Christian. We do need to be careful about making rules that God did not, adding to his word. However, the New Testament teaches us to go beyond right and wrong in our decision-making. While a thing may not be inherently sinful, it still may be foolish or unprofitable. There is nothing in all the New Testament that commends choosing our mates from among unbelievers. It is an unwise procedure from any number of standpoints.

When Christians are what they should be, they are the finest people on earth. They make the best mates. Others may certainly be good husbands or wives—loyal, caring, kind, supportive, etc.—but they will not be the best. Why? Because they cannot help with the one thing that is most important in life: living for Jesus. Those who want more than anything else to go to heaven will wisely choose a husband or wife who will help them get there.

In the Old Testament, God warned Israel against intermarriage with the Canaanite nations, part of an overall prohibition against making covenants with them. One reason was that Israel was an agent of divine punishment against these peoples. There was also the danger of apostasy. "Furthermore, you shall not intermarry with them; you shall not give your daughters to their sons, nor shall you take their daughters for your sons. For they will turn your sons away from following Me to serve other gods" (Deut. 7:3-4; cf. Exod. 23:23-33; 34:11-17). Israel disobeyed and the predicted result followed. Even wise king Solomon faltered in this regard. He loved many foreign women, accumulated wives and concubines, and when he was old "his wives turned his heart away after other gods" (1 Kings 11:4). Is this danger any less real in our day?

Most of us know of cases in which an unbeliever has been influenced by a believing mate to become a Christian. The Bible says that may happen (1 Pet. 3:1-2), although there are no guarantees (1 Cor. 7:16). But we also know of cases in which such marriages have had the opposite result: under the influence of a mate who is not a Christian, a brother or sister has abandoned his or her faith. Why purposefully put yourself under such an influence?

While an unbelieving mate *may* influence you away from the Lord, he or she almost surely *will* hold you back in some way in your service to God or others. He may resent the time you spend in assemblies, prayer, Bible study, teaching preparation, etc. He may not want to be inconvenienced with worship while traveling. Giving as you have prospered (1 Cor. 16:1-2) may be a greater challenge. You may not feel as comfortable inviting others into your home. You may be pressured to choose social occasions with his worldly friends over your brethren. These and like considerations are often subtle and are certainly not insurmountable problems. They are a burden one must bear in this situation, a burden that is absent when both mates are Christians.

Another advantage to marrying a Christian is that you have a mutual basis for solving problems. Every relationship has them. All of us have our weaknesses and quirks. When both mates are Christians, they are both molding their lives after the same model: Christ. They both understand the importance of humility, repentance, and forgiveness. They both accept God's pattern as the foundation for marriage. This mutual outlook on life not only prevents many problems, it also provides the framework in which those problems that do arise can be quickly and satisfactorily resolved as the couple grows together in Christ.

God blesses most marriages with children. Every blessing brings an accompanying responsibility. In this case our charge is to "bring them up in the discipline and instruction of the Lord" (Eph. 6:4). Will that be easier if your husband or wife is also a Christian? To ask is to answer. An unbelieving mate is always a detriment, even if he or she cooperates fully with your efforts to train the children aright. Why? Because his or her example is opposed to what you are trying to teach the children. Again, this is not an insurmountable obstacle. Only the Lord knows how many Eunices there have been, godly women who without a husband's help have reared the Timothys of the kingdom (Acts 16:1; 2 Tim. 1:5; 3:15). It is just another challenge you take on when you choose to marry someone out of Christ.

Eventually, all marriages will end. "It is appointed for men to die" (Heb. 9:27). At best, this is a most difficult time for the surviving spouse. The greatest comfort in such circumstances is the Lord's promise, "Blessed are the dead who die in the Lord" (Rev. 14:13). But what if your mate was not in the Lord? What if you have no hope of salvation for him or her? Not only must you face the pain of loneliness, you must also bear the grief of knowing that the one with whom you were closest in life, your "other half," now faces an eternity of torment. Whether your mate is a faithful Christian makes a tremendous difference in how well you will cope with his or her death.

Do you have a romantic interest in someone who is not a Christian? Teach him. Surely you want to see him be saved. Allow time for him to obey and show some growth before you commit to him in marriage. His relationship with the Lord needs to be independent of you.

One more point about spirituality. The advantages of marrying a Christian are in large measure negated if the one you marry only nominally serves the Lord. A brother of little faith or a lukewarm sister is not the target. Look for genuine spirituality, not just one who "got wet."

Character. Character is governed by spirituality. A disciple of Christ is working to be "conformed to His image" (Rom. 8:29), to "put on the new self, which in the likeness of God has been recreated in righteousness and holiness of truth" (Eph. 4:24). But some have a long way to go. You must live with whatever character deficiencies your husband or wife has, as he or she must with yours. Such flaws affect marriages in very real ways.

Ask yourself, Is this man honest? Life with a liar is difficult. "Like a bad tooth and an unsteady foot is confidence in a faithless man in time of trouble" (Prov. 25:19). Is he industrious? A good home requires that all work hard and contribute. "Like vinegar to the teeth and smoke to the eyes, so is the lazy one to those who send him" (Prov. 10:26). Is he prudent? "Common sense" is not always so common. Is he patient? Does he have self-control? What this man is will have far greater impact on you through the years than what he has or what he looks like. Good character is critical.

How can you discern character? One suggestion is to pay attention to how a person treats others, not just how he treats you. Anyone can put on a good show for one he is trying to impress. Watch him interact with others: friends, family members (his and yours), people at church, and the general public—waiters, store clerks, drivers, etc. If he is impatient, rude, or arrogant toward these people, you cannot be surprised if in time he turns out to be that way toward you, too.

Another key character issue is immoral habits. Does he use drugs? Does he drink (alcoholic beverages)? These things are usually disastrous to a happy home life. It is not at all rare for a man to be quite pleasant when he is sober but a terror when he is drinking. You will be the one to whom he comes home in that state. Does he use profanity? Is he violent or abusive? These are red flags. Is he involved in pornography? If so, there is no reason to think he will be satisfied with you.

Again, we must stress the importance of objectivity. Do not pretend that such problems do not exist or are not all that important. And do not depend on his promises to change. He may. People do improve. The Bible calls that repentance. But he may not. In fact, some of these kinds of problems tend to worsen over time. Sin is deceitful and can harden (Heb. 3:13). The question you must answer is, Am I willing to risk a lifetime of misery by hoping he will change? Before you answer yes, spend some time talking with people who married those who didn't.

Background. Another factor to consider is one's background. What do you know about it? Although it is extremely rare, some have married people who are already married, perhaps to someone in another state or country. Again it is rare, but there have been cases where only a good while after a marriage did one learn of a spouse's earlier divorce. The implications of such problems are obvious.

Speaking of divorce, marrying someone who is divorced calls for extreme care. Remember that Jesus said, "Whoever divorces his wife, except for sexual immorality, and marries another woman commits adultery; and he who marries a divorced woman commits adultery" (Matt. 19:9). In light of that, you need to be absolutely certain about the circumstance of a potential spouse's divorce. If he is not the lone exception of Matthew 19:9, you and he will be sinning if you go ahead.

There is far more to someone's background than his marital experience. In what kind of home was he reared? What influences were there? A human proverb says that "an apple doesn't fall far from the tree." It would be grossly unfair to charge anyone with the sins or faults of his parents. He may not be at all like his mother or father. On the other hand, it is naive to ignore their potential influence. This was the example he saw growing up. This is the pattern of behavior that was set before him on a daily basis. We are often more like our parents than we realize.

One's background includes the company he has kept. "Evil companions corrupt good morals" (1 Cor. 15:33). Besides whatever influences they may exert, the fact that one prefers the company of ungodly companions is a reflection of his character. "How blessed is the man who does not walk in the counsel of the wicked, nor stand in the path of sinners, nor sit in the seat of scoffers!" (Ps. 1:1).

Personality and interests. There is likely no such thing as a perfect match. Each of us is unique. It is, therefore, neither possible nor necessary to find someone just like you. As the Genesis account reads, Isaac and Rebekah met for the first time on their wedding day (Gen. 24:61-67). She had already agreed to marry him (v. 58), "sight unseen." What about personality differences—would they have them? How would they get along? Such questions may well occur to people who live in cultures in which parents arrange marriages. Yet their marriages work, proving that diverse personalties can formulate successful homes. Humility and commitment are doubtless keys.

Most of us prefer to do our own selecting. Our experience in life (including in the church) teaches us that while we *can* get along with most anyone, some are surely easier than others! Find someone whose personality is compatible with yours. Couples who frequently argue and fight while dating will likely do the same after their wedding day.

Some personality differences may actually prove advantageous. Each mate grows from living with the other's strengths. A low-keyed husband stabilizes his emotional wife, while an outgoing wife makes her reserved husband far more sociable. A frugal wife curbs her husband's carefree spending, just as his bright outlook overcomes her pessimism. Humility brings down pride, and patience conquers anger. Make the most of each other's assets.

Marriage is two becoming one. Sometimes opposites attract, but generally the blending will go much more smoothly if we share common ground. Talk extensively before you commit to marriage. Explore your views about spiritual things, money, children, jobs, recreation, your families, and more. A husband and wife certainly do not have to agree on everything. We will always have varied interests, even after learning to be accommodative (and that is a vital component of a good marriage). However, in any relationship, widely divergent outlooks pose a serious challenge to unity.

Physical attraction. Near the bottom of this list we come to what is at or near the top of many people's list of qualities in a mate: physical attractiveness. Why rank it here? Because this is where it belongs. Unless you are planning to spend your entire married life sitting on the sofa looking at each other, one's spirituality, character, background, and personality will have a far greater impact on the joy and success of your marriage than his looks will. "Charm is deceitful and beauty is vain, but a woman who fears the Lord, she shall be praised" (Prov. 31:30). Physical beauty is wasted when character is lacking. "As a ring of gold in a swine's snout, so is a beautiful woman who lacks discretion" (Prov 11:22). And as most of us are painfully aware, whatever physical attractiveness we have quickly fades.

Samson was enamored with a beautiful Philistine woman and told his father, "Get her for me, for she looks good to me" (Judg. 14:3). She betrayed him before their wedding feast was over! Early in history, "the sons of God saw that the daughters of men were beautiful; and they took wives for themselves, whomever they chose" (Gen. 6:2). The result was the almost universal corruption of mankind.

By no means must godly women be unattractive! Sarah was "very beautiful" (Gen. 12:14). Jacob fell in love with Rachel, who was "beautiful of form and face" (Gen. 29:17). Esther essentially won a beauty pageant (Esth. 2). Yet there was far more to these women than their appearance.

Let us be realistic. No one is going to marry someone whom they find physically repulsive. You will not even date them, much less marry them! We ought to do what we can with what we've got to be as attractive to our mates as possible. However, a marriage based on physical attractiveness is doomed.

Consider 1 Thessalonians 4 on this point. "For this is the will of God, your sanctification; that is, that you abstain from sexual immorality; that each of you know how to possess his own vessel in sanctification and honor, not in lustful passion, like the Gentiles who do not know God" (vv. 3-5). Commentators differ as to whether the word *vessel* here refers to one's body, as it does in 2 Corinthians 4:7, "treasure in earthen vessels," or to one's wife, as it does in 1 Peter 3:7, "a weaker vessel." Likewise, there is some disagreement about whether *possess* or *acquire* is the correct idea in the preceding verb. It may make little difference. Either interpretation points to honorable motives and conduct in sexual relations, which clearly relates to marriage.

A hedonistic world bases physical relationships on lustful passion. That is why so many go from one partner to another (perhaps they marry, divorce, and remarry, perhaps they do not bother). As soon as the thrill of a relationship begins to wane, when the passion is no longer as intense as it initially was, they are ready to start over with another who will rekindle the fire. This low-minded, carnal approach will never work. Christians are to operate on a higher plane. We must establish and maintain our marriages on the basis of character, not charm; of spirituality, not sensuality. Remember, Christ's relationship with the church is the model (Eph. 5:22-33).

Conclusion

No relationship on earth has more potential for joy than marriage. It continues long after the children, and in many cases even the grandchildren, have gone their way. The Preacher counseled, "Enjoy life with the woman whom you love all the days of your fleeting life which He has given to you under the sun; for this is your reward in life and in your toil in which you have labored under the sun" (Eccl. 9:9). An excellent wife surely is the crown of her husband. Her worth is far above jewels (Prov. 31:10).

Choose well. Do not look for perfection. You are not offering it, and you will not find it. But do not settle for second rate, either. Too much is at stake. Find someone who will help you get to heaven.

There are no guarantees, of course. Some people prove to be much different than we anticipated. Some change over time. Yet armed with God's word, prayer, and common sense, we have the best opportunity to say with King Lemuel, "Many daughters have done nobly, but you excel them all" (Prov. 31:29).

Teenagers and Sex
John A. Smith

Sex is not a dirty word. Sexual relations are not filthy. The enjoyment of a sexual relationship is not perverse. On the contrary, God designed man as a sexual being, placed a sex drive within his heart and sanctioned sexual relations. Too many people, including many Christians, treat human sexuality as if it were sinful, dirty, or shameful. This attitude is not biblical. Sexual intimacy is honorable in God's eyes. "Marriage is to be held in honor among all, and the marriage bed is to be undefiled; for fornicators and adulterers God will judge" (Heb. 13:4).

Sexual activity becomes dirty, filthy, and perverse when one takes it out of the context in which God placed it. After advising his son to find sexual

---

John A. Smith was born in Mt. Sterling, Kentucky, but raised primarily in Anderson, Indiana. He is the son of the late Arnold and Loretta Smith. He was blessed to be reared in a family where the Bible was cherished and strong stands for truth were taken regardless of the cost. He holds an AA from Florida College (1974) and a BA from Morehead State University (1976), Morehead, Kentucky.

For six years John worked as a middle school educator in Englewood, Ohio, while also being engaged in "circuit riding" preaching over a wide area of southwest and central Ohio. In 1982, John left one classroom for another to begin working full-time with the Fredericktown (Ohio) Church of Christ with whom he worked for five years. In 1987, he began working with the Winchester (Kentucky) Church of Christ and labored with them for eleven years also serving as an elder for three years. While in Winchester, John developed an abstinence based sex education curriculum that was implemented in the Clark County middle schools and taught by him. In the summer of 1998, John moved to Indianapolis, Indiana, to work with the Lafayette Heights Church of Christ and continues laboring with them today. (Continued on next page.)

179

enjoyment and fulfillment with his own wife, Solomon warned him not to seek satisfaction with "strange women." "For why should you, my son, be exhilarated with an adulteress and embrace the bosom of a foreigner? For the ways of a man are before the eyes of the Lord, and He watches all his paths. His own iniquities will capture the wicked, and he will be held with the cords of his sin. He will die for lack of instruction, and in the greatness of his folly he will go astray" (Prov. 5:20-23).

Sin, including sexual sin, complicates life, makes it more difficult and assaults one's heart. This is true regardless of the sin one commits. "Good understanding produces favor, but the way of the treacherous is hard" (Prov. 13:15). "The integrity of the upright will guide them, but the crookedness of the treacherous will destroy them" (Prov. 11:3). In describing the kind of activity that complicates life and is prohibited, God repeatedly admonished his people to avoid sexual sin. "Now flee youthful lusts, and pursue righteousness, faith, love and peace, with those who call on the Lord from a pure heart" (2 Tim. 2:22).

> Flee sexual immorality. Every sin that a man does is outside the body, but he who commits sexual immorality sins against his own body (1 Cor. 6:18, NKJV).

Why would God limit sexual activity to the marriage relationship? Why withhold this pleasure from those who are not married or why limit it to

---

John has been blessed to participate in short-term evangelism in the former Soviet Union for the past thirteen years. He has worked in three Russian cities (Moscow, Podolsk and Tula). In addition, he has made eight trips to the Republic of Moldova helping to establish churches in Chisinau and Balti. In January of 2006, he help organize and conduct a Bible Conference in Chisinau, Moldova.

John is the author of two adult class workbooks, *Teaching: The Heart of the Matter, The Sermon on the Mount* and the co-author of the teenage workbook *The Bible and Teen Dating*.

He has been happily married to Diane (Winks) for the past 30 years. They are the parents of two children, Molly Pentecost and Tom Smith both of the Indianapolis area. John and Diane have one granddaughter, Zoe Pentecost (5), one grandson, Hayden Pentecost (7 months) and one grand-dog, Lucy Smith (age unknown).

one partner? The answer certainly involves sin, but it goes well beyond the fact that such activities are sinful and will bar one from the kingdom of heaven. Truly in placing limits on our sexual expression, God was looking out for our best interest.

What Is Safe Sex?

The world promotes something called "safe sex" that abandons God's limits and restrictions. The world defines safe sex as "taking precautions during sex that can keep you from getting a sexually transmitted disease (STD), including HIV, or from giving an STD or HIV to your partner" (Medline Plus, National Institutes of Health). Further it includes taking steps to prevent getting pregnant or making someone pregnant.

The failure rate of condoms in preventing pregnancy among teenage users is somewhere between 15% and 25%. That's alarming! No one knows with certainty how often they fail when trying to prevent the spread of sexually transmitted diseases and HIV. Margaret Fischl reported that in one study of married couples in which one partner was HIV positive and condoms were consistently used after 1½ years 17% of the healthy partners had become infected. That's about one in six, the same odds as Russian roulette.

An analysis of eleven studies on condom effectiveness found that condoms had a 31% estimated failure rate in protecting against HIV transmission.

Condoms and contraceptives do not make for "safe sex." Look at it this way: If you decide to drive the wrong way down a divided highway, is it safer if you use a seat belt? You wouldn't call the process "safe." To call it "safer" completely misses the point. It's still a very risky—and a very foolish thing to do.

The fatal flaw of the world's "safe sex" message is that it condones all sexual expression as long as some kind of "protection" is used. It does not depend on any moral absolutes, but on the strength of latex. Since "safe sex" ignores all moral standards, it removes all inhibitions about sexual activity, whether "protected" or "unprotected."

God's Plan for "Safe Sex"

God's plan for sexuality is simple: abstinence before marriage and monogamy in marriage. By following God's design, you can enjoy genuine "safe sex"—a guaranteed 100% effective contraceptive that is free from all the devastating side effects of guilt, broken trusts, and shattered dreams. God's plan for safe sex will call upon you to forego the passing pleasures of sin so that you might enjoy the pleasant fruit of faithfulness (Heb. 11:25).

Premarital sexual abstinence offers true freedom from many things that are not in the young person's best interest.

- Safety from unwanted, unplanned pregnancies. Pregnant and parenting teens are less likely to obtain a high school diploma, much less a college degree. What kind of jobs and financial future is there for those who do not even complete high school? If you are the one who gets pregnant, the odds of you raising that child without any help from the father is astronomically high. Without custodial or financial support from the father, you needlessly complicate your life and compromise your future. If you are not sexually involved, you cannot get pregnant or get someone pregnant! It's that simple.

- Safety from sexually transmitted diseases and AIDS. Clearly, God knew what he was talking about. He has something better to offer! But not everyone who is sexually active outside of marriage will get an STD or AIDS. Not everyone who is sexually active will get pregnant or get someone pregnant. If these consequences are avoided, is it OK? Think again.

- Safety from the pressure to marry before you are ready. By God's design, sexual relations create a bond between the partners. It is intended to bond the couple, but does not provide a foundation for the relationship and is no substitute for genuine love. When this bond is mistaken for genuine love, a couple can be tricked into believing that the relationship is deeper than it really is, only to wake up one morning and wonder why they are no longer "in love" when they were never really in love to begin with. Mercifully God has shown us a better way. When a relationship is built upon emotional and spiritual intimacy rather than sexual intimacy, both partners will develop an inner beauty that glows ever brighter and draws them ever closer.

- Safety from the guilt, self-doubt, disappointment, worry, and ruined reputation often associated with premarital sexual activity. Guilt is one consequence of premarital sexual activity that may last longer than any other. Casual sex without deep-rooted committed love proves to be damaging to one's self-image. No pill or device can guard your mind against the terror of self-accusation. After his affair with Bathsheba, David had a terrifying experience with guilt. He became physically and emotionally sick. Describing his condition, David said: "There is no soundness in my flesh because of your anger, nor is there any health in my bones because of my sin. For my iniquities have gone over my head; like a heavy burden they are too heavy for me. . . . I am troubled, I am bowed down greatly; I go mourning all the day long. For my loins are full of inflammation, and there is no soundness in my flesh. I am feeble and severely broken; I groan because of the turmoil of my heart" (Ps. 38:1-8).

- Safe, to experience fuller communication in dating relationships. Contrary to a popular myth, you cannot get to know a boyfriend or girlfriend better by sleeping together. In fact, premarital sexual activity often inhibits communication and keeps those involved from really getting to know the other person. Premarital sex clouds the issue of true love and tends to thwart the communication process. Sex offers an easy out for those who have never learned to communicate intimacy apart from the physical. When a couple chooses to postpone sexual involvement until marriage, they allow their relationship to grow and mature. They can more easily provide themselves with opportunities to discover each other. It will be easier to find out what it is that makes the other unique and attractive. Without the pressure of sexual activity, it will be easier to communicate feelings that will lay a foundation for love that will express itself in sexual intimacy within marriage.

- Safe, to develop greater respect for yourself. One of the worst feelings many sexually active people experience is getting up the next morning and realizing that the person lying next to them is a total stranger. They rob themselves of a healthy self-image and a clear conscience. God has provided marriage as the place for sex, and a person moving within God's boundary is free to marry or not to marry. Should he decide to marry, he is able to express his sexuality in a context where no one can be hurt. There is no guilt in any of this. God protects them from destructive, shattering guilt.

- Safe, to have greater trust in marriage. God knows that marriages need trust. A marriage without trust is as unstable as a house without a foundation. One way to prove yourself to be trustworthy is to remain sexually pure prior to marriage. If you could not practice self-control before marriage, how can your mate ever be sure that you will be self-controlled after marriage?

These few consequences only begin to address the issue. Imagine sitting across the dinner table and having to tell your parents that you are pregnant, or having to tell your girl friend's father that she's pregnant and you're the father. Shattered dreams and innocence lost never to be regained are not the consequences which get publicity, but are consequences that often linger long into adulthood. The commands of the Bible are there for our protection. The Lord knows how devastating the effects of premarital sex can be, so out of his love for us he has established parameters for sex to keep it from being destructive. By insisting that we wait until marriage for sex, God protects us from that destruction. He wants our sex lives to be a point of strength and unity in the marriage relationship, not a point of division. His wisdom supersedes all our rationalizations and excuses.

I have talked with many young people who have come to regret the decision they made to become sexually active outside of marriage. But, I have never talked with a person who made the decision to wait until marriage to become sexually active who regretted it! God will forgive anyone who sincerely repents, just as he forgave David. But even though you can still have a home in heaven, your sins can create a hell on earth that cannot be escaped. "The way of the treacherous is hard." Perhaps David's second son by Bathsheba, Solomon, was thinking about this episode in his father's life when he wrote: "Can a man take fire in his bosom, and his clothes not be burned? Or can a man walk on hot coals, and his feet not be scorched? So is the man who goes into his neighbor's wife" (Prov. 6:27-29).

The Battle Against Temptation
Temptation #1

Joseph was the favorite son of Jacob and that led to jealous resentment among his eleven brothers. Eventually their hatred for Joseph prompted them to sell him into slavery. By God's providence Joseph ended up in Egypt in the service of an officer of Pharaoh named Potiphar (Gen. 39:1-2).

Genesis 39:7 says, "And it came about after these events that his master's wife looked with desire at Joseph, and she said, 'Lie with me.'" At the time of this temptation Joseph was about seventeen years old (Gen. 37:2)—a time when many young men have strong sexual impulses without the maturity to have mastered their desires. Joseph had to deal with one of man's strongest temptations at the point in life when he was most vulnerable.

Further, the temptations Joseph faced continually increased in intensity. Initially, Pharaoh's wife just spoke to him (39:7). Then, she began to appeal to him day by day (39:10). Finally, she grabbed him (39:12).

How was Joseph able to deal with this incredibly strong series of temptations?

- He simply said NO! In 39:8, the Bible says, "But he refused." There was no effort on the part of Joseph to compromise or bargain with Potiphar's wife. He plainly and flatly refused. If you want to overcome sexual temptation, never hesitate when confronted with it. Immediately and emphatically tell the Devil NO!

- He realized people were counting on him. When Joseph explained to Potiphar's wife why he could not sleep with her, he said, "Behold, with me here, my master does not concern himself with anything in the house, and he has put all that he owns under my charge. There is no one greater in this house than I, and he has withheld nothing from me except you, because you are his wife" (39:8-9a). In other words, Joseph was appreciative of the trust Potiphar placed in him, and he did not want to let Potiphar down. When you are tempted sexually, remember all the people who have placed trust in you. Think of your parents, who trust you to go out with your friends. Think of your brothers and sisters, who look up to you and want to imitate you. Think of your date, who is counting on you to conduct yourself appropriately. Think of your spiritual family, that depends on you for encouragement. Don't let all of these people down! The pleasure of sexual sin can never equal the pain and heartbreak you will cause all these people by succumbing to temptation.

- He realized all sin was a direct rejection of God. After explaining that Potiphar had been kind to him, Joseph went on to say, "How then could I do this great evil, and sin against God?" (39:9b). In one sense, all sin is against God and God only. That is not to say that we cannot sin against others, we can. But even the sinful things we do to each other are wrong only because God said so. Consequently, all sin is really a rejection of God. When David reflected on his sexual sin, he said in Psalm 51:4, "Against Thee, Thee only, I have sinned." David committed a terrible crime by having Uriah killed, but he understood that ultimately his crime was against God. We shouldn't disappoint our parents, our siblings, our date, and our brethren, but most of all we should refuse to sin because it is an offense to our Maker. And if we love him with all our heart, soul, mind, and strength (Mark 12:30), we will never want to insult God.

- He did whatever he had to in order to avoid sinning. When Potiphar's wife resorted to grabbing Joseph, "he left his garment in her hand and fled" (39:12). Joseph was not a coward running away. A coward would have betrayed his convictions and sinned. Since Potiphar's wife could not be dissuaded any other way, the bravest thing Joseph could do was run. It might be possible to stand toe-to-toe with the Devil and slug it out over some temptations, but that is not the case with sexual temptation. "Flee immorality" (1 Cor. 6:18). If you are on a date and the expression of affection becomes too physical, you need to do whatever it takes to avoid sin, even if it means literally running away. There is a secret weapon for dealing with sexual temptation—the quarter. Carry one with you at all times, and even if you are on a date where you are being tempted sexually, run away and use that quarter to call someone for a ride home. Joseph was able to live with a clear conscience free from the burden of guilt. What a blessing!

Temptation #2
David was a sincere servant of God who possessed great courage (just ask Goliath). He also displayed great self-restraint in his conflicts with Saul, twice foregoing opportunities to kill him (1 Sam. 24:3-4; 26:6-12). David was clearly an outstanding military leader, and 2 Samuel 8-10 records a series of stunning victories David achieved with God's help.

That brings us to his temptation. 2 Samuel 11:1 gives us the time for his testing: "Then it happened in the spring, at the time when kings go out for battle, that David sent Joab and his servants . . . but David stayed in Jeru-salem." Rather than leading his men into battle as he had numerous times before, David stayed at home. Perhaps one lesson we can draw from this is that if we stay busy pursuing righteousness, faith, and love with a pure heart, we won't have time to be tempted (2 Tim. 2:22).

David's temptation occurred in four stages. First, while strolling on the roof of his palace, "he saw a woman bathing" (11:2). Just looking at someone is not inherently sinful, unless the looking is done for the purpose of sexual fantasies (Matt. 5:27-28). David could have chosen to immediately turn away and get his mind on something else, but he did not. The next stage of his temptation occurred when David "sent and inquired about the woman" (11:3). David learned that the woman's name was Bathsheba and that she was married to one of his mighty men of valor, Uriah the Hittite (see 2 Sam. 23:39). At this point David definitely should have dropped the matter, because pursuing it would lead to a doubly treacherous sin—he would be breaking his marriage vows, and Bathsheba would be breaking hers. Instead, David "sent messengers and took her" (11:4). Once she came, David faced his final crossroads. He still could have avoided sin by sending her away, but instead he chose to consummate the sin. "He lay with her" (11:4).

Here are some important lessons we can learn from David's experience:

- Fornication begins with the eyes. David's descent into sin began when he looked at a naked woman. "The lust of the eyes" is one of the three avenues of temptation the Devil uses to get to us, and he knows exactly what kind of images to use. Obviously, a Christian should never delve into pornography, because Jesus taught that an impure mind is as sinful as impure actions (Matt. 5:28-29). In our society, it is impossible to avoid all images with the potential to lead one to lust. Commercials which air in prime-time on regular broadcast TV use images which would have been considered soft core porn just a few years ago. Now more than ever Christians need to follow Job's advice, who said, "I have made a covenant with my eyes; How then could I gaze at a virgin?" (Job 31:1). David himself wrote: "I will set no worthless thing before my eyes" (Ps. 101:3). If you choose to watch TV shows, or attend movies, that feature characters who are promiscuously dressed, you are taking the first step toward fornication, just like David. If you date people who dress immodestly, you knowingly place temptation before your eyes. Young men, if your date dresses immodestly, what does that say about her heart and intentions? Can you count on her to support your decision to make godly decisions and be guided by godly morals? If she dresses immodestly, can you master your thoughts? Are you fleeing fornication if you date someone who places temptation before your eyes by the way in which they dress?

- One thing leads to another. Have you ever heard that phrase? "We were just kissing, but before we knew it one thing led to another." Duh! God created us so that romantic affection between the sexes would lead to further intimacy. Once David saw the beautiful Bathsheba, he should have thought about something else. Instead, he courted disaster by going a step further and inquiring about her, and "one thing led to another." The lesson for young people is clear: be very cautious about how much affection you share with your boyfriend or girlfriend. The more quickly and more deeply you let your physical relationship develop, the more rapidly you are going to face the temptation to "go all the way." Wisely, the Shulamite maiden repeatedly asked that her love not be stirred up or awakened before the proper time (S. of Sol. 3:5). Thus, she was able to remain a "garden locked up" until the day of her marriage (S. of Sol. 4:12). Don't let things get out of control.

- Be aware of you weaknesses. 2 Samuel 3:2-5 lists the members of David's family, and in that record the Bible mentions that he had six different wives. This suggests that David had a weakness for women. If David had been more aware of this weakness, he might have been more careful in how he dealt with sexual temptation. We all have weaknesses. Honestly evaluate yourself—maybe you have a short temper, or find yourself coveting material things. Maybe you're liable to be proud or hold a grudge. All of us share a common weakness—the flesh (Matt. 26:40). Know what your weaknesses are, and then avoid anything that might play on those weaknesses.

What About Dating?

What do you hope to accomplish when you go out on a date? Sound like a silly question? Perhaps it is a bit unusual, but when that question is answered and motives are clarified you will be well on your way to spiritually healthy dating.

For far too many teens, dating is nothing more than an attempt to get their next conquest in a secluded spot for a bit of heavy breathing. What they really have in mind is discovering how far they can go hoping to have something to brag about when the weekend is over. The prospective date is little more than a thing to be used for selfish purposes. They are not at all interested in what really makes you such a unique you (intelligence, personality, values, character). They are only interested in body parts and how generous you're willing to be with them.

Dating someone who approaches each date as a safari for sex sets up a contest of wills—a contest that likely won't be over until one comes out a winner, and the other the loser. It doesn't take too many of these sexual skirmishes to leave you emotionally battered and scarred. These can be difficult scars to erase.

On the other hand, dating can be an exciting and emotionally rewarding experience without the involvement of sexual pressure. It can provide you with an opportunity to find out what makes the other person tick. It allows a friendship to develop and mature that will be a blessing in your life. You can find someone that you can care about and who will care about you. Spending time with the right person for the right reason will be a building process. Your world can come alive with new meaning when you share it with someone who respects you and God's morals.

As with any activity in life, your most important goal in dating should be to please and honor God. "And whatever you do in word or deed, do all in the name of the Lord Jesus, giving thanks through Him to God the Father" (Col. 3:17). Your personal pleasure and amusement should be secondary to honoring and pleasing God. The person who is able to approach dating from this perspective will set appropriate dating standards, communicate them clearly to prospective dates, and conduct themselves in accordance with those standards.

Some people make dating more difficult for themselves than is necessary by taking dating too seriously. For some people a Friday or Saturday night without a date is a sure sign that they are doomed to be an old spinster or bachelor. Any date is better than no date. After all who wants to stay home on Friday night and play Monopoly with their little brother? For others every date must be a production and everything go perfectly. Some people add stress to every dating situation by viewing every date as an imminent prelude to marriage. Lighten up! While you need to be cautious and set godly standards for dating, you don't need to approach the whole affair as if life and death hang in the balance with every date.

This brings me back to my point—why do you date? I hope it is to have fun, to get to know the other person, and to enjoy their company. If this is true then make dating decisions that will help you have fun while you get to know the person whose company you may come to enjoy.

Ponder the words of the wise old preacher in Ecclesiastes 11:9: "Rejoice, young man, during your childhood, and let your heart be pleasant during the days of young manhood. And follow the impulses of your heart and the desires of your eyes. Yet know that God will bring you to judgment for all these things."

When Should You Start Dating?

What is a reasonable age at which to start dating? I'm not talking about meeting a bunch of friends at a ball game and sitting dreamily with that cute guy or girl from your fourth period history class. I'm talking about serious dating when you are paired off with one other person with the intention of spending a good bit of time with them.

There is no right age for everyone. Some people mature more rapidly than others and not everyone is as responsible as others their age. It has been suggested that a person is mature and responsible enough to begin dating when they are ready to make responsible, godly dating rules and have the resolve to stick to them.

As a word of caution, there are a number of studies that indicate that the earlier a girl begins serious dating the greater the likelihood that she will become sexually involved before marriage. In *Sex Respect*, Colleen Kelly Mast shared a study that found the following:

- 91% of the girls who began dating at or before 12 had sex before they graduated from high school.
- 56% of those who began dating at 14 had sex before they graduated from high school.
- 20% of those who began dating at 16 had sex before they graduated from high school.

Setting Reasonable Dating Standards. Whatever dating standards you and your parents determine are appropriate, they should be thoroughly discussed and in place before you begin dating. Waiting until after you have begun dating may be too late and allow you to form unhealthy dating habits. Remember, it is easier to break no standard than to break some standard.

Share your dating standards with all prospective dates. If you know that there are places you are not permitted to go, whether prohibited by your parents or yourself, make sure your date knows this before the date. To do otherwise would be unfair. If your date is unwilling to spend time with you according to your standards, then he really doesn't care much for you and certainly doesn't respect you.

Whom to Date? One of the most critical decisions to make prior to dating involves whom you will date. If you choose someone who shares your core values, then many of the other critical choices will take care of themselves. Here are a couple of biblical principles that you might want to consider when choosing whom you will date:

> Do not be deceived: Bad company corrupts good morals (1 Cor. 15:33).

> Do not be bound together with unbelievers; for what partnership have righteousness and lawlessness, or what fellowship has light with darkness? (2 Cor. 6:14).

These passages should impress upon the reader the importance of making careful, cautious decisions about those with whom he chooses to associate. Paul warns us not to be deceived about this matter. Think you're strong enough to resist the influence of friends or dates who do not share your biblical morals? Think again! Do not be deceived!

Does this mean that you should only date Christians? Not necessarily. In 1 Corinthians 6:9-10 Paul wrote: "I wrote in my letter not to associate with immoral people; I did not at all mean with the immoral people of the world . . . for then you would have to go out of the world." Dating someone who is not a Christian is not forbidden by the Scriptures, but if you do choose to date a non-Christian be aware of the potential dangers.

I asked a group of young people what advice they would give others about whom to date. I found their answers interesting and reflective of the kind of caution one should take.
- Avoid people who use bad language. Remember that what proceeds out of the mouth originates in the heart!
- Avoid those who have bad reputations. Why take the chance?
- Avoid those who use drugs or alcohol. These substances may make the person more aggressive and lower any sense of inhibition.
- When choosing a person to date, be sure to look below the surface. Go beyond looks and popularity.
- Choose a person who shares your core values and standards. It is

easier to avoid compromising situations if both people share the same definition of temptation and sin.

- Choose someone that you would feel comfortable dating your little brother or sister.

Are you having trouble finding someone to date? Then "go fish!" Visit other congregations, attend gatherings of young people in other communities. Expand your horizons.

There are advantages to dating someone who is a Christian. Ultimately, you will marry someone whom you have dated. I suspect that your wedding day will not be your first date with your spouse! Do you really want to spend the rest of your life and raise children with someone who does not share your core values and commitment to the Lord? Christians should, if genuinely committed to the Lord, share your choice of moral purity relieving much of the sexual pressure on dates. However, make sure the person you are dating is genuinely a Christian in heart and not just someone who "got wet" to appease his parents. Sadly, among professing Christians there are plenty of young people who are not committed to living their faith. Make your choice carefully based on the proven content of his heart.

What are you going to do on a date? Perhaps you are familiar with the chimney corner scripture, "Idle hands are the devil's workshop." When it comes to dating these words are certainly true. When planning what to do on a date, be sure to plan enough to keep you busy for the duration of the date. If you stay busy you are less likely to occupy idle time with activities that might lead to compromising situations.

When choosing what to do on a date, remember that you should not light a fire that you can't put out. Even better, why light it in the first place? Why choose activities or places that might encourage sexual arousal or make self-control more difficult to practice? The time to look for a fire escape is before the fire begins!

The same group of young people who helped with "whom to date" also shared some excellent suggestions about what to do or not do on a date:

- Plan dates where you have to talk. Choose activities where you have the opportunity to really get to know the other person.
- Plan activities that would not tempt you to lie to your parents. Choose

activities that would not cause you to be embarrassed if your parents saw you.

- Avoid dates where you would be put in the position of being alone for long periods of time, especially if it is in the dark!
- Avoid activities and places where people may be using drugs or alcohol.
- Group dates and group activities cannot only be fun, they can also help you more easily avoid tempting situations.

How much physical contact? This is a tough one. It is unrealistic and unnecessary to expect young people to have no physical contact on a date. Holding hands, hugging, and kissing may be perfectly acceptable, or they could be the prelude to sexual immorality depending on the maturity of the people involved. Each person is going to have to develop some carefully considered guidelines for themselves.

I have talked to some young people who seem to be of the opinion that it is perfectly sane and reasonable to go just as far as they can without committing sin. This is dangerous! You will be tempted to go just a little farther and a little farther until you have gone all the way and then wonder how you got there. Why push yourself to the limits when there is the very real danger of falling off?

The Bible tells us to "flee immorality" (1 Cor. 6:18), "abstain from sexual immorality" (1 Thess. 4:3), and to not even let immorality or impurity be named among you (Eph. 5:3). All of these passages argue for careful limits that will keep one away from the kind of physical contact that will arouse one sexually.

Ladies, you need to know that males tend to get "turned on" much more quickly and easily than females. Because of the sexual make up of a male, they tend to be more visually and physically oriented than females. Ladies, you may not be aroused. You might not be frustrated by stopping what you are doing at any moment, but the male will face the prospect of interrupted sexual arousal quite differently. Why have a part in turning something on that might be difficult to turn off?

When considering how much physical contact is appropriate, try answering these questions:
- How far would I go if Christ were in the room?

- Think of someone who really respects you, someone you would never want to disappoint. What would he think of you if he saw you engaged in the behavior in question with your date?
- Is there the possibility of you regretting what you have done?
- Am I being fair with the other person?
- Would I want my son or daughter to do the same thing?
- Don't let any part of another person's body come between you and your clothes.

How should I dress? The kind of decisions you make regarding dress may be among the most important dating decisions you make. Some folks see modesty as a subject primarily concerned with swimsuits, bikinis, low cut dresses, bare-chested men, tight fitting jeans, short-shorts, and such like. But the Scriptures teach that there are two things that are to influence how a person dresses (1 Tim. 2:9). The first is an attitude of reverence and respect that would not dare challenge the limits of what is proper. The second is good judgment, defined by self-control and decency.

What we wear is an expression of character and heart. Since we will choose clothes that agree with the kind of person we are, then clearly the right place to start is on the inside. If one has built within himself a sense of modesty, respect, reverence for God, good judgment, self-control, and concern for his influence, then making decisions about dress will be far less difficult.

God has provided man with an understandable and just standard in determining how to dress. "In like manner also, that women adorn themselves in modest apparel, with shamefacedness and sobriety; not with broided hair, or gold, or pearls, or costly array; but (which becometh women professing godliness) with good works" (1 Tim. 2:9-10). This standard is neither difficult to understand nor apply.

Two things are to be with a person when they decide what to wear: (a) an attitude that would not dare challenge the limits of what is proper and (b) good judgment controlled by self-control and decency. What we choose to wear is an expression of character. What we wear should reflect well upon our identity as a child of God and reflect the moral purity for which we strive.

In light of these principles, there is no scriptural way to justify wearing any kind of sexually revealing or provocative clothing. There is nothing decent, restrained, or sound in such things as swimsuits, halter tops, bare midriff blouses, skirts with slits, low-cut blouses, or revealing shorts, etc. Such apparel shows disrespect for the wearer and places a stumbling block before those who might see them. They reveal an attitude of heart that is dangerous and ungodly.

The object is not to see how little we can get by with wearing. We are not to see how close we can get to immodesty without crossing the line. If that's your attitude or approach to dress than you have some serious spiritual problems. Certain types of dress are going to cause problems on a date. Some clothing conveys a very strong sexual message. Why light a fire you don't want to burn? What you wear will convey a message. If it is tight where it ought to be loose, don't wear it. If it is short where it ought to be long, don't wear it. If it is revealing where it ought to be concealing, don't wear it. (Better yet, don't buy it!)

Dating should be fun. It should be exciting. It should be carefree. If the time you spend together leaves you enriched, encouraged, relaxed, if it brings glory to the Lord, then you know it is time well spent.

Date Rape

We live in a different and more dangerous world than when I was a teen. Within the last decade, date rape has become a serious problem in America. Date rape is an appalling crime that is committed at a shocking rate of every two minutes in North America. Date Rape can be coerced both physically and emotionally. Some emotional tactics include: threats to reputation, threats to "not like you," name calling, saying you "brought it on" or "really want it," threats to break up and threats to say you "did it" even if you didn't. There are certain "date rape" drugs that render the victim unconscious and limit memory; using these drugs on somebody is not simply "date rape" but a federal crime with a possible twenty-year sentence. Rohypnol, GHB, "ActiveSeX," "Roofies," "Ruffies," "Roche," "R-2," "Rib" and "Rope" are all names describing a date rape drug. These drugs are odorless and tasteless and difficult to detect when in drinks or mixed with other drugs.

The introduction of date rape drugs into mainstream culture has put a very powerful weapon in the hands of sexual predators. Rapes can be easily committed behind a foggy haze of intoxication often leaving the victim oblivious to the fact she has been assaulted. It is a frightening thought that begs the question: "What, if anything, can be done to stop a person from falling victim to a rape using a date rape drug?" Let me share a few common sense suggestions that unfortunately will not eliminate the possibility of date rape, but will greatly reduce the likelihood.

- Do not attend parties where you know alcohol will be served. If you attend a party and alcohol is being served, leave immediately. Date rape drugs mixed with alcohol are extremely dangerous.
- Don't accept open drinks from others whom you do not know or do not trust; this includes drinks that come in a glass.
- Never leave your drink unattended or turn your back on your table.
- Keep your eyes and ears open; if there is talk of date rape drugs or if friends seem intoxicated, leave the party immediately and don't go back!
- Remember, any kind of beverage can be drugged; there is no taste or smell. If your drink tastes or looks differently than it should, or tastes "funny" or salty; if it is foamy, cloudy, or has residue in it, throw it away.
- Don't go to parties alone. Travel in a group of people and stick together at a party. Look out not only for yourself, but your female friends.
- Don't let your friend disappear and don't let her wander off with a member of the opposite sex. Stay by her side. Don't leave with someone you do not know well or have just met.
- Keep a cell phone with you and charged up in the event you have a problem and need help.

Drugs and/or Alcohol on Dates

Do I really need to address this? Is there anyone reading this lecture that is so naïve as to think that drug use or alcohol use on a date is a good idea? If so, wake up! Alcohol depresses one's inhibitions, lowers one's ability to make sound judgments, and makes self-control nearly impossible. If your date is trying to get you to drink, consider that they may want to do more than just "loosen you up." Consider the words of the wise man: "Wine is a mocker, strong drink a brawler, And whoever is intoxicated by it is not wise" (Prov. 20:1). Earlier allusion was made to Proverbs 6:27 and the fact that one cannot "take fire in his bosom and his clothes not be burned." Alcohol is a "fire" that will surely burn one in the end.

Making wise and morally responsible decisions while on a date can be difficult enough while stone-cold sober. Why take the risk making a fool out of oneself by introducing alcohol into the mix?

What If I Mess Up?

It might be that you have already fallen prey to temptation, and you are facing the difficult question of what to do once you have "messed up." Right from the beginning it must be emphasized that fornication is no worse than any other sin. It does have consequences that are unique, but it does not make you a "worse sinner" than anyone else. Even David, a man after God's own heart (Acts 13:22), committed sexual sin. A man (or woman) after God's own heart will still make mistakes, but he (or she) will face those mistakes in a responsible and godly manner.

The First Step: Confession

As in the case of any sin, the first thing you must do is follow David's example and confess the sin to God. After Nathan confronted David, the king made this straight forward admission. "I have sinned against the Lord" (2 Sam. 12:13). David did not make excuses or shy from responsibility for what happened. He honestly confessed his sin. David later reflected on the blessing of forgiveness which resulted from his confession (Ps. 32:1). The same blessing of forgiveness is promised to all of God's children (1 John 1:9). This verse promises that we can be cleansed from all unrighteousness. The blood of Christ is more powerful than any sin.

Reaping What You Sow

When God forgives us, he does not remove all the consequences of our actions. Even though he forgave David, God told David that his son by Bathsheba would die, and he did (2 Sam. 12:13-14). There was nothing David could do to alter that consequence. Instead, he accepted the fact that he was reaping what he sowed, and he rededicated himself to God (2 Sam. 12:20). Once you have confessed your sin to God, like David you must resolve to bear the responsibility for your choices. It will be hard, but with God's help you will make it.

It is very possible that a pregnancy might result from your act of fornica-tion. Neither abortion nor abandonment is an acceptable choice for the one striving to please God. Neither choice reflects the natural affection which should exist for a baby. The Bible teaches that "children are a gift of the Lord" (Ps. 127:3). Children are precious in and of themselves, regardless of the way they are brought into the world. The fact is, they did not choose the circumstances of their conception, but you can choose how they will be treated.

Fornication is a two-party sin, and pregnancy should be a two-party responsibility. For the young lady, this means taking care of herself during the pregnancy. For the young man, this means doing what he can to assist the girl in her pregnancy. If you and your family are unable to care for the baby, contact an adoption agency. There are thousands of couples who dream of having a baby, and you can make their dreams come true.

To Marry or Not to Marry?

I have seen this scene replayed several times. A teenage couple commits fornication and the girl becomes pregnant. They decide to "do the right thing" and get married. Both have to drop out of school, she to carry the baby and he to get a job to support them. But without a high school education, he cannot find a job that pays enough to support a family, so he has to work two or three jobs. This means that he and his new wife have no time to spend together to develop a relationship. Neither possesses the maturity to be married, much less raise a child. After the child is born, the financial strain increases dramatically. Finally, the marriage crumbles and three lives are devastated.

Is this the way all "shotgun weddings" end? No, but the undeniable fact is that most shot-gun weddings usually backfire. Just because two people were willing to spend a moment of passion together does not mean they are ready for a lifetime of commitment. How should you decide whether to get married after fornication has occurred? The answer is really very simple: just make the decision the way you would if the sin had not taken place.

The Haunting Specter of Guilt

Whether or not a pregnancy occurs after sexual sin, guilt is a problem with which everyone who sins sexually must come to grips. Sometimes it is difficult to feel forgiven even after you have confessed your sin to God and know you are forgiven. Many young people who commit sexual sin understand exactly where David is coming from when he said, "For I know my transgressions, and my sin is ever before me" (Ps. 51:3).

Guilt turns the mind into an emotional torture chamber, but through God's word we can ease its torment. In the first place, God's word teaches us that mankind is "beset with weaknesses" (Heb. 5:2). We do not have to sin, but inevitably all of us do sin. Why punish yourself with guilt? Did you think that somehow you were better than everyone else who has "fallen short of the glory of God" (Rom. 3:23)? The fact that you have made a mistake does not mean you are a failure; it means you are a human.

If guilt is tormenting us even after we have confessed our sin to God, it is because we are thinking about ourselves too much and we are not thinking about God enough! Jesus once was confronted with a woman caught in the very act of adultery. His words to her should serve as his message to everyone who struggles with guilt. "Neither do I condemn you; go your way. From now on sin no more" (John 8:11).

Talking With Your Children About Sex

OK, Moms and Dads, try this quick child-rearing quiz: When it comes to sex, your teens want to learn the details from:

a) their friends
b) the latest Leonardo DiCaprio movie
c) you.

You might be stunned, and even a bit frightened, to learn the right answer is "c"—at least according to a recent national survey of more than 2,000 teens and their parents. The simple message from the study is that, whether parents believe it or not, teens want to hear from them about sex, intimacy and relationships. Parents have an incredibly important role when it comes to their children's sexual decision-making.

With four out of every ten girls in America getting pregnant before marriage, it is obvious that parents in the United States are not doing a particularly good job of talking with their teens about sex, and conveying biblical morals in a convincing manner. Even among "church-going" families the out-of-wedlock pregnancy rates barely lags behind the national average.

When should parents start talking to their kids about sex? And what should they say? There's no magic number in terms of age, but the reality is, if your child's body has physically matured, chances are good they're also having sexual thoughts and feelings. And contrary to popular practices talking to teens about sex shouldn't be a one-shot event. Instead of having "the big talk" have an ongoing discussions about sex with your children.

Children whose parents speak openly and listen carefully to them are less likely to engage in high-risk behavior as teens than kids who do not feel they can talk with their parents about the subject. If you are uncomfortable with the subject, read some books, talk with older, successful parents or discuss your approach with a trusted friend. The more you examine the subject, the more confident you'll feel discussing it. Even if you can't quite overcome your discomfort, don't worry about admitting it to your kids. It's okay to say something like, "You know, I'm uncomfortable talking about sex because my parents never talked with me about it. But I want us to be able to talk about anything—including sex—so please come to me if you have any questions. And if I don't know the answer, I'll find out."

Start early. Teaching your children about sex demands a gentle, continuous flow of information that should begin as early as possible, rather than the trauma of the "big talk." Use anatomically correct terms when referring to body parts with your children and begin doing so at an early age. As your child grows, you can continue their education by adding more materials gradually until they understand the subject well.

Take the initiative. If your child hasn't started asking questions about sex, look for a good opportunity to bring it up. Say, for instance, the mother of an eight-year-old's best friend is pregnant. You can say, "Did you notice that David's mommy's tummy is getting bigger? That's because she's going to have a baby and she's carrying it inside her. Do you know how the baby got inside her?" then let the conversation move from there.

Talk about more than the "Birds and the Bees." While our children need to know the biological facts about sex, they also need to understand that sexual relationships involve caring, concern, and responsibility. They need to know that sexual relationships within marriage are normal and God-designed. By discussing the spiritual and emotional aspects of a sexual relationship with your child, they will be better informed to make decisions later on and to resist peer pressure.

Give accurate, age-appropriate information. Talk about sex in a way that fits the age and stage of your child. You know your children and how much information your children need to satisfy their questions. Don't overload them, yet don't leave them guessing.

Anticipate the next stage of development. Children can get frightened and confused by the sudden changes their bodies begin to go through as they reach puberty. To help stop any anxiety, talk with your kids not only about their current stage of development but about the next stage, too.

Communicate your values. It's your responsibility as a parent to let your children know your values about sex. Although they may not adopt these values as they mature, at least they'll be aware of them as they struggle to figure out how they feel and want to behave.

Talk with your child of the opposite sex. Some parents feel uncomfortable talking with their child about topics like sex if the youngster is of the opposite gender. While that's certainly understandable, don't let it become an excuse to close off conversation. If you're a single mother of a son, for example, you can turn to books to help guide you or ask your doctor for some advice on how to bring up the topic with your child. You could also recruit an uncle or other close male friend or relative to discuss the subject with your child, provided there is already good, open communication between them. If there are two parents in the household, it might feel less awkward to have the dad talk with the boy and the mom with the girl. That's not a hard and fast rule, though. If you're comfortable talking with either sons or daughters, go right ahead. Just make sure that gender differences don't make subjects like sex taboo.

Relax. Don't worry about knowing all the answers to your children's questions; what you know is a lot less important than how you respond. If you can convey the message that no subject, including sex, is forbidden in your home, you'll be doing just fine.

Be prepared for a negative reaction. Hearing their parents talk about sex is every bit as difficult as talking with your children. Appropriate, respectful humor can help ease an otherwise tense situation.

Above all talk with your children. Don't let the world influence their sexual values.

(Unless otherwise noted all Bible quotations are from the New American Standard 1995 Updated Version.)

Dealing With the Loss
of a Parent
Jesse Flowers

What the Bible Says

There is no book, chapter, or verse in the Bible that outlines for the Christian how to deal with the loss of a parent. The principles are there. Some guidance is present. Comfort, of course, can be found throughout the Scriptures for the brokenhearted. But no manual is contained within its pages that explicitly reveals to a child how to cope with the loss of his mother or father.

Parents and Death in the Bible

The death of parents has been taking place as long as the departure of the very first parents of the human race. After Adam and Eve's transgression of God's law, Jehovah informed Adam, "In the sweat of your face you shall eat bread till you return to the ground, for out of it you were taken; for dust you are, and to dust you shall return" (Gen. 3:19). After sin entered the world by Adam, "death spread to all men" (Rom. 5:12). And so it is no surprise that in Genesis chapter 5 we find the refrain "and he died" a total of eight times. In other words, mothers and fathers (i.e., parents) were dying. In

---

Jesse A. Flowers was born on June 21, 1974 in Louisville, Kentucky. He is the son of Jesse E. and Charlotte Flowers. His father, Jesse E. Flowers, was a preacher of the gospel until the day of his death. The younger Jesse preached his first two sermons with his father in the audience. He attended both Florida College and Western Kentucky University. Jesse has worked with churches in Kentucky, Indiana, Canada, Missouri, Texas, and Florida. He met his wife, April, when he moved to work with the Trilacoochee church of Christ in Dade City, Florida in May of 2003.

these pages of the Bible it does not mention any grieving or mourning by the children over the loss of their parents. It does not mention any families coming together to comfort one another or any funeral services taking place for that matter. It just simply mentions death as a fact of life. We all have an appointment with our enemy death (Heb. 9:27). Grandparents do. Parents do. Children do. Grandchildren do. And so on. No one escapes.

The Deaths of Abraham, Isaac, and Jacob. The big three; the great patriarchs of old. The enormity of the impact of the lives of these men is to some degree realized when we notice *who* it was that mentioned them in Scripture. God did so first in the burning bush passage. Four times he announced to Moses that "I am the God of your father Abraham, the God of Isaac, and the God of Jacob" (Exod. 3:6, 15, 16; 4:5). The Son of God refers to this very text when addressing the Sadducees' erroneous teaching on the resurrection (Matt. 22:32). The apostle Peter referenced the three Jewish patriarchs in his second gospel sermon (Acts 3:13). And in Stephen's fiery defense before the Sanhedrin, this Holy Spirit filled-man also made mention of Jehovah's grand affirmation to Moses in the book of Exodus (Acts 7:32).

To *Abraham* were born two sons, Ishmael and Isaac. Hagar, Sarah's maidservant, conceived Ishmael (Gen. 16). Fourteen years later Sarah, the wife of Abraham, finally conceived a child as God had promised and gave birth to Isaac (Gen. 21:1-7). These two half-brothers were not particularly close to one another, but they no doubt both loved and admired their father. We read in the book of Genesis of these two being together after the death of Abraham when they came to bury him in the cave of Machpelah (Gen. 25:9).

To *Isaac* and Rebekah were born the twin sons, Esau and Jacob (Gen. 25:21-26). As any student of the Bible knows, these two brothers had a very strained relationship. Neither had much to do with the other in their adult years. But when Isaac their father died, these two sons came together to bury the father they both adored (Gen. 35:27-29).

To *Jacob* were born twelve sons who went on to represent the twelve tribes of Israel. After Joseph had revealed himself to his brothers, he brought his father Jacob and all the family to dwell in the land of Egypt. When Jacob's time of departure came he made known to his sons his wishes concerning his burial arrangements (Gen. 49:29-33). Genesis 50 provides for the first time to readers the mention of actual weeping and mourning taking place over the loss of a parent. "Then Joseph fell on his father's face, and wept over him, and kissed him" (Gen. 50:1). In fact, "the Egyptians mourned for him seventy days" (Gen. 50:3). As the family, along with many Egyptians, traveled up to the cave of Macpelah to bury Jacob, "they came to the threshing floor of Atad, which is beyond the Jordan, and they mourned there with a great and very solemn lamentation. He observed seven days of mourning for his father. And when the inhabitants of the land, the Canaanites, saw the mourning at the threshing floor of Atad, they said, 'This is a deep mourning of the Egyptians'" (Gen. 50:10-11).

A Great and Very Solemn Lamentation. Many families have experienced "a great and very solemn lamentation" at the passing of a father or mother. One of the most heart-wrenching events to undergo in life is the loss of a parent or parents. This is not just something that I've heard or have been told, it is something that I have lived. My experience, though very real and personal to me, is but a drop in the ocean of children who have lost their parents to death. Every year, between ten and fifteen million American children experience the death of a parent (Akner 57). Grief does not discriminate. So the story I have to share with you is in no way unique or different from all others, but I relate it to you just the same.

This August it will have been fourteen years since my father, Jesse Edward Flowers, passed away. He suffered a massive heart attack in the summer of 1984, and then eight years later an aneurysm took his life. A lot of changes took place in the family's life after his heart attack in 1984. Dad could no longer preach full-time, though he preached occasionally when he was able. Mom became the primary breadwinner for the family by going to work in a factory. Dad's diet changed drastically and so did the rest of ours. As the only son in the family, I took on a lot more responsibility around the house. But soon we all adjusted to the changes brought about by Dad's heart attack. But nothing could have prepared me for the news that I received the evening of August 20, 1992. Dad had died earlier that day at the age of 51. My world, that seemed fairly normal and routine at the time, was instantly thrown upside down and into a state of confusion.

The Parent-Child Relationship

Without a doubt the relationship that exists between a parent and child is very unique and special. In God's great wisdom, he instituted the home from the very beginning of creation (Matt. 19:4). The Scriptures speak of the blessedness of the man that has many children. "Behold, children are a heritage from the Lord, the fruit of the womb is a reward. Like arrows in the hand of a warrior, so are the children of one's youth. Happy is the man who has his quiver full of them; they shall not be ashamed, but shall speak with their enemies in the gate" (Ps. 127:3-5). There is no relationship on earth that can successfully take the place of parent and child. There is a special bond between them like no other. And so when death takes one or both of the parents away, the child is dramatically impacted in a number of ways.

1. Your parents are irreplaceable. You've known your mother and father longer than anyone else. From your very first day on this earth they've taken care of you. You were entirely dependent upon them throughout childhood, and sometimes to an extent even as a young adult. ". . . when your parents die, there is no replacement. You only have one mother and father. Even the word *mother* has a special meaning; to be mothered is to be comforted, cared for, embraced. When a parent dies, an emotional umbilical cord is cut" (Akner 58).

2. Your relationship with your parents is the one upon which all others are based. From your parents is where you learn about God and your Savior, Jesus Christ. It is from them that you receive your primary spiritual instruction and guidance (Deut. 6:6-9; Prov. 22:6; Eph. 6:4). Your value system derives from them. It is in the home that you are taught to be a social being. "Every other relationship you develop is built in some way upon this foundation" (Akner 59).

3. You believe in your parents' unconditional love. A parent is the only person in the child's life who really offers him unconditional love. Most parents would gladly do anything, anytime, anywhere for their son or daughter. Even when a parent disapproves of a child's action, their love will always be present (Luke 15:20-24).

4. A parent's death is an encounter with mortality. "A parent's death only underscores what they're already feeling—that life comes to an end" (Akner 60). A child, especially a young one, never envisions his parent not being alive. I know I did not. So when a parent dies, the child is faced with a rude awakening concerning his or her own mortality as well.

In the book, *How to Survive the Loss of a Parent*, Lois Akner states:
People say the death of a parent is the toughest thing they've ever faced.

It causes emotional and physical collapse, dredges up guilt, and can spur dramatic change. Once a parent dies, you never have another chance to have the relationship you wanted. You feel regret for the missed opportunities, the absence of the parent in your life. People may try to comfort you, and even tell you it was for the best if your parent was very ill. But knowing something intellectually doesn't calm you. Logic doesn't reduce anxiety or any other strong emotion (60-61).

Young Children and a Parent's Death

There is a significant difference between a child who loses a parent who is in their 40s or 50s and a child who loses a parent that is in their 70s or 80s (Myers 53). When a parent dies young, the death is thought of as being premature and tragic. When a parent dies much later in life, it is much more expected and accepted. Based on a report in 1984 by the National Academy of Sciences, the children most deeply affected by a death in their immediate family are usually young children who have lost their mothers, or teenagers whose fathers have died (Schaefer 41).

In my family there are four children—three girls and one boy. At the time of Dad's massive heart attack in 1984 I was ten years old. The youngest was five. And my two older sisters were 11 and 15. So when Dad suddenly died in 1992, three of us children were just teenagers. We were still relatively young, and so was Dad when he left us.

In his book, *How Do We Tell the Children?*, Dr. Schaefer states:

Children grieve differently from adults. Instead of experiencing intense distress, many children are likely at first to deny the death, then grieve intermittently for many years. Experts point out that because of this, they can suffer emotional disturbances that carry over into adulthood (43).

Dr. John Bowlby worked with bereaved children at the Tavistock Clinic in London. During that time he observed that there were three basic stages of grief that most children experience: protest, pain, and finally hope (Schaefer 107). *Protest,* in that the young child refuses to accept that the person is really gone and tries to get him or her back. *Pain,* in that when the child realizes their loved one has indeed died and is not coming back, they may be overwhelmed with pain. Their pain may come in various forms such as: feelings of anger, guilt, loneliness, and depression. *Hope,* that in spite of how much love they still feel for that departed person, the child will be able to move on with his life—the good days outnumber the bad (Schaefer 108, 110).

One very interesting thing that Dr. Schaefer mentioned in his book was how different the behavior of a teenager can be in handling his or her grief. At that age in particular, teenagers are very concerned with their image and what their other peers think of them. Yes, even in the difficult circumstances of death a teenager's mind can still operate in this fashion. Sometimes when they actually are confused and screaming out on the inside, they appear quite strong, collected, and cool on the outside. They certainly do not want their classmates to see them crying (Schaefer 118-119). I remember conducting myself in a very similar way at my father's funeral. There were friends of mine from high school present that day. And I recall doing my best to keep it together in front of them; to be cool; to remain calm; to try to carry on normal conversations with them. It was very hard to do so when all I was really doing was pretending.

The Individuality of Grief

"Everyone can master a grief but he that has it," said William Shakespeare (Akner 23). Not any one person grieves in the same exact manner as another. One child may break down in loud sobs of wailing at the death of a parent, while another child may simply sit there in stone silence, seemingly emotionless, though screaming out in despair on the inside. Some children will shed a lot of tears when the death first occurs, while others do not until the actual funeral, some time beyond that event, or not at all.

In his book, *When Parents Die*, Edward Myers wrote:

> The grief process is also highly individual. There is no reason why your experience should necessarily resemble what someone else goes through. After all, your relationship with your parents was unique; when your parent dies, your sense of loss will be unique as well. . . . For this reason, you should remember that you don't owe anyone any particular emotion, expression, set of words, or gestures during the course of your grief process. If people around you imply that you seem insufficiently grief-stricken—perhaps you're not crying "enough"—then their reaction has more to do with their own expectations than with your feelings. Likewise if you get the message that you're too emotional, too upset, or too sad. . . . Nobody can decide what your parent's life meant to you, the same holds true for your parent's death (17-18).

The Emotions Experienced

Death takes away. That's all there is to it. But grief gives back. By experiencing it, we are not simply eroded by pain. Rather, we become larger human beings, more compassionate, more aware, more able to help others, more able to help ourselves (Candy Lightner from Akner 193).

Shock. At least this is the emotion that I first remember occurring at the news of my father's death. I was completely shell-shocked. Yes, Dad suffered from heart disease, but things seemed normal that morning when I told him good-bye. He certainly had his good and bad days, but that day seemed fine. It had been eight years since he almost died, and so I had no thought or feeling leading up to the day of his death that the family had but few precious moments remaining in his company. So to me, there was no warning. It happened suddenly with no indications. Dr. Beverly Raphael, an Australian psychiatrist, stated that during a period of shock, "The bereaved person feels a sense of unreality, as though . . . it must be happening to someone else. The bereaved may feel distance from the horror and its implications, frozen in time. There is a feeling of being in a dream or a nightmare from which he will awake" (*When Parents Die* 19). It is hard for a child to fathom that a parent so full of life and energy at one moment could be totally gone the next. It just doesn't seem real.

Denial and Disbelief. Connected to this feeling of shock are the feelings of denial and disbelief. When my aunt, Dad's sister, informed us of his death I just could not believe what my ears were hearing. None of us could. It sounded so foreign, so out of place, so wrong. I did not want to accept it. So I refused to at first. There had to be a mistake, some kind of mix-up. I kept expecting the facts to change. The idea, the concept, that Dad was no longer with us was entirely incomprehensible in my mind.

> How could someone who had been so thoroughly with us now be gone? How could someone who had been so alive now be dead? How could someone who was so substantial now be nothing? (Edwards 62).

Sadness and Depression. How can a child not feel sadness and depression when his mother or father is no longer with him? It is only a natural human response to express grief and sorrow when a loved one has been taken from us. David expressed his great grief over the death of his rebellious son Absalom (2 Sam. 18:33); the widow of Nain who lost her only son wept of course (Luke 7:12-12); Mary, Martha, and other friends wept over the death of Lazarus (John 11:33); even Jesus wept at the gravesite of his good friend Lazarus (John 11:35).

Almost all bereaved daughters and sons find that their sadness and depression let up after a while, and that the pain they feel gradually gives way to more comfortable emotions (Edwards 21).

Regret and Guilt. Feelings of regret and guilt in life are only intensified when a loved one dies. Perhaps you regret not spending more time with your mother or father. Perhaps you feel guilty about the last conversation you had with them, and now realize you cannot go to them to make it better. Maybe you wish you had expressed your love and appreciation of them more.

It seems almost impossible to love your parents and not end up feeling guilty when they endure a harsh illness or a sudden death. You want to make a difference for them, but can't—or at least you can't to the degree that you would have liked. And so the guilt and regret well up. They may be subtle; they may be intense. But they are there (Edwards 24).

Anger. I recognize that every child who loses a parent does not necessarily feel anger, but I did. Not far behind my feelings of shock and disbelief at the announcement of Dad's passing came anger. I was angry. I was upset. And ashamedly I directed the majority of that anger towards God. I cried out to him for the reason why he allowed Dad to die. "Why did you take him? Why God? Why?" I didn't understand. I was completely and utterly confused. And so I wanted answers right then. The feelings of anger did not last long, however, but they were present nonetheless. It just didn't seem fair for Dad to be taken from us so soon. Thus the anger.

Longing. Another common emotion many experience following the death of a loved one is longing. We miss them. We want them back. We want to enjoy their presence once again. Sometimes that longing can grow very intense. I miss my dad. Not a day goes by that he is not in my thoughts one way or another. Some days are more difficult than others when I really long to see him and talk to him once again. I miss watching sports with him. I miss hearing him describe in detail various Civil War battles. I miss his laughter. I miss his spiritual influence and guidance. I even miss him giving me jobs around the house to do. I long to be with him again!

Although the images and memories of your parent's death may haunt you for a long time, they will diminish after a while. You will eventually regain a sense of stability and continuity within your life. You will gain a sense of the past and its place in your family. You will develop a new sense of who your parent was, and of what he or she gave you during your time together (Edwards 78-79).

When those we love die, we remain poised to feel, act, think, expect, and hope as if they were still with us. We hurt as we meet their absence again and again in public places and in intimate corners of our lives. *We long for the past* (emphasis mine, jf) or for their return so that our feelings, actions, thoughts, expectations, and hopes might again find their targets (Attig 22).

The Funeral and Burial
We live by losing and leaving and letting go, and sooner or later, with more or less pain, we must all come to know that loss is indeed a lifelong human condition (Judith Viorst from Akner 99).

Solomon spoke this profound truth long ago: "Better to go to the house of mourning than to go to the house of feasting, for that is the end of all men; and the living will take it to heart" (Eccl. 7:2). Funerals are not easy for anyone, especially for those family members and friends who were particularly close to the deceased. But as the Bible teaches, one can gain more benefit from a funeral than he can from a feast. We do take such somber occasions to heart. Death has a way of capturing our undivided attention like nothing else in life. If we have been sleepwalking, it has a way of shaking us back to the reality of the brevity of life (Jas. 4:13-15). We are forced to contemplate our own mortality. And that is good for us, because it causes us to come to terms with what life is really all about (Eccl. 12:13-14).

But the funeral service can serve as a crucial step in the grief process. According to Dr. Raphael's *The Anatomy of Bereavement*, "Many bereaved people find this is a turning point where the full reality of the death hits directly home" (Edwards 107). During the funeral some, not everyone, but some finally allow their emotions to be unleashed. Sometimes during the stage of shock and disbelief, along with making the funeral arrangements, family and friends filing through the house—one does not have much of an opportunity for the death to really sink in. But often times at the funeral and gravesite the reality of it all finally settles in one's mind.

Dad died on a Thursday evening. His funeral service was on Saturday morning. He was later buried in a family cemetery the following Monday in Florida. I must admit my mind was seemingly in a thick fog during those days, especially Thursday through Saturday. It felt as if I were in a dream, a very bad dream that I hoped very much to awake from soon. I certainly have intact certain pieces of the events during that time, but much of it is still a big blur. All of which is understandable while I still existed in the shock and disbelief stages of my grief. I was asked right before the funeral services began if I would like to say anything. I was caught off guard by this question. A part of me felt like I should say something about the father whom I loved so much; that I owed that to him and those present that day. But I didn't know what to say. My mind was still in such a jumbled mess. There were times when I regretted that I didn't say something. I suppose I even felt some guilt about it in fact. However, my mind is clear now, it wasn't then.

There's no question that traditional funerals *potentially* serve an important purpose: to help you feel and express grief and loss (Edwards 109). But this did not happen to be the turning point for me in my grief; that was yet to come. Further, I believe the day Dad was buried was more difficult for me than the funeral. By that time the body that lay before us did not resemble my father. That is still not a pleasant memory for me. It was very tough to see them lower my father's casket into the ground. The reality of it all really hit home at that moment. Dad was not coming back. He was truly gone. I would not see him again. This was it, one last final goodbye.

The Sunday After

"While grief is fresh, every attempt to divert only irritates. You must wait till it be digested . . . ," said Samuel Johnson (Akner 77). The psalmist David sang: "Behold, how good and how pleasant it is for brethren to dwell together in unity!" (Ps. 133:1). I mentioned earlier, Dad died on a Thursday, the funeral was on Saturday, and then of course came the Lord's day. When we arrived at services that morning, I soon realized that this was the "therapy" and "counseling" that my heart so needed.

When I joined my family members and fellow brethren in worship to God, the thick gray clouds that had being resting upon me finally lifted. Being back at the place where my father had preached since I was a small boy meant a lot to me. I pictured him standing in the pulpit as he gave what would be his final sermons that ironically came from the Book of Ecclesiastes. Singing hymns of praise helped revive my dampened spirit (Col. 3:16). "Sing praise to the Lord, you saints of His, and give thanks at the remembrance of His holy name" (Ps. 30:4). All of God's children gathered that day sent up unified prayers that brought me "the peace of God, which surpasses all understanding" (Phil. 4:6-7). Feeding upon the eternal words of life (John 6:68) provided me the nourishment my spirit was craving (Matt. 4:4; 5:6). I remember doing the Scripture reading that morning. Just reading the words of God aloud to the saints provided an inner healing that I was in great need of. "I will praise You forever, because You have done it; and in the presence of Your saints I will wait on Your name, for it is good" (Ps. 52:9). I will never forget, and I will always cherish in my memories the Sunday after.

Don't Forget the Others

In his chapter discussing *Family Changes,* the author Edward Myers had this to say:

> No doubt you and your family members share a sense of loss. But the person who has died has a special meaning for each person within your family; each family member has an individual way of feeling and expressing his or her own sense of loss; and sometimes these differences cause conflicts instead of harmony, isolation instead of solidarity. For instance, if your father has died, you are mourning the loss of a parent. Meanwhile, your mother is mourning the loss of her spouse. Both losses are emotionally difficult. But they are different losses in many ways. Yours is the loss of the man who helped to create you and nurture you; your mother's is the loss of the man she chose to be her mate. Although you have shared certain experiences that your father and her husband brought to your lives, your sense of that person will be drastically different. Even the experiences you shared may have different meanings for each of you (*When Parents Die* 127).

Perhaps what is forgotten in the midst of our own grief, is the grief that other family members are experiencing as well. Although there is a tremendous void in your life now, don't forget there is that same void in the other children's lives, and especially in the spouse left behind. I was eighteen years old when Dad died. My sisters, Laura and Jenny, were older, while Rachel was younger. And then there was Mom of course, who had been married to Dad for over twenty-five years. When a parent (or any loved-one for that matter) passes away it is very easy to focus only on self. "Woe is *me!*" No, woe is *everyone* who has suffered such a tragic loss. But without even realizing it we may think only of ourselves, and how *our* world has been turned upside down. And think, "How could this happen to *me?,*" when in reality it happened to a number of other family members too.

I believe this especially holds true for the surviving parent. Here is one who fell in love with your mother or father. These two have spent their lives together. They have experienced the good times and bad times, and weathered the storms of life hand in hand. Your mother and father were not only close companions in life, not just best friends in fact, but "one flesh" (Gen. 2:24). They go to sleep together, wake up together, make plans and fulfill goals and dreams together. They depend on one another for comfort and support. And so, if anyone feels a keen sense of loss, it is the spouse who has been left behind. Admittedly so, these were not thoughts I had nor understood at that time in August of 1992. Only years later (and still to this day) did I come to realize this particular truth.

At the time of my father's death I was confronted with a very difficult decision. I was ready to begin my first semester at Florida College (where my parents had first met). But now my Dad was gone and that seemed to change everything. I was torn between whether I should now remain at home (Kentucky) to help Mom out and be there for her, or continue on with my original plans of attending school in Florida. I asked Mom for her advice and counsel regarding the matter. She encouraged me to go ahead with my plans to attend F.C. For a long time after that I felt guilty over that decision. Everything turned out to be okay I suppose, but even to this day I wonder if I made the right decision, the best decision.

> But try to remember that widowhood or widowerhood involves one of the most difficult transitions that people ever experience. Your parent's grief process will take a long time—probably longer than yours will (Edwards 129).

So in the midst of your own grief, heartache and devastation, try to be there for all the family members, especially for your surviving parent. All I am trying to convey here is, don't forget the others!

Death Changes Everything!

"Death ends a life, but it does not end a relationship, which struggles on in the survivor's mind toward some resolution, some clear meaning, which it may never find," wrote Robert Anderson (Akner 137).

"Her absence is like the sky, spread over everything," wrote C.S. Lewis (Attig 198).

If you doubt this, then please take the time to read the story of the parent Jacob and the child Joseph. Do you remember Jacob's reaction when his other sons convincingly deceived him that Joseph had been killed? "And all his sons and all his daughters arose to comfort him; but he refused to be comforted, and he said, 'For I shall go down into the grave to my son in mourning.' Thus his father wept for him'" (Gen. 37:35). Now that part of the story by itself does not make the point, but by adding Jacob's reaction when he learns years later that his son Joseph is indeed alive does however. Listen to these words. "But when they told him all the words which Joseph had said to them, and when he saw the carts which Joseph had sent to carry him, *the spirit of Jacob their father revived*" (Gen. 45:27). An emptiness that had existed for such a long time inside of this parent, was immediately filled up with hope and vitality at the glorious news that Joseph his son was in fact alive and well.

In his book, The Heart of Grief, Thomas Attig writes:

> Our hearts ache when . . . we experience the death of someone we love. Our feelings, desires, motivations, habits, dispositions, expectations, and hopes aim in their direction as before. It is as if our love for them is suspended in midair with no place to land. Their absence frustrates us constantly. We have lived as if they would always be with us. Our pain and anguish derive in part from reminders of how we took their presence for granted in the intimate corners and public places where we knew them; they also derive from our sense that even the smallest part of the world that we know best is not ours to control.

> We realize helplessly that our daily lives can never be as they were. We will no longer see and be seen, hear and be heard, touch or be touched, or hold or be held by them. Nor will we share a room or a view, converse or wrangle, laugh or cry, break bread, walk or dance, hope or plan with them. We will not know them as they grow older, and they will not know us. We will no longer be party to their joys and sorrows, their successes or failures. Nor will they be party to ours.

> When someone we love dies, we lose their physical presence and all that it means to us. We lose the fulfillment of many desires, expectations, and hopes centered on them that we still carry within us. We lose our abilities to interact daily and to continue into the future with them as our habits, dispositions, and motivations still incline us. We begin the rest of our lives without them ready to go on as if they were still here. But we cannot, try as we might. In losing them, we have lost the possibility of going on as

we would have had they lived. A possibility is intangible. Yet, we feel the reality of that loss in the deepest recesses of our being (10-11).

We should never allow ourselves or others to underestimate, or dismiss the significance of, the loss of another's presence. Presence is one of the most precious things we can give one another. We sometimes learn most poignantly just how precious presence is when we lose someone. We simply cannot have things as they were before death intervened. Momentous change alters permanently the worlds we experience. Our familiar life patterns are irretrievable. Whatever story captures the unfolding of the days to come, it cannot be a story of a return to life just as it was. Our hearts ache with a kind of homesickness (Attig 11-12).

Cherish the Memories

I've never spoken to anyone who mourns for someone they love who does not want to continue loving them in some way (Attig xi).

The memory of your dear Father, instead of an agony, will yet be a sad sweet feeling in your heart, of a purer, and holier sort than you have known before –Abraham Lincoln (Attig 67).

Oh, how I cherish the memories of my father! As we sometimes sing in that grand old hymn: "Precious memories, how they linger, how they ever flood my soul, in the stillness of the midnight, precious, sacred scenes unfold" (*Precious Memories* 464). In dealing with the loss of a parent, I think it is quite helpful and comforting to grab a hold of the memories of your mother or father.

Conscious remembering and shared reminiscing enrich our present living. And they enable us to carry much of lasting value into the future. Memory allows us to reclaim and revive our appreciation of those we still love and the gifts they continue to give us. We can cherish their legacies here and now. We take delight in having known and loved them. As we cherish them, we experience again the praise, gratitude, and joy they bring to our hearts (Attig 111).

What is really neat is when others who knew him in life create some new memories of Dad for me. From time to time I will run into some old college classmates of his that relate a story (often humorous) that I never knew about. Then Grandma, Dad's mother who is still living, will relate stories to me of when he was a kid growing up. Stories that only she would know about as his mother. She will at times share with me old pictures and newspaper clippings of Dad that I did not know even existed. The memories of Dad she provides for me mean a great deal to me.

As my father did, I too decided to become an evangelist of the gospel. I unfortunately did not obey the gospel until I was seventeen, so I did not do much public speaking before Dad passed away. He was alive to hear me extend a few Wednesday night invitations and preach two sermons. He helped me quite a bit with that first sermon. Shortly after Dad died, Mom shared with me how proud Dad was of me preaching. She said she would look at Dad while I was up there speaking and his smiling face would be beaming with pride. That meant (and still does) more to me than perhaps she'll ever know. Of course, I have many of his books in my library now. I cherish his notes and markings in those books. I have a number of his sermons on paper and cassette tape. I cherish all these things. I cherish the memories.

> We will always ache for those who have died. But when the ache no longer dominates our experience, they have come into view again. We can embrace them still even while we are apart (C.S. Lewis from Attig 9).

Doing Things Their Way

Isn't it amazing how much of an influence a parent has in his child's development and thinking later in life? As children, we often think and even intend to not be anything like our mother or father. And then we grow up and soon realize how much we turned out to be just like Mom or Dad. Now, depending on the example and habits we picked up, this can be a good thing or a bad thing. In at least one area in Jacob's upbringing it was bad. His parents showed favoritism to him and his brother (Gen. 25:28), and later when he had his own family he too showed favoritism to Joseph (Gen. 37:3-4). And naturally this created a number of problems. On the other hand, a parent's teaching and example can be a great blessing. For instance, consider the example of Timothy. Paul wrote: "When I call to remembrance the genuine faith that is in you, which dwelt first in your grandmother Lois and your mother Eunice, and I am persuaded *is in you also*" (2 Tim. 1:5). Timothy would not have developed into the godly man that he was if it were not for the spiritual influence of his mother and grandmother (2 Tim. 3:14-15).

Of course, our faith in God is the most important instruction and influence we can receive from our parents. But we also receive a number of other less significant things from them. Habits that I have formed in my own life (mainly good I believe), likes and dislikes, are directly tied to doing things the way Mom and Dad did them. The way I plant flowers and other plants is the way Dad showed me time and time again. Being sure to wash my hands often and be conscientious of germs is because of the continuous emphasis about that by Mom. My love for history—Dad. Writing thank you notes—Mom. Etc.

> We learn many things from those we love. Sometimes they take time and trouble to teach us skills, help us develop our abilities, and refine our routines. They explicitly share techniques, secrets, tricks, and shortcuts and help us learn their way of doing things.
>
> At other times, we learn by observing what they do. We notice their habits and dispositions, the routines they follow, the strategies they develop. We learn from them by example. Sometimes, we consciously follow their example; often, we become like them in what we do without even realizing it . . . we share many of their interests and follow them in many ways.
>
> We watch and listen as our family members and friends do their work, perform chores, or take care of everyday business. Different ones teach us how to build, maintain, and repair things. To develop good work habits. To manage our time. To manage our money. To maintain a household. To see and create opportunities and make the best of them. To improvise and make do with what is available. To lead others. To follow.
>
> We learn from family members and friends as they interact with others. Some show us how to enjoy the company of others. To appreciate the gifts others offer us. To delight in conversation and activity together. To nurture and comfort a child. To keep love alive with a spouse. To maintain friendships. To welcome and entertain guests in our homes. To respect others. To make others laugh or smile. To protect ourselves and those we love. To break tension and diffuse anger. To mediate disputes and resolve conflicts. To support others in times of crisis. To comfort those who are less well off. To care for the sick or the elderly. To find satisfaction in volunteer service (Attig 179-180).
>
> As we cherish these legacies, we pay loving tribute to those who have died. We remember them as we enjoy activities and experiences as they once did and we sense that they are still with us in what we do. We pay them additional tribute when we introduce others, perhaps our children

or friends, to these activities and experiences. We extend their influence and open others' hearts to them.

In all these ways, those we love are with us in our day-to-day practical lives. But they also touch and nurture our souls and spirits—they influence our characters, our ways of being and becoming (Attig 188-189).

Express Thanks For the Time You Had

If I could give advice to someone else who has also lost a parent it would be this: Thank God for the time you did have with your mother or father. As I mentioned earlier, this was not my first response when the family received the news that Dad had died. Rather at that time I was in a state of shock, I was upset, and I wanted God to explain to me why he had taken Dad from us. It took a while for things in my life to return to some normalcy once again. It was not until things became more settled in my mind, that I began to have these kinds of thoughts.

That was when the "light" came on for me, and I realized how foolish I had been for questioning or blaming God in some way for Dad's death. Instead, from that moment on, I began thanking God for the time he allowed us to enjoy Dad here on earth. You see, Dad could have easily died that day in July of 1984 when he had the massive heart attack. But by God's good grace Dad was with us, and was an integral part of our lives, for eight more years. Because of this fact, Dad was there to celebrate with family and close friends twenty-five years of marriage to the love of his life. And he was there for the most important day of his children's lives. He was able to witness his four children obey the gospel of Jesus Christ. For all the things related to Dad that I thank my heavenly Father for, I thank and praise him most of all for this (Jonah 2:9; Col. 4:2)!

And let me say this to those children who are still fortunate enough to have both parents alive—do not take them for granted. Spend more time with them if possible. Write more. Call more. In other words, communicate with them more than you do now. Make sure they know how much you love them and appreciate them. Because as the days quickly fly by, there is less and less opportunity to be with and express those things to your parents. Do those things today, and later when they are gone you will have no regrets or feelings of guilt.

We remember what we respected, admired, and appreciated in the richness and depth of the caring and love we saw in them. We sense how we are different and better for having known and loved them.

We make use of deep lessons in living we have learned from them about how to be, not simply how to do. We treasure the irreplaceable gifts of lives now ended that make us ever different for having known them (Attig 206, 208).

Will We See Our Parents Again?

In her book, *How to Survive the Loss of a Parent*, Lois Akner writes: "Accept that your parent has died and a reunion is impossible" (107). Well, I have accepted that my father has died, but I have not accepted that a reunion with him is impossible. It really doesn't matter how Lois Akner answers this question, but what the Scriptures reveal on the matter.

Will we recognize and know our loved ones? Will they know us? I believe there is sufficient evidence in the Bible to answer this question in the affirmative. More than likely, some brethren will disagree with me on this, and that is fine. But I would like to share with you a few passages of Scripture as to why I hold this particular conviction.

1 Thessalonians 4:13-18. The apostle Paul says that as Christians we do not sorrow like those of the world who have no hope. When Jesus returns those who have died in Christ will be resurrected. And those of us who remain alive on the earth at that time will be "caught up together with them in the clouds to meet the Lord in the air. And thus we shall always be with the Lord." There will be a reunion of sorts that day with those who have gone on before us. We will be together again. Certainly we can comfort each other with such words as these!

Matthew 22:23-33. Jesus corrects the Sadducees' mistaken view of life after death. The Lord does inform us that we will not continue in the same family units as we did upon earth. We will be like angels. God *is presently* the God of Abraham, Isaac, and Jacob. Even in death these three great patriarchs of old have not lost their identity!

Luke 9:28-36. At the Mount of Transfiguration, Moses and Elijah appeared and conversed with Christ. Is it not interesting that according to verse 33, Peter recognizes the great Lawgiver and prophet when he makes mention of them to Jesus?

Luke 13:23-28. The Lord teaches some here about the future judgment. And he says that the reason for the weeping and gnashing of teeth by the lost will be because they "see Abraham and Isaac and Jacob and all the prophets in the kingdom of God, and yourselves thrust out." Even the unrighteous knew with certainty the identity of Abraham, Isaac, and Jacob.

Based upon passages such as these in the Bible, I do believe we will not only see our parents again, but know them in our resurrected state. Will our relationship to them change? Yes, of course. The human relationship of parent and child will have ceased to be. But we will know one another in a much more glorious way!

> Let not your heart be troubled; you believe in God, believe also in Me. In My Father's house are many mansions; if it were not so, I would have told you. I go to prepare a place for you. And if I go and prepare a place for you, I will come again and receive you to Myself; that where I am, there you may be also. And where I go you know, and the way you know (John 14:1-4).

Jesus said to her, "I am the resurrection and the life. He who believes in Me, though he may die, he shall live. And whoever lives and believes in Me shall never die. Do you believe this?" (John 11:25-26).

Your father shall rise again. Your mother will rise again. Do you believe this?

My Mother: A Worthy Woman

I would be amiss if I did not say something more here about my godly mother. "A worthy woman who can find? For her price is far above rubies?" (Prov. 31:10). Without a moment's hesitation, my sisters and I would stand united in affirming that our mother's value to us is far, far above that of rubies. As children we were incredibly blessed to have parents that "were both righteous before God, walking in all the commandments and ordinances of the Lord blameless" (Luke 1:6).

As I think back upon the day that we lost Dad (and the days that followed), I think of my mother's steady, abiding strength. Yes, her heart was broken. Yes, she wept with great sorrow. But in the midst of her great pain and emptiness she remained strong for us, her children. Now as I look back on that time through the eyes of an adult it becomes abundantly clear that she was indeed a spiritual and emotional rock for us. As we all tried our best to adjust in our lives to the loss of Dad, Mom would express her concern whether we were all right. Her worries were focused more outward than inward.

She continued to work full-time at the factory. It was (and is) hard work. Ungodly co-workers surrounded her. Some treated her cruelly. And when she came home, Dad was no longer there to listen, hug her, or respond with a comforting word. Mom continued to provide very adequately for the needs of her four children: food, clothing, doctor visits, our education, etc. She has been too good to us.

I have never seen her faith in God waver. Even when she was filled with exhaustion from working overtime, she never missed assembling with the brethren to worship God. She is a faithful Christian in every sense of the word. She is our "Eunice" and always will be (2 Tim. 1:5). I have often heard Mom say that we, her children (and now grandchildren) are her life. With Dad gone, her life revolves around our lives. We may be very special in her eyes, but her price is far above rubies in our eyes!

Bibliography
Akner, Lois F. *How to Survive the Loss of a Parent.* New York: William Morrow and Company, 1993.

Attig, Thomas. *The Heart of Grief.* New York: Oxford University Press, 2000.

Myers, Edward. *When Parents Die.* New York: Viking Penguin Inc.; 1986.

Schaefer, Dan and Christine Lyons. *How Do We Tell the Children?* New York: Newmarket Press, 1993.

Stevens, R.J. and Dane K. Shepard. *Hymns for Worship.* Bowling Green, KY: Guardian of Truth Foundation, 1999.

Causes of Divorce

Stan Adams

According to the Center for Disease Control's National Vital Statistics Report for 2002, "50% of first marriages end in divorce and 60% of remarriages ended in divorce. But the Center for Disease Control also found that 96% of Americans express a personal desire for marriage and about 75% of Americans believe marriage is a life-long commitment. The statistics on a worldwide basis are similar" (see "The World's Women, Trends and Statistics" UN, 2000 and "Recent Demographic Trends in Developed

---

Stanley Warren Adams was born on August 26, 1952, the third of four living children born to Wiley (faithful gospel preacher) and Wilma Adams (deceased July 28,1990). His brothers, Keith and Art, labor in part time preaching efforts and his sister, Paige, is married to Jim Deason who is a full time preacher. Stan has been blessed to be the husband of Carla Schoonmaker Adams, a true blessing from God. They married on February 20, 1976 and are the proud parents of three faithful Christian sons: Jared Wade married to Tracy with two daughters, Ashlyn, 7 and Micaiah, 2; Shaun Wesley married to Narey (expecting our third granddaughter, Anna Elizabeth, at any moment) and Matthew Warren 23 and single. Stan attended Florida College from 1970-74 and continued with his education at Montevallo University in Montevallo, Alabama. He worked in furniture sales for three years and preached part-time for the Bloomfield church in Macon, Georgia, before beginning his first full time work with the Elliottsville Church of Christ in Alabaster, Alabama in 1977. He has subsequently labored as a full time evangelist in Calera, Alabama; Lake Jackson, Texas; Edna, Texas; and presently preaches for

the East Hill Church of Christ in Pensacola, Florida. He has held meetings in Alabama, Arkansas, California, Colorado, Florida, Georgia, Indiana, Kentucky, Maryland, Mississippi, Missouri, North Carolina, Ohio, Oklahoma, Pennsylvania, South Carolina, Tennessee, Texas, Virginia and West Virginia. He has also written articles for *Truth Magazine* and *Searching the Scriptures*. He edits *Sound Words*, the monthly bulletin for the East Hill Church of Christ.

Countries," *Population-English Edition,* Vol. 57 [January-February 2002] also www.divorceform.org).

With these statistics one can be overwhelmed when contemplating marriage. All is not lost however. At the outset of this lecture let me advise caution to all who would use statistical data alone to prove that the institution of marriage is in trouble. Many recent statistics indicate that the divorce rate is declining overall (see "The Heart of Commitment" by Scott Stanley, University of Denver at www.divorceform.org/mel/rdivorceetc.html). Before we explore the causes for divorce let us stress that marriages need not be entered into under a cloud of doom and despair. Two godly people who seek answers to all of life's challenges from God can mend any breeches any scriptural marriage may encounter. We need to also stress that God did not author the Bible from an American viewpoint. His marriage laws and all others laws are universal and adequate for all civilizations throughout time. A constant struggle in our preaching and teaching is to be very aware of the danger of Americanizing the Bible.

There can be no doubt that marriage and the home, as God's divine institution, are under attack. All must be aware that Satan is out to destroy our homes. By following God's word all couples can build a hedge against Satan in their homes. What are the reasons given by those who go through divorce for the breakdown of their relationship?

In this country (which is the focus of most data) most states have varying laws defining the difference between "fault" and "no-fault" divorce.

If we were to ask one hundred people how they define viable reason for wanting a divorce, we would most likely get one hundred different answers because they would answer from their personal perspective. Most "reasons" given for divorce are little more than excuses and, if worked on, those "reasons" could be fixed by two mature people working together to stay married instead of to break up their marriage. People start looking for ways to escape marriage when they cease being committed to the marriage and the vows they took (Eccl. 5:4—"when thou vow a vow before God defer not to keep it for He has no pleasure in fools. . .").

Often many give flimsy reasons for splitting up because they refuse to accept the hard work necessary to address their deep-rooted problems. This can cause them to feel that their marriage is hopeless and cannot be fixed.

Let me be sure to stress, however, that mending hurt marriages takes two parties working on the problems together with God. Seldom is any problem one-sided. Many marriages stay damaged because one spouse wants the other to do all of the changing. Each one must be willing to bend and adjust for growth to be achieved and for conflicts to be resolved in a marriage.

We will first deal with what the experts say and with what statistics show. These are in no particular order but represent actual reasons given in numerous surveys, polls, and Census figures (Time/CNN Poll: Divorce from telephone poll May 7-8, 2003).

Worldly Reasons For Dissolving Marriage

1. Conflicting personal beliefs
2. Tired of marriage
3. Desertion
4. Adultery
5. Cruelty
6. Bigamy
7. Irreconcilable differences
8. Lack of communication
9. Money problems
10. Lack of commitment to marriage
11. Dramatic changes in priorities
12. Failed expectations
13. Addictions and substance abuse
14. Physical, sexual or emotional abuse
15. Lack of conflict resolving skills
16. Challenges with children
17. Worldly views of marriage
18. Religious differences (even between two Christians)
19. Media influence (Oprah says that "men are just going to cheat, it is the way they are")
20. Unreasonable expectations of what marriage is to be
21. Failure to keep dating
22. Falling out of love
23. Frivolous excuses: he/she snores; he is lazy; he/she is fat; she can't hunt; she can't cook
24. Computer misuse (pornography, intimate chat rooms)
25. Breakdown in intimacy issues

(*Reasons for Divorce: What Constitutes Viable Reasons for Thinking About or Wanting a Divorce,* by Karl Augustine http://www.selfgrowth. com/articles/Augustine8.html)

This list in no way is meant to represent all the reasons that people give for divorcing their spouse. Let us further observe that all of these reasons can be resolved if both are willing to do their part in resolving the issues that trouble their marriages by hard work and an appeal to the word of God. Remember that the innocent party has the right before God to divorce their spouse and marry another (Matt. 19:9; 5:32). Sometimes resolution is not an option, especially if the guilty party is not penitent.

Generally, marriage therapists consider the top eight most common reasons given when trying to resolve and heal a marriage. These eight are the most popular reasons given for splitting up. This list is helpful to all in suggesting eight areas all need to work on to keep their marriages strong, so they do not fail.

1. Poor communications
2. Financial problems
3. Lack of commitment to marriage
4. Dramatic change in priorities (spouse feels alone)
5. Infidelity
6. Addictions and substance abuse (particularly alcohol) often leading to physical, emotional, and sexual abuse
7. Failed expectations
8. Physical, sexual, or emotional abuse
(List from "Making Marriage Last," published by American Academy of Matrimonial Lawyers at http://www.aaml.org/Marriage.Last/Marriage LastText.htm)

A recent study by the Creighton University Center for Marriage and family suggests "TIME, SEX, MONEY and RELIGIOUS differences pose the biggest obstacles to satisfaction in the lives of newly married couples. The study goes on to say that debt brought into marriage, the couples' financial situation, balancing job and family and frequency of sexual activity were of greatest concern to those ages 29 and under. Those age 30 and over shared concerns of balancing job and family and frequency of sexual activity, but also added as problem areas constant bickering and expectations about household tasks. Other concerns were parent and in-law interaction, and time spent with the spouse talking" (www.creighton. edu/MarriageandFamily).

"One in 10 of the people who receive marriage guidance from the web-site RELATE each year, now blame the Internet for their problems"("RELATE says Internet to blame for relationship breakup" Monday 15th April 2002).

So why do people get divorced? The conventional wisdom on divorce is that it only happens after both parties have tried their hardest for a long period of time to save their marriage. But the findings of this survey suggest this may not be true. When asked the questions, "Do you wish you had worked harder to save the marriage?" and "Do you wish your ex-spouse had worked harder to save the marriage?" only 33% answered "no." Also 62% of ex-wives and ex-husbands answered "yes" to the questions.

According to the findings of our survey, it appears that for both men and women there may be a "peak marriage age" in the mid-twenties. People who get married between the ages of 23-27 are much less likely to get divorces than those who marry as teens; they are also much more likely to be high-quality marriages than people who marry in their late twenties or later. Those of the 23-27 age group responded this way: 69% said their marriages were very happy and 88% said they were completely or very satisfied with their marriages.

Marriages that were preceded by cohabitation are twice as likely to fail than those who were not ("NFI Releases Report on National Marriage Survey," article by: Vincent DiCaro, Public affairs Manager, *Fatherhood Today*: Volume 10, Issue 3, Summer 2005, 4-5).

Tom Strohl, president of Marriage Works Learning Center in Allentown, PA said, "Couples who stay together typically value marriage over themselves. Research shows it's not how much you love each other that predicts the success of marriage, but how you handle the problems that come along in life. Happily married couples view problems as 'us against the problem,' they identify themselves as a team" www.divorceform.org/mel/aqualityofmarr.html)

Religious Affiliation and Divorce Rates
(AP 12/30/99 1:31 AM Eastern Birmingham, AL [AP])
Baptists have the highest divorce rate of any "Christian" denomination,

and are more likely to get a divorce than atheists and agnostics, according to a national survey.

The survey conducted by BAMA Research Group of Ventura, California found that 29% of all adult Baptists have been through a divorce. Among the Christian groups, only those who attend non-denominational Protestant churches were more likely to be divorced, with a 34% rate.

Alabama has more than one million Southern Baptists, and the state ranks fourth nationally in divorce rates.

The Bama Research Group interviewed 3,853 adults from the 48 continental states. The survey found that while just 11% of the adult population is currently divorced, 25% of all adults have been through at least one divorce.

Of other religious groups, Catholics and Lutherans have the lowest divorce rate at 21%. People who attend other mainline Protestant groups have an overall divorce rate of 25%. Jews have a divorce rate of 30% and atheist and agnostics have a rate of 21%. Mormons are near the national average of 24% (http://www.divorceform.org/mel/rbaptisthigh.html).

Most Recent Figures:

Per Capita Annual—The last-reported U.S. divorce rate for a calendar year, available as of May 2005, is 0.38% divorces per capita per year (National Center for Health Statistics). The absolute annual divorce rate for the year ending November 4, 2004 is 0.37%. This rate is only for states that keep track of the number of divorces, California, Colorado, Indiana and Louisiana do not. Since every divorce involves two people, the percentage becomes somewhat more meaningful if you double it. E.g. 0.74% of the entire population gets divorces every year (www.divorcereform.org/rates.html).

From the National Center for Health Statistics and Census Bureau's Statistical Abstract of the U.S. Divorce Rate Statistics from 1991-2002:

1991-47%	1992-48%	1993-46%	1994-46%	1995-43%
1996-43%	1997-43%	1998-42%	1999-41%	2000-41%
2001-40%	2002-38%			

About 50% of first marriages for men under age 45 are projected to end in divorce and between 44 to 52% of womens' first marriages may end in divorce for these age groups. Approximately 75% of divorced people remarry within three years.

Most Vulnerable Periods

Marriages are most susceptible to divorce in the first eight years. The number of divorced people in the population of the U.S. more than quadrupled from 4.3 million in 1970 to 18.3 million in 1996 (Census Bureau report on Marital Status and Live-in Arrangements).

In our promiscuous culture, the marriage rate has fallen 30% since 1970 and the divorce rate has increased about 40% (Ahlburg and DeVita, "New Realities," 4-12. Cited on page 5 of the *Abolition of Marriage* by Maggie Gallagher).

Changing Times

In 1880, historian Robert Griswold observed fewer than 5% of marriages ended in divorce. The reasons were adultery, abandonment, abuse, and alcoholism. He further observes that by the mid 1960s the divorce rate began to rise dramatically, fueled by a vast expansion of women moving into the work force, the rebirth of feminism and the adoption of no-fault divorce in almost every state. Although "no-fault" was intended as a progressive step to end fraud, collusion, and acrimony that accompanied divorce, it has rather had disastrous consequences for women and children (Powell, D. (2003) Divorce on Demand: Forget about Gay Marriage—What About The State of Regular Marriage? *National Review*, v55i20).

Divorce Rate Dropping

"So if you are a reasonably well-educated person with decent income, come from an intact family, and are religious and marry after the age of 25 without having a baby first, your chances of divorce are very low indeed." "It should further be observed that the 50% divorce rate refers to percentages of marriages entered into during a particular year that are projected to end in divorce or separation before one spouse dies. Such projections assume that the divorce and death rates occurring that year will continue indefinitely into the future. . . the fact is that the divorce rate has been dropping slowly, since reaching a peak around 1980 and the rate could be lower (or higher) in the future than it is today" (Taken from Barbara Whitehead and David Popenoe's, *The State of Our Unions* (2004).

State-by-state Divorce Rates for 1994
(Lowest rate to highest rate)

1.	Massachusetts	2.4	26.	Kansas	4.7
2.	Connecticut	2.8	27.	Utah	4.7
3.	New Jersey	3.0	28.	Delaware	4.8
4.	Rhode Island	3.2	29.	Montana	4.9
5.	New York	3.3	30.	Missouri	5.0
6.	Pennsylvania	3.3	31.	W. Virginia	5.0
7.	Wisconsin	3.4	32.	N. Carolina	5.1
8.	N. Dakota	3.4	33.	Colorado	5.1
9.	Maryland	3.5	34.	Georgia	5.2
10.	Minnesota	3.6	35.	Oregon	5.3
11.	Louisiana est.	3.6	36.	Texas	5.4
12.	Illinois	3.7	37.	Alaska	5.5
13.	D.C	3.8	38.	Washington	5.6
14.	Iowa	3.9	39.	Mississippi	5.7
15.	Nebraska	4.0	40.	Kentucky	5.8
16.	Vermont	4.0	41.	Arizona	5.8
17.	Michigan	4.1	42.	Florida	5.9
18.	S. Dakota	4.2	43.	New Mexico	6.0
19.	S. Carolina	4.2	44.	Idaho	6.2
20.	Hawaii	4.2	45.	Alabama	6.2
21.	California, est.	4.3	46.	Indiana, est.	6.4
22.	Maine	4.3	47.	Wyoming	6.5
23.	New Hampshire	4.4	48.	Tennessee	6.6
24.	Ohio	4.5	49.	Oklahoma	6.7
25.	Virginia	4.6	50.	Arkansas	7.1
			51.	Nevada	9.0

Source: Monthly Vital Statistics Report, Vol. 43, No. 13, October 23, 1995, CDC , Rates are per 1,000 population in specified area).

For a state by state divorce chart see end of lesson.

These statistics argue that some are not committed to the institution of marriage. Consider what a few other "experts" presented as their view of why marriages fail.

James Long, Ph.D., P.E. Analog and RF Consulting Engineer observes that "today's high divorce rate is a result of parenting failures." He believes that if parents did a better job of informing their children what type of spouse to be looking for, many marriages would never have taken place. He further observes that many parents fail to instill sound moral principles in their children, because they are afraid or too busy to talk with their children. He concludes his thought by stating that "if someone is an unhappy single, they will most likely be unhappy as a married person."

He goes on to say that there are basically three reasons for failed marriages today: (1) Mobility, (2) Affluence, and (3) Isolation. "In times past, people lived and died in one geographic region and lived and worked among many relatives. Each spouse had many years to observe the person they were marrying and also to observe the interaction of that person's family. It was more likely for marriages to take place between two people who had shared values and aspirations in life. In the early part of the twentieth century and before, a couple considered one of their primary goals in life as survival. They teamed up to fight a common enemy: hunger, poverty and nature. Men would be gone on a cattle drive for several months and the wife ran the farm and family. There was little talk or no thought given to splitting up the marriage."

Dr. Long continues to observe that these factors also contribute to failed marriages:

1. Making assumptions instead of asking and communicating.
2. Unrealistic expectations.
3. Thinking someone will change after marriage. Traits disliked before marriage will become more intense after the marriage as a general rule.
4. Failure to listen to wise counsel.
5. Cultural differences.
6. Expecting God to straighten out our foolish decisions miraculously.
7. Thinking you will be the exception to the rule—this may happen but one needs to listen and apply the collective wisdom on any given subject.
8. Cast away concepts—If you make a bad decision you can always get another one.
9. Lack of patience and sound work ethic in dealing with challenges in marriage (http://www.analog-rf.com/marriage.shtml).

Choosing Poorly
Today, many are impressed by the wrong things when it comes to choos-

ing a spouse. You get one shot at this and you must make a commitment to your choice if you want to please God. Ladies, remember that some women needed the older women to "teach them to love their husband" (Tit. 2:4). Once one becomes a husband, God commands him to love his wife as Christ loved the church and gave himself for her (Eph. 5:25). He is further instructed in verses 28, 29, "So ought men to love their wife as their own bodies, he who loves his wife loves himself." If a man stops loving his wife, he has stopped loving himself and that is sin, according to God. Wives are commanded in Ephesians 5:22: "Wives submit yourselves to your own husbands, as unto the Lord." When making our choices for marriage we would do well to choose wisely, understanding that our choice is binding for life. Listen to the advice of those wiser than you and try to think with your mind for a while before you are overtaken and blinded to faults by the "luv-bug." Do not fall into these traps:

1. The Rescuer. Many women and a few men are drawn to someone who is broken. They get married, not so much for love as pity for the other person. They see themselves as the Redeemer and Rescuer of the person who is broken in so many ways. Many, who are otherwise sensible people, will choose a spouse who has severe mental or emotional problems. The drive to fix them wears off after a few years and resentment, anger and loneliness set in and move to destroy the union, and this arrangement is never satisfied until one person has 100% of the power/attention and the other is left empty with 0%. All you can give will not be enough.

2. Affluence. Many men and women are drawn to someone who can help them have a lot of "things." They base their choice of a spouse on whether they can give them a "cushy" life, instead of whether they can give them love and devotion. They find themselves lonely, empty, and angry after a few years as they sit in their mansion with all their things and realize their relationship is empty and unfulfilling.

3. Outward appearance. Some base marriage on how handsome or beautiful someone is outwardly. While no one intentionally goes out and tries to find the ugliest person in the world to marry, the Proverb writer tells us in Proverbs 31:30, "Favor is deceitful and beauty is vain, but a woman who fears the Lord, she shall be praised." The same holds true for a man. Certainly we should all care for our appearance and try to remain as appealing as possible for our spouse, but the fact is that beauty will diminish with time, and a marriage based solely on the shallow premise of outward appearance will become sad and empty.

4. Failure to think. After a person gets starry-eyed and goofy, it is too late to talk reasonably with them. Some couples fail to think about cultural differences, differing family experiences, and so on. Others get married thinking that "luv" can handle it all. They enter into marriage with the 50/50 concept, instead of the 100/100 concept of each one giving all to the other without thought as to how much they will get from the other.

5. A fantasy princess/prince view of love. Those who hold to this concept of love labor under the delusion that marriage and love are free from any conflicts or trials. They fail to consider that marriage is a series of growing and experiencing some hard lessons and some easy ones. Trials must be faced.

After the last expert has spoken, the last statistic has been computed, and long after everyone has given his opinion as to what causes divorce, God's word will remain the definitive work on marriage and the home.

God is clear for we learn, "For the Lord, the God of Israel saith that He hateth putting away" (Mal. 2:16). God is not happy with divorce, no matter what the cause. We would all do well in the church today to work harder trying to help couples stay together and hold their marriages together. Too often in our discussions on divorce and remarriage, we lose sight of this vital point: "God hates putting away."

A Christian Lawyer's Thoughts

David Oglesby, a close friend, Christian, and senior law partner with the Boloukus and Oglesby Law Firm in Birmingham, Alabama, tells many clients who come to him considering divorce, "If I see you once, I will most likely see you two or three times." Over half of his firm's business is divorce work. After many years of dealing with numerous clients, he believes that divorce solves very little. It is merely trading one set of problems for another. He believes and advises that all couples considering divorce need to have a "cooling off" period and seek sound counsel before pursuing divorce.

I asked Mr. Oglesby what his view was on what causes divorce and he said, "Divorce increased when women left the home to go to work." He told me I could quote him on this, and he also said that he believes many may disagree. He observed that as women leave the home, they are confronted with more alternatives. They often feel empowered by their income and independence, and they become dissatisfied with what they have at home. Men who work with more and more women, also have more opportunities to make their female co-workers their "buddies," as they travel and work closely together. Many naïve men and women foolishly believe, "nothing can happen, we are just friends." This often leads to sharing discontent about spouses and before one knows or realizes what is happening, infidelity occurs. Mr. Oglesby reflected on the differences in what many jokingly call the "June Cleaver" years and our modern world. There was a time in the 1940s and 50s when mom was always found at home. She may have been hard at work running the farm, but she was there for her husband and children (Prov. 31). A woman who was divorced in a community was "whispered" about. Divorce was a disgrace and almost always was due to infidelity. Times have changed. The world we live in is an expensive world. Many women work out of the home as a necessity and not because they want to have a career. Satan truly is winning the battle with many as he "goes about seeking whom he may devour" (1 Pet. 5:8). Many women work out of the home, not due to a need, but because of a desire to be independent of a man.

Mr. Oglesby went on to say that since no-fault divorce became law in many states, there has been a rise in the divorce rate until recently. The original intent of no-fault laws on divorce was to discourage slander of one another and to protect kids from ugly divorces. It has not worked that way. There is an active effort being made in the legal community to slow down divorces. Many lawyers are advising clients to seek "spiritual" guidance first before pursuing a divorce. The state of Florida gives a discount on a marriage license for couples that will go through a "preparation for marriage" course. Most gospel preachers are eligible to sign up as instructors. It costs little and opens many doors for the proclamation of God's word on marriage and getting contacts for future home studies.

Mr. Oglesby also told me that the average divorce was around $2500-3000 per person. He went on to tell of the tremendous expense of alimony, child-support, and other expenses. He knows of very few men with children who make enough money to survive two divorces. Some may cope with one, but two will most likely bankrupt the majority of men.

Is there really any "cause" for divorce? Biblically, the Lord was wise to let us know in Matthew 19:9 and Matthew 5:32 that there is only one biblical "cause" for divorce and remarriage. That "cause" is fornication. Even that can be worked out if two people are willing to repent, forgive, and move on.

Observations of Christian Marriages That Are Surviving Infidelity

In preparing this material I interviewed several Christian couples that have weathered the storm of infidelity. Here are their observations and comments.

> It is difficult, but love, commitment to the marriage and family stability helped us in our initial healing and these things plus prayer continue to carry us through.

> We never considered divorce an option, no matter what.

> I would do this one time but not twice.

> Rebuilding trust for the guilty party is the biggest challenge. Prayer and communication are what carries us through.

> The toughest thing is not being able to tell anyone about what has happened. Living with this secret is sometimes unbearable. Who do leaders in the church go to when they suffer these things? It is a day-by-day experience but when I consider what Jesus went through, it makes it easier to bear our burdens. It is so hard not to keep talking about it. When forgiveness has been granted the real challenge is to put sin behind, but it is hard.

> Building good communications and helping the guilty person to forgive themselves, while working on your own feelings is a real challenge. Love and commitment to our marriage and "seeking the kingdom first" are major considerations.

> It takes two people who are unselfish and willing to put their respect for God and his ways, above self, to get through infidelity.

> It only works if the guilty one is truly sorry for what has been done and has a willingness to admit it, ask forgiveness and be grateful for the chance to make it right.

> The guilty person needs to understand that intimacy will be difficult for a while, until trust is built back. Both parties must be patient and handle one another with care.

I considered my role in putting a stumblingblock in his way by not being as faithful to him in our intimacy as I should have been. I was willing to give it another chance as we both repented of our sin (he of fornication and me of being a stumblingblock). Trust in the Lord and commitment to marriage and the church, has helped us survive the devil's attack on our home.

What Does God Say?

God understood the pain of infidelity and realized that the breaking of that trust is the ultimate betrayal. God understands this because he dealt with the Israelites, who left him spiritually to go a "whoring" after the nations and gods of the heathen. Jeremiah 2:19-22 tells of this; "Thine own wickedness shall correct thee, and the backslidings shall reprove thee: know therefore and see that it is an evil thing and bitter, that you have forsaken the Lord thy God, and that my fear is not in you, saith the Lord God of hosts. For of old time I have broken thy yoke, and burst thy bands; and thou said I will not transgress; when upon every high hill and under every green tree thou wanderest, playing the harlot. Yet have I planted thee a noble vine, wholly a right seed, how then art thou turned into the degenerate plant of a strange vine unto me? For though thou wash thee with nitre and take thee much soap, yet thine iniquity is marked before me, saith the Lord God."

The Book of Hosea also shows the tenderness and love that is demanded in taking one back who has committed the most serious of violations toward their spouse. Hosea loved his wife, in spite of her infidelity with so many. It took a lot for him to take her back to himself. The relationship never was the same, but it was able to continue. Make no mistake, infidelity is sin and must be repented of. No one causes another person to commit fornication. It is an action taken by individual choice. "Let no man say when he is tempted, I am tempted of God, for God cannot be tempted with evil, neither does He tempt any man; but every man is tempted when he is drawn away of his own lust, and enticed. Then when lust hath conceived it brings forth sin; and sin when it is finished, brings forth death" (Jas. 1:13,15). Someone may present many stumblingblocks but the decision to sin is our own. It should also be observed that we are better than animals. We have self-control. We do not have to act on our passions. We are not to behave as animals. We are better than that. Even if opportunity for sin presents itself, there is a way of escape (1 Cor. 10:13).

Marriage is honorable and commitment to God and one another, along with an honest desire to please God in our marriage, should be at the top of our list. If one chooses to forgive their mate for infidelity, they can no longer use that instance of unfaithfulness as a later reason for divorce. In such instances, the forgiven fornicator should not have his/her sin always brought up.

People divorce because they can. They make a conscious decision that they will be better served by departing and severing the relationship than they will be to continue it. Women file 70-80% of all divorces. There are roughly one million divorces per year in the United States. There are two parties involved in every divorce, so that means divorce directly affects two million people per year. Add to that those indirectly affected (two sets of parents, children, brothers, sisters, cousins, and grandparents) and this adds up to an estimated ten million people each year affected by divorce.

The cost to society from divorce is high. Physical, emotional, and social problems cost all of us. Divorced people have a lower life expectancy and are more susceptible to a host of physical and emotional problems than a married person.

The "causes" for divorce are as varied as the people who petition for divorce. Each one believes he has a reason. To the Christian, God's word must be the final factor in seeing if we have authority for a divorce. One needs to think long and hard before he considers going through a divorce. Many divorced people wish they had given more effort to mending the relationship before they finalized the divorce. One of the strange things about two people seeking a divorce is that they usually still love one another. That is why the divorce is so painful.

It is a fact that alarming numbers of marriages are failing. Others survive. What makes the difference?

One couple married July 1945 in Virginia, survived for 45 years, in spite of severe money problems, health issues, job-related stress, and the usual everyday challenges. What made the marriage of Wiley and Wilma Adams successful? They were a team. To think of one is to think of the other. The same is true of Nollie and Joyner Adams, my grandparents, who were married for over sixty years. Commitment to God, one another, and marriage is the key to successful marriages. In both of these relationships, you will find that both ladies considered the success of their husband to be their own personal success. They truly lived for one another and are a shining example to all of how beautiful marriage can be.

There are also examples in the Bible of couples who remained together even though one or both parties had little or no respect for God. Ahab and Jezebel were both wicked and I imagine hard to live with, but for some reason they honored their commitment to one another. Athaliah, their daughter, also honored her marriage commitment to Jehoram (2 Kings 8:16, 17). If these two couples could honor marriage, then it is hard to imagine a situation arising, short of infidelity, which would justify the severing of a marriage today.

Marriage is to be for life. People should not be seeking "causes" to destroy those unions. Most couples vow to be with one another for "better or worse, in sickness and in health." Those promises are serious and constitute a covenant between us.

We must also note here that many who truly try to work out differences with their spouses and maintain and preserve their marriages, are sometimes unable to get the other person to abide by the Scriptures. Although resolution is the desired course of action, we must recognize that God ordained that the innocent party has a right to put away the guilty party (Matt. 19:9;5:32). Sometimes, in an effort to beat one another to the courthouse for the divorce, the preservation of a marriage is suspended and given little or no thought. Our hearts go out to all who have endured divorce. The innocent party should not be made to feel like a second-class citizen by brethren. They are innocent and clean before God, and we must not call on them to constantly be defending their status.

Marriages may fail because of the view one has about marriage. Some view it as a human arrangement only, but we must remember that is was God who instituted marriage. He called it good and gave laws to regulate it. God is the one who joins two people in marriage (Gen. 2:18-24; Matt. 19:2-6).

Some undertake marriage with little or no thought given to what God desires. Many live much like animals in their marriages. They are consumed by physical desires of all sorts and seem to have no greater desire in life than to gratify self. Others are careful not to get arrested for violence against their spouse, but short of this they recognize no rules in their marriage. They simply call on the other to please them and when they do not feel pleased they betray their spouse and the Lord. Selfishness is behind all divorces. One or both parties consider "me" more important than "us." Some exist as separate entities under the same roof.

Marriage must be considered a lifetime contract (Rom. 7:1-3; Matt. 19:9). To marry someone who does not care about what God's word says is to invite trouble. The marriage may survive, but who wants to live life hoping they will be the exception to the rule?

Conclusion

I firmly believe that behind every divorce that occurs there is one basic issue that kills marriages. It is so simple that we may often miss it. It is *selfishness* and a failure to have a servant spirit in practicing love toward one another in our homes as is described in 1 Corinthians 13:4-8a. Jesus said, "He who is greatest among you shall be your servant" (Matt. 23:11). Two people who truly desire to serve one another and are not selfishly looking for anything in return will do well in marriage. When either party gets more concerned about "me, me, me" than "us" then the marriage will suffer. Jesus showed us how to live unselfishly. Some preachers would do well to pay more attention to their wives and serve them better. Many preachers and elders' homes have been destroyed due to being consumed by the welfare of others and forgetting about the helper fit for them at home. Godly wives suffer in quiet submission longing for more attention from their husbands. Faithful, good husbands survive in a world where they are lonely and longing for an encouraging word from the love of their life. The theme for this lecture is "God Give Us Christian Homes." The highest level anyone will rise to in the Lord's church is servant!

If we will learn how properly to serve our spouses then we will come a long way in reducing the divorce rate among brethren and in bringing about happier, more content, and more productive brethren.

I am thankful to God who has blessed me with Carla. We have enjoyed over thirty years of marriage together. God has blessed us with three faithful, Christian sons, two of whom have married wonderful Christian ladies. Carla and I are blessed with three grandchildren, and the joys of our marriage continue. We are empty nesters now, but we are enjoying that chapter of our marriage together as we have enjoyed all stages. There have been tough times and there have been times when our commitment to the Lord and to marriage was challenged, as all marriages are. She is my best friend and the best part of me and we look forward to aging together. God knows how to look out for men like me and he knows how to bless your marriage also. Help make your spouse your best friend and trusted companion. God only asks that you trust him enough to let him guide your home. Joshua made a choice many years ago for his family in Joshua 24:15: ". . . but as for me and my house, we will serve the Lord." May we all make the same choice.

Marriage is work, but it is to be pleasant work. The fruit of a contented marriage is truly joyful. There is to be joy in marriage. May we all work on building up our marriages and not laboring to try to find some "loophole cause" for splitting up our homes. "God hates putting away" (Mal. 2:16).

State Specific Divorce Information Chart

State	Residency Requirements	No-Fault Grounds	Waiting Period
Alabama	The filing source must be resident of the state for at least 6 months prior to filing the action if other spouse is a non-resident; no waiting period is required if both spouses are residents of Alabama.	Irretrievable breakdown of the marriage or voluntary separation for 1 year; or complete incompatibility of temperament.	30 day waiting period after filing the action before the court may issue a judgment granting the divorce.
Alaska	The filing source (the one who is filing the divorcements) must be a resident of Alaska.	Incompatibility of temperament resulting in irremediable breakdown of marriage.	
Arizona	One or either spouse must reside in Arizona for at least 90 days before filing the petition.	Irretrievable breakdown of the marriage.	After service of petition on other spouse, a 60 day waiting period is required before the divorce can be granted.
Arkansas	The filing spouse must reside in the state for at least 60 days before filing the petition.	Voluntary living separately and apart for 18 consecutive months without cohabitation.	Unless the parties shall have lived apart from each other for a period of twelve (12) months before the filing of the complaint no decree of divorce shall be rendered before the 30th day following the day upon which the action for divorce is commenced.
California	The filing spouse must reside for 6 months within the state and 3 months in the country where the divorce will be filed before filing the Petition.	Irreconcilable differences which have caused the irremediable break down of the marriage.	After the dissolution papers are served upon the other spouse or the spouse enters an appearance, the parties must wait 6 months before divorce can be granted.
Colorado	One of the spouses must be a resident of the state for at least 90 days prior to filing the Petition.	Irretrievable breakdown of the marriage.	After the responding spouse is served with the documents, the court may impose a 30-60 day wait before dissolution can be granted.

Connecticut	May be filed by either spouse if he or she is a resident of the state, but the dissolution will not be finalized until one spouse has resided in the state for 1 year (unless the filing spouse was a resident of the state at the time of the marriage and returned to the state with the intention to remain a resident—then the 1 year wait is waived).	Irretrievable breakdown of the marriage; or incompatibility and voluntary separation for 18 months with no reasonable grounds for reconciliation.	After "return date" the parties must wait 90 days before the divorce can be granted.
Delaware	Either spouse must be a resident for at least 6 months prior to tiling the action.	Irretrievable breakdown of the marriage.	
District of Columbia	Either spouse must be a resident for at least 6 months prior to filing the action.	Living separate and apart for 1 year without cohabitation; or mutual voluntary separation without cohabitation for 6 months	
Florida	The filing spouse must reside within the state for 6 months prior to filing the action.	Irretrievable breakdown of the marriage.	
Georgia	The filing souse must reside within the state for 6 months prior to filing the action (but a non-resident can file against defendant who has resided in the state for a period of 6 months prior to filing the action).	Irretrievable breakdown of the marriage.	Divorce cannot be granted for 30 days after filing of the action.
Hawaii	The filing spouse must reside within the state for 3 months prior to filing the action.	Irretrievable breakdown of the marriage; or living separate and apart for 2 years without cohabitation.	Before the divorce can be granted, one spouse must have resided in the state for at least 6 months.
Idaho	The filing spouse must reside within the state for 6 weeks immediately prior to filing the action.	Irreconcilable differences causing the irremediable breakdown of the marriage; or living separate and apart without cohabitation for 5 years.	

Illinois	The filing spouse must reside within the state for 90 days prior to filing the action.	Irreconcilable differences causing the irremediable breakdown of the marriage and the spouses have lived apart without cohabitation for 2 years (but if both spouses consent to the divorce, the noncohabitation period becomes 6 months).	
Indiana	One of the spouses must reside for 6 months within the state and reside for at least 3 months in the county where the petition will be filed	Irretrievable breakdown of the marriage.	After initiation of dissolution, there is a 60 day waiting period before the dissolution will be granted.
Iowa	The filing spouse must reside within the state for 1 year prior to filing the action (unless the other spouse is resident of the state and is served with papers and accept same).	There has been a breakdown of the marriage relationship to the extent that the legitimate object of matrimony have been destroyed and there remains no reasonable likelihood that the marriage can be preserved.	There is a 90 day waiting period after filing before the dissolution will become final.
Kansas	Either spouse must reside within the state for 60 days immediately prior to filing the action.	Incompatibility.	There is a 60 day waiting period after filing the action before the dissolution will become final.
Kentucky	The filing spouse must reside within the state for 180 days prior to filing the action.	Irretrievable breakdown of the marriage.	No dissolution will be granted until the spouses have lived part for at least 60 days.
Louisiana	The filing spouse must reside within the state for 1 year prior to filing the action.	One spouse desires a divorce.	There is a 180 day waiting period from the service of the petition or from the execution of written waiver of the service, and proof that the spouses have lived separate and apart continuously for at least 180 days prior to the filing.

Maine	The plaintiff must have resided in good faith in this State for 6 months prior to the commencement of the action; or the plaintiff has been a resident of this State and the parties were married in this State; or the plaintiff is a resident of this State and the parties resided in this State when the cause of divorce accrued; or the defendant is a resident of this State at the time of filing the action.	Irreconcilable marital difference.	
Maryland	If the grounds for the divorce occurred in Maryland, either party may file without a waiting period.	Voluntary separation, if: (I) the parties voluntarily have lived separate and apart without cohabitation for 12 months without interruption before the filing of the application for divorce ; and (ii) there is no reasonable expectation of reconciliation.	
Massachusetts	No waiting period if both the husband and wife lived in the commonwealth at the time of the grounds for divorce. If grounds occurred outside of the commonwealth, the filing spouse must reside in the commonwealth for 1 year.	Irretrievable breakdown of the marriage.	
Michigan	Prior to filing the action, one spouse must be a resident of the state for 180 days and a resident for at least 10 days in/of the county in which the action is filed.	There has been a breakdown of the marriage relationship to the extent that the objects of matrimony have been destroyed and there remains no reasonable likelihood that the marriage can be preserved.	
Minnesota	One of the parties must have resided in this state, or has been a member of the armed services stationed in this state, for not less than 180 days immediately preceding the commencement of the proceedings.	Irretrievable breakdown of the marriage, demonstrated by living apart for 180 days or serious marital discord adversely affecting the attitude of one or both of the spouses toward the marriage.	

Mississippi	One of the parties must have residence in this state, or has been a member of the armed services stationed in this state, for not less than 6 months immediately preceding the commencement of the suit.	Irreconcilable differences.	There is a 60 day waiting period after the filing of the action before the divorce can be granted.
Missouri	One of the parties must have been a member of the armed services stationed in this state, for not less than 90 days immediately preceding the commencement of the proceeding.	Irretrievable breakdown of the marriage with no reasonable likelihood that the marriage can be preserved.	There is a 30 day waiting period after the filing of the action before the divorce can be granted.
Montana	One of the parties, at the time the action was commenced, must be domiciled in this state or stationed in this state while a member of the armed services and that the domicile or military presence has been maintained for 90 days preceding the making of the findings.	The marriage is irretrievably broken, which findings must be supported by evidence: (I) that the parties have lived separate and apart for a period of more than 180 days preceding the commencement of this proceeding; or (ii) that there is serious marital discord that adversely affects the attitude of one or both of the parties towards the marriage.	
Nebraska	One of the spouses must reside within the state for 1 year prior to filing the action or if the marriage occurred in Nebraska, one of the spouses has resided in the state for the entire marriage.	Irretrievable breakdown of the marriage.	
Nevada	The filing spouse must reside within the state for 6 weeks prior to filing the action.	Incompatibility or living separate and apart without cohabitation for 1 year.	
New Hampshire	No waiting period if both parties reside in state at time of filing; the plaintiff must have resided in the state for one year if defendant was personally served with process within the state; the plaintiff must have resided in the state for one year prior to the time when the action was commenced.	Irreconcilable differences which have caused the irremediable breakdown of the marriage.	

New Jersey	One of the spouses must reside within the state for one year prior to filing the action.	Living separate and apart for 18 months with no reasonable grounds for reconciliation.	
New Mexico	One of the spouses must reside within the state for 6 months prior to filing the action and maintain a residence within state.	Incompatibility (exists when, because of discord or conflict of personalities, the legitimate end of the marriage relationship are destroyed preventing any reasonable expectation of reconciliation).	
New York	No minimum time if both spouses reside in the state at the time of the divorce. One year residency requirement when: the parties were married in the state and one party is a resident of the state when the action is commenced; when the parties have resided in this state as husband and wife and when only one party has been a resident and the cause of the divorce occurred in the state. If only one party is a resident of the state and none of the grounds above apply for the one year residency requirements, one spouse must reside in the state for two years immediately preceding the commencement action.	The husband and wife have lived separate and apart under a written Separation Agreement for a period of one or more years after the execution of such agreement and satisfactory proof has been submitted by the plaintiff that he or she substantially performed all the terms and conditions of such agreement.	One year living separate and apart.
North Carolina	One of the spouses must reside within the state for 6 months prior to filing the action.	Living separate and apart without cohabitation for 1 year	
North Dakota	One of the spouses must reside within the state for 6 months prior to filing the action.	Irreconcilable differences.	
Ohio	One of the spouses must reside within the state for 6 months prior to filing the action and a resident of the county where the action is filed for at least 90 days.	Husband and wife have, without interruption for one year, lived separate and apart without cohabitation; or incompatibility, unless denied by either party.	30 day waitng period after filing the petition.

Oklahoma	One of the spouses must reside within the state for 6 months prior to filing the petition. Also, the plaintiff must have been a resident of the county where the petition is filed for at least thirty (30) days immediately preceding the filing of the petition.	Incompatibility.	
Oregon	No waiting period if the marriage occurred in the state and either party is resident of or domiciled in the state at the time the suit is commenced. If the marriage did not occur in the state, at least one party must be a resident of the state at the time the suit is commenced and continuously for a period of six months prior thereto.	Irreconcilable differences between the parties having caused the irremediable breakdown of the marriage.	
Pennsylvania	One of the spouses must reside within the state for 6 months prior to filing the action.	The marriage is irretrievably broken (and 90 days have elapsed from the date of commencement of an action and an affidavit has been filed by each of the parties evidencing that each of the parties consents to the divorce).	
Rhode Island	One of the spouses must reside within the state for one year prior to filing the action.	Irreconcilable differences which have caused the irremediable breakdown of the marriage.	
South Carolina	If both spouses live in South Carolina, they must be residents of the state for 3 months; if only one spouse is a resident, that spouse must have been a resident for 1 year prior to filing of the action.	Living separate and apart for one year without cohabitation for one year.	
South Dakota	The spouse filing the action must be a resident of South Dakota at time of filing and at the time that the divorce is granted.	Irreconcilable differences causing the irremediable breakdown fo the marriage.	3 months waiting period after the action is filed.

Tennessee	No waiting period if the plaintiff was a resident of the state when the grounds for the divorce were committed; but one of the spouses must reside within the state for 6 months prior to filing the action if the grounds for the divorce were committed out of this state.	Irreconcilable differences between the parties; or both parties have lived in separate residences for a continuous period of two (2) or more years, have not cohabited as man and wife during such period, and there are no minor children of the parties.	60-90 day waiting period after the action is filed.
Texas	One of the spouses must reside within the state for six months prior to filing the action, plus one of the parties must be resident of County in which the suit is filed for at least 90 days prior to filing.	The marriage has become insupportable because of discord or conflict of personalities that destroys the legitimate ends of the marital relationship and prevents any reasonable expectation of reconciliation; or if the spouses have lived apart without cohabitation for at least three years.	
Utah	The filing spouse must reside within the state for three months prior to filing the action as well as being a resident of County in which the suit is filed for the same period.	Irreconcilable differences of the marriage; or when the husband and wife have lived separately under a decree of separate maintenance of any state for three consecutive years without cohabitation.	
Vermont	One of the spouses must reside within the state for six months prior to filing the action.	The spouses have lived apart for six consecutive months and the resumption of marital relations is not reasonably probable.	A divorce shall not be decreed for any cause unless the plaintiff or the defendant has resided in the state one year next preceding the date of final hearing.

Virginia	One of the spouses must reside within the state for six months prior to filing the action.	The spouses have lived separate and apart without any cohabitation and without interruption for one year. In any case where the parties have entered into a separation agreement and there are no minor children either born of the parties, a divorce may be decreed on application if and when the husband and wife have lived separately and apart without cohabitation and without interruption for six months.	
Washington	The filing spouse must (1) be a resident of this state, or (2) is a member of the armed forces and is stationed in this state, or (3) is married to a party who is a resident of this state or who is a member of the armed forces and is stationed in this state.	Irretrievable breakdown of the marriage.	90 day waiting period from the date of serving of the summons prior issuance of order granting the dissolution.
West Virginia	If the marriage was entered into within this state, the filing spouse must be a resident of this state at the time of commencement of the action; or if the marriage was not entered into within this state, one of the parties was a resident of this state for at least one year at the time the cause of action arose.	Irreconcilable differences exist between the parties (and an answer is filed admitting that allegation); or the spouses have lived separate and apart in separate places of abode without any cohabitation and without interruption for one year.	
Wisconsin	One of the parties must have been a resident of the county in which the action is brought for not less than 30 days next preceding the commencement of the action.	Irretrievable breakdown of the marriage.	

Wyoming	The filing spouse must reside in the state for at least 60 days immediately preceding the time of filing the complaint, unless marriage occurred in the state and the filing spouse has resided in this state from the time of the marriage until the filing of the complaint.	Irreconcilable differences in the marital relationship.	20 day waiting period after filing before the divorce will be granted.

Source: Standard Legal Network, LLC.

How Can A Young Man Cleanse His Way?
(Working With Young Adults)
Kurt Jones

"How can a young man cleanse his way? By taking heed according to Your word. With my whole heart I have sought You. Oh, let me not wander from you commandments! Your word I have hidden in my heart, that I might not sin against You" (Ps. 119:9-11). David, as he is writing this psalm, asks an interesting question. "How can a young man cleanse his way?" He promptly answers, "By taking heed according to Your word." This really is the focus of working with young adults. It needs to be understood that our responsibility as Christians, in local churches, is to help them to take heed

---

Kurt G. Jones was born in Altus, Oklahoma on April 8, 1979 and raised in Pampa, Texas. In 1996, at the age of sixteen, he and his family left the institutional church and began worshiping with the Central church of Christ in Pampa where they learned the truth. He graduated from Pampa High school in 1998 and attended Frank Phillips College in Borger, Texas.

Kurt worked as a corrections officer for the Texas Department of Criminal Justice for two years before beginning to preach on a full-time basis. During that time, he preached on a fill in basis, with the Central church of Christ. His first full-time work was with the Franklin Street church of Christ in Borger, Texas in November of 2001. In 2004 he moved from Borger to work with the Rosenberg church of Christ in Rosenberg, Texas. He began work with the 9th and Bliss church of Christ in Dumas, Texas earlier this year.

Kurt married Amber Ratliff on January 3, 2004. At the time of this writing, they are expecting their first child.

according to God's divine word. Paul, as he writes to the young evangelist Timothy, instructs, "And the things that you have heard from me among many witnesses, commit these to faithful men who will be able to teach others also" (2 Tim. 2:2). In this study we will notice the responsibility that Christians and local churches have in teaching young adults, as it opposes the efforts made in the denominations to entertain and provide for their social desires.

As we begin this study, we should take time to define "young adults." Webster defines "young" as, "being in the first part of life," and "adult" as, "having arrived at mature years, or to full size and strength; as an adult person or plant." For the purposes of this study we will be speaking of people from around the age of eighteen to their early thirties. A large part of our discussion will deal with those in the college age group. However, the principles we will discuss will be applicable to those of more advanced years, as well as, those who are younger.

The word of God has much to say about the young and how people should conduct their lives in youth. Solomon says, "Rejoice, O young man, in your youth, and let your heart cheer you in the days of your youth; walk in the ways of your heart, and in the sight of your eyes; but know that for a all these God will bring you into judgment" (Eccl. 11:9). In the following verse, he states that "child hood and youth are vanity." Paul, as he writes, instructs Timothy to "let no one despise your youth, but be an example to the believers in word, in conduct, in love, in spirit, in faith, in purity" (1 Tim. 4:12). And there are numerous other passages which instruct the young in their daily lives. The fact that the young have the responsibility to keep their lives pure and to "know that God will bring you into judgment" is truly the key to understanding our responsibility in working with them. Their responsibility to the Lord is to remain faithful to him.

What Do the Sectarians Have to Offer?

When we consider the various denominations round about us, it becomes evident that their focus in bringing in young adults is not centered on salvation and faithfulness, as much as it is centered around social desires and wants. They provide social groups where people in the similar age groups can "build authentic relationships" and "create an atmosphere that is filled with laughter, fun, and the presence of God" (Jackson, gatewaypeople. com). Some churches have softball, basketball, and volleyball leagues. They provide social meals and carnivals. They have elaborate orchestras and "praise bands," and they bring in famous speakers. They provide everything from "pre-marriage" and divorce counseling to tax workshops and weight loss programs. None of which is within the scope of responsibility of the church. Let us consider some of the denominations' attitudes in working with young adults. The Gateway church in Fort Worth, Texas on their website show ways they plan to "minister" (I use the term as they use it) to young people. The have a "Singles Ministry" headed up by a man named Larry Brown. Part of that ministry is a group for people in their mid-twenties to their mid-thirties called "Nexus." Larry says "every single person matters." I do not disagree with Mr. Brown, every single person does matter. He goes on to say:

> Imagine a place where you are safe at home, where you have thousands of aunts, uncles, parents, children, grandparents and grandchildren—a place of acceptance, advocacy and abundance. A group of people who challenge you to go beyond where you are, but don't judge you for where you have been. Doesn't this sound great? It is possible because at Gateway EVERY SINGLE PERSON MATTERS!

> The Singles Ministries at Gateway Church is full of life and diversity. We serve individuals from all walks of life. Some of our singles are young, some are married but separated, others have never been married, and some wish they had never been married, while a select few can't think of anything else but getting married. Many are gainfully employed and are making major contributions to society; others are looking for work and are struggling to make ends meet. A few of our young singles don't consider themselves single, they just aren't married yet. Several of our singles are a little [angry] that we use the word single. (I mean, after all, we don't refer to married people as doubles, do we?) As you can see, we have people that know where you are coming from and will meet you where you are.

He continues in describing their "nexus" ministry,

> If you are a single in your mid 20s to 30s, you are part of a diverse group of individuals who have all the marks of being the next "greatest generation." You are ambitious, informed, educated, hard working and trend-setting; yet you feel a bit tumultuous, troubled, broken and independent. You know you have great potential, but sometimes it seems society won't give you a chance, take you seriously or acknowledge that you count. Nexus is the ministry for you if you don't fit the mold, if you strive for something better, if you know you have something to offer (Brown, gatewaypeople.com).

Further, one of Mr. Brown's colleagues, Mr. Marcus Brecheen, speaks of his "pre-marriage counseling Ministry" (I understand the young adults are not the only people entering into marriage, and I do not believe that Marcus or the Gateway church believe that either. However, it is true that the majority of people getting married would fall into the young adult category.) Marcus says:

> At Gateway Church we define Pre-Marriage Ministries as "a short ministry for a lifetime marriage."
>
> Our strategy is based on the guiding principle that the long-term success of any venture can be attributed primarily to its foundation. We are more interested in the marriage than in the wedding. It is on that premise that we will only perform marriages for those couples who have fulfilled our guidelines. Our reasoning is found in today's statistics, which show that over half of all marriages end in divorce . . . and less than half of those that endure are truly happy ones.
>
> Our desire is for marriages in which both partners are truly fulfilled for a lifetime. Our experience is that the key to fulfillment in marriage is a solid foundation. We believe that with just a little effort in the present, couples can resolve differences which often pose problems for them in the future.
>
> God is the Creator and Designer of marriage and His ways work best. His intention for you is to have a marriage that grows happier each year. With that in mind, we've designed a strategy to give you the foundational tools to experience deep fulfillment from the start (Brecheen, gatewaypeople. com).

Marcus, as well as Larry, speak about their respective "ministries" as places to be "accepted" or as counseling to help have a better marriage. But notice in their descriptions or their "ministries" they make no mention of how one is to be saved, or how one is to remain faithful to God. In fact, they do not use the Bible in their descriptions at all! Brethren and friends, if you want to be part of a social club join one. I do not know, but I would imagine that the local YMCA provides similar programs. These things are not found within God's word as responsibilities of the local church. Another interesting note about both of these men, they both used to be preachers among the institutional churches of Christ. I know this because both worked at the Mary Ellen and Harvester church in Pampa, Texas when my family left liberalism and learned the truth.

The Second Baptist Church in Houston, Texas boasts the "largest singles adult ministry in the United States." They say of their "ministry, "Get connected with others by visiting one of our Bible study classes for singles. Each class, which averages between 50 and 150 people, maintains a full social calendar with parties, small groups, service projects, retreats, and sports leagues" (http://www.second.org/global/singles.aspx). There is no attempt to hide the fact that their motivation is social. They, like those at the Gateway Church, say nothing about how one is to become a Christian, or remain faithful to the Lord, in the description of their efforts with young adults. They state that their *"Bible study classes"* have a "full *social* calendar"! That is a clear sign of their motivation.

Further, let us not begin to think that only the denominations and sectarians are involving themselves in such ventures. Even those calling themselves the church of Christ desire to be "like all the nations" (1 Sam. 8:5). The Broadway church of Christ in Lubbock, Texas has a "University Ministry" which they call "Christ in Action." They say of their efforts with college students,

> Christ In Action Student Ministries is the University ministry of the Broadway Church of Christ. We seek to show students at Tech, LCU, and South Plains the joy of knowing our Lord, Jesus Christ.
>
> We are a group of people who are looking to and for Jesus in our world today. We are reminded of the passage found in Matthew 16:15: "But what about you?" he asked. "Who do you say I am?" In answering this question, we are also given the answer to our own question. We are Christians who [believe] that in order to know Christ, we must strive to be like Jesus. In fact, we must not only be like Jesus, we must "Be Jesus for Our Time and Place" (http://www.broadway-church.org/ca/default.htm).

On the surface it sounds very much like a good group to belong to. There is nothing wrong with having an attitude that a child of God should "be Jesus for our time and place." Paul in his Galatian letter even writes, "I have been crucified with Christ; it is no longer I who live, but Christ lives in me; and the life which I now live in the flesh I live by faith in the Son of God, who loved me and gave Himself for me" (2:20). Yet delving further into their Christ in Action "ministry" it becomes evident that their mission is not to preach the truth and "Be Jesus for our time." They post on their "News and Events" page their "summer news":

Sunday nights — devos and fellowship time
Each Sunday night we will schedule different events around Lubbock.
We will have a short devotional followed by fun fellowship. Examples
include Sand volleyball at the Knowlton's, swimming, Putt-Putt, movie
nights, etc. (http://www.broadway-church.org/ca/default.htm).

Once again, we notice that the Broadway church of Christ has lived up
to its name and taken the "broad way" (Matt. 7:23) which emphasizes the
social desires of man, as opposed to his spiritual needs.

What it the answer then? How is it that the local congregations are to
compete with the mega-churches and those willing to direct attention to
nearly every social desire man has? The answer is simple; the Lord's people
do not have to compete with them! We are not offering the same thing. If a
man wants to seek out things to fill his social desires, he will do so, and there
are plenty of places to find it. If a man wants to fulfill his spiritual needs, he
should seek God's word which will direct him to the Lord's church.

Many in denominations and liberal churches of Christ may not even
realize it, but this emphasis on the social desires of man has its impact
upon him spiritually. How? It down plays the spiritual responsibility. Fred
Stoeker, in "Everyman's Battle" writes,

My church in Des Moines has an excellent choir, known throughout our
region for its professional sound. Our orchestra is even supplemented by
players from the local professional symphony orchestra. In discussing
our church with a new neighbor, she said, "Oh, I've been to your church.
I really like it. It's just like going to a show!"

My church has an excellent schedule of tradition-driven events. There's
our "Super Bowl Sunday" evening service that fosters racial harmony.
We have "Honor America Night" every Fourth of July to honor our great
country, inviting renowned speakers like Elizabeth Dole, Gary Bauer, and
Cal Thomas. Our annual "Metro Night" honors the volunteers and staff of
our daughter church in the inner city. We have Christmas specials, Easter
specials, "Friends Day," "Back to School Night," and much more.

Clearly, we're striving to be "the church to belong to" in Des Moines.
Have we profited? What has come from this search for excellence?

Recently, we scheduled a week of nightly all-church prayer meetings to
begin the new year. Now hardly anyone would argue with the strategic

value of prayer or question the fact that we're commanded as believers to be faithful at it. But obedience in the matter of prayer is costly and takes commitment. On Monday night as our week of prayer began, a mere thirty-four adults showed up out of a regular church attendance of twenty-three hundred. By Thursday, only seventeen adults were praying. I was totally discouraged. Yet one week later, on Worker Recognition Sunday, one thousand people where there to be recognized for their service in the church (Arterburn, Stoeker 52).

This statement proves the point that a man is converted to what he is converted with. If he is converted to professional orchestras, special services with "big name" guest speakers, sports teams, social meals, dominos, etc. . . . then the moment that is taken away or the emphasis is pulled from these things he is likely to go elsewhere to find what he is looking for. His focus obviously is not spiritual.

What Do We Have to Offer?

That being stated, and with the understanding that the Lord's church is not in competition with those providing social desires rather than spiritual needs, what are some ways in which the Lord's church can "work with young adults"? What do we, as local congregations, have to offer young adults? Well, I will submit to you that the Lord's church has three things to offer young adults (actually, they are the same things the Lord's church has to offer all who have the ability to seek the truth). We first of all, offer truth. Second, we offer New Testament Christianity. Lastly, we offer a family.

First, we have the truth, the word of God, to offer. Notice Romans10: 17, "So then faith comes by hearing, and hearing by the word of God." When we notice that faith comes by hearing the word of God, a question could be posed. Why is faith important? The Hebrew writer points out the answer to this question, "but without faith it is impossible to please Him, for he that comes to God must believe that He is and that He is a rewarder of those who diligently seek him" (Heb. 11:6). One must have faith, if he is to be pleasing to God. Local congregations offer the word of God. Jesus as he prayed to the Father prayed, "Sanctify them by Your Truth. Your word is truth" (John 17:17). Also, Paul as he spoke to the elders of the church at Ephesus said, "So now brethren, I commend you to God and to the word of His grace, which is able to build you up, and give you an inheritance among all those who are sanctified" (Acts 20:32). God's word will lead people to salvation! James writes, ". . . receive with meekness the implanted word, which is able to save your souls" (Jas. 1:21). What a valuable thing to offer to people including young adults! The Bible shows us the road map so that we may have heaven as our home. We have the blueprint that we can offer to people that they may have the hope of eternal salvation. Peter tells us, ". . . His divine power has given us all things that pertain to life and godliness, through the knowledge of Him who called us by glory and virtue" (2 Pet. 1:3).

Some might say, "Well, don't the other churches offer the word of God as well?" The answer is "No." We can see that is the case as we notice the changes that the denominations are experiencing. The Episcopal Church recently accepted and ordained open homosexuals as "priests" and "bishops," a thing that never would have happened years ago. The turmoil that the Southern Baptist Convention has suffered with a liberal fringe pushing their agenda makes it evident that attitudes have changed. Even some of the institutional churches of Christ sponsor dances, instrumental music, adopt a more ecumenical attitude, and teach error on other things, making it evident that they are not teaching and practicing the word of God. Thus, it should be evident that folks are not being taught God's word. Remember, the Hebrew writer pointed out that, without faith, we could not please God. While all around us we see churches practicing sin, compromising, acquiescing, and perverting truth, we must be sure that we "hold fast the pattern of sound words" (2 Tim. 1:13).

In addition to offering truth, we also offer New Testament Christianity. Just before he ascended into heaven Jesus spoke to his disciples and commanded, "Go therefore and make disciples of all nations, baptizing them in the name of the Father and of the Son and of the Holy Spirit, teaching them to observe all things that I have commanded you; and lo, I am with you always even to the end of the age" (Matt. 28:19-20). Notice with me who it was that was doing the commanding. Jesus said, "*all things I have commanded you.*" Paul calls him ". . . the blessed and only Potentate, the King of kings and Lord of lords" (1 Tim. 6:15). He is the savior of the world. What do we have to offer? We offer the commands of the Lord, the very words by which we will be judged when we stand before him in judgment (cf. 2 Cor. 5:10; Rom. 2:16; John 12:48). Local congregations are helping people to be prepared for that great day. The churches that focus upon the social aspects of man are not preparing them for that day. The sad fact is, for these people when they finally stand before the Lord, that they will be lost! And not lost for a day, not annihilated, but "tormented day and night forever and ever" (Rev. 20:10). It needs to be clear in people's minds that

Jesus has made it clear that we must serve him and do so according to his teaching and pattern. Jesus stated in the Sermon on the Mount, "Not everyone who says to Me, Lord, Lord, shall enter the kingdom of heaven, but he who does the will of My Father in heaven" (Matt. 7:21). He goes on to say, "and then I will declare to them, I never knew you, depart from Me you who practice lawlessness" (Matt. 7:23).

We can read in the New Testament of how New Testament Christians worshiped. Luke records, "And they continued steadfastly in the Apostles' doctrine and fellowship, in the breaking of bread, and in prayers" (Acts 2:42). Here are a group of people who were under the tutelage of the Apostles, under the direction of the Holy Spirit, whom the Lord sent, and we can be just like them, by adhering to the commands of Christ. Local congregations offer an invaluable resource in that we offer an opportunity for those who want to worship "in spirit and Truth" (John 4:24), and a group of people who are doing the same thing to be there to strengthen and encourage them. What can be said about one who goes to a church that emphasizes social desires? He really led us to victory in basketball? He cooked the best ribs we ever ate? He was a good member of our singles group? All of that may be true, but what does that get him in eternity. When we read in the New Testament about the growth of the church, we find no mention of singles groups, chili suppers, basketball teams, etc. Yet, on the day of Pentecost we find that about three thousand souls were added to the church (Acts 2:41). In fact, throughout the book of Acts we see the church growing and multiplying, and no mention is made of any of these social programs. Paul writes to the church at Corinth, "For I determined not to know anything among you except Jesus Christ and Him crucified" (1 Cor. 2:2). This is the responsibility of the local church to remain faithful to the Lord, to teach and practice the truth. We must always remember that local churches are needed. There are lost people all around us and sadly the majority of them will not go to heaven! That is why we have to be active in trying to help people know of the New Testament church and true Christianity. That is done in our influence, our words, our worship, and our teaching.

The Lord's people also offer a family. Notice in Mark 3, we find Jesus in a house and his mother and brothers are trying to speak to him, but because of the crowd, they are unable too. They send word to him in verse 32 that they are seeking him. He answers them saying, "'Who is My mother, Or My brothers?' And he looked around in a circle at those who sat about Him, and said, 'Here are My mother and My brothers! For whoever does the will of God is My brother and My sister and mother'" (Mark 3:33-35). We find Jesus speaking to the Apostles after the account of the rich young man in Mark 10. Jesus makes this statement to them. "Assuredly, I say to you, there is no one who has left house or brothers or sisters or father or mother or wife or children or lands, for My sake and the gospel's, who shall not receive a hundredfold now in this time—houses and brothers and sisters and mothers and children and lands, with persecutions—and in the age to come, eternal life" (Mark 10:29-30). The family of God consists of the faithful. Sometimes, sadly, we are required to give up a social relationship with our physical families in order to serve God. I have known of brethren whose parents were so angry with them for obeying the gospel that it hindered their relationship. But, the child of God must realize that service to God is placed before a physical relationship. I also have known brethren who have had family members that the church was forced to discipline. They have had to sever the social relationship that they shared with them, and I understand that it is a hard thing to do. However, when we realize that our relationship with our Father is our top priority, we will be able to do his will. And, as hard as it may seem to do this, we receive a family with which we have more in common than a physical genealogy. We gain a family with whom we have a common bond, a common hope, a common joy, and a common salvation through the blood of Christ. We will spend eternity serving God together with our spiritual family!

A great deal of the time I have spent as a Christian has been spent living apart from my mother and father. There have been older brethren who have taken me and looked out for me as a son. They have been concerned about my well-being both spiritually and physically and they remain very dear to me. I have a closer relationship with my brethren in Christ than I do with some members of my physical family who are not Christians. Why? Because we share a common hope in Christ Jesus. Paul writes to Timothy, ". . . exhort [an older man] as a father, younger men as brothers, older women as mothers, younger women as sisters, with all purity" (1 Tim. 5:1-2). The Bible points out that we should foster this type of relationship with our brethren, concerning ourselves with them as our family. Peter commands, "Finally, all of you be of one mind, having compassion for one another; love as brothers, be tender hearted, be courteous" (1 Pet. 3:8). We as Christians are to "love as brothers" and to treat one another accordingly. Christians are a community of people who have the responsibility to provide this atmosphere for one another. We have this to offer those young adults who would desire to be children of God.

Why is this type of relationship valuable? Why is it important that you could go to a local church and find older men who would treat you like a son or daughter or younger men who would consider you their brother? We notice its importance when we notice the breakdown of the family in our society. It has become a common thing to hear children speak of the "step-parents." You can scarcely go into public without hearing of or seeing a "single mother." It seems that the majority of marriages end in divorce and many children are born out of wedlock. When I lived in Rosenberg, Texas I worked part-time as a security guard at a local high school and what astonished me was the number of girls in high school who were having children, just in the school where I worked. These things have their impact upon us and upon society. This results in children growing up without all of the influences needed to raise a child according to God's pattern. Thus, as children become adults it can become an invaluable relationship to have brethren who are concerned for their well-being. The local church provides a unique support system. It is an opportunity where brethren can "rejoice with those that rejoice, and weep with those that weep" (Rom. 12:15), and where they "bear one another's burdens, and so fulfill the law of Christ" (Gal. 6:2). These things are needful in our society.

In addition, the family of God concerns itself with one another's spiritual righteousness. This is the point Paul is making in Galatians 6. Paul writes "Brethren, if a man is overtaken in any trespass, you who are spiritual restore such a one in a spirit of gentleness, considering yourself lest you also be tempted" (Gal. 6:1). The inspired apostle puts a premium upon brethren helping to keep one another from sin. He later writes in the same chapter, "Let him who is taught the word share in all good things with him who teaches" (Gal. 6:6). Brethren are to share the benefits of the restoration of one another. The Hebrew writer also instructs along the same lines, "Beware, brethren, lest there be in any of you an evil heart of unbelief in departing from the living God; but exhort one another daily, while it is called 'Today' lest any of you be hardened through the deceitfulness of sin" (Heb. 3:12-13). The Hebrew writer shows the importance of exhortation. Local churches provide a family that is willing to "exhort one another daily" in order to help each other remain strong and faithful.

We must realize that local churches are very valuable! We provide something that no one else has. Local congregations provide the opportunity for people to hear the gospel in its undiluted and unabridged form—the very same gospel that Paul said he was "not ashamed of" (Rom. 1:16-17). He points out in these verses that the gospel is "the power of God unto salvation," and that "in it the righteousness of God is revealed." Brethren, as local congregations we provide this opportunity to people, the opportunity to hear the very truth that can save their souls. Further, we provide the opportunity for people to know and practice New Testament Christianity, true Christianity and not the perverted forms of it that are all around us. Also, local churches provide an opportunity for people to be part of a spiritual family. A place where there are godly people who are concerned not just with people's physical well-being, but more importantly, their spiritual health. Brethren, the only place where people are going to find these things is within local congregations. Let us, as Christians, in local churches, never forget our value and importance to the community around us.

The Importance of Godly Families in Helping to Keep Young Adults Faithful

We noticed what a valuable role that local churches have in society and to young adults, I want to consider briefly, the importance that godly families can have in helping our young people remain faithful when they become young adults. This will be particularly important to those who are raising children now who will someday be young adults. It is no doubt that there are several young adults who go into apostasy when they leave their parents' homes and go off on their own.

Young adults are like everyone else, in that they have the ability to make their own choices in regard to how they will live and what they will believe. The apostle Paul shows that we are held accountable for ourselves. "So then each of us shall give an account of himself to God" (Rom.14:12). We each will have to make the decision to become and remain faithful. Thus, in this portion of the study I am not laying all the blame of young adults leaving the church upon parents. It is not always their fault! What I do want to do is consider what God's word says concerning the responsibility of godly child rearing. What are some things that those raising children can do to instill in their children the importance of being faithful? There are three things that we will consider. First, teach your children the word of God and its relevance and importance in your life. Also, discipline them properly. Finally, be a proper example.

Paul, as he writes to the church of Christ at Ephesus, exhorts fathers, ". . . do not provoke your children to wrath, but bring them up in the training and admonition of the Lord" (Eph. 6:4). Parents and fathers specifically are given

261

the responsibility of raising children and instilling God's truth within them. This is important because one receives faith from God's word. Paul writes, "So then faith comes by hearing, and hearing by the word of God" (Rom. 10:17). Godly parents are the first line of teaching; they should spend time teaching the Bible to their children beginning when they are very young and instilling in them knowledge and love for God and his truth. In addition, it will make it easier upon their parents when their children become teenagers. If they understand God's truth, there will not be a question about whether or not it is alright to dress immodestly or dance. They will understand the importance of assembling with the saints. They will understand why not all churches are right and the list goes on and on. It is important to teach a child God's truth. The inspired apostle, as he writes to Timothy says of him, "When I call to remembrance the genuine faith that is in you, which dwelt first in your grandmother Lois and your mother Eunice, and I am persuaded is in you also" (2 Tim. 1:5). We notice three generations of faithful Christians each one passing down the "faith" to the next generation. Solomon, in his wisdom writes, "Train up a child in the way he should go, and when he is old he will not depart from it" (Prov. 22:6). The responsibility of teaching children God's truth has lasting value. It provides a child with knowledge of the "way he should go."

Secondly, proper discipline will also aid in helping "train the child in the way he should go." One who loves his child disciplines him properly. The word of God says, "He who spares his rod hates his son, but he who loves him disciplines him promptly" (Prov. 13:24). The wise man of God also writes, "Chasten your son while there is hope, and do not set our heart on his destruction" (Prov. 19:18). Proper discipline helps to teach a child what is right and wrong and what is acceptable conduct and what is not. It is part of the responsibility of bringing them up in the "training and admonition of the Lord" (Eph. 6:4). God is involved in the discipline of his children. The Hebrew writer speaks of the chastening of the Lord:

> And you have forgotten the exhortation which speaks to you as to sons: "My son, do not despise the chastening of the Lord, nor be discouraged when you are rebuked by Him; For whom the Lord loves He chastens, and scourges every son whom He receives." If you endure chastening, God deals with you as with sons; for what son is there whom a father does not chasten? But if you are without chastening, of which all have become partakers, then you are illegitimate and not sons. Furthermore, we have had human fathers who corrected us, and we paid them respect. Shall we not much more readily be in subjection to the Father of spirits and

live? For they indeed for a few day chastened us as seemed best to them, but He for our profit, that we may be partakers of His holiness, Now no chastening seems to be joyful for the present, but painful; nevertheless, afterward it yields the peaceable fruit of righteousness to those who have been trained by it (Heb. 12:5-11).

The Hebrew writer speaks of the Lord's chastening deriving from God's love for us. He shows that God chastens those who are his sons. He parallels the discipline of God with that of an earthy father, and points out that if we are trained by his chastening it "yields the peaceable fruit of righteousness." To properly discipline children at a young age will help them to remain faithful when they are young adults.

Lastly, it is vitally important to provide children with a good example, if we expect them to remain faithful when they are young adults. How many people have gone off into sin because they followed the poor example of one who was supposedly a faithful Christian? Parents need to be a godly example to their children in every aspect of their lives. Jesus said, "But whoever causes one of these little ones who believe in me to sin, it would be better for him if a millstone were hung around his neck, and he were drowned in the depth of the sea" (Matt. 18:6). I am sure you are familiar with the old cliché, "Actions speak louder than words." This is true. It is vitally important that we live out the example that we instruct in words. It is important in our attendance. Children see that serving the Lord is important to us when we are faithful in our attendance. The Hebrew writer commands it in Hebrews 10:25. Our children can see if we continually work over time on Sundays and Wednesdays. They see if we are always working instead of assembling with the saints. They see that every time there is a big football game on Sunday night Dad mysteriously gets a headache. They know if they have a t-ball game on Wednesday evening or during a gospel meeting what is more important, if we make an excuse to forsake the assembling. Let us give a proper example to our children and show them that we love Christ more than these things. Jesus said, "If you love me, keep my commandments" (John 14:15), and assembling with the saints is one of those commandments. We must be a good example in our conduct. Paul in writing to the church at Philippi commanded, "Only let your conduct be worthy of the gospel of Christ" (Phil. 1:27). Children and teenagers see what kind of drinks are in the refrigerator or cabinet. They see if Mom and Dad are picking up lottery tickets or playing slot machines. They hear the language that proceeds from their parents' mouths. How many young adults have left the Lord's church because they saw their parent's inconsistency in these things? If children have been taught the word of God they can clearly see what God's word says concerning sin. They also see the inconsistency in the lives of their parents who involve themselves in sinfulness.

Conclusion

How are we to work with young adults? We know that there are all kinds of religious and social institutions making attempts to provide for their social desires with singles and college groups, counseling programs, tax workshops, social meals, ski trips, etc. Yet, local congregations are not in competition with them. The Lord's church offers young and old alike God's truth. It provides an opportunity for people to practice New Testament Christianity. Further, it gives them a spiritual family. All of these things the social churches and organizations are unable to provide.

When we consider the importance of helping young adults whose parents are Christians, it is important to consider the grave responsibility that parents are given. They have the responsibility to instill God's divine word into the minds of their children. The Lord has commanded them to bring children up according to his "training and admonition" (Eph. 6:4). They must discipline their children properly in order that they may receive the benefit of such discipline. Through proper discipline children learn to live good and righteous lives. Also, parents must set a godly example for their children. Open inconsistencies in parents' lives can show a child or teenager that actual service to God is not as important to the parent as lip-service. Paul in writing to the young evangelist Titus spoke of those with this attitude, "To the pure, all things are pure, but to those who are defiled and unbelieving nothing is pure; but even their mind and conscience are defiled. They profess to know God but in works they deny Him, being abominable, disobedient, and disqualified for every good work" (Tit.1:15-16). Let us not display to our children such an attitude, but be a godly example to them. Being consistent in teaching, discipline, and application with children will go a long way in helping them to be faithful when they become young adults.

It is true, a young man can "cleanse his way" by "taking heed according to [God's] word" (Ps.119:9-11). Let each of us as Christians, in local churches of Christ, ensure that we remain faithful in providing all that God has made available to people, including young adults, within his church. Let parents take diligent care to train up their children in the way they should go so that children and teenagers will grow to be faithful young adults in the Lord's church.

Bibliography

Arterburn, Stephen and Fred Stoeker. *Everyman's Battle: Every Man's Guide to Winning the War on Sexual Temptation One Victory at a Time.* Colorado Springs: Waterbrook, 2000, 52-53.

Brecheen, Marcus. "Pre-Marriage Ministry Overview." 11 November 2005. http://www.gatewaypeople.com/ministries/premarriage/index.php.

Broadway Church of Christ, Lubbock, TX. "Be Jesus for our Time And Place: Christ in Actions Student Ministries." 12 November 2005. http://www.broadway-church.org/ca/default.htm.

Brown, Larry. "Singles Ministry Overview." 11 November 2005. http://www.gatewaypeople.com/ministries/singles/index.php.

Bible, New King James Version.

Jackson, Ken and Mary. "Children's Ministry Overview." 11 November 2005. http://www.gatewaypeople.com/ministries/children/index.php.

Second Baptist Church, Houston, TX. "Singles Ministry Overview." 11 November 2005. http://www.second.org/global/singles.aspx.

Webster, Noah. *Dictionary of America English.* E-Sword edition. http://www.e-sword.net/dictionaries.html.

The Historical Reliabilty of the Bible

David Dann

The psalmist directed his praise toward God saying, "The entirety of your word is truth, and every one of your righteous judgments endures forever" (Ps. 119:160). The psalmist's declaration well sums up the general claim of the Bible with regard to its own veracity and trustworthiness. The Bible consistently claims to be the divinely inspired word of God (2 Tim. 3:16), spoken and written by men guided by the Holy Spirit (2 Pet. 1:20-21; John 16:13; Eph. 3:1-5), revealing absolute truth to man (John 17:17). These claims must be borne out by the available evidence if they are to have any validity. The historical nature of the biblical narrative of both testaments makes it possible to undertake a thorough examination of the evidence relative to the claims of Scripture.

The Bible Is Rooted In History

The Bible is an historical book that rests on the integrity of the histori-

---

David Dann was born on May 23, 1973 in Miami, Florida and is the youngest of three sons born to Carl and Mary Dann. Having been brought up by godly parents, he obeyed the gospel in 1986 and preached his first sermon in 1992. David attended Georgia Perimeter College (A.S.) and Florida College and received a B.A. in finance from the University of Georgia. On July 3, 1999 he married Cynthia Crossfield of Toronto, Canada and they have two children: Olivia and Zebulon. David has worked full-time as an evangelist with churches in Canada, Indiana, and Florida. He spent seven years starting two congregations in Toronto, Canada. He has frequently contributed articles to Truth Magazine and has authored a workbook on the church in the Truth For Teens series published by Guardian of Truth Foundation. He presently works with the Northeast church of Christ in Clearwater, Florida.

cal facts revealed within its pages (Free & Vos 13). Unlike the holy books of other world religions, the Bible is not simply a collection of sayings and teachings. Instead, the Bible presents the story of a people who lived at a definite time and place in history and reveals the record of how God has dealt with mankind throughout the course of history (Price 109). The Scriptures portray real people who live real lives in the real world acting in the context of real events as they interact with a real God.

The Bible Is Not a Textbook of History
The purpose of the Bible is not to give a complete historical record of the world and its affairs.

In fact, the historical information presented in the Bible is often intentionally selective and incomplete. Critics of the Bible have attempted to use the selective and incomplete historical record of the Bible as a basis upon which to attack the historical reliability of the Bible. While the conclusions reached by the critics are unwarranted, it must be recognized that if the Bible is to validate its claim to be the word of God then it must show itself to be in harmony with known facts of history in every case where its narrative touches known history.

The Importance of the Historical Reliability of the Bible
The Bible cannot be the word of God if much that it contains is false. In this post-modern age many would like to believe that religious truth can exist independent of facts. In other words, many have the idea that one can legitimately have faith in the message of the Bible even while rejecting the historicity of the biblical narrative. This sort of thinking leads to a religion in which one simply picks and chooses the parts of the Bible he wishes to believe and rejects the rest. This approach has led to the idea that one should adopt the religious tradition that suits his lifestyle preferences. The obvious implication is that one religion is as good as another since all rest on the same flawed historical basis.

Higher criticism has promoted a post-modern view of the Bible and religion. The questions posed by higher criticism are questions concerning the integrity, authenticity, credibility, and literary forms of the writings that make up the Bible (McDowell 397). Higher criticism was first applied to the Bible beginning in the late eighteenth century (*Ibid.*). Over the course of the past two hundred years the higher critics have reconstructed and remade Bible history in their own image. Langdon Gilkey, a proponent of higher criticism, accurately characterizes the destructive results of the work of the critics as follows:

> Suddenly a vast panoply of divine deeds and events recorded in Scripture are no longer regarded as having actually happened. Not only, for example, do the six days of creation, the historical fall in Eden, and the flood seem to us historically untrue, but even more the majority of divine deeds in the biblical history of the Hebrew people become what we choose to call symbols rather than plain old historical facts . . . these "acts" vanish from the plane of historical reality and enter the never-never land of "religious interpretation" by the Hebrew people (McDowell 453).

This school of thought has come to dominate colleges, universities, seminaries, and consequently, many pulpits across the land. As a result, many have based what little faith they have on a Bible they believe is largely devoid of historical accuracy.

Can the Bible be right when it comes to religious matters if it is wrong on historical matters? The fact remains that, if the Bible is historically corrupt, chronologically confused, and culturally ignorant, then it simply cannot be the inspired word of God. Since the public has been led to believe the Bible is historically inaccurate, many have found it that much easier to reject its teachings as principles by which their lives should be governed. We live in a world that has rejected the Bible as a rule of life and conduct largely because of the widespread belief that its contents are historically unreliable. Therefore, the question of the historical reliability of the Bible is a question of utmost importance. Do the facts support the faith? This is the question that must be settled.

Archaeology In Relation To an Examination of the Historical Reliability of the Bible

Archaeology is defined as "that branch of knowledge which takes cognizance of past civilizations, and investigates their history in all fields, by means of remains of art, architecture, monuments, inscriptions, literature, language, implements, customs, and all other examples which have survived" (Free & Vos ix). Archaeologists seek to shed light on the past through the recovery of its remains (Price 26). The science of archaeology includes the study of ancient artifacts as well as ancient literary sources (Sailhamer 10). Critical to this study of the historical reliability of the Bible is an examination of ancient artifacts and documents related to the people, places, and events of the biblical record.

However, it must be noted that archaeology is limited in what it can and cannot accomplish.[1] Archaeology cannot prove that the Bible is the inspired word of God (McRay 19). The truth of the inspiration of the Bible does not depend upon secular history. In fact, the Bible would be no less true even if all historical records related to it were lost or destroyed. But archaeology can demonstrate the historical accuracy and trustworthiness of portions of the biblical narrative.

Archaeology and secular history affirm the historical reliability of the Bible. The truth of the Bible is confirmed through the known facts of history. To "confirm" is "to strengthen, to establish more firmly; to ratify; to corroborate; to verify" (Webster's Dictionary). Archaeology gives new assurance of what may already be known through the Scriptures and corroborates the biblical record. In examining the archaeological record in relation to its confirmation of the Bible a distinction must be made between general and specific confirmation (McDowell 100). General confirmation demonstrates that the historical narrative fits into the larger context of the period of which it speaks. For example, archaeology will never specifically confirm what Abraham said to Sarah on a given day thousands of years ago. But it can demonstrate that the actions and characteristics of Abraham belong in the historical time period in which the Bible places him. Specific confirmation, on the other hand, directly demonstrates the historical validity of the people, places, and events mentioned in the Bible. A tremendous amount of archaeological evidence exists which both generally and specifically confirms the historical reliability of the Bible.

General Confirmation of Old Testament History
Does the historical narrative of the Old Testament fit into the context of the time period in which it is set? Do the general environment, customs,

---

[1] The limitations of archaeology are compounded by the following five factors: a) only a fraction of what is made or what is written survives to be discovered by later generations, b) only a fraction of the available archaeological sites have been surveyed, c) only a fraction of the surveyed sites have been excavated, d) only a fraction of an excavation site is actually examined, and e) only a fraction of what is excavated is eventually reported and published (Price 46-48).

types of people, and types of events recorded in the Old Testament generally suit what is known of those ancient times?

The Historical Reliability of the Old Testament Has Been
Generally Confirmed

1. The biblical account of the flood has been generally confirmed. The
Bible describes the flood as a global event during which the water covered
the highest mountains (Gen. 7:19-20), all land animals and birds outside
the ark were killed (vv. 21-22), and only Noah and his family were spared
along with the animals in the ark (v. 23).

Ancient traditions of such a flood are preserved among nearly every
nation and tribe of the human race (Rehwinkel 127). Records from places
as diverse as ancient Babylon and Sumeria, China, India, Egypt, Africa,
the islands of the Pacific, the American continents, and Europe attest to an
ancient flood of cataclysmic proportions (Rehwinkel 128-129).

While the stories and traditions differ in detail, they agree on three key
features (Rehwinkel 128). All ancient accounts of the flood speak of: (a)
Universal destruction of the human race and all other living things by water,
(b) an ark, or boat provided as the means of escape, and (c) the preservation
of a seed of mankind in order to perpetuate the human race. It is obvious
that the flood made such a powerful and lasting impression on the generations following the event that the main points of the story were passed on
and preserved in every culture which later developed.

**2. The environment of the world of the patriarchs presented in Gen-
esis has been generally confirmed.** Genesis speaks of widespread famines
which afflicted the world of the patriarchs and led them to seek preservation
in Egypt (Gen. 12:10-20; 42:1-4; 43:1-2).

Archaeologists have confirmed that large-scale migrations did in fact take
place in the part of the world inhabited by the patriarchs in ancient times
due to the onset of sudden and severe drought (Sailhamer 38). Furthermore,
a tomb painting discovered at Beni Hassan in Egypt confirms that Asian
Semitics, like the biblical patriarchs, came to Egypt in those ancient times
(Muncaster, *Old Testament* 26).

**3. The names of the patriarchs have been generally confirmed as
representative of their time period.** The names of Abram's family mem-

bers, including his own name, have been found in ancient Assyrian and Babylonian texts of the time period (Price 95). The names Isaac, Jacob, Joseph, and Ishmael have also been confirmed as belonging to the time period of the patriarchs (*Ibid.*).

4. Abraham's behavior has been confirmed as belonging to his period of time. An ancient Egyptian papyrus document has been discovered which relates that Pharaoh had a beautiful woman brought to his court and caused her husband to be murdered (Free & Vos 50). This discovery perhaps sheds some light on what would have motivated Abraham to tell Pharaoh that Sarah was his sister rather than his wife (Gen. 12:11-13).

The ancient Babylonian *Code of Hammurabi* indicates that, according to the law, a wife may give a servant to her husband as a secondary wife in order to have children by her (Free & Vos 54). This, perhaps, confirms that Abraham and Sarah were merely following the customs of the day when Sarah gave her servant Hagar to Abraham for the same purpose (Gen. 16:1-3).

5. The biblical stories involving Isaac, Jacob, and Esau have been generally confirmed. The Bible says Esau sold his birthright to his brother in exchange for a pot of stew (Gen. 25:29-34). Ancient tablets found in the Mesopotamian city of Nuzi describe a situation in which one man sold his inheritance rights concerning a grove to his brother in exchange for only three sheep (Free & Vos 63).

Later, the Bible describes how Jacob deceived his father Isaac in order to receive the oral blessing that should have been bestowed on Esau, and once the blessing was given it could not be revoked in spite of Esau's pleas (Gen. 27:1-40). Again, the Nuzi tablets shed light on the subject by demonstrating that a father's oral blessing carried the weight of binding legal authority in patriarchal times (Free & Vos 63-64).

In another instance the Bible relates that when Jacob's wife Rachel stole her father Laban's household idols, Laban pursued Jacob for seven days in an effort to retrieve them (Gen. 31:17-42). Why was Laban so concerned over the loss of a few household idols? Once more, the Nuzi tablets shed light on the situation. One of the tablets indicates that, if a son-in-law possessed the household idols of his father-in-law he could make a legal claim to his father-in-law's estate (Free & Vos 65).

6. The biblical story of Joseph has been generally confirmed in many respects. The Genesis record states that Joseph's brothers sold him as a slave for twenty shekels of silver (Gen. 37:28). Archaeology has demonstrated that twenty shekels was, in fact, the average price paid for slaves in Joseph's day (McDowell 108). Earlier than this, slaves were less expensive, while later they would have cost more (Sailhamer 40).

Once in Egypt, the biblical record states that Joseph rose to a position of prominence in Egypt second only to Pharaoh himself (Gen. 41:39-41). Is it likely that a Hebrew slave would be given such a high-ranking position in Egypt? Ancient Egyptian records tell of foreigners who achieved prominence throughout Egyptian history, including positions comparable to that attained by Joseph (Free & Vos 71-72).

7. The historical character of Egypt's treatment of Israel and the census taken by Moses has been generally confirmed. The Bible states that the king of Egypt oppressed his Hebrew slaves by refusing to give them straw with which to make brick (Exod. 5:6-13). An ancient Egyptian document has been discovered in which an overseer of building operations states that he could not complete his work due to the fact that he lacked straw for brick-making (Free & Vos 82).

Following Israel's departure from Egypt the Bible records a census taken by Moses (Num. 1-4). It has been demonstrated that the manner in which this census was taken fits into the time period of Moses and would not fit into a later period (Free & Vos 98-99). In fact, it has been observed that the method employed by Moses in taking the census bears a striking resemblance to the method employed by the Egyptian Pharaoh Thutmose III whom many conservative scholars have concluded is the Pharaoh in whose court Moses would have been raised (*Ibid.*).

Specific Confirmation of Old Testament History

Are there specific aspects of the historical narrative of the Old Testament that are directly confirmed through what is known of the history of its time period? Do the places, people, and events mentioned in the Old Testament appear in other ancient records?

The Historical Reliability of the Old Testament Has Been Specifically Confirmed At Many Points.
1. The geography of the Old Testament has been specifically con-

firmed. Ancient clay tablets discovered in the Syrian city of Ebla mention numerous biblical cities and regions including Hazor (Josh. 11:1), Megiddo (Josh. 12:21), Jerusalem (Josh. 10:1), Lachish (Josh. 10:3), Dor (Josh. 11:2), Gaza (Gen. 10:19), Karnaim (Gen. 14:5), and the territory of Canaan (Gen. 11:31), as well as many others (McDowell 102).

The Bible names Ur of the Chaldees as the native city of Abraham (Gen. 11:27-28). The ruins of Ur have been discovered and it has been revealed to have been a fairly sophisticated walled city filled with houses (Free & Vos 46-47). Such a discovery sheds even greater light on the faith of Abraham. Though the patriarch was of a comfortable urban background, he was willing to dwell in tents as a stranger in the land of Canaan in response to God's command (Gen. 12:1; Heb. 11:9).

Additionally, the Old Testament cities of Haran (Gen. 11:31-32), Hebron (Gen. 23:2), Beersheba (Gen. 21:31), Shechem (Gen. 12:6), and Laish (Judg. 18:29) have been located and excavated (Price 96-98). Prominent Old Testament cities such as the Assyrian capital, Nineveh (Gen. 10:11), and the Philistine city, Ekron (Josh. 13:3), have been located and excavated, as well as the city of Jericho (Josh. 2:1) (Price 96-98, 226; Free & Vos 111-112, 187).

That a number of other Old Testament geographic features and locations have also been specifically confirmed may be illustrated through various examples. God told Moses that the children of Israel would be able to dig copper out of the hills of the Promised Land (Deut. 8:9) and evidence of vast amounts of copper and copper veins can be seen in southern Palestine even today (Muncaster, *Old Testament* 27). Structures believed to have served as King Solomon's horse stables (1 Kings 9:19) have been discovered among the ruins of Megiddo (Free & Vos 143). Likewise, the ruins of the "high place" of idolatrous worship built by King Jeroboam in the city of Dan (1 Kings 12:26-31) have been uncovered and identified (Free & Vos 152-153).

2. The people of the Old Testament have been specifically confirmed in numerous cases. The earliest known specific mention of the nation of Israel outside of the Bible comes from an inscription on a victory stele[2] of

---

[2] A "stele" is a stone monument engraved with a written or pictorial commemoration of an event or achievement (Muncaster, *Old Testament* 31).

the Egyptian king Merneptah (1232-1222 B.C.) in which he boasts of having defeated Israel in battle during a campaign through Palestine (Free & Vos 81). However, an even earlier inscription that likely refers to the Israelite tribe of Asher from the reign of Pharaoh Seti I (1394-1279 B.C.) has also been discovered (Sailhamer 58-59).

An ancient monument of the Moabite king Mesha, known as the "Moabite Stone," contains an inscription referring to the Israelite king Omri (1 Kings 16:16) and his son, which would be a reference to Ahab (1 Kings 21:25), who is famous for having led Israel further into the depths of idolatry (Free & Vos 160-161). Reference is also made to Ahab in the records of the Assyrian king Shalmaneser III (Free & Vos 150), and the palaces of both Omri and Ahab have been located, including Ahab's "ivory house" mentioned in 1 Kings 22:39 (Free & Vos 154-155).

A reference of Shalmaneser III which mentions Hazael, king of Syria, as one who "seized the throne" confirms the biblical account of Hazael (2 Kings 8:15), who murdered Ben-Hadad in order to usurp the throne of Syria (Free & Vos 161-162). The Black Obelisk[3] of Shalmaneser III makes reference to the tribute that king Jehu of Israel (2 Kings 9:1-10) was forced to pay the Assyrian king (Price 76-77).

The records of the Assyrian king Tiglath Pileser III confirm the events concerning him which are mentioned in the Bible (2 Kings 15:29-30) and make reference to the Israelite kings Menahem, Pekah, and Hoshea (Sailhamer 83). The records of the Assyrian king Sennacherib make reference to the tribute paid by king Hezekiah of Judah (2 Kings 18:14-16) in direct confirmation of the biblical account (Free & Vos 179). The "Taylor Prism" of Sennacherib also describes his siege against Jerusalem during the reign of Hezekiah (2 Kings 18-19), yet notably lacks any claim of victory over Jerusalem, thereby harmonizing with the biblical account of 2 Kings 19:35-36 which states that God struck the army of Assyria causing Sennacherib to return to his own land without completing the conquest (Price 272-274).

---

[3] An "obelisk" is a monument normally consisting of a tall, four-sided, tapering pillar which is finished at the top like a pyramid (*Webster's Dictionary*). A modern example of an obelisk is the Washington Monument in Washington, D.C.

The tunnel that Hezekiah constructed to bring water into Jerusalem (2 Kings 20:20) has been located (Free & Vos 182). Also in relation to Hezekiah, a tomb bearing the inscription of Shebna (Isa. 22:15), who served as his steward, has been discovered in Silwan outside Jerusalem (Sailhamer 89).

Reference to the Babylonian king Merodach-Baladan (2 Kings 20:12) has been found in the records of Sennacherib (Free & Vos 182). The records of king Esarhaddon of Assyria (2 Kings 20:36-37) tell of his subjugation of king Mannaseh of Judah (2 Chron. 33:10-11) in direct confirmation of the biblical record (Free & Vos 183).

There is a vast amount of archaeological information related to king Nebucahdnezzar, who conquered Judah (2 Kings 25) as well as a number of other nations (Free & Vos 196). Ancient Babylonian records make reference to the fact that Nebuchadnezzar captured king Jehoiachin of Judah and replaced him with Zedekiah (2 Kings 24:17) in direct confirmation of the biblical account (Price 232-233).

Seals inscribed with the names of a number of individuals mentioned in the book of Jeremiah have been found, including those of Gemariah, son of Shaphan who was king Jehoiakim's scribe (Jer. 36:10), Baruch the son of Neriah, who was Jeremiah's scribe (Jer. 36:4), Gedaliah, whom Babylon appointed governor (Jer. 40:5), and Ishmael, the son of Nethaniah (Jer. 41:2) who assassinated him (Price 235; McDowell 114).

Archaeological confirmation of king Evil-Merodach of Babylon has been found along with lists of the rations of food appointed for his captive, king Jehoiachin of Judah, during his reign (2 Kings 25:27-30), thereby specifically confirming the historical narrative of the Bible (Free & Vos 189-190).

Confirmation of the Persian king, Cyrus the Great, and his lenient policy toward captive nations (2 Chron. 36:22-23; Ezra 1:1-4) has been found in an inscription appearing on a monument known as the "Cyrus Cylinder" (Price 250-252). Confirmation of the reign of the Persian king Darius the Great (Ezra 5-6) has been found in a monumental inscription in Iran known as the "Behistun Rock" (Price 58-59). The Persian king Ahasuerus of the book of Esther has been identified in secular history as Xerxes (485-465 B.C.) who was succeeded by his son, Artaxerxes (Neh. 2:1), under whose reign Nehemiah was allowed to rebuild the walls of Jerusalem (Free & Vos 207, 211; Sailhamer 100).

The Elephantine papyri discovered in Egypt confirm the existence of Sanballat of Samaria (Neh. 4:1), while the Zeno papyri confirm the existence of Tobiah the Ammonite (Neh. 4:3), both of whom opposed Nehemiah's work (Free & Vos 211).

3. Numerous Old Testament events have been specifically confirmed through secular history. Though there is much debate over the precise location of the ruins of Sodom and Gomorrah, the cities of the plain which God destroyed with fire and brimstone (Gen. 19), the first century A.D. Jewish historian, Josephus, wrote of evidence of their destruction and stated that traces of the destroyed cities could still be seen in his day (Josephus, *Wars* 4.8.4). Perhaps even more interesting is that the first century A.D. Roman historian, Tacitus, speaks of these cities as having been "consumed by lightning" and also affirms that their ruins were visible in his day (Tacitus, *Histories* 5.7).

Widespread worship of the pagan deities Baal (Judg. 2:13), Dagon (1 Sam. 31:10), and Ashtaroth (1 Sam. 31:10) in Canaan during the Old Testament period has been confirmed through archaeology (Free & Vos 124, 128-129).

The biblical description of three successive phases of the Babylonian captivity of Judah (Dan. 1:1-6; Ezek. 1:1-3; 2 Chron. 36:15-21) has been confirmed through records found in the "Babylonian Chronicle," the "Chronicles of the Chaldean Kings," and the "Lachish Letters" (Muncaster, *Old Testament* 41).

General Confirmation of New Testament History
Does the historical narrative of the New Testament fit into the context of the time period in which it is set? Do the historical references of the New Testament generally suit what is known of the world of the first century A.D.?

The Historical Reliability of the New Testament Has Been Generally Confirmed
1. The Roman census taken at the time of Christ's birth has been generally confirmed. The Bible mentions a census decreed by Augustus

Caesar during which "all went to be registered, everyone to his own city" (Luke 2:1-3). For this reason, Joseph and Mary left Galilee and traveled to Bethlehem where Jesus was born (Luke 2:4-7).

The first century A.D. Roman historian, Suetonius (A.D. 69-140), mentions that Augustus was in the habit of census-taking (Suetonius 2.27). In fact, ancient papyrus census forms have demonstrated that a census was taken throughout the Roman Empire every fourteen years (McRay 154-155; Free & Vos 242-243). In addition to this, ancient Roman census orders have been discovered which indicate the necessity of having people return to their homes in order to be registered (McRay 155; McDowell 63). Therefore, the known facts of history correspond to Luke's account of the census.

2. The coins mentioned in the New Testament have been generally confirmed as belonging to the period. The denarius (Matt. 20:2), the shekel (Matt. 26:14-15), and the lepta (Mark 12:41-44) were all in circulation in first century Palestine (McDowell 68). While archaeologists will never be able to confirm the discovery of the very denarius Jesus used in Matthew 22:17-21, it has generally been confirmed that such a coin would have borne Caesar's image and inscription (McDowell 68; McRay 33).

3. The presence of Jewish communities in the various places listed as homes of those in Jerusalem on the Day of Pentecost (Acts 2:5-11) has been confirmed (Free & Vos 260).

4. Excavations in Nubia have confirmed that the Ethiopians did in fact refer to their queen as "Candace" (Acts 8:27) in the first century A.D. (Free & Vos 263).

5. Though it is impossible to know the exact inscription to which Paul referred in Acts 17:23, it has been confirmed that **altars and inscriptions to "unknown gods" were common in the city of Athens in the first century A.D.** (McRay 304).

Specific Confirmation of New Testament History
Are there specific aspects of the historical narrative that have been directly confirmed through what is known of the history of the period? Do the places, people, and events of the New Testament appear in the historical record of the first century A.D.?

The Historical Reliability of the New Testament Has Been Specifically Confirmed At Numerous Points

1. The geography of the New Testament has been specifically confirmed. Aside from the obvious examples of Rome, Jerusalem, and Athens, most of the important cities and towns mentioned in the New Testament have been identified and excavated, including Bethelehem (Matt. 2:1), Nazareth (Matt. 2:23), Capernaum (Matt. 4:13), Antioch of Syria (Acts 11:25-26), Corinth (Acts 18:1-17), and Ephesus (Acts 19), as well as many others (Free & Vos 242, 245, 247-248, 264, 277-280; McRay 164; Sailhamer 113).

In Corinth the very "bema," or judgment seat, where Paul stood before the proconsul Gallio (Acts 18:12-17) has been discovered (McRay 333-335). While in Ephesus, the temple of Diana (Acts 19:27) and the theater where the uproar over Paul's teaching took place (Acts 19:29-41) have been discovered (Free & Vos 279-280).

Among other significant historically verifiable locations mentioned in the New Testament, the Jordan River (Matt. 3:13-17), the Sea of Galilee (John 6:1), the Mount of Olives (John 8:1), and the Pools of Bethesda and Siloam (John 5:1-15; 9:1-11) have been identified, along with many others (Beitzel 38-40, 157; McRay 186-187).

2. The people of the New Testament have been specifically confirmed in numerous cases. The Roman emperors Augustus (Luke 2:1), Tiberius (Luke 3:1), Claudius (Acts 11:28), and Nero, to whom Paul appealed (Acts 25:10-12), are well known through secular history (Tacitus, *Annals* 1.10; Suetonius 2.27, 3.10, 5.25, 6.9-57).

The ruling family of the Herods, including Herod the Great (Matt. 2:1), Herod Archelaus (Matt. 2:22), Herod Philip (Luke 3:1), Herod Antipas (Mark 6:14-18), Herod Agrippa I (Acts 12:20-23), and Herod Agrippa II (Acts 26:1-3), is also well attested in secular history (Free & Vos 232-233, 236-238; McRay 144-145).

Historical accounts of other government officials such as Quirinius (Luke 2:2), Lysanias (Luke 3:1), Pontinus Pilate (Matt. 27:2), Sergius Paulus (Acts 13:7), Gallio (Acts 18:12), and Felix (Acts 23:23-24) agree with what is stated in the Scriptures (Suetonius 3.49, 5.28; Tacitus, *Annals* 12.53, 15.72; Josephus, *Antiquities* 18.3.1; McRay 160; Free & Vos 268-269). In 1961 a stone was discovered in the ruins of the Roman theater in Caesarea which bears an inscription making reference to Pontius Pilate (Muncaster, *New Testament* 36; McRay 203-204).

As for the Jewish leaders mentioned in the New Testament, the ossuary[4] of Caiaphas the high priest (Matt. 26:3) was discovered in 1990, Gamaliel (Acts 5:34) is mentioned in the Jewish Talmud,[5] and Ananias the high priest is known historically for his cruelty (Price 305-307; McRay 107; Sailhamer 123).

Josephus makes mention of both John the Baptizer (Matt. 3:1) and James the brother of Jesus[6] (Josephus, *Antiquities* 18.5.2, 20.9.1).

In 1929 a first century A.D. limestone inscription which makes reference to Erastus, the city treasurer (Rom. 16:23), was discovered among the ruins of Corinth (McRay 331-332).

Ancient Non-Christian Sources Make Reference To Jesus Christ
1. The Roman historian Cornelius Tacitus (A.D. 60-120) writes, in complete agreement with Scripture, that Christ was executed by Pontius Pilate in Judea during the reign of Tiberius Caesar (Tacitus, *Annals* 15.43).

---

[4] An "ossuary" is a stone box used to hold the bones of the deceased. The custom in ancient Palestine was to bury the body of the deceased in a cave tomb. The body would be allowed to remain in the cave for a year until the flesh had completely decomposed leaving only the bones. The bones would then be collected and placed in an ossuary, and the ossuary would in turn be kept in the family crypt. The cave tomb could then be used to bury the more recently deceased (http://www.rom.on.ca/ossuary/jerusalem.html).

[5] The Jewish Talmud is an ancient collection of rabbinical laws, law decisions, and commentary on the Law of Moses. The Jerusalem Talmud was compiled between A.D. 350-425, while the Babylonian Talmud was compiled about A.D. 500 (McDowell 28).

[6] The controversial "James Ossuary" may prove to be another powerful confirmation of the existence of James the brother of Jesus. The ossuary, first reported as having been discovered on October 21, 2002, bears the inscription: "James, son of Joseph, brother of Jesus." The authenticity of the ossuary and its inscription is currently the subject of intense debate (http://www.rom.on.ca/ossuary/ossuary_intro.html).

2. Another Roman historian, Gaius Suetonius (A.D. 69-140) traces a disturbance among the Jews in Rome back to the influence of Christ (Suetonius 5.25).

3. The Jewish historian Flavius Josephus (A.D. 37-100) makes reference to the ministry of Christ and to his crucifixion by Pilate at the urging of the Jewish leaders (Josephus, Antiquities 18.3.3). Additionally, he refers to the Lord as "Jesus, who was called Christ" in writing of the death of James, the Lord's brother (Josephus, Antiquities 20.9.1).

4. Pliny the Younger (62-113 A.D.), the Roman governor of Bithynia and Pontus, wrote to the emperor Trajan with questions concerning the proper treatment of Christians and provided a description of how they would regularly gather to worship Christ (Free & Vos 243).

5. The Greek satirist Lucian of Samosata (125-190 A.D.) wrote sarcastically of Christ as the originator of the cult of Christianity and mentioned that he was crucified in Palestine for having originated this cult (Free & Vos 243).

The ancient non-Christian references to Christ provide general confirmation of much of what is stated in the New Testament.

The Significance of the Historical Reliability of the Bible
1. The Bible has overcome its critics. Over the past two centuries scholars critical of the Bible have subjected the Scriptures to intense scrutiny and have sought to minimize the accuracy of the historical record contained therein. But as history has shown, the reality is that the critics of the Bible have proven unreliable while the Bible has passed the test.

The critics have said that the biblical reference to Abraham's possession of camels while sojourning in Egypt (Gen. 12:16) is an error since camels were not known in Egypt in the time of Abraham. However, camel figurines, drawings of camels, camel bones, and rope made of camel hair dating to several hundred years before Abraham's day have been found in Egypt (Free & Vos 51).

The critics have said that Moses could not have written the first five books of the Bible because alphabetic writing was not invented until later. But ancient inscriptions found in Palestine indicate that alphabetic writing was in use in that part of the world even before the time of Moses (Sailhamer 42-43).

Moreover, the critics said that Moses could not have written the law because such sophisticated law codes as that presented in Deuteronomy did not exist until much later. But the discovery of ancient law codes such as the Babylonian *Code of Hammurabi*, which dates to about three hundred years before Moses, have proven the critics wrong again (Free & Vos 103).

In the late nineteenth century critics doubted the very existence of the Hittites, who are mentioned more than fifty times in the Bible (Gen. 15:20; Deut. 7:1). Since that time archaeologists have uncovered a vast Hittite empire and many universities now offer students the opportunity to earn a Ph.D. in Hittite Studies (Free & Vos 108-109).

Critics once relegated King David (2 Sam. 5:3) to the realm of mere myth and legend. But the critics were forced to rethink their point of view when, in 1993, a three thousand year old monumental inscription referring to "the House of David" was found in northern Israel (Price 167-172).

Critics also doubted the very existence of Sargon, king of Assyria (Isa. 20:1) until his palace was discovered in 1843 (Free & Vos 170).

Likewise, critics of the Bible regarded Belshazzar (Dan. 5:1-31) as a character invented by the writer of the book of Daniel. However, inscriptions uncovered in ancient Babylonia not only confirm Belshazzar's existence, but also indicate that he was co-ruler of Babylon with his father, Nabonidus (Free & Vos 200-202). This discovery helps to explain why Belshazzar was only able to make Daniel "third ruler in the kingdom" instead of second (Dan. 5:29).

Critics have sought to cast doubt on Luke's statement that Jesus was born during the period when "Quirinius was governor of Syria" (Luke 2:2), since it is known that he served as governor in A.D. 6, which would be too late for the time of Jesus' birth. However, inscriptions have been uncovered which indicate that Quirinius actually served as governor twice, instead of only once as was previously thought (Free & Vos 243).

Furthermore, critics have raised the contention that the account of Jesus' burial (Luke 23:50-56) is not likely to be true because a crucified criminal would not have been afforded a proper burial. But in 1968 the bones of a victim of crucifixion named Yohanan ben Ha'galgol were discovered in a tomb outside Jerusalem, having received a proper Jewish burial (Price 308-311).

The critics have sought to criticize the Bible, but as it turns out, the critics have found their own work subject to criticism through the discoveries of history and archaeology. Even so, old criticisms die hard even long after they have been proven unjustifiable and many textbooks lazily persist in repeating them even still.

2. The Bible deserves the benefit of the doubt. The Bible is unique in its verifiable historical reliability.[7] The Scriptures have fended off criticism at every turn, and in the process, the historicity of the story of the Bible has been confirmed. Since thousands of biblical cities and sites remain buried and unexcavated, we should only expect further confirmation of the details of biblical history to emerge in the future (Free & Vos 293-294).

In light of the overwhelming amount of historical and archaeological evidence in favor of the accuracy of the Bible that exists today, those who view the Bible from a critical perspective would do well to reserve their judgment when tempted to denigrate the integrity of the Scriptures simply because no historical light has yet been shed on certain passages of the Bible. The obvious reality is that those passages currently lacking extra-biblical confirmation may yet be confirmed in the future. In the meantime, the Bible has earned the right to receive the benefit of the doubt.

---

[7] The uniqueness of the Bible in proving itself in the face of criticism is seen when compared to the sacred literature of other religions. For example, a striking contrast can be drawn between the Bible and the *Book of Mormon*. Though the *Book of Mormon* is filled with references to people, places, and events having to do with the American continents in ancient times, no scholarly discussion of the historical reliability of the *Book of Mormon* can be held. The narrative of the *Book of Mormon* is entirely devoid of any information that might be confirmed through history and archaeology. In fact, its narrative is everywhere contradicted by the known facts of history and archaeology. One can neither visit the ruins of cities mentioned in the *Book of Mormon* nor view artifacts and inscriptions left by those mentioned in its pages (Crane & Crane 114-120).

Conclusion

Christians must rise to the defense of the historical reliability of the Bible. The Scriptures are under constant attack. The assault upon the integrity of the Bible is not only being waged in the universities and among the academic elite. The Bible is constantly under attack in schools, in popular books, in movies, in documentary television programs, and even in the sermons of those who claim to believe it. But historical truth and historical fact are on the side of the Scriptures. The child of God must, like Paul, be "set for the defense of the gospel" (Phil. 1:17) and must "always be ready to give a defense" of the truth (1 Pet. 3:15). The battle has been joined and the faithful must uphold and guard the inspired record. In so doing, we do not seek to defend "cunningly devised fables" (2 Pet. 1:16). For that well-attested record which we seek to uphold truly is, "the word of God which lives and abides forever" (1 Pet. 1:23).

Bibliography

Beitzel, Barry J. *The Moody Atlas of Bible Lands*. Chicago, IL: Moody, 1985.

Crane, Charles A. and Steven A. Crane. *Ashamed of Joseph: Mormon Foundations Crumble*. Joplin, MO: College Press, 1993.

Free, Joseph P. and Howard F. Vos. *Archaeology and Bible History*. Grand Rapids, MI: Zondervan, 1992.

Josephus, Flavius. *The Works of Flavius Josephus*. Trans. By William Whiston. Peabody, MA: Hendrickson, 1999

McDowell, Josh. *The New Evidence That Demands a Verdict*. Nashville, TN: Nelson, 1999.

McRay, John. *Archaeology & The New Testament*. Grand Rapids, MI: Baker, 1991.

Muncaster, Ralph O. *Can Archaeology Prove the Old Testament?* Eugene, OR: Harvest House, 2000.

_____. *Can Archaeology Prove the New Testament?* Eugene, OR: Harvest House, 2000.

Price, Randall. *The Stones Cry Out*. Eugene, OR: Harvest House, 1997.

Rehwinkel, Alfred M. *The Flood*. St. Louis, MO: Concordia, 1951.

Royal Ontario Museum Website (http://www.rom.on.ca/ossuary/jerusalem.html).

Sailhamer, John H. *Biblical Archaeology*. Grand Rapids, MI: Zondervan, 1998.

Suetonius, Gaius. *The Twelve Caesars*. Trans. By Robert Graves. New York, NY: Penguin, 1979

Tacitus, Cornelius. *The Annals of Imperial Rome*. Trans. By Michael Grant. New York, NY: Penguin, 1989

_____. *The Histories*. Trans. By Kenneth Wellesley. New York, NY: Penguin, 1982

Webster's English Dictionary. New Lanark, Scotland: Geddes & Grosset, 2001.

Serving God in My Senior Years

Donald Willis

King David affirmed "I was glad when they said to me, 'Let us go into the house of the Lord'" (Ps. 122:1). What an honor one has to labor in the kingdom of God! Those who served under the law considered it an honor to serve in the house of God! God's spiritual house is his church; and all of us who labor therein should count this as an extreme honor and blessing. One must serve in purity of life and rejoice in the obligations placed therein.

God has placed upon every individual an obligation to be faithful to him. Life is filled with differing circumstances. One must learn to keep focus upon God, his will for our lives, and also to the exercise of a godly influence. One is responsible to God from the day of birth until the day of death.

Donald Fred Willis (b February 9, 1934) is one of four brothers who chose to preach the gospel: Cecil (now deceased), Donald, Lewis and Mike Willis, all children of Onan J. and Wilhemina Willis. Donald has been married to Marilyn Riggs Willis for fifty years and is the father of four children: Donald Jr.; Cathy (Price), Charles, and Christie (Estes). They have been blessed with four children, many grandchildren and great grandchildren. Don has preached since the age of sixteen in Antioch and Centralia, Texas while a senior in High School; Palatka, Florida; West End in Houston; Greenwood Village in Houston; Highland in San Antonio; Pleasant Valley in Wichita, Kansas; Floral Heights in Wichita Falls, Texas; Vivion Road in Kansas City, Missouri; Bellaire in Houston, Texas; Woodland Hills in Conroe, Texas; New Caney, Texas (started in 1981); O'Connor Road in San Antonio, Texas; and now labors with the Highway 90 church in Madisonville, Texas. Charles Willis (second son) now preaches with the church in New Caney, Texas.

Sin is a natural occurrence. ". . . all have sinned, and come short of the glory of God" (Rom. 3:23). ". . . by one man sin entered into the world, and death by sin; and so death passed upon all men, for that *all have sinned*" (Rom. 5:12). God has a plan for forgiveness, Jesus Christ came into the world as man, lived a sinless life, died upon the cross to pay the price for sin. Without Jesus Christ, we are all yet in our sins! We often sin after becoming a child of God. Again God speaks, "Repent therefore of this your wickedness, and pray God if perhaps the thought of your heart may be forgiven you" (Acts 8:22). "If we confess our sins, He is faithful and just to forgive us our sins and to cleanse us from all unrighteousness" (1 John 1:9). "There is none righteous, no, not one" (Rom. 3:10). Every individual, having reached an accountable age, has sinned and is lost without Jesus Christ. No one will earn salvation. "The gift of God is eternal life in Christ Jesus our Lord" (Rom. 3:23). Now, we are all on the same page, the ground is level, and we can commence our lesson.

Duties of an Elderly Preacher

1. Preacher means a herald, a preacher of the gospel (1 Tim. 2:7; 2 Tim. 1:11, see Vine's *Expository Dictionary*). If one preaches another gospel, he is a false preacher, a teacher of error, and is not a faithful child of God!

2. Age comes upon all people. Note some statements from the revelation: "Do not cast me off in the time of old age; Do not forsake me when my strength fails" (Ps. 71:9). "They shall still bear fruit in old age; They shall be fresh and flourishing" (Ps. 92:14). "Listen to Me, O house of Jacob, And all the remnant of the house of Israel, Who have been upheld by Me from birth, Who have been carried from the womb: Even to your old age, I am He, And even to gray hairs I will carry you! I have made, and I will bear; Even I will carry, and will deliver you" (Isa. 46:3-4). God intends for Christians to be faithful and useful until the day of death.

Rather than despise the older preacher, there should be a place of honor and respect. Listen to them, learn from their experiences. "You shall rise before the gray headed and honor the presence of an old man, and fear your God: I am the Lord" (Lev. 19:32). "The hoary head is a crown of glory, if it be found in the way of righteousness" (Prov. 16:31). Sadly, also note, ". . . fools despise wisdom and instruction" (Prov. 1:7).

Older preachers are simply described as a younger preacher who has labored diligently for over many years in the kingdom of God. Years bring experience and maturity. Proverbs 16:31 declares, "The silver-haired head is a crown of glory, If it is found in the way of righteousness." Older gospel preachers understand the trials of younger Christians. As one grows older, purity of life must continue; we become examples to younger men seeking to please God. Do not grow bitter in our older age, but rejoice in the opportunity to serve our God. Be faithful until death!

Be an example of faithfulness to the Lord and especially to our younger preachers. Rejoice in the Lord! Many influences enter the life of that younger preacher, and one will never fully realize the benefit of assisting a young preacher, directing and encouraging him in his study, supporting him in his weakness. Use empathy in listening to his problems and give reassurance. I can see all of this in the story of my own life! There are so many advantages to those whose parents and grandparents are Christians. Encouragement, uplifting statements! Anyone can find fault! The wise will attempt to assist one in overcoming and excelling. I see the duties of an older preacher exemplified in the life of the Willis family.

Let me begin my story of life! I was the second child born to Onan J. and Wilhemina Willis. Second means something; primarily, that I was not the firstborn. Cecil Willis was born in 1932 and I was born in 1934. Times were very difficult. Few had money. But the Willis family had been around for a long time. Joseph Willis, a great-great-great grandfather, migrated into the area of Alexandria, Louisiana and became a traveling preacher among the Indians. His mode of travel was often the logs floating in the river. His wife had the duties of the family, and he spent most of his life in preaching to the Indians and others who would listen. He preached throughout that area.

My family settled into Trinity County, Texas. My mother's father was a Thompson, and he died early. My grandmother married Jodie Harrott, a farmer who preached in the small church of Christ in Sylvester. This is my first remembrance of going to church assemblies. I later learned that Winslow Willis, my grandfather, also would preach in the absence of another preacher.

I did not know much about my father's religious commitment; he was so busy in the logging business and in raising a family, keeping his crew working and his trucks repaired. Dad was a very industrious individual and worked a number of men. Some years after Cecil and I had begun to preach, Dad was restored and later served as an elder in the Groveton church.

After his death, we learned of his care of other people in the area around Groveton, Texas. Mom and Dad had seven children; Homer Cecil, Donald Fred, Lewis Berton, Ouida Jean (Stover), Karen Sue (Morris), Stephen Michael, and Barbara (Coleman).

Mom always took the children to worship, first in Sylvester and later in Groveton, Texas. The church was very small and did not have a regular preacher. Ned Fairbarin preached for the church in Trinity, Texas. He would come to Groveton to teach the ladies class and to edify. Cecil and I were old enough to know the truth and this good brother taught and encouraged us, baptizing us into Christ on August 17, 1944 in a nasty old pond in Woodlake, Texas. He did not remain in Trinity very long and sadly I lost contact with him.

The church in Groveton only had a preacher every now and then. I remember when Luther Blackmon would come to preach for us. Bill Thompson was a great influence in our lives and encouraged us to memorize Scriptures and Bible history. Several Lufkin preachers encouraged us: Roy Cogdill, Luther Blackmon, etc. Upon graduation in 1949, Cecil did some campaigning in the state of Texas with the father of Dwight King. Dwight's father encouraged and assisted in the support of Cecil Willis to attend Florida College.

In my senior year of high school, I did all kinds of things to raise some money for college. Wages were always small. My dad worked about six trucks, thus I asked him if I could borrow one to attend worship in Antioch, where Aunt Mae (Dad's sister) and Uncle Jim Money attended. Another uncle, Robert Mochman (on my mother's side), attended the same church. Darwin Kerr drove to Antioch to preach the second and fourth Sundays, but he worked in the Post Office and December was a very difficult time; thus, he could not preach in Antioch that month. I asked the brethren if they would permit me to preach in brother Kerr's place on the second and fourth Sunday. They replied affirmatively and even asked, "Would you like to preach today?" I preached my only sermon! I went back the following Sunday to preach, and they asked if I would like to return the third Sunday. By then, brother Kerr heard what was happening, and he sent word to the church that he would not be coming back there to work (thus, pushing me into preaching every Sunday). With a school load, this became very difficult. I went down the road to Centralia and asked if they would permit me to preach every other Sunday. They replied in the affirmative. Now, I had an appointment for every Sunday of the month. All of this happened because brother Kerr so encouraged me at this time. I have wondered what would have happened to me without that initial encouragement.

Once graduating from high achool, I went to Houston in order to get a better job to help me toward my college education. Uncle Jim Money's daughter (Ida Bea and husband, Vestal Gaston) invited me to stay with them while I worked. They attended the Kashmere Garden church. Glenn Walker was the preacher. There was a great number of young people attending there. I dated a couple of the young ladies and became interested in Marilyn Riggs, daughter of one of the elders. There was a singing school at the Height's church, and I knew Marilyn would not attend with me so I got a group of kids to attend, Marilyn being one of those invited. You see, there was a problem—Marilyn was promised to a young man in the military. This required very immediate action upon my part. The singing school was for two weeks, which meant I would have the opportunity to be with her for several evenings. I made it a point to take her home last. We talked a lot, and I enjoyed her very much. She told me about her boyfriend. The last night of the singing school, I took Marilyn home and kissed her as she consented. I immediately told her that she did not love that young man. I "swept her off her feet." It was not long until I was away to Florida College.

College was so different from high school. I met wonderful people. All of them had religious natures, but all were human and we made many mistakes. It was good that Cecil was in Tampa. I had very little money. I developed a chronic back problem which prohibited me from working where I had been; thus, by summer time, I decided that I would not be able to return for the second year. Brother Roland Lewis worked with the school, and he heard that I was not to return. He said, "You cannot work." He encouraged me to come back and I could pay for the college later. I did return, thanks to the encouragement of this dear man. Fifty years later I worked with a church in San Antonio where some of his family attended, and I was permitted to be with him again prior to his death. It took me about five years to pay off the college debt. But, by his encouragement, I was able to receive some outstanding education. I am thankful for the interest given by older brothers and sisters in Christ.

I completed the second year of college, received an invitation from Miami to assist a church for the summer. Sure! A dream come true. As the summer drew to a close, I heard that Palatka, Florida was looking for a preacher.

I went to talk with them (they knew I was a nineteen-year old kid), and they asked me to work with them. I purchased an old Pontiac and lived in a boarding house. The work grew by baptizing many into Christ. But, Marilyn (not yet out of high school) did not much want to move to Florida. After eighteen months, I called a meeting of the men and told them my heart was in Houston and that I was going to move. Brother Bill Lambert (schoolmate) came to my rescue and moved to work with that church. I was on my way to be married.

I arrived in Houston enthusiastic, but Marilyn would not marry me without a job. Eventually, I found the West End church of Christ was looking for a preacher. An older gentleman was also interested in the work. I went to preach for them one Sunday and went home with some Trinity County people (the husband was not a Christian, but his father had worked for my dad). We studied that afternoon, and he was baptized into Christ that night. The church asked me to come labor with them. Today, some of my dearest friends were children in that church. Five years, we labored together. Two children (Cathy and Don) were born here.

R.J. Stevens preached at the Greenwood Village church. I knew his father from Lufkin. Greenwood Village was seeking a preacher, as R.J. was moving to Madisonville. I talked with them, purchased a house, and started to work. I met Jule Miller in the Houston area. Jule Miller published a set of filmstrips that were very effective for home Bible studies. I learned how to use them and baptized many into the Lord using this teaching aid. Greenwood Village did not have elders. They had some problems. I decided to move. My uncle, Alton Thompson, lived in Lufkin. He told brother Spears (from Lufkin, but by this time living in San Antonio) about my work. The Highland Boulevard church invited me to come talk with them, and they invited me to move there to work. W.L. Wharton was preaching with the church. This was a great and profitable learning period! One should encourage able churches to take a younger preacher to add to their work.

Marilyn and I moved into the house owned by the church with no air conditioning. It was hot. There was a wonderful group of young folks, and we had a wonderful work. Loren Stephens who was in the military, attended with us, and later started preaching. Rick Baughn was there, and we became closest of friends. All of this happened because someone encouraged me. While in San Antonio, Harold Trimble was preaching on base at Lackland Air Force and was having some success in teaching some of the young men.

He was involved in a terrible accident, and he asked me if I would go out and help on Saturday and Sunday. Of course. Such an opportunity. I do not know how many people were baptized, but a bunch. The base Adjutant was a member at the West Avenue church and would obtain permission to get the men off base in order to baptize them. One night I baptized sixteen young men into Christ. One of these was the son of the president of Pepperdine college, who sent me a wonderful "thank you" note. I did the work but a very short time, brother Trimble recovered. My two year's study was over.

Wichita, Kansas sought a preacher. The preacher was going to continue his education; they invited us to attend. This was the most beautiful place I had ever seen. The fields had the heartwarming green glow. The people were wonderful. They invited us to move and work with them and secured a rental property about two blocks from the building. We moved in June. I could not believe that this beautiful "oasis" was now a desert. Hot, no air conditioning. Our son, Charles, was born here. We worked hard, baptized many, and had a wonderful labor. Close friends still live in the area.

I received a call from Floral Heights in Wichita, Texas. They invited us to move and work with them. Six bountiful years were spent there. This was a highlight of my life. Some of our closest friends still live in that area and I have held gospel meetings there. Oh, yes! Christie (our last child) was born here.

Vivion Road in Kansas City invited us to move (my brother, Cecil, had preached there). They had a good eldership and a wonderful number of working Christians. The church had been using some of the Jule Miller filmstrips. I encouraged them to expand this program. We arranged a good team of workers. I think we had six or eight projectors. I would schedule homes for showing of the filmstrip and the elders/deacons/and others would present the material. On the night that one usually would be open to be baptized I went with them. We unified so many families in the Lord. It was the most fruitful work of my life. My wife took an interest in antiques. We purchased some, which I took to the basement to strip and repair. I injured my throat! I could not preach for six months. Brother Welch heard of my problem and brought me back to Wichita Falls. I hated to leave and the brethren were so dear. I began working with brother Welch in the building business, got my Real Estate license and began selling homes. I continued to get stronger. We were making good money. I received a telephone call—W.R. Jones was moving from Bellaire, Texas and the elders wanted to talk with us.

I visited and preached in Wichita, Kansas the Sunday before Bellaire, and I had voice trouble, again. But I got through the Sunday in Bellaire, and the elders invited us to move. There were so many young adults of college age. We had a delightful labor. Dr. Harold Green (deacon) recently told me that these were the most fruitful years in the history of that church. I had some trouble with one of the elders (marriage question). I was invited into an elders' meeting, and the elders thanked me for the good work and would desire that I move within twelve months. I talked with Roy Cogdill (then at Conroe), and he told me to "get up and get out. Come help us in Conroe." That was a hard time emotionally but such a blessing! We left Cathy and Donald Jr. in the Bellaire church and in 1975 moved to Conroe.

Conroe was a blessing. Brother Cogdill assisted me to purchase a home next door to him. The brethren in Conroe were wonderful people and our labors were very successful. Brother Cogdill had a young preacher from Italy move to study with him. Cecil Willis had some health and emotional problems and also moved to Conroe. Cecil later moved on to Huntsville. My children entered the Willis, Texas schools. We found out that one of our ancestors had begun the city of Willis and now our children were attending there because of the influence of brother Cogdill. Later, brother Cogdill's health began to fail him and he moved to Houston. During the time of our labor in Conroe, the Decker's Prairie church was started by Barry Pennington, and we sent two families there. The Woodlands church began a few years later, with a good number of our brethren there. We had some families attending that lived in the New Caney area, and I did some research and determined that we should begin a church there.

New Caney was primarily a mobile home community. There were a few subdivisions in the area. There were members attending in Humble, Cleveland, Porter, and Conroe. We had meetings in the home of Andy Kerr, the son of brother Kerr who assisted me while in High School. It was decided to start a church. Sister Kerr taught in the school and received permission for us to use one of the cafeterias for a meeting place. We could use this for one year, at which time (to keep using the school) we had to have begun a process for constructing a church building. In 1981 we started the church. Often the attendance was very low, but there was always that faithful few. Word came to us of available pews in northeast Texas. We went to see them, purchased them, and stored them in a trailer owned by one of the members. We purchased a piece of property with money borrowed from the mother of one of the members (who later obeyed the gospel) and sold bonds to secure the necessary monies to build the building. A member of the liberal Porter church contracted to build the building for us. We borrowed $100,000. What a delightful time! Several churches furnished my support. Steve Fontenot, from the Humble church, kept asking me if I needed additional funds. So much encouragement. We finally completed the building. It was difficult to preach, lumps in one's throat. The opening Sunday—rain! We had no parking available, no sidewalks. Lynn Farrell, newly baptized, purchased plyboard, ripped it, and made a walkway. What a wonderful service! A Conroe businessman and close friend attended the opening service. He came to me afterward and said he would like to assist us when we purchased the piano—ha! Soon the church had elders, and a solid growth was realized. We baptized so many. We added a classroom section to our building, again from borrowed money. The first Sunday after we completed the classroom addition, one of the teachers complained because there was not enough room for her students. What a joy!

In 1994, the O'Connor Road church in San Antonio invited us to move and work with them. Carolyn (Stern) Dansby attended that church. She was a member at West End in Houston and attended our wedding ceremony. We had been close friends for a long time. We moved to O'Connor and worked for nine years. We increased the eldership, started the support of several preachers in other areas. We dearly loved the work. While there, I wrote a *Truth Magazine* article and mentioned brother Ned Fairbarin who had baptized Cecil and myself. I received a call from a devoted Spanish preacher who informed me that he knew brother Ned, now rather old. I was delighted. He called me back and said brother Ned desired to come visit, and they did—spending the night and attending a Wednesday at O'Connor Road. Just a short time later, I received word that brother Ned had died, but he had positively encouraged and assisted both Cecil and me to preach the word of God. I developed knee problems and surgery followed. I had some post-surgical problems, and suggested an additional preacher. This was all right, but it meant we had to cease the support of these outside preachers. Some of the members were unhappy with this, and I ended up moving to Madisonville in 2002.

Madisonville is a very small city. A very liberal group meets in the city, they have open fellowship with the denominations within the city. There were a number of people in the faithful church that we had known over the years. We have had a wonderful three years! We moved back to our Conroe home and have an apartment in Madisonville. I am now seventy-one years of age. I have gone from the encouraged to now become an encourager. My wife and I are so happy to be back in our home, we have adequate monies to meet our expenses. We have an apartment in Madisonville and can be there any time we are needed. We started a church bulletin and print material for our classes. We have grown significantly. We love the people. It is now our duty to encourage others as we have been encouraged!

Family wise: our daughter Cathy married David Price, the son of a preacher, and they have three children and they attend Kleinwood. Our son Donald Jr. married Donna Dean (daughter of a preacher) and they have three children attending the Rosenberg church; their oldest son has been accepted into the Marine Band program. Our son Charles converted and married the remarkable Dee Hopper (two children) and Charles now preaches in New Caney. Our daughter Christie married Steven Estes (two children), the son of a deacon and now lives in Highland Village (Dallas area) while attending the church in Lewisville. God has so richly blessed our lives.

God has given work that Christians *must* do and to excel therein. There is a special work that involves the older preacher/Christian.

The Need of Aged Saints to Support and Encourage Others
Football teams hire former quarterbacks, ends, guards, place kickers. Why? Because they have done a great work? Or, do they employ them to teach the younger combatants. In Philippians 4:9, Paul declared, "The things which you learned and received and heard and saw in me, these do, and the God of peace will be with you." *Learned, received, heard, do!* That is the pattern for fidelity!

One must possess a "listening ear" in encouraging our younger preachers. Understand them. Give them a sound mind of support. Do not encourage them in the faults of youth, help them to grow and understand. All of us could say, "been there/done that." The youth are generally hesitant to appreciate the wisdom of the aged, but we still need to be faithful in teaching and encouragement.

Proper Attitudes in Spreading the Gospel of Truth
Most people are initially taught by the material presented in a special study, a gospel meeting, or a home environment. A young student in Florida College was known for cutting classes, failing to study, fishing most of the time. His grandfather (a faithful Christian) had sent him to school. He was

encouraged by teachers and fellow students, "If you plan to preach the gospel, you need to be in the classes, etc." He responded (as he lifted his purchased book of sermons, I think it was *Seed for the Sower*) that he had all the material he needed, and if they did not like the way he presented it, they could just read the book themselves.

Be positive, even in the face of negative forces. There is always a critic. We need to be the encourager! People will critically attempt to destroy the effort of the young preacher. Some will attempt to impress by their superior knowledge—most of the time they could not even give the names of the books of the Bible. But, unthinking brethren can destroy by negative input. Teach the young preacher, warn him of the attitudes of others. Fortify him to hold true.

Stand up and be counted. Do not seek the "popular" side; stand with the word of God! Your fortified stand will thereby teach and encourage the younger preacher. Just consider my physical brothers (Cecil, Lewis, and Mike) and their positive stand and how it assists to fortify me. Not a one of them sought the "popular" view!

Teach positive and negative obligations. Young people, all Christians need this! Show the work of a teacher/preacher. We all have seen those who fail to study, never take a stand on important issues, court the favor of the weak and untaught. The Bible (NKJV) uses the expression "do not" in 1081 verses. There are some things to "do" and some things "not to do."

Be the encourager. Seek positively to point the younger people to godliness. It is easy to find fault. Be patient, longsuffering, supportive, and sincere in what is being said.

Implementation (to fill up, Webster). "Train up a child in the way he should go, And when he is old he will not depart from it" (Prov. 22:6). "Your God has commanded your strength; Strengthen, O God, what You have done for us" (Ps. 68:28).

By Teaching . . .

> . . . you shall teach them the statutes and the laws, and show them the way in which they must walk and the work they must do (Exod. 18:20).

Then the Lord said to Moses, "Come up to Me on the mountain and be there; and I will give you tablets of stone, and the law and commandments which I have written, that you may teach them" (Exod. 24:12).

God ". . . has put in his (Bezaleel's) heart the ability to teach" (Exod. 35:34).

God chose Moses and Aaron ". . . that you may teach the children of Israel all the statutes which the Lord has spoken to them by the hand of Moses" (Lev. 10:11).

Now, O Israel, listen to the statutes and the judgments which I teach you to observe, that you may live, and go in and possess the land which the Lord God of your fathers is giving you (Deut. 4:1).

. . . take heed to yourself, and diligently keep yourself, lest you forget the things your eyes have seen, and lest they depart from your heart all the days of your life. And teach them to your children and your grandchildren (Deut. 4:9).

. . . Jehovah commanded me at that time to teach you statutes and ordinances, that ye might do them in the land whither ye go over to possess it (Deut. 4:14).

. . . as for you, stand here by Me, and I will speak to you all the commandments, the statutes, and the judgments which you shall teach them, that they may observe them in the land which I am giving them to possess (Deut. 5:31).

Now this is the commandment, and these are the statutes and judgments which the Lord your God has commanded to teach you, that you may observe them in the land which you are crossing over to possess (Deut. 6:1).

You shall teach them diligently to your children, and shall talk of them when you sit in your house, when you walk by the way, when you lie down, and when you rise up (Deut. 6:7).

You shall teach them to your children, speaking of them when you sit in your house, when you walk by the way, when you lie down, and when you rise up (Deut. 11:19).

Moreover, as for me, far be it from me that I should sin against the Lord in ceasing to pray for you; but I will teach you the good and the right way (1 Sam. 12:23).

I will teach you about the hand of God; What is with the Almighty I will not conceal (Job 27:11).

I said, "Age should speak, And multitude of years should teach wisdom" (Job 32:7).

Restore to me the joy of Your salvation, And uphold me by Your generous Spirit. Then I will teach transgressors Your ways, And sinners shall be converted to You (Ps. 51:12-13).

Teach me to do Your will, For You are my God; Your Spirit is good. Lead me in the land of uprightness (Ps. 143:10).

Many nations shall come and say, "Come, and let us go up to the mountain of the Lord, To the house of the God of Jacob; He will teach us His ways, And we shall walk in His paths. For out of Zion the law shall go forth, And the word of the LORD from Jerusalem" (Mic. 4:2).

And they sent to Him their disciples with the Herodians, saying, "Teacher, we know that You are true, and teach the way of God in truth; nor do You care about anyone, for You do not regard the person of men" (Matt. 22:16).

Now it came to pass, as He was praying in a certain place, when He ceased, that one of His disciples said to Him, "Lord, teach us to pray, as John also taught his disciples" (Luke 11:1).

Then they asked Him, saying, "Teacher, we know that You say and teach rightly, and You do not show personal favoritism, but teach the way of God in truth" (Luke 20:21).

. . . I urged you when I went into Macedonia—remain in Ephesus that you may charge some that they teach no other doctrine (1 Tim. 1:3).

A bishop then must be . . . able to teach (1 Tim. 3:2).

. . . the things that you have heard from me among many witnesses, commit these to faithful men who will be able to teach others also (2 Tim. 2:2).

. . . a servant of the Lord must not quarrel but be gentle to all, able to teach, patient, in humility correcting those who are in opposition, if God perhaps will grant them repentance, so that they may know the truth (2 Tim. 2:24-25).

By example—we learn so much by watching what one does.

Let no one despise your youth, but be an example to the believers in word, in conduct, in love, in spirit, in faith, in purity (1 Tim. 4:12).

For I have given you an example, that you should do as I have done to you (John 13:15).

Brethren, join in following my example, and note those who so walk, as you have us for a pattern (Phil. 3:17).

. . . you yourselves know how you ought to follow us, for we were not disorderly among you; nor did we eat anyone's bread free of charge, but worked with labor and toil night and day, that we might not be a burden to any of you, not because we do not have authority, but to make ourselves an example of how you should follow us (2 Thess. 3:7-9).

My brethren, take the prophets, who spoke in the name of the Lord, as an example of suffering and patience (Jas. 5:10).

By encouragement . . .

. . . command Joshua, and encourage him and strengthen him; for he shall go over before this people, and he shall cause them to inherit the land which you will see (Deut. 3:28).

Then David said to the messenger, "Thus you shall say to Joab (with regard to the death of Uriah, dw): 'Do not let this thing displease you, for the sword devours one as well as another. Strengthen your attack against the city, and overthrow it.' So encourage him" (2 Sam. 11:25).

The the messenger who spoke to Micaiah, said, "Now listen, the words of the prophets with one accord encourage the king. Please, let your word be like the word of one of them, and speak encouragement" (1 Kings 22:13; 2 Chron. 18:12).

By establishing . . .

Timothy was sent "to establish you and encourage you concerning your faith, that no man should be moved by these afflictions (1 Thess. 3:2-3).

. . . let the wickedness of the wicked come to an end, But establish the just; For the righteous God tests the hearts and minds (Ps. 7:9).

Of the increase of His government and peace There will be no end, Upon the throne of David and over His kingdom, To order it and establish it with judgment and justice From that time forward, even forever. The zeal of the LORD of hosts will perform this (Isa. 9:7).

Lord, You will establish peace for us (Isa. 26:12).

. . . I will . . . establish My covenant with you. Then you shall know that I am the Lord (Ezek. 16:60-62).

Now to Him who is able to establish you according to my gospel and the preaching of Jesus Christ, according to the revelation of the mystery kept secret since the world began but now has been made manifest, and by the prophetic Scriptures has been made known to all nations, according to the commandment of the everlasting God, for obedience to the faith—to God, alone wise, be glory through Jesus Christ forever. Amen (Rom. 16:25).

God will ". . . comfort your hearts and establish you in every good word and work" (2 Thess. 2:17).

. . . the Lord is faithful, who will establish you and guard you from the evil one (2 Thess. 3:3).

. . . Establish your hearts, for the coming of the Lord is at hand (Jas. 5:8).

. . . may the God of all grace, who called us to His eternal glory by Christ Jesus, after you have suffered a while, perfect, establish, strengthen, and settle you (1 Pet. 5:10).

By strengthening through assisting/empathy . . .

O God, strengthen my hands (Neh. 6:9).

God said, ". . . I would strengthen you with my mouth, And the comfort of my lips would relieve your grief" (Job 16:5).

Wait on the Lord; Be of good courage, And He shall strengthen your heart; Wait, I say, on the Lord! (Ps. 27:14).

Be of good courage, And He shall strengthen your heart, All you who hope in the Lord (Ps. 31:24).

. . . Strengthen me according to Your word (Ps.119:28).

Strengthen the weak hands, And make firm the feeble knees. Say to those who are fearful-hearted, "Be strong, do not fear! Behold, your God will come with vengeance, With the recompense of God; He will come and save you" (Isa. 35:3-4).

Fear not, for I am with you; Be not dismayed, for I am your God. I will strengthen you, Yes, I will help you, I will uphold you with My righteous right hand (Isa. 41:10).

No one will strengthen himself Who lives in iniquity (Ezek. 7:13).

Return to the stronghold, You prisoners of hope. Even today I declare That I will restore double to you (Zech. 10:12).

Jesus told Simon, ". . . I have prayed for you, that your faith should not fail; and when you have returned to Me, strengthen your brethren" (Luke 22:32).

. . . strengthen the hands which hang down, and the feeble knees (Heb. 12:12).

. . . may the God of all grace, who called us to His eternal glory by Christ Jesus, after you have suffered a while, perfect, establish, strengthen, and settle you (1 Pet. 5:10).

Be watchful, and strengthen the things which remain, that are ready to die, for I have not found your works perfect before God (Rev. 3:2).

By keeping the faith . . .

God told Adam to "dress it and to keep it" (i.e., the garden) (Gen. 2:15).

God told Abraham to ". . . keep My covenant, you and your descendants after you throughout their generations" (Gen. 17:9).

God promised to Isaac and his seed ". . . an everlasting covenant (Gen. 18:19).

God promised Moses, "If you diligently heed the voice of the Lord your God and do what is right in His sight, give ear to His commandments and keep all His statutes, I will put none of the diseases on you which I have brought on the Egyptians. For I am the Lord who heals you" (Exod. 15:26).

. . . if you will indeed obey My voice and keep My covenant, then you shall be a special treasure to Me above all people; for all the earth is Mine (Exod. 19:5).

God is "showing mercy to thousands, to those who love Me and keep My commandments" (Exod. 20:6).

God said, "Keep the Sabbath, therefore, for it is holy to you. Every one who profanes it shall surely be put to death" (Exod. 31:14).

You shall therefore keep My statutes and My judgments, which if a man does, he shall live by them: I am the Lord (Lev. 18:5).

Therefore you shall keep My ordinance, so that you do not commit any of these abominable customs which were committed before you, and that you do not defile yourselves by them: I am the Lord your God (Lev. 18:30).

. . . give my son Solomon a loyal heart to keep Your commandments and Your testimonies and Your statutes, to do all these things, and to build the temple for which I have made provision (1 Chron. 29:19).

Blessed are those who keep His testimonies, Who seek Him with the whole heart! They also do no iniquity; They walk in His ways. You have commanded us To keep Your precepts diligently (Ps. 119:2-4).

Jesus asked, "Why do you call Me good? No one is good but One, that is, God. But if you want to enter into life, keep the commandments" (Matt. 19:17).

The ones that fell on the good ground are those who, having heard the word with a noble and good heart, keep it and bear fruit with patience (Luke 8:15).

Jesus said, ". . . blessed are those who hear the word of God and keep it" (Luke 11:28).

If you love Me, keep My commandments (John 14:15).

Jesus answered and said, "If anyone loves Me, he will keep My word; and My Father will love him, and We will come to him and make Our home with him. He who does not love Me does not keep My words; and the word which you hear is not Mine but the Father's who sent Me" (John 14::23-24).

Now I praise you, brethren, that you remember me in all things and keep the traditions just as I delivered them to you (1 Cor. 11:2).

. . . endeavor(ing) to keep the unity of the Spirit in the bond of peace (Eph. 4:3).

. . . keep thyself pure (1 Tim. 5:22).

He who says, "I know Him," and does not keep His commandments, is a liar, and the truth is not in him (1 John 2:4).

By this we know that we love the children of God, when we love God and keep His commandments. For this is the love of God, that we keep His commandments. And His commandments are not burdensome (1 John 5:2-3).

Little children, keep yourselves from idols (1 John 5:21).

. . . keep yourselves in the love of God, looking for the mercy of our Lord Jesus Christ unto eternal life. Now to Him who is able to keep you from stumbling, And to present you faultless Before the presence of His glory with exceeding joy, To God our Savior, Who alone is wise, Be glory and majesty, Dominion and power, Both now and forever. Amen (Jude 21, 24-25).

By observing our behavior and approach. We are the children of God, and must walk as his people, making a difference by faithfulness and godliness.

Watch and pray, lest you enter into temptation. The spirit indeed is willing, but the flesh is weak (Matt. 26:41; cp. Mark 14:38).

Take heed, watch and pray; for you do not know when the time is (Mark 13:33).

Conclusion

Let us make a positive effort to involve our young people! These will be the older preachers of another generation. One can recall so many positive influences in our younger days and even as we have grown older! Imitate that positive influence toward our young preachers. Do not become a negative influence upon them. *Watch our attitude* as we attempt to teach. Remember how our *elderly preachers* encouraged us and duplicate!

John concluded, ". . . For I am your fellow servant, and of your brethren the prophets, and of those who keep the words of this book. Worship God" (Rev. 22:9).

The Death of a Spouse

Connie W. Adams

"And as it is appointed unto man once to die, but after this the judgment" (Heb. 9:27). Believers accept this, intellectually, as a simple statement of fact. It comes home to us emotionally when we face the death of our own companion in marriage. This is the one who changed our world: the one we vowed to cling to in prosperity or adversity, sickness or health, for better or worse "'til death do us part." And now we come to the parting. Except in rare cases, one spouse will precede the other in death while the other will be left behind to cope with all that means. When you are young and full of dreams, such a time seems far away. Yet, death sometimes severs young couples. As we age, and the infirmities of life overtake us, the fact of what will take place before long, looms larger in our minds.

Connie W. Adams was born on September 22, 1930 in Hopewell, Virginia and preached his first sermon in 1945 at Pike Road, North Carolina. He continued filling preaching appointments through high school and during four years at Florida College. He was married to Barbara Colley who passed away in 1985. To them were born two sons. In 1986 he married Bobby Hughes, who had been married to Thomas Hughes until his death in 1982. They had six children. Tom served as an elder for awhile at Berea, Ohio. Connie has done local work in Florida, Georgia, Tennessee, Ohio, and Kentucky. Two years were spent helping start the work in Bergen, Norway. Since 1975, he has been engaged in full-time gospel meeting work which has taken them throughout this country and to a dozen other countries. He wrote in the *Gospel Guardian* from 1954-65, was an Associate Editor of *Truth Magazine* from 1965-73, edited and published *Searching the Scriptures* from 1973-92 when it ceased publication. Since that time he has been Associate Editor of *Truth Magazine*. He and Bobby are members of the Manslick Road church of Christ in Louisville, Kentucky.

The Preacher in Ecclesiastes pictures two ways that we all shall "return to the earth" and "the spirit shall return to God who gave it" (Eccl. 12:7). First he describes the natural aging process with its changes: a time when the hands tremble, the legs grow weaker, teeth decay, eye sight is affected, sleep is fitful, the voice is weakened and desire fails. The hair changes color; there are fears in the way (vv. 2-5). If we live to grow old, these changes will occur. But then he turns to consider the accidental or unexpected when the head is injured or the heart fails (v. 6). Many young people, including young spouses, have died young because of accidents or tragedies. Death will come to all (unless the Lord comes first), and with it comes the need for coping with grief.

How Do You Handle Grief?

There is a difference in the grief process for the death of a spouse who has suffered a long illness and in the sudden and unexpected death of a companion. In the first case, there comes a time when you realize, ever so reluctantly, that your beloved is not going to survive. You fight the acceptance of that reality as long as you can. After my first wife was diagnosed with cancer, I asked a friend who is a doctor to level with me as to how long she had. He said, "About two and a half years."

While we both fought as hard as we could to overcome it, availing ourselves of the best medical care we could provide, the time came when I realized what was going to happen and started crossing bridges in my mind which I had been unwilling to face before. Sometimes, after a long and painful illness, death comes as a relief to those left behind, as well as to those who have struggled so hard.

But when a spouse is suddenly taken in an accident, or from heart attack, stroke or exploding aneurism, grief unfolds differently. It takes a longer time for the reality to set in. Your mind has not had time to think ahead and ask "what will I do if. . . ." "If" is here, now. There is no advance resignation.

Stages of Grief

1. Denial. "No, no, this cannot be!" This is a natural reaction that will, in time, give way to fact. Some even enter a fantasy land where they pretend the one they lost is still there. They carry on one-sided conversations.

2. Anger. "Why did this happen to me?" "It is not fair." Well, life is not always fair, is it? A Christian should be well aware of the reality of death.

Much is said about it in the Bible, and all of life has reminded us of its existence. Sometimes, the survivor aims his/her anger at the deceased. "You sure left me in a mess!" "How am I going to handle all this alone?" "I don't know how to balance the checkbook or make decisions as to what to do next." The dead can't help it and the living will have to deal with it.

3. Guilt. While this may not be true in every case, it is easy to fall into this trap. "If I had only . . . ," "I could have . . . ," "I should have. . . ." We may think of many things we wish we had said or done before it was too late. If you have not been the right kind of spouse and failed terribly in that role, then these feelings may be enlarged. But what is done is done and we cannot change it. We have to face it and go on.

4. Masking true feelings. While we do not need to be morbid or have reminders all around us of how many days, hours, and minutes have passed since our beloved left us, telling all how blue we are, there is also a false bravado which does not help you or anyone else. Some turn to medications which turn them into zombies and that only delays the process of coping.

5. Resentment. As we see others going about life with their spouses, it is easy to be envious and start feeling sorry for ourselves. After losing Bobbie, I was once at a shopping mall when I noticed a couple about my age strolling along, holding hands and obviously enjoying their time together. For a moment I had the faint beginnings of a pity party. That won't do. It is time to "rejoice with them that rejoice" (Rom. 12:15). You may find yourself excluded from events which involve couples. You are now single and not thought of as part of a couple. No injury is meant by this, but it takes some time to get used to it.

6. Acceptance. This is the time when you understand and accept the finality of what has taken place. Your loved one is dead! That is a hard word to use at first. We try to soften it by other expressions. Your companion will not be coming back. Their memories are etched in your mind and will sweeten over time so that you can muse or laugh when you recall them instead of weeping. It took awhile before I stopped wearing my wedding ring, until I suddenly realized that I was not married. That shocks your system at first. But that realization is important to the rest of your life.

Going On With Life
Beware of the shrine. Some try to cope by sealing off a room, leaving

everything as it was and resisting any effort to change a thing. This is a form of denial. But it is not healthy. Some widows have sealed a workshop and won't allow anything to be touched. We had a guest room in which my wife had made the curtains, the bedspread and arranged the furnishings. While I sometimes looked at it and stirred up old memories, we continued to use it as a guest room. One of the hardest things of all is disposing of clothing. My sister-in-law was willing (and honored) to accept her clothing. I folded each piece and placed it in a box, relived memories and wept. But it had to be done. Find someone about the same size and ask if they would like to have them. That bittersweet activity was healing for me and helped in accepting reality.

Memories

Sometimes friends think you have forgotten, especially if you decide to remarry later. But you never forget. You don't want to ever forget. Memories are painful at first and often lead to tears. But in time they brighten and sweeten.

Remarriage

Some decide to remarry. I was 54-years-old when Bobbie died. We had both told each other for years that when the time came for one of us to go on ahead, that we hoped the other could find a suitable companion, remarry and go on with life. This is not a choice all want to make. Age, health, and other circumstances must be taken into account. Paul taught that those whose spouses have died are free to marry if they choose to do so (Rom. 7:1-3). In my own case, I married a widow I had known a long time. Her first husband was a good friend of mine and I spoke at his funeral. Bobby and Bobbie (short for Barbara) were good friends. It has been an advantage to both of us to have known the other's former spouse. We have been able to merge our memories. For several years when we lived at Brooks, Kentucky, we had the walls in our basement covered with pictures of both families. After twenty years of happy marriage, we still talk freely to each other about memories of Tom or Bobbie.

But, as one in that circumstance, I will offer a few observations in the hope that others might benefit from them. First, you need to allow enough time to heal your hurt and sort out your own emotions. It is a time for good judgment, not runaway emotions. "There's no fool like an old fool" is truer than some may want to admit. Some second marriages work out well and others do not.

Please don't expect all of your old friends to be as excited about your new life as you are. That may come as a shock. It did to me. Sometimes long time friends treat you as if you have become disloyal to the spouse you lost, and their own special friend. Comparisons are inevitable. Expect them. Even when you wait a reasonable time, it will always seem short to your friends. They do not know yet what it means to dread to go home when you have been away, to walk into the emptiness. They do not know what it means to go into a bedroom alone at night (a room you shared for 35 years with a spouse who will not be coming back) and face what seems like a thousand years before daylight comes. But it always did.

She slipped into the silence of my dreams last night
Wandering from room to room, turning on each light.
Her laughter spills like water from the river to the sea
And I'm swept away from sadness, clinging to her memory.

Not only do your friends not always share your joy in deciding to remarry, neither will all your children. The merging of two families is always fraught with frustration. You will inherit a new set of in-laws. Children have a hard time accepting a step-mother or step-father. When Bobby and I married, all of our children were adults and away from home and on their own. Circumstances may be far different when there are children at home and families merge. They don't all work out as well as "The Brady Bunch." Children may feel that someone is trying to replace their father or their mother. Of course, that cannot be done. Maneuvering through family traditions and holidays can be difficult. Children do not always understand the emotional needs of their parents and parents don't always understand the struggles their children have with choices made by their parents.

Watch Out For Matchmakers
There are always some who are determined to match you with some friend. People react differently to this situation. Some appreciate it and find a good companion that way. Others resent it. I was in the latter category until I began to see the humor in it.

Pray For Wisdom
When you lose a spouse (that word seems so cold and impersonal), you need to lean upon the Lord. He is a present help in time of trouble. If you ever need to "draw nigh unto God" it is then. Bobbie died on Sunday about 1 p.m. At 6 p.m. I attended worship at the Expressway church in Louisville

where we were then members. Not only was it the right thing to do, it was also therapeutic. Songs, prayers, attention to the word of God, plus the overwhelming demonstration of love, concern, and tears from those present were strengthening and helped put things in perspective. Visitation at the funeral home brought long lines of friends, neighbors, and brethren to share in our grief. The funeral had a large crowd. Our sons and I were strengthened by the prayers, congregational singing, and words of hope and instruction from Weldon Warnock and Dee Bowman. Neighbors had a feast ready at the house after the grave side service. Funerals bring out the very best in people.

When all is said and done, it is "better to go the house of mourning than to the house of feasting" (Eccl. 7:2). You cannot go without thinking of your own mortality. "The living will lay it to his heart." That is why the gospel needs to be preached at a funeral. The "house of mourning" reminds us of our limitations. With all our vaunted knowledge and wisdom, with all our technology, we cannot prevent death. We might be able to delay it, but we cannot stop it. "There is no man that hath power over the spirit; neither hath he power in the day of death" (Eccl. 8:8). The "house of mourning" teaches us to count our blessings. The next time you go to a funeral and some man is burying his wife, and you still have yours, then thank God for her, tell her you love her, be faithful to her and "give honor" to her (1 Pet. 3:7). Or if some woman is burying her husband, and you still have yours, then be grateful. Don't take him for granted. In the loneliness of a darkened bedroom, you will think of many things you wish you had said to each other while you still could.

W. Curtis Porter wrote the following near the death of his wife who lost her battle with cancer.

The Fateful Hour
My heart is torn with sorrow,
    My mind is dulled with pain
As by your bed in sadness
    I long to see you gain;
But grief o'er me has fallen
    My soul is filled with woe
Because the dreaded reaper
    Has called for you to go.
You've manifested courage—
    Your fortitude sublime—

As with a broken spirit
    You near the heavenly clime;
Death's knell is sounding loudly,
    With pathos and with power,
And I, so sad and lonely,
    Await the fateful hour.

I know your love is fervent,
    A love so full and free—
As I pray God in anguish
    To hear my humble plea:
To grant that you may linger
    My troubled soul to bless,
But if you can't stay longer,
    That you may suffer less;
And when you reach the crossing
    That heaven be your home—
That God may give me comfort
    While sadly here I roam.

I love you still more dearly—
    Your pain but breaks my heart
This fateful hour of darkness
    Is tearing us apart.
The fateful hour approaches—
    It blinds my eyes with tears
As I without you, darling
    Must face the coming years;
But if you go and leave me,
    My love will stronger grow
As faith will look to heaven
    To which your soul will go.
And there you'll be a treasure
    To beckon still to me
To strive for that reunion
    Upon that shore with thee;
With sorrow all forgotten,
    With tears all washed away—
We'll then be home forever
    Through that eternal day.

The Pain of Divorce
Art Adams

Introduction

There is no such thing as a "painless" divorce. When the love one had expected would last forever is betrayed and rejected the familiar world which these two companions have built falls apart forever. Pain invades from every front: spiritual, emotional, familial, physical, social, financial, and career. Denial, rage, resentment, frustration, jealousy, and retaliation lurk as unwelcome guests plotting a massive invasion.

The most important human relationship in life is acknowledged to be lost. The divine institution of the home lies in ruins. The family scatters.

Art Adams is a licensed clinical social worker and certified addiction counselor in the state of Indiana. Additional certifications include: Critical Incident Stress Management, Crisis De-escalation, Trauma Specialist, and Tobacco Cessation (Tap n' Teg, Quit Smart). He holds a Masters Degree in Social Work from Andrews University in Berrien Springs, Michigan; a Bachelor of Science in Psychology from Purdue University; and a Certificate of Achievement for the completion of four years in the Bible Department at Florida College.

Mr. Adams has preached full-time for seventeen years followed by fifteen years in part-time evangelism. He currently works with the church of Christ in Plymouth, Indiana. During his eighteen years in mental health and addiction, he has served as therapist, clinical director, chief operating officer, JCAHO consultant, Corporate Vice President for Operations and Corporate Addictions/Trauma/ Recovery Specialist at Cummins Behavioral Health Systems. He is board chair for Associates in Clinical Psychology Group Homes and serves on multiple committees including the All Hazards Advisory Board to the Indiana Division of Mental Health and Addictions for Homeland Security. He was deputized and deployed by the Governor of the state of Indiana as a "first responder" for disaster relief following hurricane Katrina.

A haunting look of emptiness, guilt, disbelief, and distance covers the face and countenance of each child, replacing the smiles, the innocence and the giggles that once filled the air. Friends and brethren scatter, not knowing what to believe, where their loyalty should lie, or how to respond. The depression is crushing. Thoughts of your companion with another can erupt in bouts of rage, retaliation, and bitterness. Things one never imagined they would ever have felt begin creeping into the mind: physical violence, homicide, suicide, manipulation, vengeance, resentments, and hatred. These things lie at the door inviting and coaxing their way into your life at your weakest moments. Indeed, "jealousy is the *rage* of a man" (Prov. 6:34-35).

If there was ever a time that godly people need to support their brethren, it is at that moment and through that process. For some going through separation and divorce a supportive stance by fellow Christians has been a savior. May our God bless those who have shown hearts of compassion, ears that listen, eyes that show understanding, tongues that encourage, and minds that trust the integrity of the Christian to do the right thing when others doubt.

For others, however, that has not been the case. Some of the vilest words of judgment, mistrust, and negative decisions have come from those who should be offering the greatest support and encouragement. Unfortunately, there are those in the Lord's army that chose to shoot the wounded either by sniping from a distance having never talked to the person or by coming straight up to the hurting person and pulling the trigger at close range. Both aims are deadly. Some brethren have become a pawn in the hands of Satan to destroy otherwise good and faithful people when they are at the lowest point in their life. Is it any wonder that brethren who have stood and fought in the hottest battles, suddenly find themselves bleeding and running for cover in defeat? Attacked from within and without—unwelcome—judged—branded—the object of talebearing, reviling and suspicion. God hates "breaking faith" with your spouse and he hates divorce (Mal. 2:15, 16). I do too! It is the gift from Satan that keeps on giving!

Supposedly, time heals all wounds, but the pain of divorce like a time-release capsule continues to produce massive doses to agitate the pain over and over again. Unlike death where there is closure with a final goodbye, in divorce there are constant reappearances and interactions throughout life. The awkwardness and pain are revived at each occurrence. Numerous divorcees have told me, "Not a day goes by that I don't think about him or her" and with that I must concur. History that is written cannot be erased from the human mind.

The hardest divorces are when: (1) one is being rejected by their partner, (2) they thought the marriage was okay, and (3) parents or friends disapprove of the divorce (Thompson & Spanier, 1993). Divorce does not always deliver the results one may have thought. Although people expect to feel better soon after the divorce, in many cases the worst time is about one year after the divorce. During the first year after separating, 73% of women and 60% of men think their divorce might have been a mistake (Hetherington, Cox and Cox, 1995).

Having considered things that make for a strong home and proper communication in marital life in other lessons within this series, this lesson addresses the world in which a Christian may find himself or herself during and after the act of divorce.

General Observations

Long term effects. When one partner in a marriage decides to be unfaithful, they choose for both partners to be effected for the rest of their lives in one way or another! A principle of divine truth is that sin has enduring consequences. Choosing to sin with unscriptural divorces, as well as divorcing for the scriptural reason has long range results (Num. 32:23; Matt. 5:32-33; 19:1-12). The impact of divorce can affect the family structure even into the third and fourth generations. Families have value systems and a dysfunctional value taught in one generation can become a family "norm" for years to come. When the infrastructure of a family system is destroyed, there is a corresponding reaction by that entire family and a re-structuring of the family. It is this re-structuring that may take generations to un-do.

Interrogation. In the process and aftermath of divorce the Christian will likely have brethren who come in concern. There are others who will come in curiosity and prey on the divorcee's pain. Others will come trying to take sides, trying to intimidate and/or condemn. Brethren the divorcee has not seen or even heard from on their marital status, years later will pull a brother or sister aside and challenge their divorce status. Such happens to me when I visit meetings, am asked to speak or am otherwise involved with brethren. While I understand the need for brethren to assure they are not fellowshipping impenitent fornicators, I quite frankly do not understand where these brethren who suddenly care so much for my soul have been for all of these years. Nor, do I understand why brethren who gossip about a brother or sister have never even approached them to talk with them about those concerns. I must thank at least one good brother who when presented with gossip said, "I don't know where you got your information, but I do know him and that is not true." Thank you, brother! Brethren, we have to stop talebearing and slandering each other (Prov. 6:16; 10:18; 1 Tim. 5:13; 1 Pet. 4:15)! It does such damage to its intended victim and it damns the souls of those who practice such things—preachers and elders included! There is some serious repenting that needs to take place!

Unpredictable pain. In general the pain of divorce is unpredictable. Divorce is a situation in which two people often find their own heart full of emotional minefields. These include times when one is speaking from emotion. Either party in a divorce, innocent or not, can accrue sins related to the divorce. These can occur in subtle ways as "the dirty laundry is aired." Innocent or not, one can be guilty of gossip, slander, talebearing, bitterness, and a host of other sins that will separate him from God (Rom. 3:14; Eph. 4:31). While this is damaging when one airs his/her thoughts with neighbors and brethren, the damage is monumental and beyond comparison when one uses his/her own children as confidants. Separation and divorce are times of high vulnerability. Brethren, we would do well to remind each other of this in a gentle way (Gal. 6:1, 2). And, those separated would do well to learn that a marriage can never be repaired if one or both parties keep driving wedges. Brethren caught in the middle need to show wisdom when trying to walk the fine line between encouraging slander and helping separated partners reconcile. Marriage, with or without love, is an intimate experience. Its dissolution is highly emotional.

The intense feelings connected to a separation and divorce can result in some pretty bizarre and out of character behaviors. The level of irrationality and sheer stupidity practiced by combating divorcees is usually quite clear in hindsight. Be their anchor and not the one who "spins them up" in their irrationality. Confidants need to be part of the solution, not part of the problem. Those who can be rational need to support the divorcing persons during their irrationality.

The Process of Divorce. Usually there is both a process leading up to the divorce, a process of living through the divorce, and a process of coping after the divorce. Another chapter deals with the causes of divorce. Briefly

I would suggest marriages are likely to fail where there is a lack of commitment to the institution of marriage, a failure to mutually communicate, and an inability to effectively address issues as they arise. The greatest reason marriages fail is that the Lord is not viewed by all in the family as the supreme authority in that home in all things (Josh. 24:15).

Once the separation and divorce are in action there are sets of issues: telling the children and family, guilt toward your children and others pained by your initiative, informing the congregation, dealing with responses, attempts to reconcile, having your dirty laundry forever exposed on the public record, the personal pain of breaking your own vow, pushing it through to its formal decree, custody, missing the companionship—presence—subtle and practical support of your spouse, maintaining continency, sustaining the thought of marital failure, missing the taken-for-granted good parts of the failed marriage and what's happening with the children?

Once the decree is made there is an aftermath. There is enforcing the divorce judgment, or defending against challenges thereof by your spouse. A new financial reality becomes apparent. The one living in the museum they used to call "our home" is bombarded with constant memories. Other issues involve: coping with stereotypes of divorcees, allowing time to heal versus jumping into another or serial relationships, being "unmatched" at gatherings, loneliness, and coping with people trying to "match you up." New skills have to be learned including your feelings when you see your ex with someone new, and how to act when "the family" is back together for weddings, graduations, holidays, and funerals. Then, over time, if there is to be another relationship, one desperately needs to work not to carry unresolved issues into that next relationship.

Does time heal all wounds? Some wounds just do not heal. History once written is written. In divorce one must eventually accept that some questions will never be answered and some reasons will never be known in this life. At some point there must be closure and acceptance. Constantly picked wounds get infected—they cannot heal. I strongly advise finding a non-judgmental confidant to listen to your story, walk the distance with you, affirm you, and help you sort what you can understand from what will never be understood. People often chose to have a therapist help them in this journey, but the journey can be taken with a compassionate, wise brother or sister as well. While emotionally healthy people cannot stay healthy by living in the past, it is a good thing to visit the past occasionally and dwell on lessons learned. These can help in our own healing process and when shared can help to provide direction for others.

Supposedly, time heals all wounds, but the pain of divorce lasts and lasts. Ten years later 40-50% of women and 30-40% of men remained very angry at the former spouse and felt rejected and exploited (Wallerstein,1996). Females over forty have an especially hard time. They have less chance of remarrying (28%), inadequate income (50%), and loneliness or clinical depression (50%). After ten years, in only 10% of divorces was life reported to be better for *both* partners, in 27% of the cases both had a poorer quality of life, and 63% of the time one partner was better off but the other was unchanged or got worse (Reissman,1990: Coping with Divorce, http://mentalhelp.net/psyhelp/chap10/chap10o.htm).

Attempting to cope with divorce. There are basic differences in how men and women approach divorce. Men tend to stay in their pain deeper and longer. Women tend to move forward once the decision is made. In either case there are some maladaptive pitfalls recently separated or divorced people may encounter: (1) Retreating into a lonely state of self-pity and depression, (2) Rebounding into another love situation too rapidly, (3) Obsessing with sex or with finding the perfect man/woman, (4) Escaping through excess like alcohol, drugs, sex, work, food, shopping, etc., (5) Returning to the former spouse without adequate problem resolution, (6) Resenting the former spouse (which often rages and seethes in anger for years) (Cox et al, 1979; Queralt, 1996, 268-272).

The Innocent Ones

A party may be innocent when it comes to adultery while the couple was together and yet become a guilty party. The marriage remains as a marriage until the divorce decree is given. This means not acting single when you are still married. The "innocent party" can jeopardize his right to remarry by dating and setting himself up for temptation while he is "separated." The innocent party can become guilty of a host of sins: fornication, lust, gossip, slander, talebearing, bitterness, hatefulness, greed, strife, deceit, malice, arrogance, and failing to care for one's own (Rom. 1:29-32; 1 Tim. 5:8). Make no mistake about it—there is a vast difference in "being innocent" and "remaining innocent"! "Let him that thinks he stands take heed lest he fall" (1 Cor. 10:12). By not taking heed to these simple dangers, the innocent party and others who start out innocent can "become partakers of others sins" (1 Tim. 5:22) and fall into the devil's snare (1 Tim. 3:7).

Relatives must take heed and not become "partakers of others' sins" (1 Tim. 5:22). It is a natural thing for in-laws and parents to come to the aid of their children, but a more difficult thing to do may be to maintain reason and keep the problem where it belongs—between the married couple. It is not a time for choosing sides, but a time to help your child think rationally and scripturally through the process. In taking your child's side, you may either intentionally or inadvertently be the deciding factor in whether the home stays intact or is dissolved. My great-grandfather had a daughter who came to his house in the middle of the night after a fuss with her husband. His words are worth repeating, "Git' on back home to your husband and solve it." Hurt people look for others to take their side. It is hard to remain neutral but easy to get caught up in the problem and become a part of the problem rather than a part of the solution. Take heed in-laws, you may be driving the final wedge that destroys your child's home. Keep the problem focused where it should be focused—on the couple and their decision!

Elders must take heed to avoid becoming "partakers of others' sins" (1 Tim. 5:22). When a brother or sister comes to you to bare their soul and ask for help with their burden they are vulnerable; they need you and your wisdom. There are many good elderships that offer support, prayer, and address the Pandora's box of issues involved in separation and divorce. There are no easy fixes when something has gotten to that point. It is not a time for reaction, emotion, and lashing out. It is a time for wisdom, reason, and calm heads to work through the issues however they unfold.

Let me share two preacher stories. One preacher had an unfaithful wife. The preacher went to the elders, explained the situation and asked for their prayers and help. They responded by meeting with both parties, praying with both, encouraging both, and giving the preacher three months off with pay to address his family issues. Even when it ended in divorce, the elders and church stood beside him to encourage, support, and otherwise help him bear his burden. Brethren had questions and for the most part they asked the elders and the preacher for answers rather than producing gossip.

The second preacher also had an unfaithful wife. He, too, went to the elders, explained the situation and asked for their prayers and help. The first response was, "You've preached your last sermon here. Be out of the house by Saturday (It was Wednesday then). We cannot have a man in the pulpit that has this kind of problem at home." As the preacher began packing his stuff to move, he needed to be with his wife who was in another state and try to reconcile. The elders kept interrupting his move to talk with him. They were, also, at loose ends. Their position—one or both of you are in sin and we don't know which one. They finally decided "to stick together and none of us will meet with you alone." Then, "you need to repent." When asked what needed repentance, their response was: "You know. We cannot tell you what to repent of." Then, when a statement of repentance was finally made—"We will *not* accept your repentance."

The "innocent parties" have had similar experiences with our brethren:

1. "The men have met and decided you can pass the collection plate, but not be involved in public teaching, prayer, or serve the communion."

2. The local preacher was asked by the innocent party: "Can you go and talk with my wife?" The response, "Oh, I don't get involved in things like that. I don't know what to say." And thus, no prayer, Bible study, peacemaking effort, or other effort was made and the divorce happened.

3. Several preachers gathered at the back of the building and the local preacher told the story of a pending divorce to which another preacher said, "Sounds to me like he just needs to stay single, ha ha ha."

4. An eldership told an innocent party (lady), "You'll have to come forward and repent of divorce in order to be accepted here." She did because "right then it was more important to have their support but I didn't think I was wrong."

5. Another eldership told an innocent party, "Unless you have actual evidence (not circumstantial) of the actual act of adultery, you must go back to him." Their position was one must be "caught in the act" in spite of love notes, strange calls, reports from others, intercepted messages, and an STD.

6. The preacher from another local congregation was almost caught as a "peeping tom" trying to catch a member "in the very act" "so the innocent party would have grounds for divorce.

7. A leader from another congregation said: "The policy of this congregation is to meet with anyone who is divorced and tell them they'd probably be very uncomfortable here and would be better going somewhere else."

To clarify, the question was asked, "Even if they are the innocent party?" The reply was "that's our policy."

8. Another preacher came up to an innocent party after three years without seeing or talking with him. His first comment was, "I need to know about your divorce so I know whether to eat with you or not."

9. At another place a newcomer came to worship with his young child. Both looked very subdued. He informed one of the elders he was not a member of the church and that his wife had just left him for another man. The elder told the other elders who in turn asked the preacher to "change sermons or work divorce in and lay it on the line." The preacher did and a hurting man who came seeking spiritual hope left judged never to return.

10. Another brother was told he could share by participating on the radio program, but could not be in their pulpit due to his divorce.

What started out between a man and his wife invades the church generating sin almost everywhere it goes and keeps on for years to come. Yes, divorce is the devil's gift that keeps on giving. The Lord said, "For he shall have judgment without mercy, that hath shewed no mercy; and mercy rejoiceth against judgment" (Jas. 2:13). May our Lord grant mercy to our own brethren in the day of *his* judgment! My continuing prayer is, "Lord, open our eyes to see what we are doing to each other and to your glorious cause!"

While judgment is rampant, meaningful encouragement can be rare when a person is going through a divorce. I want to publicly thank the brother who was on a meeting and took the time to find me and invite me to lunch. He stated, "I am not here to question or condemn you, but just to see you and encourage you." After a very pleasant lunch he said, "I know you are having a tough time. I can see you are hurting. I hurt with you. Maybe this will help, too." And he placed a $50 bill in my hand. I want to thank my good family for their constant prayers, encouragment, and faith in me to do the right thing as I struggled to find my way again. They provided encouragement without pushing me. These acts of kindness and support, I believe, made the difference in where I will spend eternity.

Lessons not learned are prone to be repeated. Others will walk this path behind those who have gone before. They will need help in their hour of trial. Will our brethren be there to help them, to hold them aloof, or to crucify them? "A brother offended is harder to be won than a strong city: and their contentions are like the bars of a castle" (Prov. 18:19).

Struggles. For the divorcing one, there is an issue of facing resentment and not letting it possess them (Eph. 4:31). Feelings of betrayal, bitterness, anger/rage, jealousy, confronting the partner, explaining to the children, talking with the family and in-laws, facing the brethren, living life out of balance for days (family, finances, job, church, social, emotional roller coasters), living in a daze, forgetting basic things, feelings of "how can I go on," patience with those who judge, trying to be faithful while at your weakest, paying support that goes to the other man or woman who is with your mate (and maybe your children).

How does one survive during this? Hosea shows us how. You know the story of a wife "taken out of whoredom." The first child was Hosea's. With the second child there was doubt. The third was not his. He put her away. She ultimately became a slave and was offered at auction. Hosea bought her back. How did Hosea get through all of that? (1) He had faith in God to get him through. (2) Prayer was a constant companion. (3) Those you may least expect come forward as a support. (4) God had a purpose that Hosea could share with others (see how it feels!). (5) There were those to listen as he told his story over and over. Folks, that's how you get through, too!

Guilty Parties (Yes, that's a plural.)
The Adulterer. The pain of divorce can become more and more painful when the guilty leaves the innocent in the shadow of doubt. Consider David, the guilty party, and how he attempted to cover his sin through not owning his sin (sent for Uriah), manipulation (spend the night with your wife), head games (maybe he'll think it's his), becoming devious (death orders) (2 Sam. 11). It was a year or so later when Nathan the prophet came to David and he finally admitted his sins (2 Sam. 12). Can we see in David the tremendous power of sexual expression gone wrong? This is a man who otherwise did not flinch in doing what was right. Just look and see in David's example, the awesome power the lure of adultery has to bring down even the best.

I, also, learn from David that his sin may well have set up a family pattern. David taught by his example "take what you want." He wanted another man's wife and he took her. David repented, but his son, Amnon, "took what he wanted" by raping his half sister (2 Sam. 13). Absalom, his son, "took what he wanted" by trying to take over his father's throne. How did these boys learn to "take what you want"? I have to wonder if they learned it from dad. "My sin is ever before me" (Ps. 51:3). There are logical and natural consequences to our actions.

How does one get there? The reasons are numerous: eyes full of adultery (2 Pet. 2:14), flirtation (Prov. 5:3), gone from each other too long (1 Cor. 7:1-5), emotionally unavailable, defrauding (1 Cor. 7:1-5), sexual perversion/addiction (1 Tim. 3:7), and mid-life crisis (consider David).

Once accused of adultery there are: (1) The admitters some of whom are penitent and others not; (2) the hiders who play catch me if you can; and (3) the "wannabees" who hide in their lust—ready—but lacking opportunity.

The Innocent Party. A wise Christian lady said: "If you are innocent, don't act like you are guilty. Hold your head up and walk into that room." That's some pretty good advice. It is easy for embarrassment, shame, and depression to look like guilt. They are not!

Sometimes, the guilty party repents and the innocent party takes them back. I suggest we can learn from David again "my sin is ever before me." We learn from these brethren that damaged trust can be mended. I am not sure it can ever be made whole again.

Those who have been "cheated on" and taken their partner back have wounds, too. These spouses often feel alone and isolated by barriers that forbid them from discussing their experience openly. Some have their closure, but others remain hurt partners and at times feel overwhelmed with embarrassment, pain, and anger, but paralyzed to talk about it because "it's forgiven." Brethren, is it sinful to talk about "forgiven" things?

While sins can be forgiven, consequences of sin may linger. Understanding needs to be extended when the one betrayed questions, "Can I trust you again?" Discussions and reassurance need to be open and honest. I fear that under the guise of "forgiveness" spouses may be refusing to process the consequences and thus stall the healing process. I suggest that the event of infidelity and the forgiveness can be used in an exploitative way in the marriage on two fronts: (1) The guilty party puts a gag of silence on the innocent party since "it's forgiven," or (2) the innocent party keeps bringing the subject up to beat up the guilty party. Both extremes are equally wrong.

Once a person is forgiven of the sin of adultery, that transgression should never be used by the innocent as an excuse to harbor bitterness or engage in other sinful acts. Nor should the act of forgiveness be used to shut down further healing conversations between the couple. Through honest dialogue the couple can grow to deeper levels of love and commitment. This is a primary part of healing. The feelings of betrayal are not unlike those experienced upon a death. Trust in what was likely the most important human relationship of their life has died. Grief and recovery take a life of their own. Time, communication, and tolerance for vacillating emotions must exist before acceptance and resolution can occur. Honest dialog must occur!

The Detectives. Brethren, we are not detectives and should not demand that of others. One preacher made a practice of helping the innocent party trap the guilty by "peeping in windows to catch them." Another helped "wire the room" with camera and sound. Another put a recorder under the bed. What on earth is wrong with our brethren? This is done in the name of religion? A few of our brethren might do well to read Romans 13:1-6. Then, look up the definitions of "harassment," "stalking," and "felony" *and* start saving their money for a good lawyer. Adultery—separation and divorce are powerful emotional issues. Playing amateur detective games with emotionally charged situations is a recipe for disaster!

Circumstantial evidence is still evidence. How much evidence is enough *and* who decides? Brethren need to quit playing God and assuming they know all there is to know about a situation (Eph. 4:5, 6). Does the innocent party have to go before the judgment seat of every brother and sister *or* can brethren display some confidence that otherwise faithful Christians have the right to make their own valid decision based upon Scripture?

When going to a lawyer a person does not usually have the background or knowledge to know exactly how everything should be legally worded in the dissolution papers, the processes to file, or how to get the action through the court while complying with varying state laws. Filings for divorce are sometimes delayed due to attorney schedules, attorney practices of making a couple of trips a week to the county courthouse, and sick days among other things. Discussions and decisions at the courthouse are usually made behind closed doors with the lawyers and the judge or judge *ad litem*. Often the one filing or being filed against does not even need to be present or sits in a separate room while their divorce is being discussed. These things are at the discretion of the court and are usually treated as routine by the legal system. Most of the decisions at the courthouse are not in the hands of the person filing for divorce. Now, all of this happens at a time when the person is at his lowest, dazed, overwhelmed, and clouded in his thinking. Everything is in a whirl. The whole process at the courthouse takes place in ten to fifteen minutes. When the attorney comes out with the papers and hands them over feelings vary. For me there was a total feeling of numbness, a sense of failure, fear for my children, and disgust at my new label "divorced." In place of a home and marriage, I now had a paper.

All too frequently, the brethren start second guessing decisions made by good people who have gone through what we just described. The inquisition begins with a battery of questions: "Who filed first?", "Was 'adultery' the cause on paper?", "Did you countersue?", "Did the judge grant your petition or hers?" and a thousand other questions intended to judge, create doubt and set a platform to label an innocent party as "unscripturally divorced." The inquisition ends all too often snuffing out the last ounce of life from the victim by "binding upon others a load they cannot even bear" (Matt. 23:4). The spirit and deeds of the Pharisees are very much alive today. Do they live in you? Again, I ask: does the innocent party have to go before the judgment seat of every brother and sister or can good brethren express some confidence that otherwise faithful Christians have the right to make their own decision based upon Scripture? If we have really gotten to the point that we cannot respect the decisions of each other as fellow Christians, may God have mercy upon us all!

Children

The impact of separation or divorce varies, and can be tempered to some degree by the support of other adults who can provide stability in the child's life. When a marriage has been full of verbal abuse and even physical battles, a child's response may initially be a sense of relief. Even then there are many other complex reactions. Children often feel responsible for their parents' problems and, in some cases, may actually have been a source of parental disagreements. When a child sees that parents can stop loving each other, it is not hard for them to imagine that parents can stop loving them, as well.

Generally, the short-term effects of divorce on children are numerous and depend in part on the child's age, personality, and maturity. In the disruption of the family setting, children are prone to either act out or act in. The most unpredictable are those who "act in" hiding their thoughts and feelings. Brethren, these children need to be nurtured during this time. It is not a time to avoid contact with them, but a time a help and encourage. Common signs of confusion about the family situation and attempts to cope are:

- sadness, and even suicidal thoughts or behaviors
- feelings of abandonment
- apathy and withdrawal from family, friends, and/or activities
- anger (at self or others), rage or even violent behavior
- impulsivity, acting out, defiance, and limit-testing behavior
- self-blame or guilt; feeling responsible for parental problems
- neglect of schoolwork and drop in grades
- drug or alcohol use, or other self-destructive behavior
- sexual activity

(Gina Kemp, M.A., Jaelline Jaffe, PhD, Jeanne Segal, PhD 1996-2005 http://www.helpguide.org/mental/children divorce.htm.)

"Children of divorce are at high risk for depression and anxiety, acting out, and substance abuse problems" (Sharlene Wolchik, PhD & Irwin Sandler, PhD. Skill-building programs can have a long-term positive impact, 2004.)

That thing of "child support." Divorced women, who get custody of the children, also suffer a 33% decline in their standard of living. Men are considered "better off" (except they frequently become responsible for another family). "Only about 50% of divorced fathers pay child support regularly; 25% pay some and 25% pay little or nothing at all. Non-custodial parents (75% are men) are often depressed and anxious because they feel alienated from their children" (http://mentalhelp.net/psyhelp/chap10/chap10o.htm).

Pay your child support (Rom. 13:1-6; 1 Tim. 5:8)! The Christian who does not pay his or her child support has neglected his own, "denied the faith," and is "worse than an infidel" according to the Scriptures. With so much divorce and remarriage, we need to be preaching that divorced people still have a responsibility to care for their own. Elders may need to assure this occurs as a condition of being considered faithful. In Indiana five weeks of missed child support constitutes a felony. The law takes it seriously when a parent fails to support his children; we in the church need to take it seriously, too!

Substitute Role Models. When miles separate or situations cause a child to be virtually fatherless does James 1:27 apply? Many young men grow up in households with mom and sisters. A male role model is needed. Likewise, a young lady may be missing the male in her life—dad—and need a surrogate father figure. Daughters of divorce try to fill the lost father role by seeking a male to love them. And, too often this leads to promiscuity and/or exploitation. Now two points of caution are in order here: (1) Male role models need to have pure motives. One deacon went to a divorcing woman's home, took money, and asked to spend time with the first grade son. On the second visit he made an attempt to seduce the boy's mother. Come on—let's keep our motives pure here! (2) The single parent must be cautious for predators. I suggest for everyone's sake that the youth and adult role model only participate in activities in groups or in clearly public settings. This keeps everybody protected.

Rescuers. It should not come as a surprise to learn that many Christians qualify as co-dependent persons. These are those who give and give until they hurt and get little in return. They are the ones out there trying to right every wrong and fix things outside of their skills level or things which cannot be fixed. To them I caution that feelings of pity are often mistaken for feelings of love. Those who are on an emotional roller coaster, as are many in divorces, can be vulnerable and attempts to exploit them are all too frequent. It is not uncommon to have transference occur (i.e. seeing someone as their hero or the one to save them from their plight). Nor, is it uncommon for the rescuer to have counter-transference and mistake acceptance and pity for love. Compassion and enmeshment all too frequently give rise to pre-occupation with each other. That is how our brothers and sisters get themselves into trouble, emotional dependence and affairs. And, the cycle of divorce begins again, only this time it snares another family. Brethren, we must establish some solid boundaries and set limits! Think folks—think!

Custody. Of the eighteen million poor children in this country, over 50% live in a single-parent home caused by divorce (http://mentalhelp. net/psyhelp/chap10/chap10o.htm). One of the most critical issues in divorce regards the custody of children. While the final determination is usually made by the court, input from both parents and sometimes from children should be taken into account. Creative arrangements are sometimes incorporated, for example, the children stay in the same house and the parents take turns living there on a regular schedule. Any kind of custodial situation needs to hold the child's needs as primary. Parents must find a way to put aside their feelings about the divorce to provide a safe and secure environment for the children. Even in their own pain, parents must be sensitive to their own child's distress and find ways to avoid putting the children in the middle of their disputes. It is unfair and unwise to discuss contentious divorce issues with your children, or to badmouth the other parent, since this creates additional stress for children. Do not put the child in the position of choosing loyalties and living with secrets in order to protect parents from each other!

The worst is yet to come. A long term study was conducted by Judith Wallerstein, PhD where she followed a group of children from divorced homes in the 70s through their adulthood in the 90s. Her hypothesis was that kids bounce back from divorce. Twenty-five (25) years after the divorce: the children continued to experience substantial expectations of failure, fear of loss, fear of change and fear of conflict, heightened anxiety when forming their own romantic relationships. "Anxiety leads many (adult children of divorce) into making bad choices in relationships, giving up hastily when problems arise, or avoiding relationships altogether. Even more, those traumatized as children by divorce (and other traumas) are seven (7) times more likely to have serious health problems later in life including cancer, stroke, diabetes and cardiovascular problems (Judith Wallerstein, *et al.*, *The Unexpected Legacy of Divorce: A 25 Year Landmark Study* (New York: Hyperion, 2000), xxvii.; Catherine E. Ross and John Mirowsky, "Parental Divorce, Life-Course Disruption, and Adult Depression," *Journal of Marriage and the Family* 61 (1999): 1034-1035.

As children of divorce grow into adults they tend to "view cohabiting and premarital sex more favorably." This is a double tragedy since cohabiting couples have more breakups, greater risk of domestic violence and establish patterns of cohabiting that are more like chains of divorces (Alan Booth and David Johnson, "Premarital Cohabitation and Marital Success," *Journal of Family Issues* 9 [1988]: 255-272; Paul Amato and Alan Booth, "The Consequences of Divorce for Attitudes toward Divorce and Gender Roles," *Journal of Family Issues* 12 [1991]: 306-323.)

Children never get over divorce. It is a great loss that is in their lives forever. It is like a grief that is never over. All special events, like holidays, plays, sports, graduations, marriages, births of children, and funerals bring up the loss created by divorce as well as the family relationship conflicts that result from the "extended family" celebrating or grieving any event (Therapy group member. Used by permission).

My loss was magnified as my father remarried and adopted a new "family." His life now revolves around his new family with infrequent contact with me. This has only increased my feelings of abandonment and alienation from the divorce (an adult child of divorce. Used by permission).

Suggestions With Children

Expect a reaction. No child will happily accept a divorce. Expect him/her to be angry and sad; you need to be patient and ask about his/her feelings.

Take away blame. Tell him/her that the divorce is not his fault and that it's not his/her responsibility to fix it.

Preserve quality time. Work on your relationship with your child. Spend regular quality time together, such as meals or bedtime talks.

Provide support. Tell your child two important things: "Parents never divorce children" and "I'll always be here for you." (Note: There are special issues here *if* or *when* the parent is involved in a "next relationship.")

Enforce rules. Misbehavior is often a kid's way of saying "pay attention to me." So be sure to make time for him/her during and after the divorce. When he/she misbehaves, enforce effective and good discipline. Kids need consistency especially in a world that is falling apart. Develop as many routines as you can.

Agree together to be partners in parenting although not partners in marriage. Avoid catching kids in the middle—using them to "spy," demanding loyalty or being on "my side," belittling the other parent, reprimand any carrying of "spy" information. Don't exploit your kids in this process!

Elderships

Elders need the wisdom of Solomon in dealing with some of the entanglements brought before them. The function of "watching for souls" can be tedious and stress provoking, but throughout the process, elders, do not ever forget you "shall give account" (Heb. 13:17). A proverb is "he that is first with a cause seems just" (Prov. 18:17). Please, be wise and know that the first spouse with the story sets up a good offense and puts the other spouse in a defensive role. Elders, be careful that you don't get played. Give each person a chance to tell their story objectively. A fact shown in research over and over is that men tend to believe the woman's story before the man's story. As men, be sure you listen to the facts and not the gender. Do not get caught up in the emotions and heart-breaking stories of either. If you are to be wise, you must not get your own issues enmeshed in either of theirs. Make every attempt to be fair and impartial. If you cannot, back off and let others handle it!

There is a time to *act* and a time to *react*. When these issues come before an eldership it is not a time for quick response, but a time for gathering of the facts, a time for prayer, and a time to enlist support within the congregation. If a marriage is to be spared, the keys to healing that marriage lie within every faithful congregation. The resources are there in terms of older women who can teach younger women to "love their husbands" and be "keepers at home" (Tit. 2:5). We speak of preaching the whole truth of God's word, but how often do we keep certain Scriptures silent in our teaching programs? Where are God's instructions presented on sexuality in our teaching programs both inside and outside of marriage? Where is Proverbs 2:16-19; 5:1-23; 7:4-27; Song of Solomon; Galatians 5:19; Romans 1:18-32; 1 Corinthians 7:1-5; 6:12-20; 1 Thessalonians 4:3-8 and numerous other sections of Scripture in our teaching programs? Where are the lessons on Old Testament abominations involving promiscuity and perversion in our programs? Part of what is happening with immorality in our congregations today is that the world is offering sexual excess in great detail while the Scriptures on these things remain unknown to many of our members. In short, the world is pulling harder than the church in matters of infidelity. It is destroying our youth and defiling our marriage beds (Heb.13:4). Elders must be both *proactive* and *reactive* on this issue as they watch for the welfare of souls.

As people come to elderships with their marital issues involving divorce, elders will hear many "secrets" of a marriage. To get to the core of issues one may need to listen to things they would rather not hear. And, brethren may need to set road blocks when conversations are heading in a non-productive direction. Please, keep in mind that *hurt people hurt people*. In their emotions, they may take unfair shots at each other. Elders must remain neutral with the parties involved, but never neutral on holding to God's truths. As you work with cases of separation and divorce, consider *both* the innocent party *and* the guilty party. You watch for both of their souls *and* their children as well. If you do not know what to do, seek counsel!

How do we treat anyone caught up in sin? It should be with meekness and consideration that we avoid getting caught in sin ourselves (Gal. 6:1-3). In "watching for souls" is the "guilty party" treated with the same compassion (John 8:3-11)? Could anyone of us get "caught up in sin in a weak moment"? Do we just write off "the guilty party" and let the devil have them (even if they have five failed marriages and the person is currently "living with" someone? John 4:17ff)?

Dear elders, you know that sooner or later you will have feuding, separating, cheating, and divorcing couples in your congregation. Why wait and become reactive? A proactive approach is highly recommended to pre-determine your process in dealing with these divorce situations before the emotions of the situation get interjected.

Mutual Friends and Peers
In divorce part of the isolation felt by divorcees is when church families, to whom we were close, back away and their children may avoid our children at the very time we need them to draw closer to us all. People often do not know how to respond to the individual when they have been used to responding to the family unit. Some want to be "friends" to both parties and so they keep their neutral distance. Others do not want to get caught in triangulation or to be quoted when divorcing couples try to recruit their allies and quote them. Unfortunately, all of this "divorce thing" is exciting to some and they may want to know all the details. Please, do not get caught in the trap of satisfying your own curiosity by dining on someone else's pain. Remember that your advice whether shoddy or wise just might be taken and made the direction for your friend's life and eternity. Be sure your advice is what God would have you give. Say what the divorcing person needs to hear, not what they want to hear.

Final Remarks
If divorce is so awful, then why do people choose that alternative so often? Three common reasons are: (1) A person may not realize the problems they will face alone or with a new partner. (2) It would be hard to choose to continue living with an unloving, hateful, uninterested partner for another

forty or fifty years. (3) It is so easy to dream of a wonderful future with an ideal partner, but how many ideal partners are there?

Consider this before giving up on your marriage:

1. Are you sure the awfulness of your marriage is not a product of your own thinking and attitudes? Or, is it a justification for your anger and urge to leave? If so, the same process is likely to re-occur in 4-7 years with another spouse. Fix this one.

2. Are you pretty sure you can and will select a better partner for your next time? The facts are that you will likely be attracted to a person with the very same traits.

3. What are the consequences to others, especially your children?

4. Are you staying in the marriage because you are dependent and afraid to change?

5. Consider the Scriptures:

- Was there "defrauding"? Was it with consent (1 Cor 7:1-5)?
- Did you "rejoice with the wife of thy youth" (Prov. 5:17-20)?
- Were you "captivated by her love" (Prov. 5:17-20)?
- What emotional distancing happened (Eph. 5:22-32)?
- Did you give "honor unto the wife as unto the weaker vessel" (1 Pet. 3:1-7)?
- Were you in subjection to your own husband (Eph. 5:22)?
- Did you treat your husband with respect (1 Pet. 3:1-6)?

If divorce is being considered . . .

1. Most of us by ourselves cannot rationally handle the complex and emotional questions involved in divorce. We need to be told things we may not want to hear. Talk with a trusted spiritual advisor. (For those advising, this is a sacred trust. Do not let your reaction destroy souls. This is not a time for a lynch mob—let's go get 'em boys!) It is a time for wisdom.

2. There are many helpful books about divorce, with the Bible being *first* (Hosea; Prov. 5:1-23; 7:1-27; 1 Cor. 6:12-20; Matt. 5:31-32; 19:1-12).

3. Trust the power of prayer—for yourself, your spouse, your children, and a supportive congregation.

4. If the divorce involves emotional conflict over marital property or children, consider using mediation. Children deserve access to both parents under usual circumstances. Stuff is just stuff; it only has the value we assign to it.

5. Children should have equal representation in a divorce (in an ideal world). They have a birthright to two parents, their time, love, and resources. They will remain sons and daughters forever with both parents. Consider grandparent's rights and those of extended family members.

6. The congregation must help "the saved" stay saved during the process of their pain and reach out to the family member(s) who is "lost."

Conclusion

Know that divorce is a life-changing decision with eternal consequences. The next time you see a divorced person, please see him as a person first. We are not objects to be talked about. We are not numb to the gossip and slander. We are people, God's people, and we hurt. In my darkest hours of pain I wrote these words:

> His lonely heart ached to be with the one he loved
> But he grew tired and weary
> A lonely soul yearning for his mate
> And finally giving up
> He cried out in pain.
> An empty heart is a lonely place
> Time and energy can be spent and yet the void is never filled.

Divorce! Satan's gift that keeps on giving. God hates it! I do, too!

Bibliography

Amato, P. and A. Booth. "The Consequences of Divorce for Attitudes toward Divorce and Gender Roles," *Journal of Family Issues* 12 (1991): 306-323.

Booth, A. and D. Johnson. "Premarital Cohabitation and Marital Success," *Journal of Family Issues* 9 (1988): 255-272.

Cox *et al*, 1999. http://mentalhelp.net/psyhelp/chap10/chap10o.htm.

Goldberg, H. and I. Goldberg. *Counseling Today's Families.* Pacific Grove, CA: Brooks/Cole Publishing Co., 1998.

Hetherington, Cox and Cox, 1995 http://mentalhelp.net/psyhelp/chap10/chap10o. htm.

Isaacs, M.B. and B. Montalvo, D. Abelsohn. *The Difficult Divorce.* New York: Basic Books, Inc. 2001.

Kemp, Jaffe, Segal. http://helpguide.org/mental/children divorce.htm 1996-2005.

Keyes, K. Jr. *A conscious person's guide to relationships.* Marina del Rey, CA: Living Love Publications,1999.

Queralt, M. *Social Environment and Human Behavior.* Boston:Allyn and Bacon, 1996.

Reissman, R. Coping with Divorce. http://mentalhelp.net/psyhelp/chap10/chap10o. htm1990.

Ross, C. and J. Mirowsky. "Parental Divorce, Life-Course Disruption, and Adult Depression," *Journal of Marriage and the Family* 61 (1999): 1034-1035.

Thompson & Spanier. *The Life-Long Pain of Divorce.* New York: Guilford Press, 1993.

Wallerstein, *et al. The Unexpected Legacy of Divorce: A 25 Year Landmark Study.* New York: Hyperion, 2000, xxvii.

Wolchik S. and I. Sandler. Skill-building programs can have a long-term positive impact, 2004 presentation.

God Hears the Cry of the Weak

Ron Halbrook

David often praises God for delivering him from his sins and his enemies, and thus from danger and suffering. Such praises are expressed in Psalm 40:1-5:

Ron Halbrook was born in Indianola, MS in 1946, moved to Belle Glade, FL in 1951, and grew up and graduated from high school there. He preached for the Southside Church of Christ in Belle Glade in the summer of 1964. During his years at Florida College (1964-67), his preaching continued with the Central congregation near Live Oak, FL (fall 1965), the West Sixth St. church in Pine Bluff, AR (summer 1966), and the Hercules Ave. church in Clearwater, FL (1966-67).

During 1967-73 Ron labored with the Wooley Springs church near Athens, AL, taught high school at Athens Bible School, and finished a degree in history at Athens College (1969). He labored with the Broadmoor church in Nashville, TN 1973-78 (and completed a master's degree in church history at Vanderbilt University, 1979), the Knollwood church in Xenia, OH 1978-82 (with Mike Willis in a two-preacher arrangement), the church in Midfield, AL 1982-84, and the West Columbia, TX church in 1984-97. In August of 1997, he began work in a two-preacher arrangement with Andy Alexander at the Hebron Lane Church of Christ in Shepherdsville, KY. Andy moved to Bowling Green, KY in 2003 and Steven Deaton took his place at Hebron Lane in June 2004. This arrangement allows Ron to hold about ten gospel meetings and make 2-3 trips to the Philippines each year. He has made fifteen trips to the Philippines since 1995. Ron's articles have appeared in such religious journals as *Truth Magazine, Searching the Scriptures*, and *The Preceptor.* Other writing includes tracts (*Unity With Christ & Christians; Honorable Marriage*), booklets (*Trends Pointing Toward a New Apostasy; Understanding the Controversy*), and books (*The Doctrine of Christ & Unity of the Saints; Halbrook-Freeman Debate on Marriage, Divorce, & Remarriage*). Ron married Donna Bell in 1967. They have three children: Jonathan, David, and Deborah.

I waited patiently for the LORD; and he inclined unto me, and heard my cry. He brought me up also out of an horrible pit, out of the miry clay, and set my feet upon a rock, and established my goings. And he hath put a new song in my mouth, even praise unto our God: many shall see it, and fear, and shall trust in the LORD. Blessed is that man that maketh the LORD his trust, and respecteth not the proud, nor such as turn aside to lies. Many, O LORD my God, are thy wonderful works which thou hast done, and thy thoughts which are to us-ward: they cannot be reckoned up in order unto thee: if I would declare and speak of them, they are more than can be numbered.

David's distress was like that of a man trapped in "an horrible pit," helplessly sinking in "the miry clay," but God delivered him from certain death and set his feet "upon a rock." As David now will sing God's praises, other men will learn of the wonderful works of God and learn to "trust in the Lord." Numberless are the times God has delivered his people from danger and suffering.

It is the common lot of man to suffer in this world. We suffer because of our own sins. We also suffer as innocent victims of the sins of other people, which is the focus of this study. All sin is the result of man misusing his free will, but we must understand that all sin is the choice of man and not the will of God. Men choose to sin in ways that abuse and harm innocent victims, contrary to the will of God. God is not the source of abuse and suffering but is the source of deliverance from abuse and suffering to those who trust in him.

Knowing that enemies were abroad seeking to do him harm, David trusted in God as the source of deliverance and comfort. We hear David's prayer of faith in Psalm 59:1-4:

Deliver me from mine enemies, O my God: defend me from them that rise up against me. Deliver me from the workers of iniquity, and save me from bloody men. For, lo, they lie in wait for my soul: the mighty are gathered against me; not for my transgression, nor for my sin, O LORD. They run and prepare themselves without my fault: awake to help me, and behold.

It was not the consequences of his own sins which David feared, but rather men who acted as enemies and worked to wound or destroy him "without my fault." Where can we turn when endangered and victimized by such men, except to the Lord? David pled with God and trusted in God to observe his precarious and perilous circumstances and to "awake to help me."

Those who have suffered and been delivered like David will praise God as David did. They will also rejoice to tell others who suffer the good news that they can trust in God as the God who delivers. That is the purpose and motivation for this study. This will be a Bible study, not an emotional and extended testimonial, but this lesson will reflect my own experience like David's in learning that God hears our cries of distress.

Our suffering reminds us that we are weak, and we desperately need God's help. Is there an answer to the cry of the weak? Yes, a thousand times, yes! There is a true and living God who sees, hears, cares, delivers, and comforts the weak and wounded who seek him!

A Horrible Pit

In Psalms 40 and 59, David speaks out of the terrible experience of fears and dangers created by men and circumstances beyond his control. He felt like he was trapped in a horrible pit. Wicked men were planning and plotting selfish schemes which put him in harm's way through no fault of his own. His praise to the God who delivers was genuine and real because he had lived in the shadow and fear of dangers which were genuine and real. These psalms awaken and captivate my heart because I was trapped in a horrible pit from which there seemed to be no escape as a child.

In spite of my father's good qualities, he acted the part of a wicked man by putting his wife and children in harm's way through no fault of our own. One of my earliest childhood memories is being startled out of my sleep by my father's late appearance at home with his explosive temper. Flipping on the light in the bedroom where we three children slept, he would shout that the toys were not all stored in the toy box or were not properly stored. Picking up the box and turning it upside down, he would violently jerk it up and down catapulting the toys onto the floor. It was horrifying to hear this volcanic eruption and to see my mother pleading for him to calm down, only to have him scream in anger toward her. It was a horrible pit.

Many times I was awakened through my growing up years late at night to witness the scenes of my father berating, belittling, and bullying my mother. Many a time I saw through the doors barely cracked open in my parents' room and my own room as my father screamed into the face of my mother lying in bed. Many a time I saw her weeping as he ranted over nothing, and as he badgered her to engage the battle, I often heard her tender words, "It takes two to argue, and I have nothing to say," or, "Be ye kind one to another," using the beautiful words of Ephesians 4:32, which often enraged him even more. In that horrible pit, my father's tyrannical tirades made him appear powerful and my mother weak in my childhood eyes, but I later realized he was weak and she was strong. As I matured, his demeanor seemed all the more wicked against the kind and beautiful attitude and words of my mother. I never heard her respond in kind to his insulting tirades. It is possible to hear beautiful words and witness beautiful character even in the horrible pit. Yet, it is a horrible pit.

When I was about sixteen, my youngest sister was standing and rocking in a rocking chair, causing it to tip over and break. My father's volcanic temper erupted as he grabbed her by one leg and held her upside down while he flailed her unmercifully. The cumulative effect of this incident and others caused me to bolt from the house, partly out of pity for my sister, partly out of disgust for my father, and partly out of fear that I was about to say or do something untoward. After a while, my father came out into the cool night air demanding to know what "my problem" was. Shocking myself, I crossed a line by telling him that his conduct was completely out of order for a Christian, that my sister should have been punished properly, but that his constant outbursts and overreactions were harmful to our home. He cut me off by saying, "This is my house and I'll run it any way I want to. When you get married and have your own house, you can run it however you want to." Though disappointed by his rebuff, I was strangely and strongly motivated by those words from that moment, and the effect continues to this moment: I was then and am now determined not to live in such a wicked, disruptive, and destructive environment, but to strive with all my might to have a godly home by the grace of God. That was a crucial night for me, but it was also a horrible pit.

I do not mean to sound self-serving and self-righteous, but I hope to ac-complish what David hoped to accomplish by those psalms: to lift up the heart of someone who lives in a horrible pit, to give that someone hope that God can deliver anyone who trusts in him no matter how horrible the pit. I have to admit I was influenced by this environment and had a huge problem with my own temper, with fighting with friends, and with foul language, especially during my junior high school years. But it began to dawn on me that, if my father's lack of self-control was disgusting, shameful, and destructive, my own sins were equally so. It was a horrible pit and I looked to God for a way out.

The constant verbal and emotional abuse took its toll on us as children and later as adults, but there was an even more horrible experience for me. The most demeaning, shameful, and discouraging part of all was the sexual abuse and molestation. It is hard and horrible enough to push myself to call to mind the incidents already recounted, and I have neither the emotional energy nor the desire to pursue the incidents and experiences of sexual abuse. Suffice it to say that this horrible pit involves the crassest selfishness, the crudest carnality, the self-destructive hardening of the conscience, the most calculating manipulation of a child's mind and emotions, and a dark world of secrets the abuser must keep hidden from his mate and from the larger community of family, church, and neighbors. Sexual abuse, sexual manipulation, and sexual molestation create a pit which becomes more and more horrible with time. It is a pit, and it is horrible.

The same carnal rationalizing which justified the secret of sexual molestation bred other secret sins as well. Beer and wine were hidden in the bedroom closet, appropriately stored near the stack of pornographic magazines. Alcoholic drinks, I heard it said, are relaxing, and, as for pornography, it promotes a healthy sex life for husband and wife. These rationalizations came from the same mind and mouth which proclaimed the gospel of Christ in the public arena and decried the corruptions of alcohol, pornography, and sexual abuse! I regarded this as hypocrisy then, and I regard it as hypocrisy now.

That brings me to the last segment of this selective biographical sketch of life in a horrible pit. Four of us children grew up in a home where we were taught the sinfulness of sin, the saving power of the gospel of Christ, the inestimable value of spiritual blessings, and the preeminent priority of going to heaven to spend eternity with God. In spite of all that teaching, the emotional and spiritual effects of living in this horrible pit were, and are, treacherous to the children who grew up in this environment. Two of us drew closer to God and found him to be the God who delivers. Two of us have abandoned the faith, partly out of frustration, discouragement, and disgust at the hypocritical conduct witnessed in this horrible pit.

Some of you will wonder whether my father repented, truly and genuinely repented of his carnal attitudes and hypocritical conduct. I hope and pray that he did, because I wish no harm on him, but God knows and we must simply trust him to handle all cases perfectly, justly, and mercifully.

The Tears of the Weak and Wounded

When the innocent suffer at the hands of wicked people, they must know that God sees and hears all things in all places at all times. "The eyes of the LORD are in every place, beholding the evil and the good" (Prov. 15:3). Such evil deeds are often practiced under the cover of darkness, but "the darkness and the light are both alike" to God (Ps. 139:12).

Women and children are often victims. Malachi accused the men of his generation of divorcing their wives and taking new wives. The abandoned, anguished wives came before God in worship pouring out their hearts in grief, "covering the altar of the LORD with tears, with weeping, and with crying out" (Mal. 2:13). God rejected the worship of their heartless husbands. Throughout the ages, abused wives have wept rivers of tears over the bitterness and rancor of their husbands (Col. 3:19). Likewise, abused children have been frustrated, angry, discouraged, and depressed because of the uncontrolled temper of their fathers (Eph. 6:4; Col. 3:21).

The innocent victims weep because of how their wounds are inflicted, because of who inflicts them, and because of the pain and torment resulting from their wounds.

Here are some of the ways the wicked wound the innocent. They practice verbal, physical, and sexual abuse. They berate, belittle, and demean through unloving attitudes, piercing words, and disrespectful conduct. This may include unfounded suspicions and ridiculous accusations. Temper explosions are triggered by incidents small and large, sometimes instantaneously, sometimes like a gathering storm, with shock waves of screaming, irrational and violent outbursts, and even severe beatings of family members.

How Wounds Inflicted
- Verbal, physical, and sexual abuse
- Berate, belittle, demean
- Screaming, anger fits, severe beatings
- Manipulate, flatter, betray, false promises
- Fondle, rape
- Slam doors 'til wall shakes, throw chairs, etc.
- Menace, threaten—atmosphere of fear
- Create tight, closed circle: do not talk, live in fear

Manipulation is practiced as a way of controlling rather than nurturing relationships, including flattery, betrayal, and false promises. Sexual touching, fondling, and rape may occur. Doors may be slammed repeatedly with increasing force until the walls shake. Chairs and other objects may be thrown or broken. The abuser will menace and threaten so as to create an atmosphere of fear. The family learns or is forced to create a tight, closed circle so that no one who knows about the abuse will report it or seek help. In fact, it may never occur to those who live in this atmosphere to seek help. They live in a maze from which there appears to be no escape. All their mental faculties and energies focus on coping, on self-preservation, and on protecting the other victims as best they can. I did not learn this from a book, I lived it.

Who inflicts such wounds? It might be one's mate in marriage. A parent may wound the child, or a child the parent. A sibling may be wounded by a sibling. Other relatives such as an uncle or an aunt or a cousin may be guilty. Someone in a circle of brethren and friends may abuse others in the circle. The person inflicting wounds may be a non-Christian or a Christian. The wounds are deeper, more daunting, more damaging when inflicted by someone very close who should be the source of protection and security, such as a parent.

All too often we who are men, husbands, and fathers are the abusers. To our shame we have betrayed our God-given trust. We have broken our vows to "love, honor, and cherish." Rather than protecting our wives and children from harm, we are often the very ones inflicting harm upon them. How shall we escape the wrath of God in such cases? In homes cursed by abusive men, wives can be "enablers" by defending their husbands, thus betraying the trust of their children. In some cases, the wife may be guilty of overt abuse, especially verbal abuse and emotional manipulation.

Who Inflicts Wounds
• Mate wounds mate
• Father, mother wound child
• Child wounds parent
• Brother wounds brother or sister; sister wounds brother or sister
• Other relatives
• Brethren, friends
• Strangers
• Person not a Christian
• A Christian

The wounds torment the victim in a variety of cruel ways. The damage may be physical, emotional, or psychological—or all three. Discouragement and depression may haunt the victim. Many people struggle with repressed anger, which may be directed toward persons who have nothing to do with the problem. In that way some abused people become abusers themselves. Some souls will suffer from self-doubt, self-loathing, and self-hatred because they feel tainted and contaminated by the filthy or destructive acts inflicted on them. Irrational fears and phobias may appear. Nightmares taunt and horrify in some cases.

How Wounds Torment Victim
- Physical, emotional, and psychological wounds
- Discouraged, depressed
- Repressed anger
- Self-doubt, self-loathing
- Irrational fears, phobias
- Nightmares
- Suicidal thoughts
- Try to hide bruises
- "Did I invite or deserve it?"
- Hide, cower, crawl, avoid the abuser
- Obsessive, compulsive conduct
- Lifelong struggle

Suicidal thoughts and actions plague those who carry unbearable memories and scars. People who suffer physical bruises and scars use ingenious methods to hide them as marks of shame. Some victims are tormented by recurring questions such as, "Did I somehow invite the abuse or deserve the wound?" Victims devise means of avoiding the abuser's attention such as hiding, cowering, or pretending to be asleep. For instance, as a child I learned to silently slide from the bed at night and crawl to the toilet, and then to urinate into the commode near the top lip on the inside of the bowl, immediately against the bowl, so that not a sound was made.

The torment of the wounds may be manifested in many forms of obsessive, compulsive conduct (constant washing of hands or other cleaning obsessions, constant arranging of objects in certain patterns, etc.).

Most victims face a lifetime of struggle in coping with the pain of their wounds and in attempting to make some sense of how and why they were abused.

A good friend, whose experience was similar yet somewhat different from my own, penned poignant words reflecting the pain of abuse in childhood after many years have passed. She quoted in full the passages which are only cited here (capitalization, punctuation, and spacing original):

there are truths that i know
my father taught them to me

proverbs 11:29
proverbs 11:17
proverbs 20:1

i know a home that isn't as God would have it
wreaks havoc in the heart of the child
i know a father who salves his pain with alcohol inflicts
harm on the people he loves
i know a father fleeing from his demons
turns them loose on his family
i know those who love him scatter to the safe places of the heart
a refuge of the mind   prepared by God
i know   'til i die there is comfort in this place

there are truths that i know
my father taught them to me

proverbs 23:29-35
proverbs 19:19
proverbs 10:7
proverbs 15:13

i know my father   drunk in misery   in sadness
gave the gift of terror
i know he threatens the rest of my life
i know the past   the present   the future   are the same place
i know his hand is cruel   wielding weapons of fear
i know his hand is perverse   visiting where it ought not
i know his hand is gentle
sometimes his hand is gentle
i know i love him

Only those who have experienced such a curse can understand the conflicting emotions it breeds, and they will spend a lifetime trying to understand their own wounded emotions. God alone could truly understand the
cry of the weak, the wounded, the innocent, the defenseless, the helpless.
God hears. God understands. God delivers.

The Innocent Suffer at the Hands of the Wicked
The innocent suffer at the hands of wicked men and women. This sad

reality does not reflect God's will but is provoked by the malicious character of Satan. The Bible is replete with examples of such tragedies, and they have occurred again and again, and are occurring this very moment.

When Abel worshiped according to God's instruction, and Cain substituted his own will for God's instruction, God accepted Abel's worship and rejected Cain's. Cain experienced resentment, rage, and hatred toward his brother because of his righteous life and murdered him (Gen. 4:8-10).

Job was deprived of his possessions, his family, and his friends as the result of Satan working behind the scenes to destroy his faith in God. Satan sneered at God and denigrated Job's righteous life (Job 1:8-9). After losing his wealth and children, Job suffered the loss of his wife's moral support, as she told him to "curse God, and die" (2:9). His misguided friends wounded him with baseless charges of grievous sins (4:7-8).

Lot was the victim of his conniving daughters who caused him to become drunken so that they could commit incest with him (Gen. 19:30-38). If Lot was vexed and distressed by the sins of his neighbors in Sodom (2 Pet. 2:7), how much more so by his daughter's disgusting conduct!

Sarah was despised and mocked by Hagar because she conceived when Sarah was barren (Gen. 16:4). After Sarah bore Isaac and he grew as a child, he was despised and mocked by his half-brother Ishmael (21:9).

Joseph was hated by his brothers because of his father's favoritism toward him. They envied him, could not speak a kind word to him, quarreled with him, threw him into a pit, and sold him to merchants bound for Egypt (Gen. 37).

King Saul tried to manipulate his own children—Jonathan, Merab, and Michal—as a means to capture and murder David, who served him so faithfully (1 Sam. 18-20). His children were used as bait in an effort to catch David, beginning with Merab (18:17-19). When his plans to utilize Michal and Jonathan failed, Saul railed not only at them but also slandered his own wife (19:17; 20:30-33).

David was the victim of jealousy, intrigue, and betrayal by Saul, by his own sons, and by close friends. Regarding Saul's hatred, David echoed the cry of the innocent who have suffered at the hands of the wicked throughout the ages, when he asked his dear friend Jonathan, "What have I done? What is mine iniquity? And what is my sin before thy father, that he seeketh my life?" (1 Sam. 20:1). There was no rational answer, only Saul's irrational envy and abusive anger. David's words of distress in Psalm 55:12-14 memorialized the grief and anguish of God's people in every age who have been subjected to similar trials:

> For it was not an enemy that reproached me; then I could have borne it: neither was it he that hated me that did magnify himself against me; then I would have hid myself from him: But it was thou, a man mine equal, my guide, and mine acquaintance. We took sweet counsel together, and walked unto the house of God in company.

As David learned that the deepest wounds are inflicted by people closest to us, he learned to focus his faith all the more in God not man.

Sweet, kind, considerate Abigail was married to arrogant, unthankful, stubborn, selfish, bickering, foolish Nabal (1 Sam. 25). While David hid from Saul in the area of Mt. Carmel, he had protected Nabal's shepherds and flocks from harm. Later, needing food for his men, he sent messengers to greet Nabal and to ask for any help which he might wish to offer. Nabal refused and insulted David. In turn, David organized his men to attack Nabal. Meanwhile, a young shepherd reported to Abigail what Nabal had done, and that David was preparing to attack. Nabal's despicable disposition was common knowledge; in the words of the young man, "He is such a son of Belial, that a man cannot speak to him" (25:17).

Abigail quietly sent provisions to David with profuse apologies for her husband's misconduct without telling him. Like many a wife trying to clean up her husband's senseless mess, she pled, "Upon me, my lord, upon me let this iniquity be" (25:24). Her kindness caused David to spare Nabal's life. When Abigail later revealed to her husband what she had done on his behalf, he became so enraged that he suffered a stroke—"his heart died . . . he became as a stone"—resulting in his death (25:37-38).

Only God knows how many have walked and are walking the path of Abel, Job, Lot, Sarah, Isaac, Joseph, Jonathan, Merab, Michal, David, and sweet Abigail. Their number is legion! Many suffer in silence among men, but their hearts and prayers cry out unto God. If God numbers every hair on our heads, in like manner he numbers every tear that falls, he sees every bruise that scars the heart. He hears every cry of anguish and every prayer for help. God hears the cry of the weak and wounded.

Trust God and Seek Help

1. Help in the God who delivers. As we saw in Psalm 40, the true and living God is the God who delivers.

> I waited patiently for the LORD; and he inclined unto me, and heard my cry. He brought me up also out of an horrible pit, out of the miry clay, and set my feet upon a rock, and established my goings.

All of the innocent who trusted in him from Abel to Abigail were delivered. Their deliverance did not always come in the manner or time they might have thought or planned. Men must learn to trust in God to work in his own time and way. Today, we serve the same God they served. He has delivered me and many others in his own time and way! He is still the God who delivers and brings stability to the life of the abused!

2. Help in prayer. We must trust God and seek his help in prayer. He is always near at hand and ready to help his people in distress who call upon him:

> For this shall everyone that is godly pray unto thee in a time when thou mayest be found: surely in the floods of great waters they shall not come nigh unto him. Thou art my hiding place; thou shalt preserve me from trouble; thou shalt compass me about with songs of deliverance (Ps. 32:6-7).

Those who seek and find in God their hiding place also find themselves in the company of the saints who are singing songs of deliverance.

When the people of God are faced with overwhelming dangers, they flee to God as the rock, the tower, and the fortress who is greater than ourselves and greater than the gravest enemies. David prayed,

> Hear my cry, O God; attend unto my prayer. From the end of the earth will I cry unto thee, when my heart is overwhelmed: lead me to the rock that is higher than I. For thou hast been a shelter for me, and a strong tower from the enemy. I will abide in thy tabernacle for ever: I will trust in the covert of thy wings (Ps. 61:1-4).

To find rest in God is to find rest atop a majestic rock which towers above the raging storms of the sea and the frightful cries of the enemy. Truly, God is "the rock that is higher than I," to which the weak may flee to find strength, deliverance, and security.

During the years when wounds were being inflicted, I like others learned to draw near to God in prayer. In this prayerful fellowship with God, I found consolation, strength, and hope even without knowing how he would answer. "Tribulation brings us to God, and brings God to us" as we seek his help in prayer (C.H. Spurgeon, *The Treasury of David* III:105). Prayer draws us closer to the heart of God in our suffering and our sense of helplessness.

3. Help in God's word. Those who trust in God seek and find his help in his word. As we learn to love and meditate more and more upon the word of God, we find his word to be more and more a source of strength, guidance, and comfort. The Psalmist exclaimed in Psalm 119, the great psalm of praise for God's word,

> O how love I thy law! It is my meditation all the day. Thou through thy commandments hast made me wiser than mine enemies: for they are ever with me. I have more understanding than all my teachers: for thy testimonies are my meditation. I understand more than the ancients, because I keep thy precepts. I have refrained my feet from every evil way, that I might keep thy word. I have not departed from thy judgments: for thou hast taught me. How sweet are thy words unto my taste! yea, sweeter than honey to my mouth! Through thy precepts I get understanding: therefore I hate every false way. Thy word is a lamp unto my feet, and a light unto my path.

As the word of God yields its growing light to our troubled souls, the darkness which troubles us first fades and finally flees away. We find true wisdom and true delights which our carnal minded enemies can never experience as they pursue power and pleasure by victimizing the helpless.

As a young man reading and meditating upon the word of God, and as I have continued that study and meditation through the years, I have found the strength, guidance, and comfort of God's word stronger than the pain of my wounds. "Trouble and anguish have taken hold on me; yet thy commandments are my delights" (Ps. 119:143). "Great peace have they which love thy law: and nothing shall offend them" or cause them to fall (Ps. 119:165). The word of God is a healing balm for the wounded soul.

4. Help in God's people. Trusting in God, we learn to seek God's help in his people. We will find the same strength and consolation the psalmist found by cultivating close friendship with people who serve God: "I am a companion of all them that fear thee, and of them that keep thy precepts" (Ps. 119:63). Fellow Christians can be sources of great blessings by sharing the wisdom they have gained in serving God: "He that walketh with wise men shall be wise: but a companion of fools shall be destroyed" (Prov. 23:20).

Proverbs 24:6 has been my safety rope from the days of my youth until the present hour: "For by wise counsel thou shalt make thy war: and in multitude of counsellors there is safety." Countless times I have sought wisdom and insight from God's people in striving to resolve in some measure the questions, doubts, and struggles which resulted from the wounds of abuse inflicted in my youth. Many Christians have helped me find strength and healing through the years. Little could they have known what a great blessing they have been in my life by patiently listening to me ramble in an effort to describe and define these thorny issues from my painful past. Little could they have known how much their own comments, observations, and advice truly helped me to sort through these thorny issues, to resolve some of them, and to lay others aside. A partial list of these precious souls would include my mother (Nelwyn Nason Halbrook), my wife (Donna), Homer Hailey (deceased 2000), Bobby and Karen Graham, Leonard (d. 1999) and Ruth Tyler, Roy E. Cogdill (d. 1985), Gilbert Savely (an elder at the Broadmoor church of Christ in Nashville, Tennessee, d. 1983), Mike and Sandy Willis, Larry and Marilyn Hafley, Raymond and Wanda Maxwell (West Columbia, Texas), Andy and Joy Alexander, Steve and Bette Wolfgang, Harry Osborne, and many others.

5. Help in people with special qualifications. We trust in God by seeking help from people with special qualifications made available to us by God's providence. Such people are included in the "multitude of counsellors" who contribute to our safety and victory in the midst of the trials of life (Prov. 24:6). There are Christians with professional training and experience in counseling, such as Art Adams (Indianapolis, Indiana) and Bette Wolfgang (Danville, Kentucky). Other trained professionals may not be Christians but may be people of good character and respect for God and the Bible. Sources of advice may include teachers and school officials, doctors, nurses, and legal authorities. Books, articles, and web sites which may help abound.

(For example, a list of such resources appears in a book by Paul T. Mason and Randi Kreger, *Stop Walking on Eggshells: Taking Your Life Back When Someone You Care About Has Borderline Personality Disorder.*)

I was an adult before I realized help is available through such avenues. I was well on the way in the process of healing and recovery before coming into contact with them. My contact came primarily through seeking help for other people. In the process of finding such sources and resources, I have learned how valuable they can be.

6. Help when we obey the gospel, grow as Christians. No step is so important as obeying the gospel of Christ and beginning the process of growing as a Christian (Matt. 28:19-20). God helps us put the past in the past when we become new creatures in Christ (2 Cor. 5:17; Phil. 3:13). God constantly leads us on to higher ground, teaching us to press onward and upward toward heaven (Phil. 3:14). On the one hand, that growth might include seeking resolution with the person who wounded us, confronting him in a proper spirit (Matt. 18:15; Gal. 6:1). On the other hand, that growth might include seeking resolution with the person we have wounded, if we have been guilty of abuse. Our worship cannot be accepted until this sin is corrected (Matt. 5:23-24).

As we grow in Christ, our identity and painful memories as victims of abuse are replaced more and more by our identity and precious memories as children of God.

God Hears the Cry of the Weak: We Sing a New Song!
We learn in Psalm 40 that God heard David's painful cry of distress and anguish: "He brought me up also out of an horrible pit, out of the miry clay, and set my feet upon a rock, and established my goings." Because God delivered David, he said, "And he hath put a new song in my mouth even praise unto our God: many shall see it, and fear, and shall trust in the LORD." God still puts the new song in our hearts and mouths today as he delivers us from our sins and our enemies, from every source of danger and suffering. Often enough, we suffer as a result of our own sins, and God addresses this need. Also when we cry to God as victims of the sins of other men, God addresses this tragedy so that it will not destroy us. With David, we flee and fly to "the rock that is higher than I," and in the safety and security of God's love, we sing the new song of praise to him and we teach others to sing with us.

Above all, the great gifts of the gospel of Christ and salvation in Christ redeem us from our own sins and from a world cursed by sin. "For ye are all the children of God by faith in Christ Jesus. For as many of you as have been baptized into Christ have put on Christ" (Gal. 3:26-27). In union and fellowship with Christ, we sing of pardon from our own sins. We sing of the strength he gives us to press forward and to grow regardless of the wrongs we have done and regardless of the wrongs others have done against us. We sing of the divine comfort and consolation which heals the pain inflicted on us by others and the pain we have inflicted on others.

Yes, God hears the cry of the weak, and we sing a new song! He helps us each day, each step of the way, so that in the end we will sing the new song in heaven with all the saints and all the angels through all the ages!

Morning Classes

The Headship of Man
Steve Curtis

"Run to and fro through the streets of Jerusalem; see now and know; and seek in her open places if you can find a man?" (Jer. 5:1). What is God asking of Jeremiah? Obviously, Jeremiah could find people of the male gender in Jerusalem. So for whom is Jeremiah looking? God was not looking for just a man, but one "who executes judgment, who seeks truth" (Jer. 5:1). Jeremiah could find those of the male gender, but finding a person who was a man in the eyes of God was more difficult.

Name any town or city in America, run to and fro through its streets, and seek in her open places if you can find a man. If we are talking about finding the male gender, obviously we will not have any trouble. If we are talking about finding a godly man who is the head of his house, then it is more challenging. In this lecture, we are talking about those of the male gender whom God recognizes as men. According to the National Fatherhood Initiative in the year 2000, thirty-three percent of all births occurred out of wedlock and thirty-four percent of all children lived without their

---

Steve Curtis was born in Shelbyville, Tennessee on January 12, 1969. He is the son of Clayton and Ann Curtis. His parents are both members of the Lord's church and his father serves as an elder. Steve married Kim Leeman, the daughter of Melvin and Judy Leeman from Manchester, Tennessee in 1993. They have twin daughters, Laurel and Lindey (3). Steve attended Middle Tennessee State University and Florida College before he began full-time preaching at the age of twenty-two. He has worked with congregations in Arkansas, New Mexico, Kentucky, and Alabama. He has also been involved in preaching the gospel in Lithuania and the Philippines. Steve is currently working with the Wooley Springs church of Christ in Ardmore, Alabama. He is working on a business degree at Athens State University and as the assistant manager at the CEI Bookstore in Athens, Alabama.

biological father (Horn 15). Ask these children to find godly men and it would be as difficult for them as it was Jeremiah.

Whom does God recognize as a man? The answer is found in Jeremiah 5:1. A man is one who seeks judgment (justice) and truth. Though this definition applies to every area of a male's life, our focus is on the individuals who are in the position of head of the household. Can godly men be found who seek justice and truth in their marital bond? Can godly men be found who seek justice and truth in their role as fathers? Can godly men like Abraham be found? "For I have known him, in order that he may command his children and his household after him, that they keep the way of the Lord, to do righteousness and justice" (Gen. 18:19). Can godly men like Manoah be found? When he learned he was going to be a father, Manoah wondered, "What will be the boy's rule of life, and his work?" (Judg. 13:12). "Then Manoah prayed to the Lord, and said, 'O my Lord, please let the man of God whom You sent come to us again and teach us what we shall do for the child who will be born'" (Judg. 13:8). Can a godly man be found who will not "deal treacherously with the wife of his youth" (Mal. 2:14-15)?

In the past few decades, cultural shifts concerning the headship of man have been taking place in the United States. Society's view of a husband and a father has gradually been changing. Unfortunately, these cultural changes have taken our society farther away from God's original design for the marital relationship and the home. These changes are not without cost. Like Israel of old, the iniquity of the fathers may be visited "upon the children, and upon the children's children, unto the third and to the fourth generation" (Exod. 34:7). What will happen when the thirty-three percent of children born out of wedlock and the thirty-four percent of children living without a father become parents themselves? What kind of husbands and wives will they be? Only time will tell.

Certain items have influenced our society's values and have helped to trigger these cultural shifts concerning the headship of man. It is important to identify these items and reinforce God's original design for the godly man. As we consider these things, keep in mind the importance of the family unit to our society. "Righteousness exalts a nation, but sin is a reproach to any people" (Prov. 14:34). Our future lies not in the power of our government, our economic growth, nor in the strength of our military. Our future depends upon the righteousness of the people.

The Cultural Shift of the Role of Head of Household in America

From a biblical standpoint, there are some obvious cultural changes in regards to the position of man in the home. God defined the role of the husband in the marital relationship in the very beginning with Adam and Eve (Gen. 2:18-24; 1 Tim. 2:12-13). As husband, the man is "head of the wife, as also Christ is head of the church" (Eph. 5:23). As father, the man is head over his children to "provide for his own" and to "bring them up in the training and admonition of the Lord" (1 Tim. 5:8; Eph. 6:4). Culturally, this patriarchal rule of man in the home is archaic and barbaric to those who desire a more egalitarian or matriarchal rule. However, God's law supersedes cultural trends. Today, our culture has so confused people that some do not know if the term marriage applies to same sex relationships or not. Is it any wonder some are confused about the role of man as husband and father?

To say that the institution of marriage, the roles within the marital relationship, and the family structure have changed is to state the obvious. In the introduction to her book, *Raising Boys Without Men*, psychologist Peggy Drexler writes:

> In a country in which one in two marriages will end in divorce, and 40 percent of babies are born out of wedlock, the mom-dad-and-kids version of family is now less than definitive. Moreover, ideas of how children are conceived and what kinds of relationships add up to a "family" are being redefined. More and more children in the Western world are being raised not in the traditional nuclear family but by single mothers who are single and who have not divorced a husband or been abandoned by a man; these mothers are single by choice and have made a conscious decision to have a baby and find a sperm donor to do it. Lesbian couples and single mothers by choice are pioneering new ways of getting pregnant via donor insemination (vii).

Drexler identifies three things that are affecting society's view of the head of the household: high divorce rates, out of wedlock births, and single mothers by choice. In similar tones Barbara Dafoe Whitehead writes, "In the postwar generation more than 80 percent of children grew up in a family with two biological parents who were married to each other. By 1980 only 50 percent could expect to spend their entire childhood in an intact family. If current trends continue, less than half of all children born today will live continuously with their own mother and father throughout childhood" (50). More and more, divorce, absentee fathers, and out-of-wedlock childbirths have redefined the responsibilities of the head of the house as outlined by the Bible and held traditional in America. The role and responsibilities of the head of the household are now more than ever being minimized, shifted to women, or altogether vacated.

Everyone from psychologists to journalists to rock groups support the cultural changes. In 1992, then vice president Dan Quayle was criticized for his comments about absentee fathers in child bearing in relationship to the fictional character on the television show "Murphy Brown." Dan Quayle feared that this portrayal would glamorize what was already a growing problem in our society. Many in the news media, entertainment industry, and politics severely criticized him for making these comments.

A year after Dan Quayle's "Murphy Brown" speech, Barbara Dafoe Whitehead published an article, "Dan Quayle Was Right," in *The Atlantic*. In that article she writes, ". . . the United States has made divorce easier and quicker than in any other Western nation with the sole exception of Sweden—and the trend toward solo motherhood has also been more pronounced in America." Not only is this "trend toward solo motherhood" fueled by easier divorce, this trend is also influenced by out-of-wedlock births. According to Whitehead, in 1960, five percent of the births were out-of-wedlock births, but that number jumped to twenty-seven percent in 1990. In this thirty-year period, out of wedlock births grew twenty-two percent despite increased sex education in schools, condom distribution, abortion, and the scare of the AIDS epidemic. It seems that none of these things deterred the growth of out-of-wedlock births. Indeed, Dan Quayle may have been right. During this time having a baby outside the marital relationship was "glamorized" because more people were choosing to do it.

Since the sixties, Americans have been indoctrinated with freedom and rebellion against all institutions of authority. Our culture is obsessed with individual rights, individual freedom, individual choice, and individual happiness. There was a time when people did not get a divorce for the sake of the children, but this is not the case with the spirit of individualism. It sounds like a romantic fairy tale but "once upon a time in a far off land" marriage was the only honorable way to bring children into the world. We do not live in that world any more. Both men and women driven by individualism have children at the slightest whim. Whatever is good for the individual must be defined as good by society. Whitehead writes:

354

Survey after survey shows that Americans are less inclined than they were a generation ago to value sexual fidelity, lifelong marriage, and parenthood as worthwhile personal goals. Motherhood no longer defines adult womanhood, as everyone knows; equally important is the fact that fatherhood has declined as a norm for men. In 1976 less than half as many fathers as in 1957 said that providing for children was a life goal. The proportion of working men who found marriage and children burdensome and restrictive more than doubled in the same period. Fewer than half adult Americans today regard the idea of sacrifice for others as a positive moral virtue (56).

Is it any wonder then that a high divorce rate and higher out-of-wedlock births reflect a change in attitude toward the role of the head of the household? Ever wonder why divorce, to a great extent, has lost its shame? When is the last time you read or heard the word "illegitimate" used to refer to a child born to a single mom? It has probably been a while. Why? Is a child who is born and raised without a father present illegitimate? Yes he is. However, unless one wants a tongue-lashing the likes of which Dan Quayle received, it is best not to use the "i" word.

This is not a personal attempt to be harsh, cruel, or unkind toward anyone. Unfortunately, calling attention to the cultural shifts that diminish the role of man as head of the household is unpopular. Children born out-of-wedlock do not have a choice. Children living without a father in the home do not have a choice. Neither is this an attempt to say all divorces and all out-of-wedlock childbirths are the result of the culture's rejection of husbands and fathers. It is simply stating the obvious.

In the second half of the twentieth century there has been a dramatic expansion of the range of individual choice and a relaxation of the social prescriptions and proscriptions for many dimensions of family and personal behavior. There has been a substantial and widespread weakening of the normative imperative to get married, to stay married, to have children, and to maintain separate roles for males and females. In addition, attitudes and norms prohibiting abortion, premarital sexual relationships, and childbearing outside of marriage have dramatically receded. Thus, many behaviors that were previously restricted by prevailing social norms and personal attitudes have become accepted by substantial fractions of Americans (Thornton 201).

Relaxing values toward out-of-wedlock childbirths do not occur without relaxing values toward parenting in general and fatherhood in particular.

Besides absentee fathering and out-of-wedlock births, the diminishing role of the man in the home is a result of the diminishing role of the man in society as a whole. In an article entitled "Why Johnny Isn't Going To College," Phyllis Schlafly discusses college enrollment and reports that "by the time this year's college freshmen are seniors, the ratio will be 60 percent women to 40 percent men. . ." (Schlafly). Concerning educational attainment, the U.S. Census Bureau reports from the 2000 census that of those with a bachelor's degree or higher women outnumber men (Educational Attainment by Sex: 2000). What does this information tell us? If "education pays," it tells us more and more in our society women will have greater earning potential than men. From the standpoint of discrimination, this is wonderful. However, if we consider the relationship between the husband and wife, there is obviously going to be a strain on the head of the house when he is bringing home the bacon and his wife is bringing home the filet mignon.

In fact, studies now show that households are recognizing that some wives can earn more than their husbands. As a result, people have taken the next logical step—change the traditional roles of the husband and wife. Now there is a trend of "stay at home dads," "homebound fathers," or "full-time dads." Amy Saltzman writes, "No one is sure how many men have primary responsibility for taking care of their children. The U.S. Census Bureau estimates the number who stay home with their children while the mother works at somewhere around 2 million" (71). From a cultural standpoint, some will say that the wife should work when she has greater earning potential and that the husband can stay home with the children. From a biblical standpoint, this cannot occur without people setting aside what God has divinely prescribed.

Another interesting consideration concerning the role of man in society is the fact that women also outnumber men in politics as well. Men may outnumber women in elected and appointed positions. However, women outnumber men in both registered voters and active voters (Reported Voting and Registration, by Sex and Single Years of Age). What difference does this make? Should not women have the right to vote? I believe they should. So, what is the significance? For an elected politician, votes are the significance. Therefore, issues that are important to the biggest voting demographic in our country are going to be important to the politician. Whether a person is being nominated for the Supreme Court or to represent a party's presidential candidate, they must be right on certain hot topics. No topic is hotter than a female's right to control her own body and reproduction with abortion. This is not to accuse all women who vote of supporting abortion. Without question there is a correlation between women who choose to keep men out of their reproductive lives when it comes to insemination and when it comes to termination. These women want politicians and judges who will protect their "rights." In the last presidential election, feminists clamored against re-electing President Bush. They equated voting for Bush with voting for rape. In the appointment of the two newest Supreme Court justices, the primary concern is "what is their view of Roe vs. Wade."

This cultural shift regarding the role of the man as head of household is not happening accidentally. Something drives the divorce rate and the number of absent fathers in the lives of their children. It is important to recognize what these driving forces are. Again, we turn to the American Fatherhood Initiative and refer to comments to the question "What caused this great upheaval in marriage and fertility patterns?" Here is their answer:

> Most explanations factor in many forces, including: the transition to the post-industrial (or "information") economy that resulted in diminished economic opportunities for lower-skilled men, especially in inner cities; greater women's participation in the labor force, weakening their economic dependence upon marriage; the sexual revolution, aided by technological advances in contraception; welfare policies that discouraged marriage; the onset of "no fault" divorce laws; a materialistic consumer culture; and the cultural ascendance of expressive individualism and an emphasis on self-fulfillment over community and family obligations (Horn 11).

No one would deny that there are advantages to transitioning from an industrial economy to an information economy, greater economic opportunities for women, technological advances in contraception and fertilization, or in making life easier in general. In many areas these changes have improved our lives. Unfortunately in some ways, the changes have negatively affected marital relationships, child bearing, and fatherhood. Our challenge is to recognize the benefits of these changes while not allowing them to change that which is divinely prescribed by God.

The Divine Arrangement of the Head of the Family

As the head of the family, man has unique responsibilities to his wife and children. We must recognize that God assigns these responsibilities, not cultural trends. Therefore, God must define them. The Bible contains the definition. In the beginning, God created man and woman equal, but

357

different. "So God created man in His own image; in the image of God He created him; male and female He created them" (Gen. 1:27). Out of all the things God created, nothing enjoys the compliment of being created in the image of God except man and woman. In this sense, male and female were created equally. No role in the home, in the church, or in society can destroy this equality. Even despite the obvious physical differences, men and women are created equally in the likeness of God.

When God created the plants and animals, they were created with the ability to reproduce "according to its kind" (Gen. 1:11-12, 21). The same is true for humans. For Adam, there "was not found a helper comparable to him" (Gen. 2:20). God recognized that it was not good for man to be alone and made him a "helper comparable to him" (Gen. 2:18). Eve was Adam's perfect complement and Adam was Eve's. Adam could not say that Eve was inferior to him because she was also made in the image of God. Neither could Adam say that he was better off without Eve because God said it was not good for him to be alone. Indeed, Adam recognized that Eve was his perfect complement. "And Adam said, 'This is now bone of my bones and flesh of my flesh; she shall be called Woman because she was taken out of Man'" (Gen. 2:23). Adam and Eve's physical differences complemented each other that they might also reproduce after their kind, and "be fruitful and multiply" (Gen. 1:28).

God's word tells us that despite being equal and complements of one another Adam and Eve did not have the same relationship to each other. In 1 Timothy 2:12-13 Paul writes, "And I do not permit a woman to teach or to have authority over a man, but to be in silence. For Adam was formed first, then Eve." Adam was head over his wife and Eve was subject to her husband. This is not as a result of sin. These roles of husband and wife were designed by an all-wise God. In his wisdom God made man and woman differently and gave them different roles to fulfill. We may not be able to comprehend his wisdom and know why. However, we do not question God's wisdom for making male and female in his image. We do not question God's wisdom for seeing that it was not good for man to be alone. We do not question God's wisdom for making a helper suitable to Adam. So, why would we question God's wisdom that Adam was head of his wife?

In our society, when one speaks of the husband being the head of the wife, many view him as outdated as the cave man. Many associate being the head in the marriage as being a tyrant or a dictator. For many the headship of man in the marriage destroys the equality of the sexes. "In today's equal-opportunity culture, leadership abilities in men are often defined as macho or arrogant, giving these mutual instincts and gifts negative connotation. It must be understood that machoism and arrogance are not leadership qualities; they are character flaws that are usually rooted in insecurity or immaturity" (Hammond 31). No matter how culture views the leadership role of the husband, we must not be ashamed of what God has designed for our well-being.

Like the husband-wife relationship, God also prescribed a divine arrangement for having children and the roles between the parents and child. First of all, there is an order. Notice that a man and woman would leave father and mother, cleave unto one another, and then become one flesh (Gen. 2:24). Second, as husband and wife, they would "be fruitful, multiply, and replenish the earth" (Gen. 1:28). The divine order is plain—marriage first, then children.

As previously discussed, men and women are ignoring this divine order. When men father a child with no intention of fulfilling their role as a father, they are assaulting the role of fatherhood. When women choose to have children without marriage and without a father present, they are assaulting the role of fatherhood. Both are showing their contempt for God by violating his divine arrangement. Furthermore, it is the children who are robbed of what is rightfully theirs—a home. Children have a right to a home where they are cared for, nurtured, and prepared to become responsible adults. Both the mother and father have responsibilities in assuring that these rights are fulfilled. Particularly, the father is the key figure for guidance, decision-making, and leadership in the home as the children mature.

Husband as the Head of the Wife
There are two main reasons why the husband is the head of the wife. As has already been noted, one of the reasons is that God designed it that way (1 Tim. 2:12-13). This principle is consistently reinforced in both the Old and New Testaments. A second reason is based upon the fact that woman was deceived. "And Adam was not deceived, but the woman being deceived, fell into transgression" (1 Tim. 2:14). Because of her role in the transgression, God told Eve, "Your desire shall be for your husband, and he shall rule over you" (Gen. 3:16).

The New Testament specifically assigns the role of head to the husband. In 1 Corinthians 11:3, Paul writes, "But I want you to know that the head of every man is Christ, the head of woman is man, and the head of Christ is God." In Ephesians 5:23, we read, "For the husband is the head of the wife, as also Christ is the head of the church; and He is the Savior of the body." One can also see that the man is to be head of his house from God's qualifications for elders. In order to be an elder, a man must "know how to rule his own house" (1 Tim. 3:4).

Thayer's *Greek-English Lexicon* says of "head" that it is used metaphorically of anything supreme, chief, prominent; of persons, master, lord (345). Thayer also says of "rule" that it means to be over, to superintend, preside over (539). It is evident that the role of husband is one of authority, rule, and leadership. "Head" and "rule" define the relationship between husband and wife, not the value of each. Therefore, husband and wife are still equal, but have different roles. When a husband is guided by the word of God, his position in the marriage will not turn to one of dictatorship, tyranny, or feelings of superiority in value. A godly man assumes his role of headship without these attitudes.

How is the wife able to subject herself to the rule of a husband without losing her equality? This question can be answered by looking to Christ. Christ is in the role of being in submission to his Father's will. Yet, he was equal with him. Even though his role required great humility on his part, even to the point of suffering physical death, Christ did not consider it robbery (Phil. 2:5-8). Equality between husband and wife can still exist even though there is one role of headship and one of subjection. If Christ could be in subjection to his Father without losing his identity and equality, then a wife can be in submission to her husband without losing her identity and equality.

How can a husband be head over his wife without being a tyrant? Consider the husband of the virtuous woman in Proverbs 31. How could the inspired word of God commend the wife, whose price is far above rubies, unless she was also a woman who was in subjection to her husband? Yet, consider the facts that she was a diligent worker at home (vv. 13-15), an entrepreneur (vv. 16, 24), and she spoke with wisdom (v. 26). She even received praise for her works (v. 31). She was a "real go getter." What type of husband and father would have such a wife? Clearly, it would not be one who is domineering or dictatorial. Neither would the husband of this woman be a spineless jellyfish, henpecked by his wife and run over by his children. Here is what the Bible says about this man. He trusts his wife and is prosperous (v. 11). He is known as a wise man (v. 23). He praises his wife (v. 28). Seeing that this "Proverbs 31 woman" is priceless in the eyes of God, one ought to appreciate the value of the "Proverbs 31 man" who can rule his home without being a dictator.

When the headship of man is based upon the right foundation, a husband can be a wonderful blessing to his wife, the family, the church, and society as a whole. From the word of God, one can see that the right foundation for the headship of man is love. Primarily, this is seen in three areas: love for his wife, as Christ loved the church, and as he loves himself.

First, a man's role as head of his wife is based upon his love for his wife. "Husbands, love your wives, just as Christ also loved the church and gave Himself for her" (Eph. 5:25). "Husbands, love your wives and do not be bitter toward them" (Col. 3:19). "Husbands, likewise, dwell with them with understanding, giving honor to the wife, as to the weaker vessel, and as being heirs together of the grace of life, that your prayers may not be hindered" (1 Pet. 3:7). These passages teach a husband to love and honor his wife. Thayer says "love" is "to be full of good-will and exhibit the same . . . to have preference for, wish well to, regard the welfare of" (3). "Honor" means, "to show honor to" (Thayer 624). Clinton Hamilton writes of honoring the wife, "This showing of honor results from the opinion that one holds of the other person to whom it is shown: the value or the estimate of the person; in this case, it is the wife" (139). From these definitions, one must understand that both love and honor require activity, an expression. Both are based on knowledge and understanding, not emotions and feelings. This means that a husband can learn how to love and honor his wife and that his love and honor for her grows as his knowledge grows.

How will this love and honor be shown? God has given us the standard by which love and honor behaves which is the second area of love on which the headship is based. A man's role as head of his wife is based upon Christ's love for his bride. Husbands are to love their wives "just as Christ also loved the church and gave Himself for her" (Eph. 5:25). Is there a greater standard of love to which a husband's love for his wife can be compared? This elevates love above emotions, affections, companionship, and even sexual desires. A husband may never be able to love and honor his wife to the degree that Christ loved the church, but every husband can learn to love and honor his wife according to the manner in which Christ loved the church.

Christ manifested his love for the church. His love was selfless (Luke 22:42). It was not in his personal best interest to be despised, rejected, and crucified. Yet, he endured these things for the sake of the church. His love was sacrificial (Eph. 5:2, 25). He completely gave himself for the interests of the church. His love was shown as the expression of his estimate of the worth of the church. His love was shown "that He might sanctify and cleanse her with the washing of water by the word, that He might present her to Himself a glorious church, not having spot or wrinkle or any such thing, but that she should be holy and without blemish" (Eph. 5:26-27). Christ's love for the church is without end (Heb. 7:23-25). The church can confidently trust in Christ's unwavering, unending love.

Maybe a husband cannot manifest his love to his wife to the same degree that Christ does to the church, but he can manifest his love in the same manner that Christ does. A husband can put his wife first and not be selfish and self-centered with his time, money, and interests. A husband will not work ill will toward his wife, but seek her best interest. A husband, who loves his wife as Christ loved the church, learns and appreciates the value of his wife. His wife trusts him and feels secure because his love is not fickle. A man who manifests this love will be the kind of head his wife will appreciate.

The third love on which the foundation of headship is based is the love a husband has for himself. "So husbands ought to love their own wives as their own bodies; he who loves his wife loves himself" (Eph. 5:28). A husband should treat his wife the way he would want to be treated. The husband and wife are one, not two. In this case, one plus one does not equal to two, but to one. By "leaving and cleaving," the husband and wife destroy self and become one new entity. What relationship does this have to a husband loving his wife as himself? Paul states, "For no one ever hated his own flesh, but nourishes and cherishes it, just as the Lord does the church" (Eph. 5:29). "To hate one's wife is as irrational as to hate one's own flesh, and as, on the other hand, men constantly nourish and cherish their flesh, protecting it from hurt, seeking to heal it when hurt, and generally to promote its welfare and comfort, so ought husbands to act towards their wives" (Spence *et al.* 212). As the head, the husband will nourish and cherish his wife as he leads, rules, and governs in the home.

When a godly man assumes the role of headship and loves his wife as Christ loves the church and as he loves himself, he will not be abusive or use his role for selfish gain. He will easily lead godly women to submit. He will be a blessing to all who know him.

Father As Head of the Children

"Behold, children are a heritage from the Lord, The fruit of the womb is a reward. Like arrows in the hand of a warrior, so are the children of one's youth. Happy is the man who has his quiver full of them; they shall not be ashamed, But shall speak with their enemies in the gate" (Ps. 127:3-5). Two things are evident from these verses. First, children are a gift from God. Fathers and mothers are stewards of a gift for which they will one day give an account to God the Giver. Second, children are blessings to their parents. They should not be considered a burden, but an investment. Knowing these two things ought to impress upon parents the tremendous responsibilities they have to their children and to God. Unfortunately, many parents fail to appreciate what God has designed.

Consider Abraham again. God chose Abraham to be the father of his people because Abraham would be a good father. "For I have known him, in order that he may command his children and his household after him, that they keep the way of the Lord, to do righteousness and justice, that the Lord may bring to Abraham what He has spoken to him" (Gen. 18:19). Notice Abraham would command his children, not abandon or be commanded by them. He would be an example for his children and household to follow. He also would teach them to keep the way of the Lord and to do righteousness and justice. God wants fathers to be "Abrahams" today, but this type of father is becoming more difficult to find.

In an interview published in *Christianity Today*, Nancy Madsen asked Bill Glass, a former NFL football player and founder of Champions of Life, "What is our country's biggest problem?" He replied, "A lack of the father's blessing. The FBI studied 17 kids that have shot their classmates in little towns like Paducah, Kentucky; Pearl, Mississippi; and Littleton, Colorado. All 17 shooters had only one thing in common. They had a father problem" (Madsen 48-50). Bill Glass has learned from thirty-six years of prison ministry what many others are learning, that a father's absence from his children's lives increases the likelihood of problems. These problems go beyond violence and affect children in many ways.

The National Fatherhood Initiative reports, "Children who live absent their biological fathers are, on average, at least two to three times more likely to be poor, to use drugs, to experience educational, health, emotional, and behavioral problems, to be victims of child abuse, and to engage in criminal behavior than those who live with their married, biological (or adoptive) parents" (Horn 15). In her book *Home-Alone America*, Mary Eberstadt, a research fellow for Stanford University's Hoover Institution, writes:

> Today's juveniles, among the most materially prosperous ever to walk the earth, are either suffering or thought to be suffering from unprecedented levels of mental affliction. . . . In January 2001, the Surgeon General issued a report declaring that the United States is facing nothing less than a "public crisis in mental care for children and adolescents." The report further predicted that childhood neuropsychiatric disorders will become one of the five most common causes of morbidity, mortality, and disability by the year 2020. Similarly, the National Mental Health Association now estimates that one in five American children have diagnosable mental, emotional, or behavioral disorder and that up to one in ten may suffer from a serious emotional disturbance (57).

All these problems referred to by Eberstadt cannot be solely attributed to the absence of the father. However, when our country's divorce rate is around fifty percent and out-of-wedlock childbirth is around thirty-three percent, it would be impossible to deny that there is a relationship between the father's absence and these problems.

Another interesting connection that Eberstadt makes in her book relates to the music industry. It is easy because of generational gaps to disregard the music that young people are listening to these days. This is the way it has always been with music and young people. However, Eberstadt points out a notable change. Whereas previous generations' music "rebelled against parents *because* they were parents—nurturing, attentive, and overly present. . . . Today's teenagers and their music rebel against parents because they are *not* parents—not nurturing, not attentive, and often not even there" (21).

Eberstadt writes:

> . . . If yesterday's rock was the music of abandon, today's is that of abandon*ment*. The odd truth about contemporary teenage music—the characteristic that most separates it from what has gone before—is its compulsive insistence on the damage wrought by broken homes, dysfunction, checked-out parents, and (especially) absent fathers. Papa Roach, Everclear, Blink-182, Good Charlotte, Eddie Vedder and Pearl Jam, Kurt

Cobain and Nirvana, Tupac Shakur, Snoop Doggy Dogg, Eminem—these and other singers and bands, all of them award-winning top-40 performers who either are or were among the most popular icons in America, have their own generational answer to what ails the modern teenager. Surprising though it may be to some, that answer is: dysfunctional childhood.

Again, the father's absence is not the sole contributing factor to dysfunctional family problems. No doubt it is one of the contributing factors.

As previously noted, God in his infinite wisdom designed the marital relationship between a husband and a wife and the relationship between parents and their children. God has designed this family unit in such a way that each individual member contributes to the well being of the whole. If one member should suddenly and untimely be removed involuntarily by death, the absence would affect the whole family. Would not the same be true for voluntary removal of a family member, particularly the father? Voluntary removal of the father includes a number of things such as divorce and out-of-wedlock births. If one denies this, then one might as well challenge God who designed the family and the relationship of its members.

God has designed the role of the father to be one of providing. Going back to the first father, God told Adam "in toil" and "in the sweat of your face you shall eat bread" (Gen. 3:17). Paul said that a man who does not provide for his own has denied the faith and is worse than an unbeliever (1 Tim. 5:8). As a provider, the father's responsibility includes, but is not limited to, physical care. A father's provisions care for the entire well being of his children—mentally, spiritually, socially, and physically. The point is that a father's responsibility as a provider involves more than just a paycheck. It involves his time, emotions, intellect, and his interaction with his children. Even if children living without their father's presence receive financial support from him, it still does not furnish them for all their needs.

God has also designed the role of the father to be one of a disciplinarian. Concerning this the Hebrew writer asks a good question, "If you endure chastening, God deals with you as with sons; for what son is there whom a father does not chasten?" (Heb. 12:7). The divine answer to this question is found in the next verse. "But if you are without chastening, of which all have become partakers, then you are illegitimate and not sons" (Heb. 12:8). A child, whose father does not discipline him, is like a child who does not have a father.

God appointed the father to "bring them up in the nurture and admonition of the Lord" (Eph. 6:4). This involves positive and negative discipline. From a positive standpoint, a father can "Train up a child in the way he should go, and when he is old he will not depart from it" (Prov. 22:6). Here discipline suggests teaching. A good way to reinforce teaching is to set the example. If a father lives by what he teaches, he can avoid provoking his children to wrath. From a negative standpoint, a father can "not withhold correction from a child, for if you beat him with a rod, he will not die. You shall beat him with a rod, and deliver his soul from hell" (Prov. 23:13-14). The rod is not the only form of negative discipline, but it is an attention getter. As the Hebrew writer says, "No chastening seems to be joyful for the present, but painful; nevertheless, afterward it yields the peaceable fruit of righteousness to those who have been trained by it" (Heb. 12:11). What a statement of shame to say of a father that "his sons made themselves vile, and he did not restrain them" (1 Sam. 3:11).

Conclusion

Many factors are contributing to the breakdown of the family, and in particular the role of the head of the household, such as no fault divorce, out-of-wedlock childbearing, materialism, and individualism. Involved in that breakdown is a lack of respect for the Bible as the word of God by allowing culture to redefine what God has divinely instituted. Stopping the tide of culture from overtaking our families takes strength and courage.

"Watch, stand fast in the faith, be brave, be strong" (1 Cor. 16:13). Throwing more money into government programs will not help lower the divorce rate, the number of children born out-of-wedlock, or the number of children who live in a house without a father. Strengthening the economy, the military, and public education is not the answer. Men need to be godly men, who seek justice and truth. We need men who will not forsake the covenant of their marriage bond, nor abandon their children. We need men like Abraham, Manoah, and Joshua.

Works Cited

Drexler, Peggy, Phd. *Raising Boys Without Men.* Rodale, 2005.

Eberstadt, Mary. *Home-Alone America: Why Today's Kids Are Overmedicated, Overweight, and More Troubled Than Ever Before.* New York: Sentinel, 2004.

"Educational Attainment by Sex: 2000." *U.S. Census Bureau American Fact Finder.* U.S. Census Bureau. 14 Jan. 2006 <www.factfinder.census.gov>.

Hamilton, Clinton D. *Truth Commentaries: 1 Peter*. Bowling Green: Guardian of Truth Foundation, 1995.

Hammond, Michelle McKinney. *In Search of the Proverbs 31 Man*. Colorado Springs: WaterBrook, 2003.

Horn, Wade F., PhD. *Father Facts*. 4th ed. Gaithersburg: National Fatherhood Initative, 2002.

Madsen, Nancy. "The Power of a Father's Blessing: What former NFL pro Bill Glass has learned after 36 years of prison ministry." *Christianity Today*, Jan. 2006: 48-50.

"Reported Voting and Registration, by Sex and Single Years of Age." 15 2005. U.S. Census Bureau. 14 Jan. 2006 <www.census.gov/population/www/soc-dem/voting.html>.

Saltzman, Amy. "When dads stay home." *U.S. News & World Report*. March 3, 1997: 71-72.

Schlafly, Phyllis. "Why Johnny isn't going to college." Townhall.com. 16 Jan. 2006. 17 Jan. 2006 <www.townhall.com>.

Spence, H.D.M. and Joseph S. Exell, ed. *The Pulpit Commentary*. Peabody: Hendrickson Publishers.

Thayer, Joseph Henry, ed. *Thayer Greek-English Lexicon of the New Testament*. 4th ed. Grand Rapids: Baker Book House, 1991.

Thornton, Arland. "Attitudes, Values, and Norms Related to Nonmarital Fertility." Report to Congress on Out-of-Wedlock Childbearing September 1995: 201.

Whitehead, Barbara Dafoe. "Dan Qualye Was Right." *The Atlantic*, April 1993, 47.

The Pain of a Wayward Child

Prodigal Son and Prodigal's Father
Melvin Curry

Heartbreak and agony over wasted lives are common experiences of parents today. Children leave home, usually intending to go far away, and carrying with them inflated dreams and great expectations. The parents' concerns are evident. Will the children be faithful to the Lord? Will they be safe? Will they have the self-discipline to achieve positive goals? The children, however, are confident they will make good; they see no real dangers. They are anxious to get out on their own, away from parental restraints, free to make their own choices about life, and believing they will succeed. They have plenty of money; the parents have seen to that. Most of them get off to a good start, but soon things go wrong for some of them. They get caught up in the exciting activities of the world and begin to "live it up." Soon their lives are ruined, and their supply of money is exhausted. The realities of "the school of hard knocks" begin to set in.

Melvin D. Curry and his wife Shirley reside at 11912 Pasco Trails Blvd., Spring Hill, Florida 34610. Curry retired in 1997, after thirty-four years of teaching in the Biblical Studies department of Florida College. He has been preaching since 1952 and currently works with the West Citrus congregation in Crystal River, Florida. Evangelistic work has carried him throughout most of the United States, Eastern Europe, Scotland, Ireland, and Ethiopia. His published works include articles for the *New Smith's Bible Dictionary*, a book entitled *Jehovah's Witnesses: The Millenarian World of the Watchtower*, numerous articles for religious journals, and contributions to the Florida College Annual Lectures, fifteen volumes of which he edited. He and Shirley have five children and twelve grandchildren, all of whom currently reside in the central part of Florida.

The children are determined to tough it out; the last thing they want to do is go home and face alienated parents, disappointed brethren, and hometown gossip. But one of them, a young man, falls on extremely hard times and hits rock bottom. No money! No food! Nobody where he now lives really cares! He finally has to beg for work that entails doing something contrary to his religious convictions. But the pay is not enough to cover his bare necessities. He is still starving. There is nothing else left to do but eat crow and face the music. "There's no where else to turn. I'll have to go home," he says. "My older brother is still there, and he's doing alright. Maybe Dad will forgive me and give me a job. I'll do anything he wants. And I'll straighten out my life." The long journey back gives him time to think and prepare what he wants to say, but he doesn't really know what to expect.

The story sounds familiar to Bible students. It should. The parable of the *prodigal son* (Luke 15:11-32) describes all the above, and more. It is a story that is bound up with two others in a larger context, and this larger context helps us to understand its meaning. Those other parables are about a *lost sheep* (vv. 4-7) and a *lost coin* (vv. 8-10). At the least, then, one should expect the third to be called the parable of the *lost son*. But the complexity of the story indicates that such a title is inadequate. The parable is about *a man who had two sons* (v. 11), and it is told in two parts. Only the first part tells the story of the father and his prodigal son (vv. 11-24); the second part centers on the older brother and his relationship both to his loving father and to his wayward brother who has returned home to a festive reception (vv. 25-32). In two-part parables, moreover, the second part receives the greater emphasis. And, truly, the pain experienced by the elder brother, although caused by entirely different forces than that of either his father or his younger brother, is paramount in this parable. It is more appropriate, therefore, to call it *the parable of two lost sons*.

Luke devotes a large section of his Gospel to the Lord's journey to Jerusalem (9:51-19:27), in which there is a complex interaction between Jesus and the Pharisees. Let's go back to the beginning of chapter 14, where Luke describes an occasion in which Jesus is eating in the house of a prominent Pharisee (vv. 1-6). The Lord tells the invited guests a parable about those who choose the best seats at a wedding feast (vv. 7-11), and he counsels the host about inviting the infirm, not friends, to his next feast (vv. 12-15). These words are followed by a parable that describes guests who offer lame excuses for not attending a great banquet (vv. 16-24), a discourse on the cost of discipleship (vv. 25-33), and a lesson about salt that has lost its tang

(vv. 34-35). The last segment ends with the admonition, "He who has ears to hear, let him hear!" And jumping forward to chapter 16, Luke records another parable of Jesus, which tells about a steward that is *wasting* a rich man's goods (vv. 1-13), an indictment of the Pharisees as "lovers of money" (vv. 14-18), and the story of the rich man and Lazarus (vv. 19-31).

In between, however, Luke 15 records the three parables described above and introduces them with the startling revelation that "all the tax collectors and the sinners" gather around Jesus "to hear him" (v. 1). Sinners have ears to hear. But *not* the Pharisees and scribes; instead, they grumble, saying, "This man receives sinners and eats with them" (v. 2). In Luke, Timothy Johnson observes, listening to Jesus is a prominent theme of Luke's Gospel (see 5:1, 15; 6:17, 27, 47, 49; 7:29; 8:8-18, 21; 9:35; 10:16, 24, 39; 11:28, 31) (*Luke* 235), and the complaint of self-righteous individuals about *eating with sinners* serves as the "compositional frame" for the parables of the lost sheep, the lost coin, and the prodigal son (242).

The Pharisees and scribes surely think they are on the right side of the law when they complain that Jesus eats with sinners (Prov. 1:10, 15; 4:14-16; Isa. 52:11; see 2 Cor. 6:14-18). Non-participation with sinners, including both those within Israel and those without, becomes a basic tenant of Jewish legal tradition: "Let not a man associate with the wicked, even to bring him near to the law" (*Mekilta de Rabbi Ishmael*, tractate *Amelek* 3.55-57 on Exod. 18:1, quoted by Bock, *Luke* 1299). After all, the tax collectors work for the Romans. This makes the tax collectors as bad as the Romans. Pharisees can't fellowship anyone who fraternizes with the enemy. Moreover, the scribes, who are the best students of the law, have determined that toll collectors are all dishonest: they lie, cheat, and steal in order to enrich themselves. Everybody should know this, especially one who claims to be the Messiah.

Luke records that the scribes and Pharisees begin to grumble when Jesus attends a feast in the house of Levi, asking, "Why do you eat and drink with tax collectors and sinners?" To which question Jesus replies, "I have not come to call *the* righteous, but sinners, to repentance" (Luke 5:27-32; compare 7:34). In fact, one of the main themes of Luke is that "the Son of Man has come to seek and to save that which was lost" (19:10), a statement specifically applied to Zacchaeus, "a chief tax collector," "a son of Abraham," a brother in the faith. In the eyes of Pharisees, scribes, and lawyers, however, tax collectors and sinners are classed as undesirables, either people who lead "an immoral life" or people who follow "a dishonorable calling," like shepherds, donkey-drivers, peddlers, and tanners (Jeremias 132). But Jesus reverses the spiritual status of these divergent groups in the assessment he makes of them. He chooses tax collectors to be his disciples, one even to be an apostle, and accuses the self-righteous Pharisees of busying themselves in cleansing "the outside of the cup," while their "inward part is full of greed and wickedness" (11:39). They trust in themselves that they are "righteous" and despise others (18:9). The tax collectors and "sinners"—whether really sinners or just considered to be such by others—are treated by Jesus as being on the inside; however, he considers the "righteous" who need no repentance as being on the outside with respect to the attitude they have toward God's saving purpose (Bradley 255). Earlier in Luke's narrative, the tax agents submitted to John's baptism; the Pharisees did not and "rejected the will of God for themselves" (7:29-30).

In the first of the three parables of Luke 15, Jesus forces the Pharisees and scribes to make a decision about the action of the characters in the stories. "Which man of you having a hundred sheep," he asks, "if he loses one of them, does not leave the ninety-nine in the wilderness, and go after the one which is lost until he finds it?" (v. 3). And at the end of the third parable, his elder-brother character even represents their self-righteous attitudes. In all three parables, Jesus portrays everyone as making personal choices, some wise and some unwise, some bad and some good, some right and some wrong.

The parable of the Pharisee and the tax collector provides an appropriate parallel here: "Two men went up to the temple to pray, one a Pharisee and the other a tax collector. The Pharisee stood and prayed thus with himself, 'God I thank You that I am not like other men—extortioners, unjust, adulterers, or even as this tax collector. I fast twice a week, I give tithes of all that I possess.' And the tax collector, standing afar off, would not so much as raise *his* eyes to heaven, but beat his breast, saying, 'God, be merciful to me a sinner!' I tell you, this man went down to his house justified *rather* than the other; for everyone who exalts himself will be humbled, and he who humbles himself will be exalted" (Luke 18:10-14). No wonder Jesus said, "Beware of the leaven of the Pharisees" (12:1; compare 20:45-46).

All three parables of Luke 15 share the common themes of "lost-found" (vv. 4, 8, 24, 32) and "joy" (vv. 5, 6, 7, 9, 10, 32). To these may be added "repentance," a concept that is explicit in the first two (vv. 7, 10) and implicit in the third (vv. 17-18, 21). Furthermore, the magnitude of the loss increases as Jesus moves from one parable to the next: one sheep out of a hundred (= 1%), one coin out of ten (= 10 %), and one son out of two (= 50 %). In the first two stories something that is lost is sought and found, but in the third story the seeking is done by the lost son (Morgan 181). And only the first story finds a parallel in another Gospel (Matt. 18:12-14), where Jesus associates the lost sheep with one of his disciples who might stray (read v. 14 in the light of v. 1 and vv. 15-17).

The Prodigal Son

The first part of the third parable is about the prodigal son and his return home (Luke 15:11-24). Its main point, however, actually comes at the end of part two: "It is necessary that we should make merry and rejoice, because this brother of yours was dead and came to life, and having been lost was found" (v. 32, my translation; see v. 24). Remember, when the shepherd finds the lost sheep, he calls together his *male* friends and neighbors to rejoice with him (v. 6). And when the woman finds the lost coin, she calls together her *female* friends and neighbors to rejoice with her (v. 9). So, too, the elder brother must rejoice with the father because the lost son has returned home (v. 32). Moreover, there is at least one lesson common to all three parables: "Rejoice with the heavenly Father and his angels when a sinner repents" (paraphrase of vv. 7, 10).

The attitude of the younger son when he leaves home must cause his father great pain, although the parable does not elaborate on this fact. The whole episode evokes negative feelings. The son will inherit one-third of the estate when his father dies (Deut. 21:17). To ask for his part while the father still lives cuts across the grain of Jewish legal advice: "As long as you live, give no one power over yourself—son or wife, brother or friend. Do not give your property to another, in case you change your mind and want it back. It is better for your children to ask of you than for you to depend on them" (Ecclus. 33:20-21, *NEB*). The *Mishna* provides specific details as to how the father should protect himself in such a circumstance (*Baba Bathra* 8:7). Although the estate provides the father's livelihood, he graciously divides it between the two sons (v. 12). The younger son might as well wish his father to be dead as to ask him for his inheritance. Bailey observes:

> it can be documented that often the father before his death did "divide his living between them." But the startling fact is that, to my knowledge,

372

in all of Middle Eastern literature (aside from this parable) from ancient times to the present, there is no case of any son, older or younger, asking for his inheritance from a father who is still in good health (164).

Derrett also points out that herein the prodigal commits a great wrong, namely, "forgetting that his father had a moral claim on his property, that his father, as long as he lived, had a right to call, in case of necessity, upon the son's labor and his savings" ("Law in the New Testament" 64). But let's not beat up on the younger son too much. He may have made a simple request from his father rather than "an impertinent demand" (Linnemann 75).

One might wish there were more details than Jesus offers, more answers to nagging problems. Did the father try to talk his younger son out of taking his cut and leaving town? Did the elder son protest against his brother's request? Did he assume "the traditional role" of a third-party "reconciler," which was normally filled by one of the sons (see Bailey 168)? But the story that our Lord tells stands as recorded without these questions being answered.

"Not many days after," the younger son gathers up his possessions and travels "to a far country" (Luke 15:13). Why he departs so quickly and goes so far are questions not answered in the text. Restlessness, family tensions, the lure of the world, the desire to make his own way—all would be within the realm of possibility. For whatever reason, however, this is what he does. And in order to accomplish his aims, he appears to convert his assets into cash (see *sunagô,* BAGD 782; MM 600). As far as we know, "he leaves nothing behind that can minister to his desires; nothing to guarantee his return" (Plummer 372). He could have been going to Babylon, Egypt, or Rome; the geographical location of his destination would add little to the story.

The youth's lack of self-control eventually results in the loss of *all* he has. Jesus says that he wastes his possessions (v. 13). Literally, the term *diaskorpizô* means "scatter" or "disperse," but in reference to property signifies "waste" or "squander" (*BAGD* 188). He does not retain anything; he throws everything away in "prodigal living" (*asôtôs zên*), in other words, in a "reckless," worldly lifestyle (Morris 241). The term *asôtôs* literally describes an unhealthy kind of existence. One lexicon gives the meaning "dissolutely, loosely," as in "debauched, profligate living" (*BAGD* 119). Its noun form *asôtia* sometimes designates a way of life characterized by various forms of drinking (Eph. 5:18; 1 Pet. 4:4) and gluttony. Foerster says the phrase *asôtôs zên* "speaks of the dissipated life of the Prodigal without signifying the nature of this life . . . It is simply depicted as care-free and spendthrift in contrast to the approaching dearth" (TDNT 1:507). And Johnson adds, "The term *asôtôs* has the sense of carelessness but does not by itself suggest sexual excess in contrast to the interpretation of the elder brother (15:30)" (230). An interesting example by Josephus supports the conclusion of Foerster and Johnson. A steward named Arion accuses Hyrcanus of being reckless with money, rebuking him "for having chosen a dissolute (*asôtôs*) way of life" because he wants to spend an extravagant sum to buy presents for King Ptolemy (*Antiquities* 12.4.8). At the least, however, in New Testament usage "*asôtôs* is not associated with positive values for life, but with negative choices leading away from obedience to God" (Latham 45).

Fun is not as important as foresight, as the prodigal soon learns. He runs out of money about the time "a severe famine" ravages the land. Everyone is in dire straights, and he cannot even meet his basic needs (v. 14). In desperation, he attaches himself "to a citizen of that country." Probably, in order to get rid of this "hanger on" the man assigns him a task that surely will be refused. He sends him into the fields "to feed pigs" (v. 15; see Bailey 170). The *Mishna* says, "None may rear swine anywhere" (*Baba Kamma* 7:7). Such work will further defile this wayward Jew (Lev. 11:7; Deut. 14:8), but he takes the job anyway. Here he is in a Gentile land, working for a Gentile, feeding unclean animals. How much worse could it get? But this young man is not the first person, nor will he be the last, to compromise his religious convictions in order to get a job.

Finally, he hits the bottom of the barrel: "he would gladly have filled his stomach with the pods that the swine ate, and no one gave him *anything*" (Luke 15:16). On no given day can he get enough to eat. Even if he tries to beg, as some contend he does, he is unsuccessful. His plight reminds me of a friend of mine who became a severe alcoholic. As long as anyone would come to his assistance, he says that he would keep on drinking. But the turning point in his life was the same as that of the prodigal son, in other words, *when no one gave him anything*. The situation eventually comes down to changing one's life or dying. The prodigal has chosen to ask for his inheritance; he has chosen to convert his assets into a form he can carry with him; he has chosen to go far away from home; he has chosen to waste his resources and suffer the consequences; and now he chooses to live.

Jesus continues, "But when he came to himself, he said, 'How many of my father's hired servants have bread enough and to spare, and I perish with hunger!" (Luke 15:17). So the young man plans what he will do and says, "I will arise and go to my father, and will say to him, 'Father, I have sinned against heaven and before you, and I am no longer worthy to be called your son. Make me like one of your hired servants'" (vv. 18-19). Both the phrase, "when he came to himself," and the confession, "I have sinned before heaven" (probably a paraphrase to avoid the mention of God's name) imply repentance, especially when read in the light of vv. 7 and 10, and comprise the structural turning point in the first part of the parable (see Bailey 160).

Some expositors think that the prodigal's intention to return home and become his father's "hired servant" suggests that he plans to give up any legal rights that attach to sonship (Bock 1313). Furthermore, as a day laborer he may be able to earn wages and begin to make restitution of the money he has wasted. He will live in the village, not in his father's house, and avoid further offense to his brother (see Bailey 176-79; Derrett 65).

The younger son's resolve is not "a mere flash of remorse" (Farrar 307), but there is no time for delay. Both physical and spiritual reasons press him to get up, go home, and face his father. So he does (Luke 15:20).

The Father's Love

The Lord says that "when he [the younger son] was still a great way off, his father saw him and had compassion" (Luke 15:20). The father is aware "of the gauntlet the boy will have to face as he makes his way through the village"; therefore, he "runs the gauntlet for him, assuming a humiliating posture in the process!" (Bailey 181-82). He knows that his son "will be subject to taunt songs and many other types of verbal and perhaps physical abuse" (181). The verb translated "had compassion" (*splanchnizomai*) describes a feeling deep within one's inner parts. Jesus himself has this feeling for the widow of Nain, whose son is dead (Luke 7:13). And the Samaritan demonstrates the same compassion for the man that is robbed, wounded, and left half dead (10:33). The father now sees his own son, who has been the same as dead, walking toward him, and his reaction shocks those who are listening to the parable. He has *waited* for his son long enough, now he *runs* to meet him. "An Oriental nobleman with flowing robes never runs anywhere," writes Bailey (181). To do so is disgraceful. "A man's clothes, and the way he laughs, and his gait, reveal his character" (Ecclus. 19:30).

But forgiveness is shameless. Before the boy can say a word, his father embraces him and kisses him again and again (implied by the intensive form of the verb). Jesus portrays the father as waiting longingly for this moment (Plummer 375).

The son, then, begins to deliver his prepared speech: "Father, I have sinned against heaven and in your sight, and am no longer worthy to be called your son" (Luke 15:21). But either he decides to drop the proposal that he be made a day laborer as inappropriate in the light of his father's loving reaction or the father unexpectedly interrupts the young man's words. The addition of this proposal in a few manuscripts appears to be influenced by the reading of verse 18. The way Jesus tells the story, "'I am unworthy' is now the only appropriate response" (Bailey 184). The boy is on the accepting end of his father's merciful forgiveness. Rather than responding verbally to his son, however, the father addresses his servants, "'Bring out [quickly] the best robe and put it on him, and put a ring on his hand and sandals on his feet. And bring the fatted calf here and kill it, and let us eat and be merry; for this my son was dead and is alive again; he was lost and is found.' And they began to be merry" (vv. 22-23). They are to bring the finest robe in the house, the one reserved for special occasions. The ring appears to be a signet ring, a symbol of restored trust and "membership in the family" (Bock 1315; see BAGD 170). The sandals are "marks of a free man, for slaves went barefoot" (Plummer 376). The calf to be slaughtered is no ordinary animal that is grazing in the fields; it has been fed grain and fattened to eat with friends and neighbors and special guests. The father's desire seems to be "to reconcile the boy to the *whole* community" (187). He wants everyone to share with him this joyful moment.

The Elder Brother

Although Jesus began the parable of the prodigal son, saying, "A certain man had two sons," the character of the older brother has not been developed until now. Part one (Luke 15:11-24) recounts the story of the younger son's relationship to his father. It describes how the boy squanders both his heritage and his inheritance in a far country, sinks to the lowest depths, resolves to repent and return home, and is graciously and joyously accepted back at the father's table with the full honors of sonship. The tax collectors and sinners can empathize with this part of the parable. Part two (15:25-32) introduces us to the elder son and his conversation with his father about their relationship to the younger brother. And his character evokes negative feelings within us because of his similarity to the scribes and Pharisees. Furthermore, the location of the elder brother outside in the field (v. 25) rather than inside the house is probably a literary touch of irony. "The brother who had been on the outside," observes Bock, "is now on the inside, while the brother who had been on the inside is now on the outside" (IVP Commentary on *Luke*, commenting on v. 25, see http://www.biblegateway.com). As the fellow approaches the house he hears "music and dancing" (v. 25). He is puzzled and asks a lad (*pais*) what the celebration means (v. 26). The boy replies, "Your brother has come, and because he has received him safe and sound, your father has killed the fatted calf" (v. 27).

If the younger son humiliated his father by asking him to grant him his inheritance, the older brother's boiling anger (*orgizô*) and persistent unwillingness (imperfect tense of *thelô*) to enter the house to join the festivities are equally humiliating. They "are profoundly deep public insults against the father" (Bailey 196). In fact, his refusal to participate is "a symbolic act of gargantuan proportions in a culture where kinship boundaries are secured through the sharing of food" (Green 585). But we are not informed as to the reason for his rage. Perhaps he strongly disagrees with his father's instant and unconditional forgiveness of his brother. He could also be concerned that his brother will deplete even more of the family assets, in which case he will lose part of his own inheritance. But such possibilities are only speculations. Although characters in a parable may represent real people, they exist only in the speaker's mind and do not think beyond the text (Robert H. Stein, *Luke* 408).

When the father realizes that his older son refuses to come into the house, he goes out and repeatedly pleads (imperfect tense of *parakaleô*) with him, only to be "met with a torrent of words as the pent-up feelings of years [come] tumbling out" (Morris 244); however, he displays no indication of rancor or rebuke. Once again he acts honorably by humiliating himself in hope of reconciling the family.

One can sense the deep resentment as the older son addresses his father without even using a polite title. He complains about both his father's treatment of him and his father's favoritism toward the younger brother. His complaint not only forms the structural center of the parable's second division but also echoes the murmuring of the Pharisees and scribes about receiving sinners and eating with them (Luke 15:2). Indeed, this is the main point of the parable of the prodigal son.

The elder brother expresses three negative feelings toward his father (Luke 15:29): (1) "Look!" he says, "All this time I have worked like a slave for you." He views his working conditions at home to be nothing more than *slavery*. (2) "I never sidestepped your command." The verb that Jesus puts in his mouth is *parerchomai*, which means "pass by," "ignore," "neglect," "disregard," or "disobey." Although he thinks of his father as a taskmaster, he rates himself as a perfect son who has scrupulously done everything expected of him. (3) "And yet you never gave me a young goat, that I might make merry with my friends." He accuses the father of slighting him. No fatted calf, not even a goat! He is miffed that his father has not prepared a feast *for him* so that he can make merry with *his own circle of friends*.

The elder son completely distances himself from "the fellowship of the family": "But as soon as this son of yours came . . . you killed the fatted calf for him" (Luke 15:30a; see Bailey 199). He expresses contempt that the father has joyfully welcomed the younger brother back home. One senses hostility in his words: "He's not my brother; he's *your son!*" And he puts the worst possible spin on the younger brother's activities in the "far country." "This son of yours," he continues, "has devoured your livelihood with *harlots*" (v. 30b, emphasis mine, MDC). Is he trying to get the father on his side by saying, "Your living" (Farrar 310)? Or is he suggesting that the father shares a good part of the blame in giving the inheritance to the younger son? Or is he slamming the prodigal for wasting money that right- fully should have been part of the father's livelihood? We pointed out in the comments on verse 13 that *asôtôs* does not necessarily imply immoral living. But whatever the elder brother knows about the younger brother's conduct while in a distant place, the term *harlots* carries the negative im- plication that serves his purpose. His assessment of the whole situation is that "the wages of sin is a lavish party for the sinner" (Taylor, "Prodigal Son," http://www.explorefaith.org/LentenHomily03.05.99.html). He will have no part of it.

The father responds graciously, not with rebukes but reassurances. He addresses his older son with deep affection: "*Child (teknon)*, you are always with me, and all that I have is yours" (Luke 15:31). He reminds him that their relationship as father and child has not changed because his prodigal brother has reentered the family circle. Nor have his legal rights been affected; he is *now* and *always will be* both his son and his heir. The father gives assurance that he has never considered him to be either a hired hand (*misthios*) or a slave (*doulos*). He also reminds him that as a son he is bound by strong family ties to the *entire* family: "'*Child . . . your brother'* has come home" (vv. 31-32). "The older son," writes Latham, "represents the tragedy of one who stands on the verge of shutting out the father by shutting out the brother" (52). The father lets him know that the family's reception of a wayward member is not an option but an *obligation*: "It was right (*edei*) that we should make merry and be glad" (v. 32). *Edei* is the imperfect indicative form of *dei*, "*it is necessary, one must* or *has to*, denoting compulsion of any kind" (BAGD 172). The outward celebration ("make merry") must arise spontaneously from joyful hearts ("be glad"). The shepherd rejoices with his friends and neighbors when he finds the lost sheep. The woman rejoices with her friends and neighbors when she finds the lost coin. How much more, then, should the elder brother now rejoice with his father over the return of the prodigal— "your brother was dead and is alive again, and was lost and is found" (v. 32b). The point is so obvious that Jesus does not feel compelled to repeat the spiritual implication drawn from the first two parables as he concludes the third one: "Likewise there is more joy in heaven over one sinner who repents than over ninety-nine just persons who need no repentance" (v. 7; see v.10).

Finally, Plummer observes, "We are not told whether the elder brother at last went in and rejoiced with the rest. And we are not told how the younger one behaved afterwards. Both those events were still in the future, and both agents were left free" (379). The parable of the prodigal son is not a rebuke; it is an invitation to tax collectors and sinners, to Pharisees and scribes, and to us. The Lord is saying, "Come! Join with me in the celebration!"

Some Possible Applications

Christians through the centuries have applied the parable of the prodigal son to the tragic situation that occurs when a young person leaves home, wastes much of his life in sin, decides to repent, and returns to face the loved ones who have been forced to share his pain and humiliation. If some of us have not personally experienced such a trauma, either as troubled children or as distraught family members, we are acquainted with someone who has. What principles does the story teach us about handling this kind of situation?

The character of the wayward child reveals how strong the love for the world can be. All young men and women—in fact, all of us—should take seriously some New Testament exhortations and warnings:

> Do not love the world or the things in the world. If anyone loves the world, the love of the Father is not in him. For all that is in the world—the lust of the flesh, the lust of the eyes, and the pride of life—is not of the Father but is of the world. And the world is passing away, and the lust of it; but he who does the will of God abides forever (1 John 2:15-17).

> Now godliness with contentment is great gain. For we brought nothing into this world, *and it is* certain we can carry nothing out. And having food and clothing, with these we shall be content. But those who desire to be rich fall into temptation and a snare, and *into* many foolish and harmful lusts which drown men in destruction and perdition. For the love of money is a root of all *kinds of* evil, for which some have strayed from the faith, and pierced themselves through with many sorrows (1 Tim. 6:6-10).

Furthermore, when one of us who has lived a prodigal life finally realizes that "the wages of sin is death," *not* a lavish party, when desperation says there is nowhere to turn, let us remember the way back home. Godly sorrow is painful, but it produces repentance. And repentance results in remission of sins, so let us begin our arduous journey with full assurance that spiritual life can be renewed. What really counts is not a good reception by earthly family and friends—elder brothers are lurking everywhere—but the absolute conviction that our heavenly Father is waiting there for us. He will run to greet us, fully accept us as his child, and joyfully celebrate our return.

The gracious father in the parable demonstrates the true nature of love, and loving parents must not let pride stand in the way of reclaiming a prodigal child. Obviously, this is easier said than done. *Scepticism* may cause parents to be overly cautious about complete acceptance or unrealistic about the conditions they demand. *Resentment* may ignite rage for wrongs done and losses sustained. And *an unforgiving spirit* may drive a child further away from both the family and the Lord. Love allows for none of these negative responses.

> Love suffers long and is kind; love does not envy; love does not parade itself, is not puffed up; does not behave rudely, does not seek its own, is not provoked, thinks no evil; does not rejoice in iniquity, but rejoices in the truth; bears all things, believes all things, hopes all things, endures all things. Love never fails (1 Cor. 13:4-7).

Parents must understand, however, that love cannot control the will of another. "Love never fails," but children do—time and time again. But fathers and mothers must not allow the possibility of their child's future failure to diminish their joy; rather, they should kill the best calf for the son or daughter who has come home and encourage family and friends to join the celebration.

The elder brother helps us to see the wrong in setting ourselves on a pedestal of virtue and vanity. Virtue is that quality of character that exemplifies excellence in all that is good, and the capacity for love is the greatest good that God has bestowed on his children. Virtue does not give us bragging rights to judge ourselves superior to others and to act condescendingly toward those who have wasted part of their lives in reckless behavior, especially when they are our siblings. Self-righteousness leads the elder son to view both his younger brother and his father as prodigals: the brother, for wasting the father's livelihood in the company of harlots; the father, for wasting his love on a worthless child. It also leads many of us who claim to be Christians to act contemptibly toward our siblings who have sinned in ways that make both restitution impossible and loving them difficult. And it creates resentment toward parents who are willing unconditionally to forgive our brother or sister who is attempting to make a new start. Why can we not empty ourselves of self-centeredness, self-pity, and self-righteousness? Why can we not join the celebration and rejoice that the family is together again? Unfortunately, too many of us are content to remain outside the house and criticize what is going on inside.

As parents and children we must support one another in trying to reunite dysfunctional or divided families. It is never easy, but it must be done. And love is the only adhesive that is strong enough to mend broken relationships.

Now to the *main application*. Jesus tells the parable of the prodigal son in response to the criticism that he "receives sinners and eats with them" (Luke 15:1). The story is about a father who graciously receives his sinful but penitent son back home with full honors and the negative reactions of the older son who withholds fellowship from his younger brother by refusing to eat with him.

Christians have a tendency to apply the parable to our relationship with people of the world and the extent to which we may associate with them in order to bring them to God. When aliens become penitent believers and are baptized into the body of Christ, what restitutions must they make if we are going to accept them into fellowship? But the tax collectors and sinners with whom Jesus eats are individuals like Levi, Zacchaeus, and the fellow who was praying in the temple in remote proximity to the Pharisee. They are brothers in the faith, although some of them are estranged from their brethren because of "unclean occupations" or "ungodly associations."

The Lord intends that by means of this simple story we may better appreciate some of the complexities of fellowship within the family of God. As Christians, he wants us to know that God is our heavenly Father and Jesus himself is our elder brother. In turn, we are their beloved heirs and joint heirs, and some of us squander our inheritance in all kinds of sinful ways. But a penitent spirit helps us come to understand how undeserving we are in the presence of our benevolent Father and loving Savior and leads us to plead for their mercy and grace in hope that our spiritual siblings on earth will participate with us in a joyful family reunion in the divine kingdom.

On the one hand, some of us are as shocked as the Pharisees and scribes were by the father's lack of demands concerning sanctification, probation, and restitution. Indeed, as Taylor senses, this episode "has been an offensive story all its life":

> Tertullian, an early defender of the faith, insisted that the parable of the prodigal son must never apply to Christians. If it did, he said, then not only "adulterers and fornicators," but also "idolaters, blasphemers, and renegades" would use the parable to pardon their sins. "Who will worry about losing what can so easily be regained?" he asked, and others agreed with him—especially those who had to decide what to do with Christians who had knuckled under to the Romans. . . .
>
> And, Novation, a near contemporary of Tertullian, allowed that while God certainly had the power to forgive such apostasy, the church should not—indeed, could not—re-admit them to the body of Christ without a long and public period of humiliation. If the church really was Christ's body, Novatian reasoned, then it was supposed to be without sin. To welcome a tainted person back into fellowship was to defile the whole body ("The Parable of the Prodigal Son," http://www.explorefaith.org/LentenHomily03.05.99.html).

On the other hand, some of us are as relieved as the tax collectors and sinners were to rejoice in the father's gracious spirit toward his reclaimed son, because we see in him a symbol of the heavenly Father who has compassion on us.

Of course, one parable does not equal the entire teaching of the New Testament. We all struggle to resolve the tensions that the parable of the prodigal son creates. But some things are quite clear. The restoration of an erring brother is a loving work: "Brethren, if anyone among you wanders from the truth, and someone turns him back, let him know that he who turns a sinner from the error of his way will save a soul from death and cover a multitude of sins" (Jas. 5:19-20). Moreover, those who are "spiritual" must undertake the responsibility "in a spirit of gentleness, considering yourself lest you also be tempted" (Gal. 6:1, notice how Paul personalized the matter). Especially, one should keep in mind that the attitude of the elder brother can be a source of temptation to one who is spiritual or righteous. Also, we should remember that every persons's situation is different. Jude reminds us, "On some have compassion, making a distinction; but others save with fear, pulling them out of the fire, hating even the garment defiled by the flesh" (v. 22). We must never, however, demand a pound of flesh! "On the contrary, we must "forgive and comfort" the penitent, "lest perhaps such a one be swallowed up with too much sorrow" (2 Cor. 2:7). It is important to "reaffirm" our love . . . lest Satan should take advantage of us; for we are not ignorant of his devices" (vv. 8, 10). Paul's request to "reaffirm" our love uses the verb *kuroô*, a legal term that means "to confirm, ratify, validate," usually by a formal decision or vote (BAGD 461). As he has previously commanded the church at Corinth to take formal disciplinary action on the immoral man, so here he calls for a formal, public acceptance of the man back into fellowship.

The climax of the parable of the two sons is the loving father's appeal to the elder brother. He has allowed a spirit of resentment to build up in himself to the point that he refuses to participate in the feast in honor of his younger brother. He remains outside the house. He does so because he cannot condone his brother's actions: "This son of yours . . . has devoured your livelihood with *harlots*" (Luke 15:30, emphasis mine, MDC). Perhaps his concern for the way his brother has wasted what belonged to his father is justified, but he distances himself from his family and puts the worst possible spin on his brother's lifestyle. Wasteful? Yes. A fornicator? Well, maybe. But he means for his words to polarize the differences between himself and his brother. How often do we hear the worst kind of interpretations hurled at others within the family of God today? All too easily we attach unnecessary, derogatory labels on brethren and their teaching. Or we drag out a brother's past actions, of which he has repented long ago. Sometimes we distance ourselves too quickly from other brethren because we fear the direction they are going, thereby losing all hope of reconciliation. Carelessly we take statements out of context, or we do not accept a brother's own explanation of the intention of his words. Sometimes, like Diotrephes, we not only refuse to eat with "sinners" but deny fellowship to those who do, when perhaps we may have misjudged their motive for continuing their association. And, yes, I am aware of Matthew 18:17 and 1 Corinthians 5:11.

Most of us are struggling honestly to resolve the difficulties and tensions associated with the question of fellowship, but our application of the New Testament data has thus far only fractured us into numerous splinter groups that will have little to do with each other because of convictions, suspicions, and hostilities. Why do you suppose the Lord did not tell us the elder brother's response to his father's appeal to join the celebration? Perhaps, it is because he wants to force each one of us as hearers to decide for himself what must be done. But the freedom of will is both our best and worst enemy. We must make up our minds on the basis of what God's word says, what our conscience dictates, and do so in the best interest of others first and ourselves last. Above all, we must not allow ourselves to think that "we have dominion over (another person's) faith" (2 Cor. 2:24). Our appeal to biblical authority should be "for building up" our brothers, not for tearing them down (2 Cor. 10:8).

In conclusion, I exhort all of us to reexamine our personal relationship to the family of God, especially toward those we consider to be "sinners." As Paul says, "Examine yourselves *as* to whether you are in the faith. Test yourselves" (2 Cor. 13:5). Not that I expect any sudden changes in many of us; we all have enough of the elder brother in us to believe that we are doing the right thing. As for myself, when I reflect on my life, I see some characteristics of both the prodigal son and the elder brother, and I find it increasingly difficult to be like the gracious and forgiving father. Perhaps, as someone has said, we all need to see Jesus Christ as a third brother in this parable, the one who is telling the story for our benefit. Our hope lies in being like him. This means that we will empty ourselves of pride and be willing to endure pain and humiliation, whether caused by the wastefulness of the lives and teachings of our spiritual siblings or through the bitterness of their actions toward us. Our heavenly Father is having a difficult time in persuading his children to sit down together at the table and "make merry and be glad." I truly believe we desire to be a loving family, but surely we can be more gracious to one another and fulfil his joy.

Sources Used

Bailey, Kenneth Ewing. *Poet and Peasant: A Literary Cultural Approach to the Parables in Luke.* Grand Rapids: Wm. B. Eerdmans Publishing Co., 1976.

Bauer, Walter. *A Greek-English Lexicon of the New Testament.* Translated by William F. Arndt and F. Wilbur Gingrich. Revised and augmented by F. Wilbur Gingrich and Frederick W. Danker from Walter Bauer's fifth edition, 1958. Chicago: University of Chicago Press, 1979.

Bock, Darrell L. *Luke.* Baker Exegetical Commentary on the New Testament. Vol. 2:9:51–24:53. Baker Book House, 1996.

_____. *Luke.* The IVP Commentary on the New Testament. Http://www.biblegateway.com.

Bradley, Chance J. "Luke 15: Seeking the Outsiders." *Review and Expositor* 94 (1997): 248-257.

Derrett, J. Duncan M. "Law in the New Testament: The Parable of the Prodigal Son." *New Testament Studies* 14 (1967): 56-74.

Farrar, Frederic W. *The Gospel According to Luke.* Cambridge Greek Testament for Schools and Colleges. Cambridge: University Press, 1899.

Foerster, Werner. "*Asôtos, asôtia.*" *Theological Dictionary of the New Testament.* Ed. Gerhard Kittel. Grand Rapids: Wm. B. Eerdmans Publishing Co., 1964. Vol. 1: 506-507.

Green, Joel B. *The Gospel of Luke.* Grand Rapids: Wm. B. Eerdmans Publishing Co., 1997.

Jeremias, Joachim. *The Parable of Jesus.* Rev. ed. New York: Charles Scribner's Son, 1963.

Johnson, Luke Timothy. *The Gospel of Luke.* Sacred Pagina 3. Collegeville, MN: Liturgical Press, 1991.

Latham, Tony. "The Role of Jesus' Parables in Luke's Gospel: Luke 15:11-32." A research paper submitted to Dr. Lorin L. Cranford at Southwestern Baptist Theological Seminary, Fort Worth, TX, February 7, 1994. See pp. 28-53.

Linnemann, Eta. *Jesus of the Parables: Introduction and Exposition.* Trans. John Sturdy. 3rd ed. New York: Harper & Row, Publishers, 1966.

Morgan, G. Campbell. *The Gospel According to Luke.* New York: Fleming H. Revell Co., 1931.

Morris, Leon. *The Gospel According to St. Luke: An Introduction and Commentary.* Tyndale New Testament Commentaries. Grand Rapids: Wm. B. Eerdmans Publishing Co., 1974.

Moulton, James Hope and George Milligan. *The Vocabulary of the Greek Testament.* Grand Rapids: Wm. B. Eerdmans Publishing Co., 1963.

Plummer, Alfred. *A Critical and Exegetical Commentary on the Gospel According to St. Luke.* International Critical Commentary. 5th ed. Edinburgh: T. & T. Clark, 1922.

Stein, Robert H. *Luke.* The New American Commentary. Nashville: Broadman Press, 1992.

Taylor, Barbara Brown. "The Parable of the Prodigal Son." Http://www.explorefaith.org/Lenten homily03.95.99.html.

Teenagers For Christ
Steven F. Deaton

At what age one becomes responsible before the Lord, no one but the Lord knows. Most agree it varies from one person to another. Generally, folks believe the "age of accountability" is somewhere in the teenage years. If not before, then somewhere in their teen years a person is aware of his or her own moral failings. Whether or not they are consciously aware of God is another matter (cf. Rom. 1:18-32). For the sake of this study, however, we will assume they are aware of God's existence, though their understanding of him may be immature or warped. We will also assume the "age of accountability" has been reached.

The Bible shows us that many young people served the Lord. Both the Old Testament and the New Testament alike give examples of young servants of God. Samuel, David, Solomon, Shadrach, Meshach, Abednego, and Jesus are all held forth as men to emulate and admire. The wise man gives this admonition:

Steven Deaton spent four years in the United States Air Force before beginning full-time work as a preacher. To help him get started, he worked with the church in West Columbia, Texas where Ron Halbrook was serving as the local evangelist. From there Steven went to central Kentucky where he preached by appointment and attended the classes offered by the church in Danville for one year. His first work as the sole preacher was in Mineola, Texas. In 1997 he moved to Lufkin, Texas where he spent seven years with the Loop 287 church of Christ. Steven is again working with Ron Halbrook in a two-preacher arrangement with the Hebron Lane church of Christ in Shepherdsville, Kentucky.

Remember now your Creator in the days of your youth, before the difficult days come, And the years draw near when you say, "I have no pleasure in them" (Eccl. 12:1).

Teenagers for Christ will take this exhortation to heart and keep it in mind daily. They understand that "youth" is a time to enjoy, but also a time for which they will give an account to their Creator (Eccl. 11:9). Hence, they will take their duties before him seriously.

Start Young

Teenagers need to understand the value of developing righteousness while they are young. Solomon indicated the need for this when he said, "Remember your Creator in the days of your *youth*." If the Lord does not return first, young people will grow older and their health will deteriorate (Eccl. 12:1-5). Their ability to travel and work will become limited. Their ability to concentrate and read may be hindered. Eventually, they will pass from this world into the next and face God in the judgment (Eccl. 12:6-14; Heb. 9:27). Therefore, they need to establish godly habits in their youth—habits that will take them through their old age and provide for a fulfilling life all along.

The first thing a teenager ought to do is obey the gospel plan of salvation. When young people come to the point of understanding their personal offense to God, because of their sins, and a belief in Jesus as the Christ, then they should repent, confess him, and be baptized (Rom. 3:23; 10:9, 10; Acts 2:38). There is danger in putting this off until they have reached an older age. It is like Felix who told Paul to go away. He said, "When I have a more convenient time I will call for you" (Acts 24:25). This type of reaction suppresses the spirit of obedience and makes it more difficult later on. There is no more convenient time than when one first realizes his guilt before God and what is required of him to get rid of it.

After obeying the gospel, there are many habits a young person can develop in service to God. Teenagers will be greatly benefitted if they study the Bible on a regular basis. Paul said Timothy knew the Scriptures from childhood (2 Tim. 3:15). No doubt, this was due in large part to his mother and grandmother. Do you suppose, though, that Timothy was also personally motivated to study the Scriptures apart from his mother's prodding or his grandmother's urging? Paul further admonished him when he said, "Be diligent to present yourself approved to God, a worker who does not need to be ashamed, rightly dividing the word of truth" (2 Tim. 2:15). The only way to rightly divide the word of truth is to study it. As the young Christian studies God's word, he or she will be stronger in the faith, better able to resist temptation and peer pressure, as well as lay the foundation for future service as an elder or elder's wife, Bible class teacher, preacher, and Christian in general.

Teenagers also need to get in the practice of praying without ceasing (1 Thess. 5:17). The Hebrew writer said, "Let us therefore come boldly to the throne of grace, that we may obtain mercy and find grace to help in time of need" (Heb. 4:16). Teens need this help and can look to Daniel whose custom from "early days" was to pray three times a day (Dan. 6:10). David declared, "*Evening* and *morning* and at *noon* I will pray, and cry aloud" (Ps. 55:17). Habitual prayer while young will help draw one closer to God through the years. As the young person grows older and faces increasingly greater problems, prayer will help him overcome. It will give him the "peace of God, which surpasses all understanding" (Phil. 4:6, 7). Those with a weak prayer life will feel increasingly isolated and fearful because their confidence in and closeness to God will be lacking.

Another habit to start young is attendance at worship services and Bible study. The Hebrew writer said it is mandatory (Heb. 10:25). The younger this starts, the easier it will be to do as one grows older. If the teenager for Christ will determine that attendance is a priority, then many of his decisions will be simpler as time goes by. For instance, if a seventeen-year-old young lady has attendance as a priority, then when it comes time to choose a college to attend, she will be able to rule out all schools where there is not a sound church nearby. A young man will not take a job that requires him to work every other weekend—thus missing 37 percent of the services each year. Teenagers will be blessed by developing the habit of regular attendance.

Further, teenagers need to practice charity, that is, serving their fellow man. They need to do this, because like the other things we have discussed, they will be held accountable for it (Matt. 25:31-46). If the habit of helping those in need is established while young, then in later years it will not seem like such a burden. Too, it will help the young person appreciate his blessings. James said, "Visit orphans and widows in their trouble" (Jas. 1:27). Going to see an orphan will help the teenager appreciate the home in which he lives. While visiting with a "senior," teenagers will realize what a blessing it is to have energy, good eyesight, hearing, mobility, and many other things. They may even appreciate the fact that they have all their teeth!

The younger a person starts, the better. No one will get to the judgment day and say, "I wish I had waited longer to serve the Lord." Therefore, our admonition to teenagers is to start right now and never look back.

Faithful Children

David. The Bible gives us many good examples of those who served God in their youth, like David. It is generally accepted that he was a teenager when he faced Goliath the giant (1 Sam. 17:4-11). He was able to do this because he put his trust in God, not flesh (1 Sam. 17:38-51). David's experience provides us with several useful lessons.

Teens should not be discouraged by the criticisms of others who are unwilling to rise to the challenge. David's brother, Eliab, criticized David for inquiring about the reward for the one who would fight the giant (1 Sam. 17:28). David protested and went on with his determination to stand up against the enemy. Teenagers for Christ need to adopt this attitude. There will be times when their friends or family will criticize them for taking a stand. They should not allow this to depress or hinder them from doing what is right.

Young people will be doubted, just as Saul doubted David's ability to fight a giant who had been "a man of war from his youth" (1 Sam. 17:31-33). David was confident because of God's help in the past. His fight with the lion and bear prepared him for Goliath (1 Sam. 17:34-37). Teens may be doubted by older Christians at times. It is not that older Christians do not love or trust young folks, but simply they do not know their true abilities. However, a young Christian with the right heart can face tremendous challenges and conquer the enemy. Each hurdle they face will better prepare them for the next. They can do all things through Christ (Phil. 4:13).

Teenagers for Christ need to depend on what God gives them for the battle, not what man offers. Before David faced Goliath, Saul tried to get him to put on his armor, but it only encumbered David (1 Sam. 17:38, 39). He then took up the weapons of a shepherd with which he would slay the giant (1 Sam. 17:40). Instead of fighting with the carnal weapons of man, teens need to take up the armor provided by the Chief Shepherd (Eph. 6:10-18). The gospel armor is what will help them defeat sin and Satan, not name calling, slander, lies, or back stabbing (cf. Eph. 4:31; Gal. 5:15).

Young Christians also need to learn that the enemy will severely threaten them, but with trust in God, it need not intimidate them. As David went out to fight Goliath, the giant cursed David, said he would kill him and feed his "flesh to the birds of the air and the beasts of the field" (1 Sam. 17:43, 44). Yet, David remained unfazed by this because he put his faith in God (1 Sam. 17:45-47). Enemies of truth will try to intimidate all Christians, especially the young. Threats and curses will be hurled at teens, but if they depend on God for their strength, they will not be shaken.

Further, teens need to be willing to stand alone. David stood up to Goliath in spite of the fact that the whole army of Israel was too afraid to fight the giant, including the king who stood "head and shoulders" above the rest (1 Sam. 17:11; cf. 9:2). There are times when teens will find themselves standing alone against the enemy. They may be by themselves because others are not around or, like David and Israel, others are too afraid to take a stand. This may happen at school, when out with their friends, or when they go away to college. Nevertheless, if they will stand with God, they can overcome.

Shadrach, Meshach, and Abednego. Shadrach, Meshach, and Abednego also serve as excellent examples for young people. They were "young men in whom there was no blemish . . . gifted in all wisdom" dwelling in a foreign land, serving before the king (Dan. 1:1-4). Though they were commanded to serve idols and threatened with death, they refused (Dan. 3:1-18). Teenagers for Christ will be blessed if they learn from their example.

Sometimes there is pressure to compromise from those in authority. Though the king commanded and threatened the three young Israelites, they did not give in. Principals, teachers, and coaches may try to push teens into compromising their faith. A coach may want them at the regional tournament on Sunday. The band leader may want a teen to skip Wednesday night services to be at a recital. However, one who is dedicated to serving God will not give in, even if it means being kicked off the team or out of the band—or a bad grade on the report card. Taking a stand while in school will help them later when they face pressure to compromise in the work place.

Young people face great challenges when it comes to peer-pressure as well. Shadrach, Meshach, and Abednego were not exceptions. All the people around them were bowing down to idols. Yet, they refused. Teenagers for Christ will not give in or give up because of peer pressure, whether it is sexual immorality, drugs, or rebellion toward parents.

There has always been the pressure and temptation to commit sexual immorality, but it seems more prolific today. Hard-core pornography is readily accessible via the Internet and satellite or cable television—and soon on cell phones. Soft-core pornography is found nearly everywhere, including broadcast television shows and commercials, men's and women's "health" magazines, and music videos. This is in addition to the immodest clothing worn by many young people. There is a culture among the young that it is exciting to be involved in all this "forbidden" and "naughty" stuff. Teenagers for Christ must remember that the Spirit condemned all such things as works of the flesh (Gal. 5:19-21).

Teens also face peer pressure to "experiment" with drugs, including alcohol. The advertising campaigns for beer and whiskey companies target young people. They make them think it is all "fun-and-games." The peddlers of poison do not show the young woman vomiting on herself because her body is trying to expel the poison. They do not show the young man's mangled body being cut out of his car after a drunk-driving "accident." It is hip and cool to drink and be part of the crowd, according to worldly teens. However, teenagers for Christ will keep in mind that God says it is sinful to use drugs or alcohol recreationally (1 Pet. 4:3, 4). The wise man said,

> Who has woe? Who has sorrow? Who has contentions? Who has complaints? Who has wounds without cause? Who has redness of eyes? Those who linger long at the wine, Those who go in search of mixed wine. Do not look on the wine when it is red, When it sparkles in the cup, When it swirls around smoothly; At the last it bites like a serpent, And stings like a viper. Your eyes will see strange things, And your heart will utter perverse things (Prov. 23:29-33).

Moreover, teenagers will be influenced by their peers to rebel against their parents; to disrespect them and the role God has given them. Many entertainment media send the message that children are smarter than their parents. Rarely is there a father figure on television who is wise, competent, loving, and helpful to his family. The mother is head of the father, and children run the whole house. Yet, the Bible still says children need to listen to and respect their father and mother (Eph. 6:1-3). They can give them much needed wisdom and advice that help them avoid many of life's pitfalls (Prov. 6:20-22). Even Jesus submitted to his earthly parents (Luke 2:51). God takes this so seriously that he authorized the death penalty in the Law of Moses for children who rebelled against their parents (Deut. 21:18-21). Teenagers for Christ will honor their father and mother.

Teens can also learn from Shadrach, Meshach, and Abednego, that it helps to have others standing with you. Each one had faith in the one true God. Hence, they did not even debate the matter among themselves. They knew God could deliver them, but if he chose not to, they would rather die than betray him. Who can doubt that there was a measure of comfort in the fact that they stood together? Teenagers for Christ need to develop friendships with peers who serve Christ. Just as companions can have a negative impact, so can they have a positive one (1 Cor. 15:33). Young people need to "note" others who serve the Lord and spend time with them (Phil. 3:17).

Young people will eventually travel away from their home and have their faith tested without the immediate help of parents and others they normally depend on. The three young Israelite boys did not allow the fact that they were away from home to cause them to compromise. They knew that God sees all (Heb. 4:13). The Psalmist said,

> Where can I go from Your Spirit? Or where can I flee from Your presence? If I ascend into heaven, You are there; If I make my bed in hell, behold, You are there. If I take the wings of the morning, And dwell in the uttermost parts of the sea, Even there Your hand shall lead me, And Your right hand shall hold me. If I say, "Surely the darkness shall fall on me," Even the night shall be light about me; Indeed, the darkness shall not hide from You, But the night shines as the day; The darkness and the light are both alike to You (Ps. 139:7-12).

Teenagers for Christ will know that being away from home on a school trip, summer vacation with friends, or a move to college does not mean God is not watching. Rather, they know they will give an account for all their deeds.

Another lesson to learn from Shadrach, Meshach, and Abednego, is that just because something is a law does not mean it is right. The law of Babylon was that all bow down to the idol—with the death penalty attached. The three friends did not care that it was the law of the land. Young people today need to know that a law made by man is valid only if it does not violate God's will. Just because drinking, gambling, prostitution (in some areas), abortion, and so on, is legal, it does not make it right. As Peter said, "We ought to obey God rather than men" (Acts 5:29).

Jacob's Children. The story of Dinah ought to hit teenagers hard, especially the young women. Dinah "went out to see the daughters of the land"

(Gen. 34:1). It seems she went out innocently. When she was out visiting, she was raped by one of the men of the land (Gen. 34:2). Young people today need to know that not all people have noble intentions.

There is a reason children are told by their parents to be in at a certain time at night or stay away from certain people or places. The parents know trouble thrives during the night. Too, it may be mom and dad do not think it is a good idea for their child to hang around someone with tattoos and body piercings. Yet, the child cannot see the problem since their friend is so nice. He or she may resent having to come home so "early" when "everybody else" is out so late. Teenagers for Christ will know their parents are looking out for their best interest and respect their parents' decisions.

Joseph is another young person from whom teens can learn much. He fell into disfavor with his brothers because of his dreams and the fact that his father showed so much favor toward him (Gen. 37:1-11). His brothers wanted to kill him, but ended up selling him into slavery instead—at the age of seventeen (Gen. 37:18-28). Many young people would allow such events to make them bitter at the world. They would say, "Life is so unfair." Yet, Joseph pressed on by becoming the best slave he could be (Gen. 39:1-6). Just when things were going well, Joseph was falsely accused of trying to rape his master's wife and was thrown in jail (Gen. 39:7-20). Again, this would be an excuse for many young people to hate everyone and everything around them. However, Joseph continued to be diligent and was elevated in the prison (Gen. 39:21-23). This eventually led to an opportunity to stand before Pharaoh and inform him on the meaning of his dreams (Gen. 41:1-36). At this point he was lifted up to the second highest position in Egypt (Gen. 41:37-45). Because he did not give up when life was unfair, God blessed him.

Teenagers for Christ need to be like Joseph. Though their home-life may not be good, because of their siblings or even parents, they can still serve the Lord. Though their boss or others in society may wrongly condemn them for something they did not do, they ought to continue doing their best. And, like Joseph with his brothers, they should not hold a grudge against or be bitter toward those who did them wrong (Gen. 45:1-15).

Solomon. As teens face peer pressure, temptations, and troubles, they must lean on God for help. Solomon realized his lack of wisdom and experience when he ascended to the throne of Israel. Thus, when given the opportunity to ask God for something, Solomon asked for an "understanding heart" (1 Kings 3:9). Teenagers today need an understanding heart to deal with the turmoil and temptations of life. They must acknowledge that they do not have all the answers. They need to know "the fear of the Lord is the beginning of knowledge" (Prov. 1:7). Prayer and study of God's word, as mentioned before, will greatly aid teens to make the proper decisions and set the right example. Remember, "Trust in the Lord with all your heart, And lean not on your own understanding" (Prov. 3:5).

Rebellious Children

Further, the Bible shows us rebellious children and the consequences of their actions. Teenagers would do well to take these examples to heart. By so doing they will save themselves much trouble and be a blessing to those around them.

Absalom. Absalom is an example of one who rebelled against the authority of his father, the king. He was an arrogant young man who believed he could and should run the kingdom better than his father, David (2 Sam. 15:1-6). This young man, however, over estimated his strength, wisdom, and ability. During the battle with his father, Absalom's hair became entangled in a tree. The Bible indicates he took great pride in his hair, and it became his hang up—literally (2 Sam. 14:25, 26; 15:9). As he was hanging there, Joab, the leader of David's army, killed him (2 Sam. 18:10-15). The young man's rebellion against his father ended up costing him his life.

Teenagers for Christ will know that arrogance and pride end up in destruction (Prov. 16:18). They will not be puffed up and think they know more than their parents. Rather, they will hear the wise man when he says, "My son, hear the instruction of your father, And do not forsake the law of your mother; For they will be a graceful ornament on your head, And chains about your neck" (Prov. 1:8-9). The young Christian will not try to usurp the authority God has given to parents. He will gracefully accept discipline, knowing that it will refine his soul (Heb. 12:7-11). A teen will believe the Spirit's words that honor shown toward father and mother yields a happy, content life (Eph. 6:1-3).

The Youth. Sometimes there is the temptation among teens to mock and ridicule one who is in a position of authority, including religious authority. This happened when Elisha was on his way to Bethel (2 Kings 2:23). The youths of the area, no doubt influenced by idolatry, ridiculed

Elisha the prophet of God. The prophet turned and cursed them, then "two female bears came out of the woods and mauled forty-two of the youths" (2 Kings 2:24).

Teenagers for Christ will not become involved in mocking Bible class teachers, elders, deacons, or preachers. They will recognize it as an affront to God and avoid it, no matter how much pressure their peers put on them. They will treat the older men and women as fathers and mothers and look to them for advice and counsel (1 Tim. 5:1, 2). They will have respect for the age, wisdom, and experience of older Christians.

Amnon. Amnon serves as another negative example. He loved his half-sister Tamar so much that he became sick (2 Sam. 13:1-4). He listened to his cousin's scheme of getting Tamar and ended up raping her (2 Sam. 13:5-14). As Tamar described him, he was a "fool" in Israel. After he had his way with her, his love turned into hatred (2 Sam. 13:15). Tamar's full brother, Absalom, was extremely angry about this, but patient. After two years passed, and not saying a word to Amnon, he arranged for Amnon to be killed (2 Sam. 13:21-29). Amnon's lusts ended up being his downfall and death.

Teenagers for Christ will control their lusts, remembering their body is a temple for the Holy Spirit (1 Cor. 6:18-20). Young ladies will take note that when young men are being nice, complimenting them, and giving them presents or flowers, while pressuring them to have sex, their attitude often changes after they get what they want. As Paul told Timothy, "Flee youthful lusts; but pursue righteousness, faith, love, peace with those who call on the Lord out of a pure heart" (2 Tim. 2:22).

Eli's Sons. Eli's sons stand out as an example of what corrupt religion can do. Eli's sons perverted the sacrificial system in Israel (1 Sam. 2:12-16). As a result, "men abhorred the offering of the Lord" (1 Sam. 2:17). Eli's sons did not heed their father's chastening, "because the Lord desired to kill them" (1 Sam. 2:25). And that he did (1 Sam. 4:1-11).

Teenagers for Christ will know that they are "priests" for the Lord (1 Pet. 2:9). In such a position of importance, they must recognize their influence on others—for good or ill. If they pervert the religion of Jesus, it will cause men to abhor the truth. If this happens, the Lord will desire to kill them, that is, the wrath of God will abide over them. Then they must either repent or be cast into hell (cf. Luke 13:3).

Whether the example is positive or negative, young Christians will learn from them. They will imitate the good and avoid the bad. By so doing, their influence for truth and impact on others will increase.

Evangelism

Teenagers for Christ have a unique opportunity to teach others. God wills that all his children teach the gospel to the lost (Mark 16:15, 16). Some Christians have opportunities to reach certain people that others cannot. Teens, of course, have contact with other teens—with whom they hold great influence. Thus, these young Christians can study with their friends or invite them to church. Their friend might not otherwise contact the truth or attend an assembly of the saints. They can reach those who are generally searching for the meaning of life and open to new ideas.

Picking A Partner

By the time the teen years come along, young men and women are well aware of each other. They now willingly brush their teeth and hair, take baths and put on deodorant. Eventually, these young people want to impress the right guy or gal and convince them to marry. Teenagers for Christ will take great care in this process.

Take Heed Whom You Marry. God established marriage and, therefore, has the right to regulate it (Gen. 2:18-25). His law is basically one man for one woman for life, with one exception (Rom. 7:1-3; Matt. 19:1-9). Young Christians must realize they have one choice of a lifelong mate and must be careful in the choice they make. Perhaps a good way to illustrate it is with a car. What kind of car would a young person choose if they could have only one and must keep it for life? Would it be sporty, fast, high maintenance, get poor mileage, and be the first one that caught their eye? Or, would it be a comfortable four door that is reliable, gets excellent mileage, a good reputation, and is a well thought out decision? Similarly, they need to determine what qualities and characteristics are best for a lifelong mate: best looking or best character, high maintenance or down to earth, first one or well thought out. They must keep in mind that the person they marry will have great influence over them for the rest of their lives. They will avoid people with a worldly mindset; people who will:

- Mire their morality (Gen. 6:1, 2).
- Corrupt their commitment (Judg. 14:1-3).
- Ravage their religion (1 Kings 16:30-33).

Young Christians must keep in mind that the person they marry will be a parent to their children (Eph. 6:4). The right choice can help them get their children to heaven. The wrong choice may result in them going to hell.

The marriage relationship is the most intimate. After God made Adam and Eve, looking forward he said, "Therefore a man shall leave his father and mother and be joined to his wife, and they shall become one flesh" (Gen. 2:24). Jesus repeated this truth when he taught on marriage (Matt. 19:5, 6). Paul reinforced it when he described the relationship between Christ and the church, likening it to the marriage of a man and woman (Eph. 5:28-31). Thus, the relationship between a husband and wife is to be nearer and dearer than the relationship between the husband/wife and his/her:

- Best friend.
- Brothers or sisters.
- Parents.
- Children.

Take Heed Why You Marry. Various people get married for various reasons. The man and woman do not normally get married for the exact same reasons, though they may overlap. The following points were taken from Steve Curtis' lesson titled *Respectable Worldliness: In The Home*.

Wrong Reasons: Carnal
- Good looks.
- Money.
- Fame.
- A Name.

Wrong Reasons: Emotional
- Friends are doing it.
- Avoid loneliness.
- Get away from parents.
- Spite parents.
- It is what is expected.
- To give a sense of self worth.
- To change the other.
- On the rebound.
- To cover sin (like out of wedlock pregnancy).
- Pity the other.

Right Reasons: Spiritual
- To please God (Prov. 18:22).
- To get to heaven (1 Pet. 3:7).
- To raise godly children (Ps. 127:1-5).
- To be an influence for good in this world (Matt. 5:13-16).

No, it is not wrong to marry a person of good character who also looks good. A faithful Christian is not to be rejected just because he or she comes from money. Rather, the idea is that the primary, overriding reason is based on biblical principles.

A Word To Parents
What can parents do to help ensure their teenagers are teenagers for Christ? No doubt, just dealing with a teen is a challenge for most parents. It is a time when their child wants to establish his own identity—"find out who he is"—and the world is trying to do that for him. Still, parents can persuade their children to do right.

The first thing parents must do is start training their children when they are young, even from birth. The Spirit says, "Train up a child in the way he should go, And when he is old he will not depart from it" (Prov. 22:6). This is not a law set in concrete. Rather, it is a general principle that, when followed, usually turns out correct. Various practices in the home will aid the parent in fulfilling this principle. The habit of praying together will train children how and for what to pray. It will also teach them to depend on and be thankful to God. Regular Bible study not only teaches the children how to study and what God's word teaches, but it also affords an opportunity to make practical application to their lives and answer questions they may have. Consistent attendance at worship services will help the children learn that God comes first, before baseball, homework, time with family, television, and vacation.

The example parents set will also greatly determine the spiritual character of their teenagers. The wisdom or foolishness with which the parents conduct themselves from day to day will "rub off" on their children (Prov. 13:20). All the teaching and training in the world will likely fail if mom and dad are not faithfully serving the Lord. Teenagers need to see consistency in the lives of their parents. Hypocrisy turns them off just as quickly as it does anyone else.

Teenagers also need discipline. They need to know the limits. Too many mothers and fathers try to be a "friend" instead of a parent. It is not unloving to discipline a child, but the opposite (Heb. 12:5-11). Parents should not be fearful that they are too strict. While they do not want to provoke their teens to anger by being arbitrary, inconsistent, hypocritical, or biased, they do want to set the rules and stick to them—religiously (Eph. 6:4).

Parents need to have rules touching all areas of the teen's life. Yes, teens have a mind of their own and parents cannot control their every action, but they must have some control or there will be chaos in the home. To help their teenagers be teenagers for Christ, parents need to set the rules on the type of clothing their children can wear. It needs to be modest and befitting a Christian (1 Tim. 2:9, 10). It should not be clothing similar to what the latest "pop tart" like Britney Spears wears. Neither should it be clothing that gives people the impression your teen is a vampire or has lost 70 pounds in the last week. Some parents protest that their teenagers have money and buy their own clothing—so there is nothing mom and dad can do. The Bible still says parents are in charge of the children, including the children's money. Besides, every home has a pair of scissors and a trash can.

Parents also need to control their children's recreational activity. Whether it is television, movies, video games, music, or the Internet, moms and dads need to know what is going on. Teenagers have access to every form of vile and degrading "entertainment." If they are allowed, either through permission or neglect, to ingest sexual immorality, vulgar language, or wholesale graphic violence, then it will eventually come out in their behavior. Jesus said,

> What comes out of a man, that defiles a man. For from within, out of the heart of men, proceed evil thoughts, adulteries, fornications, murders, thefts, covetousness, wickedness, deceit, lewdness, an evil eye, blasphemy, pride, foolishness. All these evil things come from within and defile a man (Mark 7:20-23).

Teenagers are especially impressionable and must keep their heart with all diligence (Prov. 4:23). Mom and dad need to help guide them in this process.

Another area where parents need to be conscientious with their teenagers is education. Moses was taught in Pharaoh's house, but he was also taught by his mother. His mother's influence led him to make the decision to reject Egypt and embrace Israel (Heb. 11:23-28). Even in this day when many schools are teaching anti-God messages, parents can educate their children on the truth. Some may choose to home-school their children, while others may choose not to. Either way, a godly, righteous home devoted to serving God will forever mold the beliefs and character of the children. As they grow up and go off to college, parents need to continue to work to counteract error that is being pushed on their teens. Whether it is teaching them about the creation of the universe, relationship of man and wife, or inspiration of the Bible, those who will be teenagers for Christ must be taught and reminded of the truth (Gen. 1:1-31; Exod. 20:11; Eph. 5:22-25; 2 Tim. 3:16, 17).

A Final Word

There is room in the kingdom for teenagers. They have energy and enthusiasm. If they start early, they have a better foundation to face greater challenges as life unfolds. Their faith can have a tremendous impact on their family, the local church, and their friends. Parents and others need to be there for them, help them overcome troubles, and encourage them to stay the course. As Paul told Timothy, let us admonish teenagers for Christ to "fight the good fight of faith, lay hold on eternal life" (1 Tim. 6:12).

Open Forum:
Drawing the Young to Christ

Drawing the Young to Christ
Jason Hardin

Potential. It is a word that expresses optimism. It is a hope-filled ideal. It carries promise for the future. If something has potential, it may not yet be in existence, but the possibility exists. Power and opportunity are present. There is a capacity for growth and development. The only question is, "Will that potential be reached?"

Just as every tiny seed has potential (Matt. 13:1-8, 18-23), so also does every generation of human beings. What better example of unadulterated optimism for the future could there be than the first couple, Adam and Eve? They are surrounded by a perfect world of beauty. They enjoy a pure, harmonious relationship with their Creator. He has granted them "dominion over the fish of the sea and over the birds of the heavens and over the livestock and over all the earth and over every creeping thing that creeps on the earth" (Gen. 1:26). Their potential is God-breathed: "Be fruitful and multiply and fill the earth and subdue it and have dominion over the fish of the sea and over the birds of the heavens and over every living thing that moves on the earth" (Gen. 1:28). The divine seed has been sown and blessed. "And God saw everything that he had made, and behold, it was very good" (Gen. 1:31). And yet, just as seed "sown among thorns" is choked

---

Jason Hardin was born in Louisville, Kentucky to Steve and Donna Hardin. He worked in a preacher training program with the church in Plainfield, Indiana in 1997-1998 while also attending IUPUI. From 1998-2002 he worked as an evangelist with the North Ridgeville church of Christ in North Ridgeville, Ohio. In 2002, Jason moved to Akron, Ohio where he continues to labor with the Thayer Street church of Christ. Jason is married to Shelly (Cummins), of Plainfield, Indiana. They have one daughter, Chloe.

out (Matt. 13:7, 22), the potential of the first couple was tragically hindered by their own sin (Gen. 3). Optimism was replaced with despondency. Hope was exchanged for hardship. Promise for the future was overshadowed by regret for the past.

With Adam and Eve's children naturally comes fresh promise for the future—until Cain's anger blossoms into murder. Genesis 5 subsequently records the rising and falling of one generation after another. But as history develops further away from God's initial design, so mankind drifts further away from his Creator's ideal. A type of climax is reached in Genesis 6:5-6 when we are told, "The Lord saw that the wickedness of man was great in the earth, and that every intention of the thoughts of his heart was only evil continually. And the Lord was sorry that he had made man on the earth, and it grieved him to his heart." Those words, in one way or another, characterize so many individuals, tribes, and nations of people throughout history. The Old Testament provides a type of roller-coaster ride through Israel's story. One generation will humbly receive Jehovah's instructions and stand strong in his statutes. Another arises with little regard for reverence and servitude. The promise of potential is dashed with disrespect and disobedience.

A prime example of the degeneration is Joshua 2:7-12: "And the people served the Lord all the days of Joshua, and all the days of the elders who outlived Joshua, who had seen all the great work that the Lord had done for Israel. . . . And all that generation also were gathered to their fathers. And there arose another generation after them who did not know the Lord or the work that he had done for Israel. And the people did what was evil in the sight of the Lord and served the Baals. And they abandoned the Lord, the God of their fathers, who had brought them out of the land of Egypt." Optimism has been lost. Hope has been confused. Promise for the future has been forsaken. If the successive generation is to reach their full potential, a hard battle of restoration must be fought. But far from an isolated event, this vicious cycle has been in existence for thousands of years.

Drawing . . .
At this point, we find the proverbial "ball in our own court." With new and impressionable generations knocking on our doorstep, how will we respond? To what will we draw this people of potential?

When a fisherman "draws in" his catch, he is applying force to cause his prize to move toward the shore. When a team of horses "draws" a wagon, they are working to pull their cargo in a given direction. When the leadership of a city decides what will be developed within their territory, they must be mindful of whom they are trying to "draw" or attract, based on what they intend to provide.

We also, whether deliberately and consciously or not, will draw the generations that follow us in very specific directions. Granted, the strength of our influence may not be as strong as the fisherman with his fish or the horses and the wagon. Each generation (as the account from Joshua revealed) will ultimately make its own decision. But we cannot discount the impact of the influence we will produce on the lives of those who come after us.

Therefore, before we take another step in the journey, we must ask ourselves, "From what point of spiritual development are we drawing those who are younger, weaker, and more impressionable? What impact will our own foolish decisions toward . . .

• Worldliness	• Hypocrisy
• Materialism	• Rivalry
• Selfishness	• The sanctity of marriage
• Pride	• Roles within the home
• Authority	• Shallow spirituality

. . . have on those who are just beginning their journey?"

It is truly commendable to be concerned with drawing others toward a higher ideal. But before we make another tug on the line of influence, we must make sure that we are drawing from stable spiritual ground. Such was one of Jesus' points of condemnation toward the Pharisees: "But woe to you, scribes and Pharisees, hypocrites! For you shut the kingdom of heaven in people's faces. For you neither enter yourselves nor allow those who would enter to go in. Woe to you, scribes and Pharisees, hypocrites! For you travel across sea and land to make a single proselyte, and when he becomes a proselyte, you make him twice as much a child of hell as yourselves" (Matt. 23:13-15).

Whom Are We Trying To Draw?

It is imperative that we grasp this point. We are seeking to draw the young of the twenty-first century. The young of the 1950s, 60s, and 70s have grown and matured. They no longer exist as "the young." Prudence would seem to dictate that we make sure we are working to draw a generation of young people that still exists. If our efforts are characterized by success, we must be willing to ask some hard questions and earnestly seek for accurate answers:

- In what way are the young of the twenty-first century different than those who were young in the twentieth century?
- How do the young of the twenty-first century think? What is important to them? How do they communicate?
- What kind of effectiveness are our nineteenth and twentieth century evangelistic methods showing in the lives of twenty-first century young people?
- Is what was determined to be expedient in the twentieth century still advantageous and useful in drawing the young of the twenty-first century?
- If not, are we willing to adapt our efforts, within the realm of expediency, for our changing culture?

The apostles grasped the importance of seeking to understand their audience. Peter, James, and John "seemed to be pillars" in their apostolic ministry "to the circumcised" (Gal. 2:7-9). They worked primarily to draw the Jews to Jesus as the Messiah. In doing so, a great deal of their reasoning was founded upon the Old Testament Scriptures. Why? They understood their audience and sought to meet them at the appropriate level of comprehension. In Acts 2, Peter reasoned with his Jewish audience from the writings of Joel and of David. In his speech before the Jewish council, Stephen quoted Amos, David, and Isaiah (Acts 7). Even Paul, in the Jewish synagogue of Antioch in Pisidia, appealed to his "brothers, sons of the family of Abraham" from David, Isaiah, and Habakkuk.

It is extremely significant, however, that as Paul stood in the midst of the Areopagus and addressed the "men of Athens" that he did not base his message on the writings of Habakkuk or Isaiah. Acts 17:22-31 is a masterful display of taking the time to understand and address a specific audience. Notice the tactfulness with which Paul addresses his purely Gentile hearers:

> I perceive that in every way you are very religious. For as I passed along and observed the objects of your worship, I found also an altar with this inscription, "To the unknown god." What therefore you worship as unknown, this I proclaim to you (vv. 22-23).

"The God who made the world and everything in it, being Lord of heaven and earth, does not live in temples made by man" (v. 24). How many temples would have been in plain view from Mars' hill?

In him we live and move and have our being"; as even some of your own poets have said, "For we are indeed his offspring" (v. 28).

Paul's very deliberate efforts to conscientiously approach his audience are perhaps best articulated in 1 Corinthians 9:19-23:

For though I am free from all, I have made myself a servant to all, that I might win more of them. To the Jews I became as a Jew, in order to win Jews. To those under the law I became as one under the law (though not being myself under the law) that I might win those under the law. To those outside the law I became as one outside the law (not being outside the law of God but under the law of Christ) that I might win those outside the law. To the weak I became weak, that I might win the weak. I have become all things to all people, that by all means I might save some. I do it all for the sake of the gospel, that I may share with them in its blessings.

Paul took the time to appreciate the kind of person he was trying to draw. The last thing he wanted to do was to place a "stumbling block" between that person and Christ.

As the apostle "to the Gentiles" (Gal. 2:8), Paul was willing to studiously recognize that "not all things are helpful (expedient, KJV) . . . not all things build up" (1 Cor. 10:23). Even though he was more mature in his under-standing, he had enough humility to discern that "knowledge puffs up, but love builds up" (1 Cor. 8:10). Despite his recognition that "food will not commend us to God. We are no worse off if we do not eat, and no better off if we do" (1 Cor. 8:8), he was sensitive enough to command, "But take care that this right of yours does not somehow become a stumbling block to the weak" (1 Cor. 8:9). He was mature enough even to refrain from exercising his own rights for the spiritual benefit of others: "Therefore, if food makes my brother stumble, I will never eat meat, lest I make my brother stumble" (1 Cor. 8:13).

His conclusion to the Corinthian Christians is simple and straightforward: "So, whether you eat or drink, or whatever you do, do all to the glory of God. Give no offense to Jews or to Greeks or to the church of God, just as I try to please everyone in everything I do, not seeking my own advantage, but that of many, that they may be saved" (1 Cor. 10:31-33). Paul had developed a Christ-like obsession of concern for others.

Does that mean that Paul was "soft"? Was he then exhibiting a willingness to compromise on matters of truth? Not for a moment. In Galatians 2, we read of his stand for truth regarding those that would forcefully bind circumcision on the Christian: "To them we did not yield in submission even for a moment, so that the truth of the gospel might be preserved for you" (v. 5). In the same chapter he tells of his stand for the truth regarding the inclusive nature of the gospel and the hypocrisy of some: "But when Cephas came to Antioch, I opposed him to his face, because he stood condemned. For before certain men came from James, he was eating with the Gentiles; but when they came he drew back and separated himself, fearing the circumcision party. And the rest of the Jews acted hypocritically along with him, so that even Barnabas was led astray by their hypocrisy. But when I saw that their conduct was not in step with the truth of the gospel, I said to Cephas before them all, 'If you, though a Jew, live like a Gentile and not like a Jew, how can you force the Gentiles to live like Jews?'" (vv. 11-14).

Paul earnestly contended for the faith. He refused to compromise in matters of the truth. But it is equally evident that he would not allow his personal feelings, preferences, or opinions to hinder, in any way, the salvation of souls outside of Christ, or the spiritual progress of brethren weak in the faith. Quite simply, Paul was not seeking his own advantage.

Likewise, if we are successful in drawing the young of the twenty-first century to Christ, it will require prayerful evaluation and discernment. It will demand our willingness to examine ourselves honestly. Like the apostles, we must be willing to regard our impact as individuals in our daily contact with the young. Like Paul, we must be willing to consider our influence as God's people on the faith of others. As those who are more advanced in the faith, we have been called to consider whether or not our actions are "helpful" and "edifying" (1 Cor. 10:23) to those we are trying to reach. We have been instructed to evaluate whether or not our actions are:

- Hindering young people from becoming Christians.
- Hindering our younger brethren from greater spiritual growth in Christ.

- Destroying the peace and unity between young and old that ought to exist within the church.

May we have enough humility and concern in our hearts for others to say with Paul, "So then let us pursue what makes for peace and for mutual upbuilding" (Rom. 14:19). "I try to please everyone in everything that I do, not seeking my own advantage, but that of many, that they may be saved" (1 Cor. 10:33). And if we do, the end result will be a people who "do nothing from rivalry or conceit, but in humility count others more significant than (themselves). Let each of you look not only to his own interests, but also to the interests of others" (Phil. 2:3-4).

The best reasoning can be shamefully wasted by failing to understand the people we are trying to draw. The most earnest of efforts can be pointlessly squandered on a target audience that no longer exists. Our task is to draw the young of the twenty-first century. If we are trying to reach a world that is past and gone, is that not akin to taking our "talent" and burying it in the ground (Matt. 25:14-30)?

Who Are the Young of the Twenty-First Century?
Anytime one sets out to characterize in just a few words an entire generation, he is treading on very "general," and sometimes very dangerous territory. As with every generation, there are multiple exceptions to the rule. However, to this 27-year-old, there seem to be a number of qualities and traits that generally define the young at the dawn of the twenty-first century. With broad strokes, the following is how I would describe those currently in their teens, twenties, and thirties:

1. They are information savvy. Young people have access to more information at the touch of a button than anyone could have possibly imagined fifty years ago. Consider just a few examples:

- As of December 15, 2005, a Google search of the word "Bible" produced 74,400,000 results in 0.09 seconds. "Truth" produced 163,000,000 results in 0.28 seconds. "God" produced 152,000,000 results in 0.08 seconds. "Jesus" produced 73,100,000 results in 0.11 seconds.

- During the week of November 28-December 5, 2005, the average American logged on to the Internet ten times. He visited twenty-five different websites. He spent eight hours and fifty-seven minutes online (Nielsen//NetRatings: http://www.netratings.com).

- During that same week, Microsoft had 58,546,000 unique hits to their website. Yahoo! had 53,592,000. Google had 41,328,000. eBay had 23,762,000. Amazon had 16,551,000. MySpace.com (a blogging site specifically geared towards young people) had 12,458,000 (Nielsen// NetRatings: http://www.netratings.com).

- According to another Nielson Media Research study conducted in 2005, an estimated 204.3 million people, or 74.9% of the U.S. population above the age of two and living in households equipped with a fixed-line phone, have Internet access (http://www.protectkids. com/dangers/stats.htm).

- A Henry J. Kaiser Family Foundation Study conducted in March 2005 reported that nearly all young people have used a computer (98%) and gone online (96%). In a typical day, just over half (54%) of all young people will use a computer for recreation. Nearly one-third (31%) of 8- to 18-year-olds have a computer in their bedroom, and one in five (20%) have an Internet connection there. One in ten young people (13%) reports having a handheld device that connects to the Internet. According to the study, the most common recreational activities young people engage in on the computer are playing games and communicating through instant messaging (http://www.protectkids. com/dangers/stats.htm).

- On October 30, 2005, *USA Today* reported that at least eight million teens blog (keep an online diary). MySpace, a hybrid site that allows people to post their personal interests, write blogs, put up video and set up ways to communicate with their friends has exploded to 34 million users in just two years—and is dominated by 14- to 34-year olds (http://www.usatoday.com/tech/news/techinnovations/2005-10-30-teen-blogs_x.htm).

- On November 2, 2005, The Associated Press reported that 1 in 5 school aged teens have a blog. About a quarter of girls, aged 15 to 17 do so, compared with 15 percent of boys in that age group. Among adults, 7 percent of Internet users have created their own blogs, or online diaries. And while 26 percent of adults say they read blogs, 38 percent of young people with online access said they do so. The study also found that the main reason teens have a blog is for communication (http://www.bloggersblog.com/statistics/).

2. They are technologically savvy. As the above would seem to indicate, the young of the twenty-first century acquire their information and communicate with one another in a drastically different way than those who grew up in the twentieth century. Consider the following reports:

- On October 11, 2005, The Minneapolis *Star Tribune* reported, "Newspaper readership is down. Fewer young people are picking them up, and the average age of a newspaper reader is now 55, according to a Carnegie Corporation study" (Average Age Of Newspaper Readers: 55, *Star Tribune*, Eric Black).

- On October 31, 2005, MediaDaily News reported "It's official: 2005 will be the newspaper industry's worst year since the last ad industry recession. And things aren't looking much better for next year either, according to a top Wall Street firm's report on newspaper publishing. 'Sadly, 2005 is shaping up as the industry's worst year from a revenue growth perspective since the recession impacted 2001-2002 period,' says the report from Goldman Sachs, adding a warning that meaningful growth in 2006 is 'very unlikely'" ('05 Proving To Be Worst Newspaper Year Since Recession, Ross Fadner, MediaPost Publications, http://publications.mediapost.com/).

- On November 13, 2005, The Associated Foreign Press predicted "Dark days are ahead for American newspapers, as sales tumble, a warp-speed news culture leaves lumbering dailies behind and scandals over flawed reporting taint heavyweight titles. US papers are battling an explosion in online information, a news agenda powered by bloggers and 24-hour cable news, and they can't seem to connect with young readers. . . . In a survey last year, the Pew Research Center for the People and the Press found only 23 percent of people under 30 read a daily newspaper, compared with 60 percent of older people" (A Future Of Empty Doorsteps? Dark Days For US Newspapers—http://www.breitbart.com/news/na/051113145312.o7xd4zz6.html).

3. They are very open to new ideas. A logical consequence of such a flood of information readily available seems to be that young people of the twenty-first century are very open to new ideas. In the mind of the modern young person, information is power. Hours upon hours are spent online soaking up details from innumerable sources. Little is taken for granted. Young non-Christians are often willing to engage in religious discussion, if for no other reason than to increase their general knowledge and awareness.

4. They are seeking to make "their faith their own." Like many before them, the typical young person of the twenty-first century is struggling with the evolution from "this is what my parents believe" to "this is what I believe." They are immersed with more information than ever before and have revolutionary tools to access it, but still they are faced with that most basic question: "What do I believe?"

5. As a result, they are not afraid to ask hard questions. With new information often comes the questioning of that which is "old." The typical young person of the twenty-first century is not afraid to question that which is settled in the minds of those who are older. They are not afraid to ask "Why?"

6. As they wrestle with these hard questions, they crave real, open, and honest discussion. They are anxious to test their personal opinions and conclusions in a "give-and-take" kind of crucible. In their minds, "discussion" is much more preferable than "debate." The primary vehicle for discussion is the Internet, and more recently, blogs. In the minds of many young people, posts to blogs are invitations to "discussion," rather than efforts at wide-spread "teaching."

7. As is evidenced in a great many of these "discussions," the typical young person of the twenty-first century is unsatisfied with the "status-quo." They are skeptical of those who do not see a need for continued advancement and progress. They will tune out those who are more anxious to "debate" than "discuss." They are frustrated by those who do not appreciate the asking of "hard questions." They will quickly divorce themselves from those who would alienate them for speaking out. They believe that there is much room for physical, social, political, and spiritual improvement and, in many cases, are willing to work to bring about such improvement.

8. As a result, they are optimistic and zealous about the future. Many young people, particularly in their twenties and thirties, believe that the work of "progress" is ongoing. The typical young person believes that through a humble willingness to evaluate ourselves and our beliefs while engaging in open and honest discussion, improvements can continue to be made.

To What Are We Drawing the Young of the Twenty-first Century?

The conscientious efforts of anyone who would seek to draw another to the Savior must always be founded upon the apostle Paul's words to the Galatians: "I have been crucified with Christ. It is no longer I who live, but Christ who lives in me. And the life I now live in the flesh I live by faith in the Son of God, who loved me and gave himself for me" (Gal. 2:20). It is imperative that we keep that goal at the forefront of our minds: we are seeking to draw the young to Christ.

To the Corinthians, Paul wrote: "I do not write these things to make you ashamed, but to admonish you as my beloved children. For though you have countless guides in Christ, you do not have many fathers. For I became your father in Christ Jesus through the gospel. I urge you, then, be imitators of me. That is why I sent you Timothy, my beloved and faithful child in the Lord, to remind you of my ways in Christ, as I teach everywhere in every church" (1 Cor. 4:14-17). Those words are simply and beautifully rephrased in 1 Corinthians 11:1: "Be imitators of me, as I am of Christ." If we are intent upon "drawing" others, particularly the young, in the right direction, we must make sure that we are drawing them to Christ.

Our children are not called to obedience before God based upon our faith. They are called to develop a faith of their own. A parent's or grandparent's faith will not safely navigate them through periods of tribulation and distress. Only a personalized faith, a faith that has developed based upon their own convictions, will propel them towards a heavenly home. We are not seeking to draw the young to "our" faith. We are seeking to help them develop a faith of their own, based on Christ.

We are not seeking to draw them to a social club. Millions throughout the denominational realm automatically gravitate toward gimmicks and physical gratification when considering the subject of "drawing" the young. As we seek to understand our evolving culture and the young people that make it up, our task is not to adapt some new and clever form of the "social gospel" for the twenty-first century. As has been the case since the days of the apostle Paul, "the kingdom of God is not a matter of eating and drinking but of righteousness and peace and joy in the Holy Spirit" (Rom. 14:17).

We are not seeking twenty-first century American Christians as much as we are seeking Christians that happen to live in the United States of America in the twenty-first century. Paul appealed to Christians in first century Rome "by the mercies of God, to present your bodies as a living sacrifice, holy and acceptable to God, which is your spiritual worship. Do not be conformed to this world, but be transformed by the renewal of your mind, that by testing you may discern what is the will of God, what is good and acceptable and perfect" (Rom. 12:1-2). God has placed the church within culture and asks us to be an influence for good. Far too frequently in both Testaments, God's people have lost sight of their mission and ended up being the very ones who were changed. Instead of permeating culture with the fragrance of Christ, or even being counter-cultural when necessary, they have become captive to culture. What greater danger could a people be in when they do not even recognize such when it happens? What disastrous consequences are on the horizon for a people who do not even realize it when they have begun to read the Bible through the lens of culture rather than through the lens of faith? "Back to the Bible" is still the right call and back to the God of the Bible, in spite of the cultural shifts around us.

We are not seeking to draw the young to human tradition. The young are called to be "Christians" (Acts 11:26) by God, not "Campbellites." Our chief objective is not to perpetuate the Stone-Campbell Movement. Of course, there is nothing wrong with the young learning of the efforts of Thomas and Alexander Campbell, Barton W. Stone, Walter Scott, and others like them. But the faithful Christian of the twenty-first century must always remember the words of Paul in 1 Corinthians: "What I mean is that each one of you says, 'I follow Paul,' or 'I follow Apollos,' or 'I follow Cephas,' or 'I follow Christ.' Is Christ divided? Was Paul crucified for you? Or were you baptized in the name of Paul? . . . I have applied all these things to myself and Apollos for your benefit, brothers, that you may learn by us not to go beyond what is written, that none of you may be puffed up in favor of one against another" (1 Cor. 1:12-13; 4:6). Our goal is not to draw the young to "the way things have always been" within our own congregations. Our great privilege is to draw them to the Scriptures, and the Scriptures alone. That is the very essence of "speaking where the Bible speaks and remaining silent where the Bible is silent."

Our task is not to guide young people into the path of denominationalism. However, from both young and old, it is not difficult to hear the language of denominationalism among us:

- "I'm Church of Christ."
- "That's Church of Christ doctrine."
- "He's a Church of Christ preacher."
- "The Church of Christ is right."

In contrast, we must make sure that we are seeking to draw the young using the language of the word of God. "Whoever speaks, is to do so as one who is speaking the utterances of God . . . so that in all things God may be glorified through Jesus Christ, to whom belongs the glory and dominion forever and ever" (1 Pet. 4:11). With that as our goal, we read of "Christians" (Acts 11:26; 26:28; 1 Pet. 4:16), "saints" (Rom. 15:25-26), and "children of God" (Gal. 3:26; 1 John 3:2). When asked, "What is 'Church of Christ' doctrine?" some, without really thinking about it, might say, "Church of Christ doctrine is:

- "You have to be baptized for the remission of your sins."
- "The Bible is the inspired Word of God."
- "You assemble together on the first day of the week."
- "You partake of the Lord's supper every first day of the week."
- "Women can't be preachers or elders."
- "Instrumental music is unscriptural."
- "Miracles have ceased."
- "You don't observe Christmas or Easter as a religious holiday."

. . . and on and on we could go. When we are asked by our friends, our co-workers, our family, as well as the young, what "Church of Christ doctrine" is, would we try to formulate a list like this? Would we say, "I am trying to teach him our position—the Church of Christ position. I want to tell him about Church of Christ doctrine." Or, would we determine to humbly "speak where the Bible speaks"? Beyond a shadow of a doubt, we read of the "doctrine" or "teaching of Christ" (2 John 9), of "sound doctrine" (Tit. 2:1) and "the word" (2 Tim. 4:2), but let us make sure that we have not fallen into the trap of using denominational language that betrays a denominational mind set. The young of the twenty-first century have not been called by God to denominationalism.

Let there be no mistake: We must seek to draw the young to Christ. We are seeking to introduce them to the Christ of compassion and commands. In order to realize our goal of declaring "the whole counsel of God" (Acts 20:27), we must proclaim the "whole Christ"—the Christ who exhibited amazing grace and profound concern for the people around him (Luke 19:10; John 3:16), but who also spoke with authority and expected people to humbly receive and diligently obey his commands (Matt. 7:21-23; 28:18-20; Luke 6:46-49).

Ultimately, we are attempting to draw the young into the visible manifestation of the kingdom and rule of God on earth. We are seeking to persuade them to be active, diligent, faithful members of the church, the body and bride of Christ (Matt. 16:18-19; Heb. 12:23, 28; Eph. 1:22-23; 5:23-24). God is Ruler over all. Our great task as citizens of his kingdom is to help others acknowledge and submit to his rule.

What Do the Young of the Twenty-first Century Desperately Need?
1. They need you to be honest. They are seeking people of intellectual honesty. Be honest when you don't know. Be honest about your own struggles of faith. They don't expect you to have flawlessly perfect answers all of the time, but they do expect you to be honest with them and they will be able to perceive if you are "uttering what you do not understand" (Job 42:3).

They are seeking people of moral integrity. The young of the twenty-first century have grown up watching public figures who have made a laughing stock of the word "integrity." They are unimpressed by hypocrisy. They recognize that you are not sinlessly perfect. But they do expect you to be honest about your failures. In an age of extreme skepticism and cynicism, honest integrity shines brightly as a light in a very dark place. May we all take Jesus' words in Matthew 18:6 very seriously when it comes to our integrity: "Whoever causes one of these little ones who believe in Me to stumble, it would be better for him to have a heavy millstone hung around his neck, and to be drowned in the depth of the sea."

So many of them want to be a part of an honest church. They crave challenging exhortations from the pulpit and meaningful discussions in the classroom. They respect honest confession of sin. They admire people who seek out one another to deal with differences in a spirit of reconciliation rather than a group that talks behind one another's backs. Their hearts rejoice when they are able to carry someone else's burdens before the throne of their Father in prayer. They genuinely appreciate Christians who share the attitude of Paul: "Not that I have already obtained or am already perfect, but I press on to make it my own, because Christ Jesus has made me his own. Brothers, I do not consider that I have made it my own. But one thing

I do: forgetting what lies behind and straining forward to what lies ahead, I press on toward the goal for the prize of the upward call of God in Christ Jesus" (Phil. 3:12-14).

2. They need to be able to talk with good Bible students who are willing to listen to their thoughts and discuss their new ideas and hard questions with care and concern. This past summer I was in the audience when a speaker asked a large group of young people, "How many of you have questions you would be afraid to ask in Bible class?" I would estimate that 90% of the people raised a hand.

There is certainly a time and a place for the discussing of certain issues, and our Bible classes may not always be the most conducive opportunities to raise such questions. However, we must recognize that our young people have questions. Remember, generally speaking, they are not afraid to tread in difficult theological territory. "The gate is narrow and the way is hard that leads to life, and those who find it are few" (Matt. 7:14).

We have often commended the Bereans for being "more noble than those in Thessalonica; they received the word with all eagerness, examining the Scriptures daily to see if these things were so" (Acts 17:11). Let's make sure that when our young people manifest a willingness to examine the Scriptures for themselves and come back to us with genuine questions and difficult doubts that we listen, that we commend them for thinking for themselves, and that we lovingly seek to guide them in "the paths of righteousness" (Ps. 23:3).

3. They need people who care. They need spiritual role-models in their lives who care about God, who care about other people, who care about the "good news" of the Christ. In a world engulfed with darkness and selfishness, they need people around them who are a "refreshment" to the people around them (Phile. 7).

We all know people that are a drain to others:

- People who seem to open their mouths only to complain.
- People who cannot rejoice in the good because they are obsessed with the bad.
- People who are too immersed in negativity to open their hearts to that which is positive.

- People who find it shameful or weak to be optimistic.
- People who could not care less about trying to understand before they sought to be understood.
- People who seem to automatically assume the worst about every person in every situation.

Young people have to put up with more than enough of that kind of attitude in the world. They are in desperate need of people like Philemon as described by Paul: "For I derived much joy and comfort from your love, my brother, because the hearts of the saints have been refreshed through you" (Phile. 7).

4. They need to be able to follow people who love God and love his word with all of their heart and all of their soul and all of their mind (Matt. 22:37). Our young people, and the Lord's church as a whole, are in serious need of men that are willing to step up and lead. A great void exists, to the shame of so many, of "older men" who are "sober-minded, dignified, self-controlled, sound in faith, in love, and in steadfastness" (Tit. 2:2). So many younger women yearn to interact with "older women" who are "reverent in behavior, not slanderers or slaves to much wine." There are still young women who are looking for older women to actively "teach what is good."

In many places throughout this country, we are experiencing an elder shortage of epidemic proportions. If we are ever to be successful in restoring that vital element of God's design for the health and growth of his people, a generation of reverent men that are willing to "stand in the gap" and "build up the walls" must rise up (Ezek. 22:30). There is a younger generation of people anxiously waiting to follow your lead. May God be patient with us, gracious to us, and bless our efforts.

Drawing the Young to Christ

Daniel Ruegg

How do we draw the young to Christ? How do we draw the mother or father or elderly widow to Christ? The wonderful thing about the gospel is its universal appeal to anyone who is capable of weighing evidence to produce a verdict of simple belief. "I am under obligation both to Greeks and to barbarians, both to the wise and to the foolish. So, for my part, I am eager to preach the gospel to you also who are in Rome. For I am not ashamed of the gospel, for it is the power of God for salvation to everyone who believes" (Rom. 1:14-16). Paul declares the gospel draws all who believe in it to the saving grace of God. This is a universal concept and appeal. There are no age specifications here. As its appeal extends from the Jew even to the Greek, so does its widened appeal to the audiences extending from the young to the old. Paul's audiences were comprised simply of anyone who would lend an ear to listen. "For we are not overextending ourselves, as if we did not reach to you, for we were the first to come even as far as you in the gospel of Christ; not boasting beyond our measure, that is, in other men's labors, but with the hope that as your faith grows, we will be, within

---

Daniel L. Ruegg was born May 6, 1979 in Barberton, Ohio. He was taught the word of God by his mother and grandparents (Robert and Alice Bills), and the Bible class teachers of the Southeast Church of Christ and Brown Street Church of Christ in Akron, Ohio under the influential gospel preaching of his grandfather, Ed Holcomb, and Vernon Teagarden (at Southeast) and Lewis Willis (at Brown Street). Daniel attended Florida College for one year (1998-99). He preached by appointment from 1997 to 2002 and then began preaching full time at the Winding Road Church of Christ where he worked for two and a half years. Currently, Daniel preaches at Burbank Road in Wooster, Ohio. He married Beth Morrison on June 1, 2005.

our sphere, enlarged even more by you, so as to preach the gospel even to the regions beyond you" (2 Cor. 10:14-16).

In Paul's letter to the Colossian brethren, he indicates those whom he targeted with the preaching the gospel were any who could hear and understand the grace of God. "Because of the hope laid up for you in heaven, of which you previously heard in the word of truth, the gospel which has come to you, just as in all the world also it is constantly bearing fruit and increasing, even as it has been doing in you also since the day you heard of it and understood the grace of God in truth" (Col. 1:5-6). There is no age to whom the gospel makes an extra special appeal. Its contents, power, and transforming ability are universal in nature and penetrate best those who have a beating heart and an ear to hear. "If indeed you continue in the faith firmly established and steadfast, and not moved away from the hope of the gospel that you have heard, which was proclaimed in all creation under heaven, and of which I, Paul, was made a minister" (Col. 1:23). "And I saw another angel flying in mid-heaven, having an eternal gospel to preach to those who live on the earth, and to every nation and tribe and tongue and people" (Rev. 14:6).

Perhaps the reason that no specific age group is given in regards to who best fits as a candidate to be drawn by the gospel to Christ is because the three simple components of the power and appeal of the gospel can reach the hearts and minds of anyone who is willing to listen. Those three components are quickly summed up in the famous verse within John's gospel. "For God so loved the world, that He gave His only begotten Son, that whoever believes in Him shall not perish, but have eternal life" (John 3:16).

1. Love—"For God so loved the world."
2. Sacrifice—"He gave His only begotten Son."
3. Life after death—"Whoever believes in Him shall not perish, but have eternal life."

All three of these components of the power of the gospel will prick the heart and conscience of any young person willing to open his ears and listen as it would anyone else of any other age group. Can the concept of love be any more moving or appealing to the young than it is to the elderly? Certainly we all learn to experience different types and degrees of love throughout the various stages of our lives. The child who is taught to love and honor his mother and father will one day mature to fall in love with a mate who, together, will learn what it is to love unconditionally their own child. But with respect to the love that God has demonstrated to the sinner, what age group can appreciate or identify with that any more than another? Sin attacks all who come to an age of accountability of knowing the difference of right and wrong. "For all have sinned and fall short of the glory of God" (Rom. 3:23). And the very same fate is attributed to all who are guilty of sin. "Behold, the Lord's hand is not so short that it cannot save; nor is His ear so dull that it cannot hear. But your iniquities have made a separation between you and your God, and your sins have hidden His face from you so that He does not hear" (Isa. 59:1-2). "For the wages of sin is death, but the free gift of God is eternal life in Christ Jesus our Lord" (Rom. 6:23). What an amazing God! One who was willing to sacrifice his only begotten sinless Son to save us sinners from our own wretchedness simply because he loves us! "He made Him who knew no sin to be sin on our behalf, so that we might become the righteousness of God in Him" (2 Cor. 5:21). "By this the love of God was manifested in us, that God has sent His only begotten Son into the world so that we might live through Him. In this is love, not that we loved God, but that He loved us and sent His Son to be the propitiation for our sins" (1 John 4:9-10). This type of amazing sacrificial love is certainly understandable and appealing to every generation of any age.

The powerful images of the way God sacrificed his Son for us through humiliating beatings, mocking, and crucifixion are capable of moving anyone who is willing to hear. Just recently I was preaching on the crucifixion of Jesus and began to describe in detail the awful humility of Jesus to allow his accusers to spit upon him in hatred. As I described that awful scene, I suddenly noticed the eyes of a young girl open wide in horror as she listened attentively and was moved with compassion and tenderness when I saw tears falling down her cheeks. It quickly caused me to realize the universal appeal and powerful moving that scene draws to all, and of the statement Jesus made that we all must become as children in their innocence. "And He called a child to Himself and set him before them, and said, 'Truly I say to you, unless you are converted and become like children, you will not enter the kingdom of heaven. Whoever then humbles himself as this child, he is the greatest in the kingdom of heaven'" (Matt. 18:2-4). While those who are young may not exactly be contemplating what is to become of them after death, seeing that they have just begun to experience life in its very earliest stages, eternity is still something in their heart that can be summoned to the forefront of their thoughts by the preaching of the gospel. "He has made everything appropriate in its time. He has also set eternity in their heart" (Eccl. 3:11).

The idea of targeting a specific age group in the preaching of the gospel is both unwise and unscriptural. The very blueprint for evangelism and spreading the message of the grace of God to lost souls teaches us of a universal target audience with the hopes of drawing out those with sincere and honest hearts.

> Behold, the sower went out to sow; and as he sowed, some seeds fell beside the road, and the birds came and ate them up. Others fell on the rocky places, where they did not have much soil; and immediately they sprang up, because they had no depth of soil. But when the sun had risen, they were scorched; and because they had no root, they withered away. Others fell among the thorns, and the thorns came up and choked them out. And others fell on the good soil and yielded a crop, some a hundredfold, some sixty, and some thirty. He who has ears, let him hear (Matt. 13:3-9).

In further explanations by Jesus to his inquiring disciples as to the meaning behind this parable, he explained that the seed being used to produce fruit is the gospel of God's word (Luke 8:11). Its universal message of love, sacrifice, and eternal life is being sown and spread about in a widespread fashion ranging anywhere from beyond the tilled area beside the road to the fertile, thorny, and rocky soil (Mark 4:14). Rather than carefully placing the gospel in a specific targeted area, Jesus paints the picture of randomly tossing the seed of the gospel as far as you can, much like the way a farmer would sow his field with seed. When we evangelize and spread the gospel in this fashion, the result will always be the producing of fruit to God based upon who is willing to open his ears and listen rather than any specific age or group of people.

It has been the result of man's wisdom throughout many religious groups, including various congregations, that special alterations and gimmicks be accompanied with the preaching of the gospel to draw a younger audience to Christ. One such religious group is the Momentum Christian Church, which just started up as of January this year. Momentum Christian Church is interested in drawing and appealing to a younger audience by transforming the message of the gospel into a rap song or popular pop culture icon that will be more easily swallowed and accepted by the younger audiences. Unfortunately, many among the churches of Christ have been impressed with this plan of attack and are attempting to adopt these same methods.

Here is a sample of how the Momentum Christian Church is attempting to appeal to a younger audience from the Frequently Asked Questions section of their website: http://www.momentumchurch.com/:

What will a typical Sunday morning look like?
Great question! We'll be asking that same question each week. Each Sunday morning will have a very unique thumb print, including great live music, high-quality videos, a relevant message (you'll enjoy this way more than you're expecting), and maybe a few good belly laughs. We hope to be very creative (as Jesus was) in how we communicate our weekly topics. One Sunday, there might be a painter creating something on a canvas while the band is playing, another week there might be a funny Top Ten List or an improv skit that sets up the sermon. We talk about real-life issues . . . but we also believe that God is the creator of joy. It's okay to smile here.

What's the deal with the song "Baby Got Book"?
(This is a rap song about how the singer loves big Bibles, a parody of a rap song by Sir Mix-A-Lot about a much more offensive topic which many young people would be able to identify with.)

Dan Smith created the "Baby Got Book" video to be used at the church he worked for in the Washington, D.C. area called New Life Christian Church. The church loved it and when it was put on the Internet, people started passing it around like crazy and it exploded!

Momentum has put together a DVD featuring "Baby Got Book" and ten other funny videos that Dan had a part in creating so that it could be enjoyed by the droves of interested people.

What style of music will you be playing on Sunday mornings?
We'll be rockin' a full band and playing worship tunes that are pretty much the same style as what you would hear on a good radio station. Our music will often be a mix of modern rock and urban.

We will also be covering songs from the radio every week (i.e., Dave Matthews, Linkin Park, Jay-Z, Alicia Keys) that tie in with the topic we are tackling that Sunday. Religious or not, mainstream music is often asking questions about, or suggesting answers to, the spiritual questions that our whole culture is also asking.

It is pretty obvious what age group is the target audience here. Aside from dealing with the obvious issue of a complete lack of authority for conducting an act of worship of the Almighty God in such a fashion, where does this attempt to reach a younger audience leave other age groups? Instead of a universal appeal to any who will listen to the saving message of the gospel of Christ, it alienates others while honing in on a specific group. The sower does not plant his field this way, and neither does the evangelist who wishes to spread the gospel according to the pattern set forth by Jesus and his Apostles (Heb. 8:1-6).

Rather than drawing the young to Christ, we are in danger of losing the young to artificial, feel-good, entertaining imitations of the gospel. Fortunately, not all young people are willing to fall for these charades, but rather are hungering and thirsting for what only Christ and his pure gospel message can quench. Over the past several months I have had the opportunity to study and talk with a young man in prison. He is twenty years old and serving out a term given to him for armed robbery. He is also a Christian who fell away for a time. He indicated to me that for a short while he attended services at the congregation where I preach, but quickly left to attend services at places which he described were more "entertaining" to him. After several months of studying the gospel and New Testament worship and the subject of authority, I was encouraged to hear his remarks about the worship services which were more geared towards entertaining and attracting young people. "Knowing now the manner in which God has prescribed to be worshiped," he relinquished, "I would much rather attend the services where you preach and be pleasing to God than to fill myself with fun and entertainment and be in sin." It has been my good pleasure and delight to see many other young souls with the same desire to be found pleasing to God without the appeal of entertainment or fun.

A young thirteen year old boy who lives in the neighborhood of an older couple from our congregation recently asked if they could take him to church so he could be a part of the Bible classes. He continues to assemble with us on Wednesday evenings; he is full of questions and a firm desire to learn about God and his word. It is obviously not any source of entertainment or social activity that might appeal to a young person that has been drawing this young man back to our services time and time again, since our activities on Wednesday evening consist solely of singing, praying, and studying the Bible. From observations and various personal conversations I have had with this boy it is obvious he is yearning and searching for something greater, purer and holier than what he can find among his own surroundings in his own community, something that he knows he can only find through seeking God. It wasn't anything of an entertaining or social nature that caused these desires and hungering to surface. It obviously wasn't the appeal of being surrounded by a great number of other young people to socialize with, since we have only a handful of young people in our number and none that is anywhere close to his age group. No, but rather he was drawn by the life lived by an older godly couple in his neighborhood who demonstrated a life that is clearly affected by the powerful attributes and blessings found in the gospel. "But sanctify Christ as Lord in your hearts, always being ready to make a defense to everyone who asks you to give an account for the hope that is in you, yet with gentleness and reverence" (1 Pet. 3:15).

Another misconception and attempt to attract more young people to Christ is to have young people together for activities for young people with only young people at all times. I can certainly see the benefit of having get-togethers for young people to get to know one another and get closer together. I volunteer my time to serve as a counselor at various camps for the young to be together for a week. I have helped entertain and chaperone at various Youth Banquets and other activities involving young Christians. But when that is the constant focus, for young people to always be together with only other young people, it is neglecting the atmosphere that God truly wants us to have, and that is to be his spiritual family.

> While He was still speaking to the crowds, behold, His mother and brothers were standing outside, seeking to speak to Him. Someone said to Him, "Behold, Your mother and Your brothers are standing outside seeking to speak to You." But Jesus answered the one who was telling Him and said, "Who is My mother and who are My brothers?" And stretching out His hand toward His disciples, He said, "Behold My mother and My brothers! For whoever does the will of My Father who is in heaven, he is My brother and sister and mother" (Matt. 12:46-50).

A family is not solely comprised of a bunch of young people who are constantly surrounded by each other at all times. But rather a mix of ages, from old to young, to sons and daughters, to mothers and fathers. "Do not sharply rebuke an older man, but rather appeal to him as a father, to the younger men as brothers, the older women as mothers, and the younger women as sisters, in all purity" (1 Tim. 5:1-2). "Older women likewise are to be reverent in their behavior, not malicious gossips nor enslaved to much wine, teaching what is good, so that they may encourage the young women to love their husbands, to love their children, to be sensible, pure, workers at home, kind, being subject to their own husbands, so that the word of God will not be dishonored" (Tit. 2:3-5). This is the type of atmosphere and image we are to be drawing anyone into when drawing them to Christ. We are to be drawing them into a spiritual family, comprised of all ages, who genuinely love one another with a pure heart fervently.

Another atmosphere and image the Lord's church is to manifest which will be especially appealing to the young perhaps more than anyone is to be culturally and socially unbiased. For a young person in today's society, it can sometimes be nearly impossible to find acceptance and a sense of belonging among their peers. Within the powerful elements of the gospel is the representation of the very image and character of God. "And even if our gospel is veiled, it is veiled to those who are perishing, in whose case the god of this world has blinded the minds of the unbelieving so that they might not see the light of the gospel of the glory of Christ, who is the image of God" (2 Cor. 4:3-4). Among the great attributes of the Heavenly Father of whom Jesus was the very image, was his breaking down of social barriers and acceptance of those who were shunned by others. One great example of this is recorded in John's gospel as Jesus initiates a conversation with a Samaritan woman. "Therefore the Samaritan woman said to Him, 'How is it that You, being a Jew, ask me for a drink since I am a Samaritan woman?' (For Jews have no dealings with Samaritans)" (John 4:9). In this cultural context, indeed the Jews commonly had no social ties or dealings with anyone who was a Samaritan. But this is not the case with Christ. And if it's not the case with Christ, then it should not be the case in his church. Unfortunately, whether or not we are willing to admit it, too often we are guilty of the same sin Peter was reprimanded for by the Apostle Paul. "But when Cephas came to Antioch, I opposed him to his face, because he stood condemned. For prior to the coming of certain men from James, he used to eat with the Gentiles; but when they came, he began to withdraw and hold himself aloof, fearing the party of the circumcision" (Gal. 2:11-12).

How many times have you seen a brother or sister in Christ who seems to be somewhat uncomfortable in social situations or seems to be unique in their own character or personality who is therefore commonly left by themselves or abandoned by others since they don't seem to have as much in common or likeness as others? I have seen it enough to know it needs to be repented of and corrected. This will push the young away rather than draw them to the image of Christ. Notice, this behavior of social desertion on the basis of character or personality is not simply bad manners, it is sinful! Those at a young age are especially in need of a sense of belonging and feeling safe to allow themselves to let their natural character and personality to be seen without fear of ridicule. We see the jealousy that arose in the hearts of Joseph's brothers when he received special recognition from his father and they did not. We see the reaction of Jesus to those who thought the Kingdom of Heaven was too important to include young children. "And they were bringing children to Him so that He might touch them; but the disciples rebuked them. But when Jesus saw this, He was indignant and said to them, 'Permit the children to come to Me; do not hinder them; for the kingdom of God belongs to such as these. Truly I say to you, whoever does not receive the kingdom of God like a child will not enter it at all.' And He took them in His arms and began blessing them, laying His hands on them" (Mark 10:13-16). We even see Jesus bringing special attention upon a young child as an example in his teaching. "Taking a child, He set him before them, and taking him in His arms, He said to them, 'Whoever receives one child like this in My name receives Me; and whoever receives Me does not receive Me, but Him who sent Me'" (Mark 9:36-37).

Clearly set forth in the parable of the sower, Jesus demonstrates in what way we are to draw lost souls of this world to him. There are no special candidates, and no special ways to direct the message to specific ages or groups. Simply put, "He who has ears, let him hear."

Drawing the Young to Christ
Steven F. Deaton

Christians are concerned with drawing men to Christ. "All have sinned and fall short of the glory of God" (Rom. 3:23). This includes young people who have reached the age of accountability. Their souls need to be saved as well as people in the 30s, 40s, or older. Too, it is helpful to reach young people before they enter their teenage years, when their hearts are more pliable and their minds more pure. The question is: How is this done? How do we draw the young to Christ?

Ancient Methods

Long ago God commanded evangelism (Matt. 28:19, 20). The apostles practiced it from the very beginning (Mark 16:19, 20; Acts 2, 3). Disciples engaged in it as they spread out from Jerusalem (Acts 8:4, 5). Every generation since the first century has had the obligation to draw men to Christ. The manner in which men were drawn was determined by God.

God did not choose to draw men to Christ through an ambiguous feeling, amazing experience, or fleshly appetite (John 6:22-40). Rather, he used his word, the truth (John 6:44, 45). They had to hear and learn from the Lord. The process by which this was done is evident in the Bible. The Holy Spirit inspired certain chosen men to reveal the gospel (John 16:13). These men were to go and teach others (Mark 16:15). Those who were taught were then to teach others also (2 Tim. 2:2). The book of Acts confirms this pattern of using words to draw men to Christ.

> "heed my words" (2:14).
> "hear these words" (2:22).
> "with many other words" (2:40).
> "gladly received his word" (2:41).
> "heard the word" (4:4).

"number . . . came to be about five thousand" (4:4).
"the word of God spread" (6:7).
"number of disciples multiplied" (6:7).
"went everywhere preaching the word" (8:4).
"men and women were baptized" (8:12).
"begged that these words might be preached" (13:42).
"came together to hear the word of God" (13:44).
"when the Gentiles heard this" (13:48).
"believed" (13:48).

We know that this method of drawing men to Christ worked on young people as well as older ones. Timothy was converted by the preaching of Paul and Barnabas (Acts 14:8-21; 16:1). Who can doubt that there were young Christians in many places during the first century? When Paul commanded children to obey their parents, these were old enough to understand the command and obligation, and young enough to be at home (Col. 3:19; Eph. 6:1-3). Inasmuch as he wrote the letters to the "saints" at Colosse and Ephesus, he wrote it to "children" who were Christians (Col. 1:2; Eph. 1:1). The word worked on the young.

Modern Methods
In modern times men have forgotten or abandoned the Bible pattern for drawing men to Christ. Maybe it is because they do not have faith in the power of the gospel (Rom. 1:16). Or, maybe they are just not satisfied with the way God designed it. Or, maybe they just don't think the old way is fast, hip, or cool enough. Whatever the reason, whether intentional or not, men have replaced God's will with theirs. In order to draw men to Christ they have invented all kinds of tricks and gimmicks. This is especially true when it comes to drawing in young people—who seem to be the "holy grail" when it comes to drawing men in.

Denominations have long used the "social gospel" approach to attract young people. Everything from bicycle give-aways, to free pizza, to puppet shows, to "Christian" rock concerts have been used. Institutional churches of Christ have also employed social gospel tactics in an attempt to bring in young people. Some of their gimmicks are:

Bug Safari with "live ladybugs while you catch the buzz about God's love" (Wills Point [TX] church of Christ).

Father/Daughter Date Night (North Main church of Christ, Belton, Texas).

429

Renewal 01
Drama: Revival
Concert: Firemen & Vocal Union
Free T-shirts (South Baton Rouge [LA] church of Christ).

East Texas Youth Summit
Theatron
The Core
Entertainment: Big Britches and Boogers (North Street church of Christ, Nacogdoches, TX).

Non-institutional Liberals

Some non-institutional churches of Christ are not far behind the institutional camp when it comes to the social gospel. What once would have been almost universally condemned, is now being accepted and practiced by some liberal, non-institutional churches. They play fast and loose with God's pattern for drawing in young people. The following are actual announcements for "youth events," supposedly Bible studies, seminars, or lectureships.

Fun social events (Church in the Northwest).

Praise Worship.
Bring your sleeping bag.
Magical World of Arthur [who has] performed from Hollywood to Puerto Vallarta.
And the rest of the night is filled with all sorts of fun and fellowship, too.
Field trip.
"Light the fire" with a laid-back devotional and old-fashion bonfire.
Games, Movies, Karaoke, Hoops, Volleyball, etc. (Church in Texas)

Modern Day Parables
Lessons from Michael Jordan
The Great One—Lessons from Wayne Gretzky
The Death of Princess Diana (Church in Texas)

As far as I know none of the "social events" was paid for from church funds. Many are very careful to place a disclaimer in their advertisements. It usually says something like, "The expenses for the various social activities will be covered by individual Christians at _____," or "Friday, Lock

In (hosted by individual Christians from _____).” Do you suppose non-Christians paid any attention to such disclaimers?

A few comments and questions are in order about these events. First, why are “fun social events” advertised along with the Bible studies? If it is not to help attract the young people, then what purpose does it serve? Do these events make the occasion more holy and reverent?

Second, what is the essential difference between what institutional churches advertise and what the above non-institutional churches advertise? Growing up in institutionalism, I cannot tell a big difference. In fact, the only thing that distinguishes a few of them is the fact that they put in a disclaimer about the church not paying for the social events. Again, this is a meager attempt to differentiate themselves from their counterparts in institutionalism.

Third, what happened to “Lessons from Daniel,” “The Great One—Jesus Christ,” or “The Death of the Prince of Peace”? Must we now look to worldly people for spiritual lessons? I understand that illustrations from current events sometimes help make a point. However, is it necessary to construct an entire lesson or series of lessons based on these modern-day examples?

Finally, liberal-minded brethren can offer any excuse or explanation they wish, and perhaps feel justified in their mind, but I don’t buy it. When the social and spiritual are promoted together, it is the “social gospel.” *The social events are advertised for one purpose—to draw in young people who would not otherwise be inclined to attend if the activities were purely spiritual.*

Arguments and Answers For the Social Gospel Approach
“Jesus used food. We can too” (John 6)
Jesus did not use food to attract people. Jesus’ use of food was out of compassion and an opportunity to confirm his word by a miracle (Mark 6:34; Acts 2:22). When the people followed Jesus and demanded more food, he refused to give it to them (John 6:22-27). It was a perfect opportunity for him to practice the social gospel, keep his audience and “win some converts.” However, he did not see it as today’s liberals see it.

Further, if the use of food in John 6 justifies using food to attract young people to Christ, then perhaps other events of the Lord’s labors provide additional means of bringing in the sheaves. We can give them catchy titles and really grab the attention of youngsters.

Relax With the Redeemer

Jesus called his disciples to "rest a while" (Mark 6:31). Come refresh your whole mind, body, and soul in our "Resort Spa Ministry."

Messiah Medicine Ministries

Our Savior healed men of their physical ailments (John 5:5-9). Now we have a ministry designed to heal the body and soul in our state-of-the-art medical facilities.

Cadavers for Christ

The Lord was very concerned about those who lost loved ones and help them overcome their sorrow (Luke 8:41-55). Our "Time-of-Sorrow" funeral home ministry helps individuals and families through their grieving period.

"Plays and puppet shows simply portray the
Bible in a dramatic way."

We wonder, then, why did Paul not use plays to convey the gospel? He could have used the theater at Ephesus. Instead of "reasoning and persuading" in the Synagogue, he could have stirred and swayed the hearts of men with a production of "JESUS: Nattering Nitwit or Marvelous Messiah?" Perhaps if Paul had done this, he would have drawn in the young people and avoided causing a riot in the city.

The idea of putting on plays did not come from the word of God. Rather, it came from the world. Those who use them are like Israel when it looked to other nations for their governmental organization (1 Sam. 8:4, 5). They wanted to be like the nations around them. This attitude and desire meant they rejected God and his way of ruling them. Those who love the Lord and respect his word will not adopt worldly tactics to spread the gospel.

Further, if a play is to be used, will only male Christians act in it? Let's say we do a play around October 31 to impress teenagers about the awfulness of hell. If any females act in the play, and the purpose is to deliver a Bible message, then women are teaching men. This is a direct violation of 1 Timothy 2:11, 12, "Let a woman learn in silence with all submission. And I do not permit a woman to teach or to have authority over a man, but to be in silence." Many plays also have musical numbers in them. This would be a problem because it sets up a "choir" type environment instead of congregational singing (Eph. 5:19; Col. 3:16).

"What's Wrong With It?"

What's RIGHT with it? What's wrong with infant baptism? What's wrong with offering young people money to attend? We could give a dollar for every year of age up to nineteen. A bonus could be given for attending four consecutive weeks.

The Bible says, "Test all things; hold fast what is good" (1 Thess. 5:21). It also says we must have authority for all we do (Col. 3:17). Where is the authority for the social gospel? Where is the direct statement, approved example, or necessary inference that gives God's stamp of approval for drawing the young by carnal means?

Emphasis

The fact of the matter is that fun, food, and frolic turn the attention away from God and toward man. The Lord used teaching and preaching as the means of conveying the gospel. If he wanted social-gospel methods used, he would have used them. However, he did not.

Worship that is not prescribed by God is sinful (Matt. 15:7-9). Today, men who follow their own pattern for worship are no less guilty than the Pharisees and their worship is just as worthless. It matters not that they do it in service to the Lord. Saul spared the best of the flocks to sacrifice to God, but in so doing disobeyed the Lord (1 Sam. 15:10-23). Disobedience, no matter how well intended, is always sinful.

What happens when "fun social events" supported by individual Christians are not enough? Will non-institutional liberals advertise a "Christian Rock" band comprised of teenagers from area congregations? Will they offer door prizes, an X-box or Play Station? Where will it end?

Renewed Faith

We need a renewed faith in the word of God. It is his power unto salvation (Rom. 1:16). Young people can be drawn to Christ by the gospel. If it does not have an appeal to them, then adding a pizza will not save their souls. If "fun social events" draw young people in, then any faith they may develop will be short-lived if not shallow.

Let us be convicted that God's word still appeals to the hearts of men, including young people. Let us give them Bible stories about Noah, David, Shadrach, Meshach, and Abednego. Let us show them Jesus as a boy and teach them about Timothy. Let us have faith in the faith.

Ladies Classes

Winning Your Children For Christ

Elma Monts

Introduction

In today's society we have many types of homes to raise children. For the purpose of our study I will address the Christian homes our children are brought up in. Some of these homes have parents who are united in Christ and other homes have parents who are divided by religious matters or divorced. In whatever home a Christian parent may be found, raising children for God's glory will come with many challenges. There are many challenges that are harder to meet because of quickly changing traditional family values in our society. Whatever the type of home in which a Christian can be found, whether united, divided, divorced, or a single parent home, he has the same resource to adhere to, that is God's word, the Bible. The teachings found in the Bible will help us identify our problems of life, promote a solution, and resolve our conflicts. And ultimately, these teachings will help us as Christians reach our final goal, that is to have an eternal home in heaven with the Lord.

Elma Monts was born in Pearsall, Texas to Alberto and Anita Rivas in 1946. She attended Southwest Texas State University and graduated in 1969 with a degree in elementary education. She has lived in Issaquah, Washington for the last fifteen years and is currently working as a supervisor in a child care facility at a health club. She is the mother of Stephen Monts who preaches in the 31-W North Church of Christ in Franklin, Kentucky and of Justin Monts who preaches at Peters Creek in Glasgow, Kentucky. Shannon Monts, her daughter, lives and works in Seattle, Washington. Elma and Shannon are members of the Manitou Park Church of Christ in Tacoma, Washington.

As for my own household, it was a religiously divided home that ended in divorce after thirty-two years. It was through this difficult situation that my three children were raised and survived to become faithful Christians. It is for this purpose that I have this study. I want to assist others who may be in the same situation and give them hope and encouragement to hold to the faith (1 Tim. 6:12).

As parents, we have a short time in which to lay a Christian foundation to help our children live in this world. *Winning our children for Christ* is a worthy goal that is worth all of our efforts. The word "winning" is derived from the old Anglo-Saxon word "winnan" (*Webster's Unabridged Dictionary*). It means to "to fight, to endure, struggle, hence to gain by struggling." Winning your children for Christ is the highest and most worthy goal that any Christian parent would ever hope to achieve. We all want our children to be happy, financially secure, and successful in life, but can we know of any goal, any aspiration, any hope that would rival or come close to the goal of being a true child of Christ?

Consider earthly wealth and its treasures (Matt. 6:19-21), worldly fame or acclaim (John 12:43), academic knowledge and human wisdom (1 Cor. 2:13; Acts 17:21), or carnal, physical beauty (Jas. 4:14). All of these will in time pale, fade, or corrode and eventually die. In contrast, heavenly treasures, the praise of God, spiritual wisdom, and inward Christian beauty are profitable not only for this present life, but for the eternal life to come (1 Tim. 4:8). Knowing this, it is imperative that we learn what is the will of the Lord (Eph. 5:17) and in learning his will, to concentrate on what it means to be a new creature in Christ (2 Cor. 5:17). We can no longer do as we please, but must do as the Lord commands since we were purchased at a great price (1 Cor. 6:19-20). Our lives must be centered in Christ. His words and his works are to be studied and manifested in our daily lives. Our ultimate goal is to gain eternal life in Christ, which has been promised to those who love and obey him (John 3:15; Matt. 25:46).

We then prepare ourselves to obey him regardless of the cost to ourselves. Knowing that there is a price that must be paid, we count the cost and acknowledge that we are willing to forsake all in order to be found in Christ (Luke 14:26). If we, as parents, believe and obey Christ, our lives will surely reflect this belief and our children will certainly see our faith in God. Do we, as parents, love the Lord and make every sacrifice to be found in him? If we love the Lord with all of our heart, soul, mind, and strength, and if we love our neighbor as ourselves, then it follows that we will also make every effort to win our children for Christ. Are not our children our most valuable possession for those few years that we have them? We must be concerned with our stewardship, especially with our children. As a parent you will be providing them with the tools to succeed in this life and preparing them for eternity.

Raising Our Children in a United Home

In Genesis 2:24, the book of beginnings, we read of how God instituted marriage between a man and a woman and created the first home. In Mark 10:6-9 the Bible says, "For this reason a man shall leave his father and mother and be joined to his wife, 'and the two shall become one flesh'; so then they are no longer two, but one flesh. Therefore what God has joined together, let not man separate." In marriage a home is created.

A Christian home that is united and structured under God's plan is indeed a blessing for its parents and their children, and not only to themselves, but also to the local church and their community. Such homes that abide under God's design and plan are a haven of peace, calm, and security for rearing and guiding children to a wholesome life in the Lord. Godly homes bear and reflect the fruit of the Spirit: "love, joy, peace, longsuffering, kindness, goodness, faithfulness, gentleness, self-control. Against such there is no law" (Gal. 5:22-23). Such godly homes have love, respect, and appreciation for the members of the household. There is agreement, cooperation, and success in a home as God intended and expects. It is in such an ideal home that God would want his "heritage" to be raised. "Behold children are a heritage from the Lord" (Ps. 127:3).

Parents have an immense influence in shaping the lives of their offspring. They are their first figures of authority and first teachers. Mothers, especially in their early years, since they are around their children twenty-four hours a day, can have a significant influence. There is an old proverb that says, "The hand that rocks the cradle is the hand that rules the world." A mother's daily presence, protection, and affection are great comforts and security to the child. As tiny babes, mothers are their first instructors. We teach them nursery rhymes and their first spoken words. We are diligent to teach them the names of animals, colors, clothes, tools, and as they mature we teach them the alphabet, numbers, and how to read books.

Not only are we influential as teachers of our children, but our actions and our attitude that we exhibit also can have a great impact. Mothers and fathers impart volumes of unspoken lessons to their children by their be-havior and conduct. Sometimes we do not realize how much we say or do things until we see our children repeat it to others. What is our example or pattern of behavior? What can be said of our attitude? Our children are ob-serving and will model our behavior whether good or bad. In 1 Corinthians 11:1, the apostle Paul said, "Imitate me, just as I also imitate Christ." In Philippians 3:17, the apostle Paul writes, "Brethren, join in following my example, and note those who so walk, as you have us for a pattern." "Let us examine ourselves as to whether we are in the faith. Let us test ourselves" (2 Cor. 13:5). Are we serving God without hypocrisy? Are we serving God in a haphazard way? Are we giving our service and our worship to God in a half-hearted way? Are we going through the motions because others expect it of us? Our children see and observe and are not fooled. They will know if our commitment and loyalty to God are genuine. Our children know if Christ has priority in our life.

We, as parents, need to be careful as to how we behave and remember: "Whatever you do in word or deed, do all in the name of the Lord Jesus giving thanks to God the Father through Him" (Col. 3:17). The old saying of "do as I say, not as I do" is ineffective and hypocritical. Parents, the des-tination of you and your children's souls must be taken seriously. We need to be careful not to be negligent or careless of such a great and priceless treasure as our souls and the souls of our children. 1 Timothy 4:16 records a worthy principle: "Take heed to yourself and to the doctrine. Continue in them, for in doing this you will save both yourself and those who hear you." Be genuine, honest, true, consistent, and persistent when it comes to serving God and your children will take your example to heart.

As parents, we need to see to it that we are "running with endurance the race that is set before us, looking unto Jesus, the author and finisher of our faith" (Heb. 12:1-2). At the same time we should encourage our children to do likewise. We should strive to guide our children in life's journey of faith one step at a time, being careful not to cause them to stumble along the way. Are we assisting our children in keeping their "eyes on Jesus"? Are we teaching, disciplining, advising, counseling, warning, rebuking, and reprimanding our children through God's word and in his way (2 Tim. 3:16-17)? Are we preparing our children to make wise decisions in life? Are we helping them build a strong relationship with the Lord and to be ultimately accountable to him? Make every effort as parents to be united in God's word and to work in unison in the instruction, discipline, and preparation of your children to face life independent of you, but totally dependent on God as their spiritual father. Let us heed well to the Lord's commandment in Ephesians 6:4 which states, "And you, fathers, do not provoke your children to wrath, but bring them up in the training and admonition of the Lord." As parents let us be diligent to obey this commandment.

If your children are found in a united Christian home under God's direction, be thankful and grateful to God. Thank God for the spiritual, physical, emotional, and financial support that this environment provides for your family. James 1:17 reads, "Every good gift and every perfect gift is from above, and comes down from the Father of lights." If you and your spouse have created a united home, you have done well and your children will surely reap its rewards and you shall be blessed (Prov. 31:28).

In the Bible there are many examples of godly parents working together for the good of the children. One important example is Abraham and Sarah. In Hebrews 11:8-11 and verses 17-19, the Scriptures speak of their faith in God to perform as he had promised. In Genesis 18:19 God says of Abraham, "For I have chosen him, in order that he may command his children and his household after him to keep the way of the Lord by doing righteousness and justice." Another example is Amram and Jochebed who were not afraid of the king's command (Heb. 11:23), but took Moses and hid him and, after Pharaoh's daughter placed Moses under their care, they continued to teach him the Scriptures (Heb. 11:26). In the New Testament we read of Zacharias and Elizabeth, parents of John the Baptist, who were said to be righteous and blameless before the Lord (Luke 1:6). Time and space would prevent the listing of many biblical parents whose examples are to be emulated.

Raising Our Children in a Divided Home
We are all familiar with the statement, "United we stand; Divided we fall." In Luke 11:17 and Matthew 12:25, Christ laid down the foundation of that truth: "A house divided against itself will not stand." There are homes that are divided or destroyed by sin and its effects. There are households separated by religious beliefs, worldly living, or divorce even among Christian families. In these homes all the members of the household suffer. Tragically, the children suffer the most because they have little or no control of their family environment. Unfortunately the calamity of broken and divided homes seems to be a growing epidemic nationwide. It is depressing to see how many lives are affected by broken homes. Sadly, we see this trend growing in our communities, at our work place, and even in the local church.

There is a biblical example of a child raised in a religiously divided home and that is the young disciple Timothy. In Acts 16:1, we read of Timothy's mother being a Jewish woman and his father a Greek. While his mother and grandmother were believers, his father was not. While we do not know much of how this religious division affected their home, we know that as a babe, Timothy was not permitted to be circumcised which was a crucial condition of the Mosaic Law. However, Timothy, as a child, was still taught the Scriptures and in time was able to demonstrate a "sincere faith" which first dwelt in his grandmother Lois and his mother, Eunice (2 Tim. 1:5). In 2 Timothy 3:14-15, Paul exhorts:

> But you must continue in the things which you have learned and been assured of, knowing from whom you have learned them, and that from childhood you have known the Holy Scriptures, which are able to make you wise for salvation through faith which is in Christ Jesus.

We see that his training in the Scriptures upheld his faith in the gospel and the apostle Paul calls Timothy, "my true child in the faith" (1 Tim. 1:2). From the example of Timothy, Lois, and Eunice, we draw hope and encouragement not to give up.

My own children were raised in a religiously divided home. My former husband attended an institutional church and I attended a faithful, conservative church. He gave our children no choice in which congregation to attend. They had to go to the congregation of which he was a member. I too attended with him and our children for a period of time, rationalizing in my mind that it was better for us to be together. I would speak up against error that was taught and would not participate in unscriptural social events, but by my presence I was supporting error. In trying to keep peace in our household and to be submissive to my husband, I had ultimately compromised my beliefs and turned my back on Christ. The truth that one cannot be in fellowship with error rang through my conscience (2 John 9-11; 2 Cor. 6:14-18).

The time soon came when I could no longer justify being a member of an unscriptural church. I had to serve and worship God to the best of my ability because I would one day have to give an account of myself to him (2 Cor. 5:10). I could not in the Day of Judgment say, "My husband made me go to church with him." Excuses did not work for Adam or Eve and it surely would not work for me (Gen. 3:12-13). I left the institutional church of Christ and went alone to attend a faithful congregation.

I remember my eldest son, who was five years at the time, crying and being punished by his father because he wanted to attend church services with me. At another time he expressed his frustration and anger of the situation by saying to me, "When I grow up, I will not go to church." While this attitude would sadden and frighten me, I hoped and prayed that time would bring a better change in our family home life. The others were younger and could not articulate their thoughts well, but I could sense that they were confused and distressed by the situation. Trusting in the Scripture of Matthew 10:37: "He who loves father or mother more than Me is not worthy of Me. And he who loves son or daughter more than Me is not worthy of Me," and trusting in God to do what is right, I held to the hope that things would change and get better (Ps. 27:14).

Throughout these troublesome years, I tried to instill in my children the need to obey God's laws and instructions. While I could not control what they were being taught and practicing in the congregation they attended, I still would try to exert as much influence as possible. Eventually they would have to decide for themselves and chose to do what was right because God revealed the right thing to do, not because mom or dad said so. I wanted them to think for themselves as they studied God's word and then to be faithful to his word. In this way I wanted to impress upon them that they were accountable to God. In developing a relationship with God, in strengthening their love for their Creator and keeping their focus on Christ, they could endure anything in life—even the disappointing disintegration of their family relationships.

I believe my children are committed to the cause of Christ because they have had to experience many conflicts and struggles in their young lives. At a young age they experienced trials of life that I could not take away or shield them from. I would do my best to support them and encourage them. I would tell them that these trials of life would either make them stronger in the faith or break their faith. The choice was up to them. Thankfully, they chose to endure and mature in Christ.

I must also mention three other things that I believe helped in my children's spiritual development through all of these years. These are personal Bible studies, prayer, and encouragement received from faithful brethren as they came to hold gospel meetings. During this time my children heard many excellent sermons preached, participated in many good Bible studies, and observed many good examples of godly preachers as they worked with the Tacoma church. These lessons helped their spiritual development in the early years. Isaiah 55:11 declares: "So shall My word be that goes forth from My mouth; It shall not return to Me void, But it shall accomplish what I please, and it shall prosper in the thing for which I sent it." God's word always has an effect in a person's life. It could be a good and wholesome result or a destructive and condemning consequence. It is up to the hearer to choose, but choosing not to hear does not change its results. Therefore, as parents, make every effort to take your children to gospel meetings, debates, and to Bible studies conducted in your area. Much good will be achieved from such opportunities.

In addition, the countless prayers offered in their behalf (1 Thess. 5:17), both from myself and many faithful brethren (Jas. 5:17), cannot be overlooked. In 1 Peter 5:7 the apostle exhorts, "casting all your anxiety upon Him, because He cares for you." Prayers are the balm for the soul. Through prayer a mother's fears and thoughts are released to a Heavenly Father who is able to do what she cannot do by self-reliance (Phil. 4:6). Let us always remember to "Pray without ceasing" in all situations (2 Thess. 5:17).

In Remembering the Eternal Home

While our earthly home is not perfect, we teach our children that there is a perfect home awaiting all who love the Lord. As Christians, we must be diligent to enter this eternal home. Ecclesiastes 12:5 reads, "For man goes to his eternal home while mourners go about in the street." And again in Ecclesiastes 3:20, Solomon declares, "All go to one place: all are from the dust, and all return to dust." This is the end of all men. Hebrews 9:27 states, "And as it is appointed for men to die once, but after this the judgment." Since the Bible reveals that this earthly life is transitory and brief we would do well to seek and be found in the eternal home when this life is over. In John 14:2 Christ declares, "In My Father's house are many mansions . . . I go to prepare a place for you." This is the home that is promised to Christians who love and obey him. This is what all Christians look forward to when this short life is over: an eternal abode with an eternal Father.

The apostle Paul tells the brethren in Philippians 3:20, "For our citizenship is in heaven, from which also we eagerly wait for a Savior, the Lord Jesus Christ." We need to make every effort to enter into this home not made with hands (2 Cor. 5:1). In Luke 13:24, Christ urges us, "Strive to enter by the narrow door, for many, I tell you, will seek to enter and will not be able." How are we preparing our children, others, and ourselves for heaven? The choice has been given for us to make. The time to choose, to strive, to work is now while we have breath and life.

In order to reach this heavenly home we must teach our children to be diligent to study God's word (2 Tim. 2:15). While Bible classes in the local congregation are important and necessary, the home Bible study cannot be over emphasized. Even then it is very sad when those few hours of assembling with the saints are given up to school activities or recreation. What message are we giving to our children when we place secular activities over spiritual matters? We see the high priority of parents teaching children God's law in Psalms 78:5-8:

> For He established a testimony in Jacob, and appointed a law in Israel, which He commanded our fathers, That they should teach them to their children . . . That they may arise and tell them to their children, That they may set their confidence in God, And not forget the works of God, But keep His commandments . . .

And in Deuteronomy 6:6-7:

> And these words which I command you today shall be on your heart. You shall teach them diligently to your sons and shall talk of them when you sit in your house, when you walk by the way, when you lie down, and when you rise up.

These Scriptures demonstrate how important home studies are in the development of children. When they are babes we should teach them Bible characters and Bible stories, Bible songs and hymns, and how to pray. As teenagers we should ask them to read the Bible out loud to us and help them memorize Bible verses. As young adults we should take the time to study with them on doctrinal issues. We buy our children school supplies but are we willing to help provide resources for them such as new Bible translations, a concordance, commentaries, or whatever can aid in their biblical studies?

How about our time? Do we set time aside from our busy life for a Bible discussion? We all need to be careful, unless we weaken or lose our faith in this hurried life. Our world seems to get busier and busier each passing day. There are many activities in school programs, in community meetings and services, in recreational sports and camps, in television shows, in electronic gadgets, and in more working overtime in our secular jobs that it seems there is little or no time left for our families to be together. Yet we need to make every effort to find the time to study the Bible with our children until the time when they can come to see its value and study the Bible on their own.

We need to always remember that our life is short and temporary, and as we see how fast our children grow we realize just how short our time is with them. In James 4:14, the Bible says, "You are just a vapor that appears for a little while and then vanishes away." What manner of life should we be living in Christ and for Christ? Are we equipping our children for the life to come? We all want to go to this eternal home and be with Christ when this life is over, but are we working toward that end? Christ is preparing a place for you (John 14:2). He has given us many abundant blessings to use and to reflect his nature as his redeemed children. Are we being good stewards of his blessings? Are we using our time, our talents, our wealth, and our health for his glory? Remember there is nothing that we will take from this world but our souls and the "works" that follow us (Rev. 14:13).

Be resolved to save yourself and those who hear you (1 Tim. 4:16). If there is no one else but your family you can save, you have done well. Noah saved only his family from the worldwide destruction of the flood and Lot only saved some of his children from the destruction of Sodom and Gomorrah. "Seeing then that all these things shall be dissolved, what manner of persons ought ye to be in all holy conversation and godliness" (2 Pet. 3:11). Even when you as a parent have done everything in your power to instruct and discipline your children in the Lord, a child may still choose to rebel so as to be lost (Ezek. 18:10). The decision to follow Christ is ultimately a personal one. I can think of no greater happiness, pleasure, delight or comfort than to know that one's own children have chosen to commit their lives to Christ and his kingdom.

Conclusion

When they are on their own, we will see the wisdom in teaching and communicating well with our children while they were young and under our control. We need to firmly anchor them in Christ before they grow up and are influenced by their peers and the world. Soon they will be grown and on their own facing the world without your care or watchfulness. Have we prepared them adequately?

Any mother who has had children knows the strong bond that exists between mother and child. We can recall the joy of having in our arms a living, breathing babe. Our children did not have a choice in being born in this world nor did they choose their parents. We, as parents, took part in that decision. Along with the great joy and anticipation of having a child come the sober and serious obligations in raising the child for the Lord.

You are the first and most influential example and teacher. Teach your children the Scriptures well. There is no substitute for knowledge of God's word. Show them to support faithful gospel preaching and to encourage sound faithful brethren. Let them learn not to shy away from doctrinal controversy, but to be prepared for it (Jude 3). And, lastly, instruct them to stand firm in the truth (1 Cor. 16:13). In winning your children for Christ, you shall surely say as the apostle John said in 3 John 4, "I have no greater joy that this, to hear of my children walking in the truth."

Subjection of Women
Sandra Nite

There is much controversy in today's society over the roles of men and women in the home and in the church. But an examination of the Scriptures will allow us to clarify and define the roles as God designed them in the beginning until the end of time. First, we must acknowledge God's authority and his right to define those roles. If one does not believe in God or does not accept the Bible as his word, then he or she will not understand the purpose for the male and female genders or their roles. Unfortunately, there is controversy and division about the subject even among those who claim to believe in God and his word.

The mere fact that God is I AM (Exod. 3:14), the Almighty, all-powerful God (Rev. 4:8), should be sufficient proof that he has the right to dictate to man in all matters. In addition, as the Creator and giver of life (Gen. 1:1; Heb. 3:4), he understands us better than we understand ourselves. He has not left us to direct our own steps (Jer. 10:23), nor do we have the right to question his decisions and judgments (Rom. 11:34). God is the one who will judge man in the last day (2 Cor. 5:10), so it would be foolish to ignore his will.

Sandra Nite resides with her husband Michael in College Station, Texas. Michael, Sandra, and daughter Stephanie are members of the Twin City congregation in College Station. Sandra has taught Bible classes for various ages over the past thirty years. She has a Master of Science in Mathematics and a Master of Music in Music Education from Texas State University. She has taught high school and college level mathematics for the past thirty years. She served as Mathematics Coordinator at Sweeny High School for eight years and currently teaches mathematics at Texas A&M University. She is coauthor of a mathematics textbook, *Mathematical Modeling with Applications*, and a beginning piano book using the Kodály concept.

But From the Beginning It Hath Not Been So

And there came unto him Pharisees, trying him, and saying, Is it lawful for a man to put away his wife for every cause? And he answered and said, Have ye not read, that he who made them from the beginning made them male and female, and said, For this cause shall a man leave his father and mother, and shall cleave to his wife; and the two shall become one flesh? So that they are no more two, but one flesh. What therefore God hath joined together, let not man put asunder. They say unto him, Why then did Moses command to give a bill of divorcement, and to put her away? He saith unto them, Moses for your hardness of heart suffered you to put away your wives: but from the beginning it hath not been so (Matt. 19:3-8).

The phrase "but from the beginning it has not been so" is found in Matthew 19 as part of Jesus' response to the Pharisees' questions about the putting away of a spouse. He directs us to the creation and God's plan in the very beginning for an understanding of God's law regarding divorce. He implies that God's plan and his law regarding any subject can be better understood if we can attain an understanding of the plan God began unfolding at the very beginning of time when he created male and female. Implicit in his response is also the concept that God's purpose and plan for men and women has not and will not change over time. A close study of his purposes for us in the very beginning can help us today in trying to apply biblical passages regarding roles of men and women in the home and in the church. A study of some passages in Genesis and the creation is a good place for us to begin our study of God's plan for men and women from the beginning even until now.

It Is Not Good That Man Should Be Alone

And Jehovah God said, It is not good that the man should be alone; I will make him a help meet for him. And out of the ground Jehovah God formed every beast of the field, and every bird of the heavens; and brought them unto the man to see what he would call them: and whatsoever the man called every living creature, that was the name thereof. And the man gave names to all cattle, and to the birds of the heavens, and to every beast of the field; but for man there was not found a help meet for him. And Jehovah God caused a deep sleep to fall upon the man, and he slept; and he took one of his ribs, and closed up the flesh instead thereof: and the rib, which Jehovah God had taken from the man, made he a woman, and brought her unto the man. And the man said, This is now bone of my bones, and flesh of my flesh: she shall be called Woman, because she was taken out of Man. Therefore shall a man leave his father and his mother, and shall cleave unto his wife: and they shall be one flesh. And they were both naked, the man and his wife, and were not ashamed (Gen. 2:18-25).

There are several points to consider from this passage: (1) God says that man needed a helper suitable for him; (2) God brought all the animals for Adam to observe and name; (3) there was no suitable helper for man found among the animals; (4) God made a creature from one of Adam's ribs; (5) Adam named the creature Woman; and (6) Woman was deemed a suitable helper for man. These points are crucial to our study and understanding of God's plan for men and women today.

Submission is a Bible Theme
There is a hierarchy of submission and of responsibility in all relationships. Jesus willingly submitted to the Father's plan for our salvation. The Hebrew writer says of Christ in chapter 5, verses 8-9, ". . . though he was a Son, yet learned he obedience by the things which he suffered; and having been made perfect, he became unto all them that obey him the author of eternal salvation." In Philippians 2:8, Paul writes, ". . . and being found in fashion as a man, he humbled himself, becoming obedient even unto death, yea, the death of the cross." Jesus gave the perfect example of submission and obedience for us to follow.

God designates the head in many relationships. There are numerous commands given by both Paul and Peter in regard to submission to those in leadership positions. In 1 Corinthians 11:3 we read, "But I would have you know, that the head of every man is Christ; and the head of the woman is the man; and the head of Christ is God." In Ephesians, a parallel is drawn between the headship of Christ to the church and that of husband to wife.

> Wives, be in subjection unto your own husbands, as unto the Lord. For the husband is the head of the wife, and Christ also is the head of the church, being himself the saviour of the body. But as the church is subject to Christ, so let the wives also be to their husbands in everything (Eph. 5:22-24, ASV).

In Colossians 1:18 we read of Christ, "And he is the head of the body, the church: who is the beginning, the firstborn from the dead; that in all things he might have the preeminence." Members of the local congregation are to be in subjection to the elders, according to Hebrews 13:17, "Obey them that have the rule over you, and submit to them: for they watch in behalf of your souls, as they that shall give account; that they may do this with joy, and not with grief: for this were unprofitable for you." Christians are to subject themselves to the government, as described at some length by Paul in Romans 13:1-7. Peter wrote, "Be subject to every ordinance of man, for the Lord's sake: whether to the king, as supreme; or unto governors, as sent by him for vengeance on evil-doers and for praise to them that do well" (1 Pet. 2:13-14). Paul wrote to Titus, "Put them in mind to be in subjection to rulers, to authorities, to be obedient, to be ready unto every good work, to speak evil of no man, not to be contentious, to be gentle, showing all meekness toward all men" (Tit. 3:1-2). Slaves are to be in subjection to their masters, "Servants, be in subjection to your masters with all fear; not only to the good and gentle, but also to the froward" (1 Pet. 2:18). Paul also instructs slaves to be submissive to their masters, "Exhort servants to be in subjection to their own masters, and to be well-pleasing to them in all things; not gainsaying; not purloining, but showing all good fidelity; that they may adorn the doctrine of God our Saviour in all things" (Tit. 2:9-10). The same instructions are given in Ephesians 6:5, Colossians 3:22, and 1 Timothy 6:1. Children are in subjection to parents, "Children, obey your parents in all things, for this is well-pleasing in the Lord" (Col. 3:20; see also Eph. 6:1-3).

An understanding of the theme of subjection throughout the Bible according to the position of an individual helps clarify Paul's statement that "there can be neither Jew nor Greek, there can be neither bond nor free, there can be no male and female; for ye all are one man in Christ Jesus" (Gal. 3:28). Some have misunderstood this passage to mean there is no order of subjection, but in light of the clear passages we have studied regarding subjection and leadership, it is evident that this is not the case. A closer study of the context of the passage reveals that the idea that all are equal in terms of availability of salvation and importance in God's eyes is the better interpretation. Another verse sometimes misinterpreted is Ephesians 5:21, ". . . subjecting yourselves one to another in the fear of Christ." Some claim the verse means that men must also subject themselves to women. However, there is no Scripture anywhere to bear that out. Immediately after that verse, Paul goes on to specify that women are to be in subjection to men. Again, the interpretation that fits the clear passages we have already considered is that Christians are to subject themselves to one another as befitting their roles. It is true, in some sense, that Christians can all submit to one another by serving one another. But the passage in Ephesians 5 discusses leadership roles and submission to those in leadership.

Man Is Designated Head of Woman

In God's plan throughout the Bible, preeminence is a recurring theme. In the Old Testament, the firstborn in families received the greater inheritance as a birthright (Deut. 21:15-17). The New Testament teaches about Jesus' being the firstborn from the dead and what that implies (Col. 1:18). Likewise, God gives as one of the reasons for man's headship or leadership the fact that he was created first. Paul writes in 1 Timothy 2:12-13, "But I permit not a woman to teach, nor to have dominion over a man, but to be in quietness. For Adam was first formed, then Eve." A second reason is given in verse 14, "and Adam was not beguiled, but the woman being beguiled hath fallen into transgression." If God had given no reason for his choice of leader, we would still have no right to question or change it. However, by giving the reasons, he shows us that the reasons are not culturally dictated but rooted in the very beginning of time when he created us. We know, then, that his choice is not for a particular age or time or culture but for all men in all places for all time. There is nothing in the Scriptures that gives any indication that God considers the second-born inferior, nor is there any indication that he considers women inferior mentally, morally, or spiritually. He does, however, designate man as the leader in the home (Eph. 5:23-24; 1 Pet. 3:1, 5-6) and the church (1 Tim. 2:11-14) under Christ and God.

> But I would have you know, that the head of every man is Christ; and the head of the woman is the man; and the head of Christ is God (1 Cor. 11:3).

The role of leader carries with it a responsibility and accountability. After Adam and Eve sinned and hid in the garden, God called for Adam, "And Jehovah God called unto the man, and said unto him, Where art thou?" He knew that Eve had sinned first and Adam had followed, but he questioned Adam first. The man is given the responsibility to lead and to love with a sacrificial love, in a similar relationship to Christ and the church. He is to honor his wife as the weaker vessel or body (1 Pet. 3:7). He is to cherish her (1 Pet. 3:19), value her, and esteem her. There is much more that could be said about man's responsibility, but our discussion here centers on the woman. A woman's responsibility is made much easier by a leader who follows Jesus' example, but she is responsible to God's law whether or not he leads appropriately.

Woman Is Designated Follower

In like manner, ye wives, be in subjection to your own husbands; that, even if any obey not the word, they may without the word be gained by the behavior of their wives; beholding your chaste behavior coupled with fear. Whose adorning let it not be the outward adorning of braiding the hair, and of wearing jewels of gold, or of putting on apparel; but let it be the hidden man of the heart, in the incorruptible apparel of a meek and quiet spirit, which is in the sight of God of great price. For after this manner aforetime the holy women also, who hoped in God, adorned themselves, being in subjection to their own husbands: as Sarah obeyed Abraham, calling him lord: whose children ye now are, if ye do well, and are not put in fear by any terror (1 Pet. 3:1-6).

Peter, by the inspiration of the Holy Spirit, instructs women in regard to their actions and demeanor. Actually, the two are tied together because a submissive and quiet character is the root of the behavior described in this passage. A woman should dress herself in a becoming way, not drawing undue attention to herself, and she should respect her husband and his position in the home. She remains strong in her convictions to obey the word of the Lord, even if her husband is not a Christian. By her submissive attitude she may be able to influence him to become obedient to Christ.

Wives, be in subjection unto your own husbands, as unto the Lord. For the husband is the head of the wife, and Christ also is the head of the church, being himself the saviour of the body. But as the church is subject to Christ, so let the wives also be to their husbands in everything. Nevertheless do ye also severally love each one his own wife even as himself; and let the wife see that she fear her husband (Eph. 5:22-24, 33).

In his letter to the Ephesians, Paul gives the same instruction to women as Peter did. They are to be in subjection to their husbands and to be respectful to him. For those who would try to minimize the teaching in 1 Peter, this passage emphasizes the instruction by comparing the relationship of Christ and the church to the relationship between husband and wife in regard to headship and submission.

. . . that aged women likewise be reverent in demeanor, not slanderers nor enslaved to much wine, teachers of that which is good; that they may train the young women to love their husbands, to love their children, *to be* sober-minded, chaste, workers at home, kind, being in subjection to their own husbands, that the word of God be not blasphemed (Tit. 2:3-5).

Again, in Paul's letter to Titus, instruction to women includes the command to be in subjection to their husbands. Paul here adds that improper demeanor and behavior of women would cause the word of God to be blasphemed, emphasizing the importance of following God's plan for women. Although they are in subjection to husbands, women are not slaves. God made woman as a helper suitable for man, not a slave for him. Husband and wife should work together to plan for the home and to solve problems, but she must defer to his leadership. The wife often has insight or areas of expertise which the husband does not have. She can offer advice and make suggestions about a variety of matters. A discerning husband will use his wife's special abilities as his helper rather than lording it over her and making decisions arbitrarily simply because he has the right to do so. The husband will often give the wife certain duties to fulfill as his helper. As the head, he has the right to put her in charge of handling financial affairs (preparing a budget for his consideration, selecting and purchasing items, paying bills). He is still the head and can oversee these activities as he chooses. If women and men both understand God's plan for providing a leader for the woman and a helper for the man, they can work together in a harmonious way for the benefit of all in the home.

The fact that there are so many passages that speak of the leadership of the man and the subjection of the woman makes it impossible for individuals to ignore the teaching as if it did not exist. Too often, self importance gets in the way of listening to and following God's plan. Men sometimes want to make sure everyone knows they are in charge, so they are condescending and harsh to the woman God has given as a helper. Perhaps this is why Paul writes, "Husbands, love your wives, and be not bitter against them" (Col. 3:19). Women sometimes think that submitting makes them inferior, so they want everyone to know that the man is not the boss to tell her every little thing she must do. When that happens, God's plan for the roles of men and women does not work effectively. Those who do not want to follow God's word must find some way to discount it. They may try to use the verses in Galatians 3:28 and Ephesians 5:21 as was mentioned above. They use human reasoning to declare that women are as smart as men, and some are as strong as men; therefore, God could not have intended her to be in subjection throughout time. If we understand the concepts behind God's commands, we can apply them better and recognize the traps set by those who refuse to submit to God as our Creator. Two important concepts regarding men and women and their roles are (1) God's choice of man for leader was rooted in the very creation, not in which one is more or less intelligent; and (2) Headship does not infer superiority. Jesus is equal with the Father, and he willingly submitted to the Father. If we can remember those concepts as we apply the passages regarding the roles of men and women, we will have less difficulty following God's plan.

Not only are women to be in subjection to their husbands at home, but they are to be submissive to the leadership of the men in the church. Women are instructed to keep silence in the church.

> As in all the churches of the saints, let the women keep silence in the churches: for it is not permitted unto them to speak; but let them be in subjection, as also saith the law. And if they would learn anything, let them ask their own husbands at home: for it is shameful for a woman to speak in the church (1 Cor. 14:34-35).

Paul gives similar instruction in his letter to Timothy, "Let a woman learn in quietness with all subjection. But I permit not a woman to teach, nor to have dominion over a man, but to be in quietness" (1 Tim. 2:11-12). When we understand the concepts we have discussed about the headship of the man, it is not hard to understand this application of that principle.

Women Are To Be Keepers at Home
Although woman is not the leader in the home, she has been given a very important role. We will look at passages which give her direct instructions and those which give approved examples to follow.

> But speak thou the things which befit the sound doctrine: that aged men be temperate, grave, sober-minded, sound in faith, in love, in patience: that aged women likewise be reverent in demeanor, not slanderers nor enslaved to much wine, teachers of that which is good; that they may train the young women to love their husbands, to love their children, to be sober-minded, chaste, workers at home, kind, being in subjection to their own husbands, that the word of God be not blasphemed: the younger men likewise exhort to be sober-minded: in all things showing thyself an ensample of good works; in thy doctrine showing uncorruptness, gravity, sound speech, that cannot be condemned; that he that is of the contrary part may be ashamed, having no evil thing to say of us (Tit. 2:1-8).

In Paul's letter to Titus, instruction is given to different ages and genders. The women are to be respectful in demeanor and to be in subjection to their husbands. Women are also commanded to be workers at home. Their primary responsibility is to keep the home. They are to be in charge of the household, under the direction of the husband. Paul says, "I desire therefore that the younger widows marry, bear children, rule the household, give no occasion to the adversary for reviling: for already some are turned aside after Satan" (1 Tim. 5:14-15). Notice the work that was done by the worthy woman of Proverbs 31.

A worthy woman who can find? For her price is far above rubies. The heart of her husband trusteth in her, and he shall have no lack of gain. She doeth him good and not evil all the days of her life. She seeketh wool and flax, and worketh willingly with her hands. She is like the merchant-ships; she bringeth her bread from afar. She riseth also while it is yet night, and giveth food to her household, and their task to her maidens. She considereth a field, and buyeth it; with the fruit of her hands she planteth a vineyard. She girdeth her loins with strength, and maketh strong her arms. She perceiveth that her merchandise is profitable: her lamp goeth not out by night. She layeth her hands to the distaff, and her hands hold the spindle. She stretcheth out her hand to the poor; yea, she reacheth forth her hands to the needy. She is not afraid of the snow for her household; for all her household are clothed with scarlet. She maketh for herself carpets of tapestry; her clothing is fine linen and purple. Her husband is known in the gates, when he sitteth among the elders of the land. She maketh linen garments and selleth them, and delivereth girdles unto the merchant. Strength and dignity are her clothing; and she laugheth at the time to come. She openeth her mouth with wisdom; and the law of kindness is on her tongue. She looketh well to the ways of her household, and eateth not the bread of idleness. Her children rise up, and call her blessed; her husband also, and he praiseth her, saying: Many daughters have done worthily, but thou excellest them all. Grace is deceitful, and beauty is vain; but a woman that feareth Jehovah, she shall be praised (Prov. 31:10-31).

She is trustworthy; she can be trusted to be faithful to her vows and to carry on the affairs of the home. She makes sure her household has the necessary food and proper clothing for the winter. She rises early and works late to provide for their needs. Although many women today do not sew and preserve food because clothing and food are readily available to buy, they are still responsible to see to the needs of the household for food and clothing. The worthy woman is financially responsible. She should have the skills necessary and the willingness to work to prepare healthy food for the family. She needs some knowledge of nutrition to see to those needs. She needs to be able to cook tasty, healthy food. Even though there are frozen dinners and prepared foods readily available today, very few have either the good taste or the nutrition of food the wife can prepare at home. Scientists have found that the preservatives used in many foods today are not healthy in large quantities and should not be consumed on a daily basis. The wife and mother needs some mending skills to make the best use of the clothing her family owns rather than having to throw it away for a small tear. At times when modest clothing is not readily available in the stores, she needs sewing skills or the means to purchase appropriate clothing. The fact that fashions of the time are not modest is not an excuse for Christians to dress immodestly. The wife is responsible to see that she and the children have appropriate clothing. The worthy woman places the interests of her husband and children ahead of her own. She is supportive and unselfish with her husband's time. She watches after her children. She "worketh willingly with her hands." Although she is not the family breadwinner, she finds ways to supplement and stretch the family income. She is hardworking and organized. She is well prepared for the future. She trusts in God. She is compassionate, sympathetic, and concerned for the needy. Her speech manifests her kindness. She dresses becomingly, and her clothing reflects her character and self-respect. She has the respect of her children and praise of her husband. Her beauty is one that is not skin-deep.

Although we live in a different age, the principles from the passage in Proverbs have not changed. A modern-day rendition of the passage in Proverbs might look like this:

> A worthy woman who can find? For her price is far above rubies. The heart of her husband trusts in her, and he shall not come to poverty because of her extravagant spending. She does good and not evil to him all the days of her life. She purchases materials and works willingly with her hands to provide items for the household. She searches for the best quality, economically priced merchandise for her family. She rises early to prepare food for her household, and lay out her tasks for the day. She plants a garden to provide fresh produce for her family. She works hard to keep her body strong in the service of her family. She works late at night to provide for her family. She mends and sews clothing for her family. She economizes so that she has means to give to the poor and needy. She makes sure her family is well-clothed and warm for the winter. She sews becoming clothing for herself and adorns her home with items she has crafted. Her husband is well known in the community. She supplements the family income as needed, through her industriousness. Strength and dignity are her clothing; and she has prepared well for her family's future. She speaks wisely and kindly to all with whom she comes in contact. She takes care of her family well and fills her time with useful endeavors. Her children and husband respect and love her. Her husband says, "You are

the best wife a man could have and a wonderful mother to our children."
Grace is deceitful, and beauty is vain; but a woman that fears Jehovah
shall be praised.

Today's worthy woman may not necessarily provide all the homemade
items or have the space to plant a garden, but she still works hard to economically provide all that her family needs. It is still useful today to have
homemaking skills because society does not always readily provide what the
Christian needs, especially in the area of modest and appropriate clothing.
The examples of the worthy woman in Proverbs 31 and of Lydia, the seller
of purple, in Acts 16:14 show that women may work outside the home. But
they must be very careful that they take care of the work at home first and
foremost, since that is the primary responsibility God has given them.

Women Are To Be Teachers
God instructed the Israelites to teach their children continually about
God's law.

Hear, O Israel: Jehovah our God is one Jehovah: and thou shalt love Jehovah thy God with all thy heart, and with all thy soul, and with all thy
might. And these words, which I command thee this day, shall be upon
thy heart; and thou shalt teach them diligently unto thy children, and shalt
talk of them when thou sittest in thy house, and when thou walkest by
the way, and when thou liest down, and when thou risest up. And thou
shalt bind them for a sign upon thy hand, and they shall be for frontlets
between thine eyes. And thou shalt write them upon the door-posts of thy
house, and upon thy gates (Deut. 6:4-9).

God made physical promises to them about the land they were to possess,
if they would keep his commandments and teach their children to do so. He
reiterates these instructions in Deuteronomy 11:18-23. He has made spiritual
promises to us if we keep his commandments. In the New Testament the father is specifically given the responsibility to see that his children are taught
properly (Eph. 6:4), and much of the teaching is done by the mother.

We are all aware of the tremendous influence a mother has on her children. Even mothers who spend relatively little time with their children
wield great influence, usually to their detriment. Paul credits Timothy's
mother and grandmother for teaching and providing an example, "having
been reminded of the unfeigned faith that is in thee; which dwelt first in
thy grandmother, Lois, and thy mother Eunice; and, I am persuaded, in

thee also" (2 Tim. 1:5). Later in the chapter, Paul comments, "that from a babe thou hast known the sacred writings which are able to make thee wise unto salvation through faith which is in Christ Jesus" (2 Tim. 3:15). Timothy's father was a Greek, but his mother and grandmother made sure he was well grounded in the Scriptures. Mothers and grandmothers today can be an influence for good in the lives of their children and grandchildren by their example and teaching. Mothers should begin early to teach their sons about the role they will have as adult men. The father should also be involved in the teaching and should provide the good example for his sons. Mothers should teach their daughters the Scriptures, but they should also spend time teaching their daughters the homemaking skills they will need in order to be workers at home when they have a family. Although it is not wrong for girls to obtain education, and it may even be necessary for them to support themselves, mothers should emphasize the qualities that God wants them to have as wives and mothers. They should spend time teaching them nutrition, cooking, sewing, and craft skills that they can use in the home. Daughters can take pride in helping around the house, and fathers can commend them for the work they do in preparation for ruling their own households some day.

Grandmothers can also work with granddaughters to teach them about the Bible and teach them homemaking skills. There is a special bond between grandparents and grandchildren that can be used to full advantage in teaching godly principles and applications. They can enjoy time together learning to bake or create crafty items for the home. Sometimes other ladies in the congregation enjoy working with girls, teaching them to crochet or knit or do other handwork. Although every wife and mother does not have to have all these skills, it is good for the girls to learn some of them and experience the joy and accomplishment that comes from being able to provide something special for their home. It tends to ground them more in the home and help them take pride in their work as keepers of the home, especially in a time when many in society would scoff and denigrate them for wanting to fulfill God's pattern for them. Grandmothers often have more time and patience to teach their grandchildren about the Bible. By reason of age, they tire more quickly and will not easily be able to take over the parents' job. But they enjoy their grandchildren and can build some very special bonds by spending time studying the Bible with them. Some grandmothers will keep the grandchildren for a time in the summer and devote an entire week to a study of the Scriptures. As the grandchildren grow older, they will retain a close relationship with the grandmother. They have someone in addition to the parents to whom they can feel free to come for advice. Grandmothers are perfectly suited for this role because they have years of experience beyond even the parents. As the grandchildren mature, they will realize the value of the teaching and time so generously given, and perhaps they will follow the example set by the grandmother when their time is come.

There are several passages that tell us that women are to be teachers. Their role in that capacity is clearly defined by Scripture. Paul tells Titus that older women are be "teachers of that which is good; that they may train the young women to love their husbands, to love their children, to be sober-minded, chaste, workers at home, kind, being in subjection to their own husbands, that the word of God be not blasphemed" (Tit. 2:4-5).

> In like manner, that women adorn themselves in modest apparel, with shamefastness and sobriety; not with braided hair, and gold or pearls or costly raiment; but (which becometh women professing godliness) through good works. Let a woman learn in quietness with all subjection. But I permit not a woman to teach, nor to have dominion over a man, but to be in quietness. (1 Tim. 2:9-12)

The instructions about how to dress and what demeanor women should possess fits well with her attitude of submission. The demeanor of shamefastness and quietness affects the way a woman acts and dresses. Some would contend that this passage forbids women from teaching at all, but we know this is not the case from other clear passages. When the church at Jerusalem was scattered, as recorded in Acts 8, they taught the gospel wherever they went. We know that Priscilla worked with her husband, Aquila, in teaching Apollos more perfectly (Acts 18:26). A woman can help teach a man if she does it without teaching over or having dominion over a man. If Paul were saying that a woman is not permitted to teach at all, he would be contradicting his own writing in Titus 2:3-4 in which he instructs older women to teach the younger women. 1 Timothy 2:11-12 must be interpreted in harmony with the clear instructions in Titus 2:3-4. The necessary inference is that the woman is not to (1) teach over a man, nor (2) have dominion over a man. Women are responsible to teach in any capacity that does not violate that principle. To further clarify that principle, Paul instructs,

> . . . As in all the churches of the saints, let the women keep silence in the churches: for it is not permitted unto them to speak; but let them be in subjection, as also saith the law. And if they would learn anything, let

them ask their own husbands at home: for it is shameful for a woman to speak in the church (1 Cor. 14:33-35).

Women Today Have a Challenge to Meet

The culture in which we live is very worldly-minded, filled with people selfishly seeking their own pleasures. It is so easy for us to become "fashioned according to this world" and to forget our goal to be "transformed by the renewing of your mind, that ye may prove what is the good and acceptable and perfect will of God" (Rom. 12:2). We face challenges dealing with the effect the feminist movement has had on our society. Although it seems natural that women and men should receive equal pay for the same quality job, that is not really the agenda of the movement. That is only a small legitimate part of a very invasive, destructive way of thinking leading to the complete denigration and dissolution of the home as it was designed by God. Christian women are challenged as we work for respect in our world to stay within God's plan. The principles of Exodus 23:2 are valid instructions for us today: "Thou shalt not follow a multitude to do evil; neither shalt thou speak in a cause to turn aside after a multitude to wrest justice." Solomon's observation fits our world today as well as it did the world of his time when he wrote, "Behold, this only have I found: that God made man upright; but they have sought out many inventions" (Eccl. 7:29). As we strive today to live in the world, but not to be of the world, we must heed John's words,

> Love not the world, neither the things that are in the world. If any man love the world, the love of the Father is not in him. For all that is in the world, the lust of the flesh and the lust of the eyes and the vainglory of life, is not of the Father, but is of the world. And the world passeth away, and the lust thereof: but he that doeth the will of God abideth forever (1 John 2:15-17).

Women today need to be discerning of the philosophies put forth in our society. Many seem to be innocent on the surface, and perhaps even beneficial, but after closer inspection we find that they will lead us farther and farther from God and his word. The feminist movement is just one of these. We must be aware of these and learn to become women "who by reason of use have their senses exercised to discern good and evil" (Heb. 5:14). We must teach our children and grandchildren to discern good and evil and not be deceived by a society of which the following can be said:

> Woe unto them that call evil good, and good evil; that put darkness for light, and light for darkness; that put bitter for sweet, and sweet for bitter!

Woe unto them that are wise in their own eyes, and prudent in their own sight! (Isa. 5:20-21)

Some women today are challenged to live with husbands who are immature, irresponsible, or abusive. Extra care must be taken to deal with these men in a godly manner, hoping and praying for the day they will follow God's plan for them individually and in their relationships in the family. Women can cultivate the husband's faith and sense of responsibility by encouraging him to lead the family in prayer and Bible study and praising and encouraging his efforts to participate in activities of the local congregation. In 1 Samuel 25 we read of a woman who had to deal with a husband the Bible calls "churlish and evil in his doings" (v. 3). Abigail faced and dealt with the challenge of avoiding her husband's wrath and doing what was right. She acted in a way that benefitted him in spite of his attitude. Women today who face similar challenges can read and reread that story for encouragement to continue to do right. Women who deal with men who are abusive in attitude, word, and deed can derive benefit from the instruction given in Matthew 5:43-48 dealing with loving enemies. The abusive husband is an enemy to his wife no matter how much he declares his love. Paul's letter to the Romans includes instructions that can be very helpful in this situation as in many others.

Render to no man evil for evil. Take thought for things honorable in the sight of all men. If it be possible, as much as in you lieth, be at peace with all men. Avenge not yourselves, beloved, but give place unto the wrath of God: for it is written, Vengeance belongeth unto me; I will recompense, saith the lord. But if thine enemy hunger, feed him; if he thirst, give him to drink: for in so doing thou shalt heap coals of fire upon his head. Be not overcome of evil, but overcome evil with good (Rom. 12:17-21).

If a husband is physically abusive, subjection does not include providing cover stories for bruises or ignoring the duties of self-preservation and protection for the children. In that case, help should be sought from mature brethren, qualified counselors, medical services, and civil authorities as necessary to protect the wife and children.

Both men and women will grow in character and in the Christian graces as they learn to be in subjection to God and to others according to God's plan. Learning to submit as God instructs will help control the selfish, stubborn will that is at the root of our disobedience to God.

Yea, and for this very cause adding on your part all diligence, in your faith supply virtue; and in your virtue knowledge; and in your knowledge self-control; and in your self-control patience; and in your patience godliness; and in your godliness brotherly kindness; and in your brotherly kindness love. For if these things are yours and abound, they make you to be not idle nor unfruitful unto the knowledge of our Lord Jesus Christ. For he that lacketh these things is blind, seeing only what is near, having forgotten the cleansing from his old sins. Wherefore, brethren, give the more diligence to make your calling and election sure: for if ye do these things, ye shall never stumble: for thus shall be richly supplied unto you the entrance into the eternal kingdom of our Lord and Saviour Jesus Christ (2 Pet. 1:5-11).

As we meet the challenge to make godly subjection a central part of our feminine character, we become better people, better wives, better mothers, and better Christians. As we live so as to make our lives a blessing to our husband and to others, we ourselves will be enriched with the blessings of God for time and eternity.

Overcoming An Abusive Parent

Sandra C. Willis

Godly Fathers

Fathers are told, "And, ye fathers, provoke not your children to wrath: but bring them up in the nurture and admonition of the Lord" (Eph. 6:4). The Old Testament Law said, "Only take heed to thyself, and keep thy soul diligently, lest thou forget the things which thine eyes have seen, and lest they depart from thy heart all the days of thy life: but teach them thy sons, and thy sons' sons" (Deut. 4:9).

There are many blessings of a good father: He loves you, cares for you, and protects you. Unfortunately, not all children grow up in homes with fathers like this. I knew of fathers like this only by seeing other people's fathers. My cousin was very close to her dad. She adored him and he was so good to her. I felt like a child looking into a toy store window—seeing all of the wonderful joys a happy home and family could bring and knowing in reality that I would never be able to have this in my family. Thankfully, my husband is that kind of father to my children. They ran to meet him when he came home; they couldn't wait to be with him. He is truly everything a father needs to be to his children.

Sandra C. (Parson) Willis was born December 20, 1947 to Earl and Pauline Parson. She was the oldest of four children. She attended Florida College in 1965-66 where she met and married Mike Willis in June 1966. They have two children, Jennifer Lynette Mann and Corey Michael Willis. She is blessed to have four wonderful grandchildren who are the loves of her life.

Dad always worked very hard to provide for us and we never lacked any necessities. He had a strong sense of right and wrong, especially about telling the truth. He had been brought up in the church but never attended much after he became an adult. His parents were the ones who taught me about the Bible, about Bible characters and Bible facts.

But my relationship with my father was not a good one. Dad had an uncontrolled, violent temper. He seemed angry all of the time. I never wanted to be near him. You could be in trouble and the object of his wrath and have no idea why. Even a wrong look would be enough to set him off. As I said of my husband, when Daddy came home, my children would run from every corner of the house to see Dad, expecting a hug. When my dad came home, it was just the opposite. We may have been laughing and having fun, but when we heard him drive up, everyone scattered away from his presence, away from his sight.

Discipline
The Bible teaches the need for disciple in such passages as the following:

He that spareth his rod hateth his son: but he that loveth him chasteneth him betimes (Prov. 13:24).

Chasten thy son while there is hope, and let not thy soul spare for his crying (Prov. 19:18).

Train up a child in the way he should go: and when he is old, he will not depart from it (Prov. 22:6).

And ye have forgotten the exhortation which speaketh unto you as unto children, My son, despise not thou the chastening of the Lord, nor faint when thou art rebuked of him: For whom the Lord loveth he chasteneth, and scourgeth every son whom he receiveth. If ye endure chastening, God dealeth with you as with sons; for what son is he whom the father chasteneth not? But if ye be without chastisement, whereof all are partakers, then are ye bastards, and not sons. Furthermore we have had fathers of our flesh which corrected us, and we gave them reverence: shall we not much rather be in subjection unto the Father of spirits, and live? For they verily for a few days chastened us after their own pleasure; but he for our profit, that we might be partakers of his holiness. Now no chastening for the present seemeth to be joyous, but grievous: nevertheless afterward it yieldeth the peaceable fruit of righteousness unto them which are exercised thereby (Heb. 12:5-11).

The Bible even warns about the danger of parents exercising the wrong kind of discipline, saying:

> And, ye fathers, provoke not your children to wrath: but bring them up in the nurture and admonition of the Lord (Eph. 6:4).

> Fathers, provoke not your children to anger, lest they be discouraged (Col. 3:21).

A father who abuses his family, using as his defense that he is "disciplining" them, misunderstands what the Bible teaches about discipline.

My father's discipline provoked in me a deep-seated anger. When Dad "disciplined," he *hit* in anger—with a slap, a slug, or a push. It was violent. He disciplined with brute force. This is how he "ruled" our home, with domination which created fear. I couldn't imagine what a loving father was like, but I knew it wasn't this.

I know that in the eighteen years I lived in my home there had to have been good times and happy times. But unless they were with other people outside my home, I really do not remember them or if Dad was present for them. I am not saying they did not exist. I just don't remember them! Maybe that is another result of abuse—that it blocks out all of the pleasant memories and leaves your memory full of hurt and nightmares.

Examples of Abuse

I am going to mention several examples of what our home life was like to show you that I am not talking about normal discipline. I do not tell you these things to get your sympathy, but only to try to help you understand what our home was like.

I remember a time when Dad got angry at me and shoved me hard up against a piece of furniture. I was in junior high school and went to gym with a bruise on my side from my waist to my knee. When I was asked what happened, I made up a lie. There was no way that I could have told the truth. I don't know what Dad would have done if I had told school authorities what happened.

Another incident which I vividly remember happened on a night when we had company. We had a dog that, for some reason, Dad had tied on the porch. The dog didn't like to be tied up and barked that night. Dad went out, mad at the dog because of the barking, and kicked him; I am sure that it was repeated kicking, not just one time. The next night when we came home, there lay my dog—dead! I don't think my dad said anything, at least if he did, I don't remember it. You can imagine how devastating that was to a child.

Another vivid memory I have occurred when my mom was about seven months pregnant with one of my brothers. I was awakened one morning by Dad yelling at her. The next thing I knew, he came in the bedroom and grabbed my brother and left with him in the car. I suspect that I pretended to be asleep. When he was gone, I went to check on my mom. She was doubled over because he had hit her in the side with his fist. I ran down the road to get my Papaw. They took Mom to the hospital. She was okay and did deliver a healthy boy at the proper time. I need to tell you that my father had been drinking when most of these incidents happened. He was abusive without liquor, but with liquor, he was even worse.

These incidents happened before I was fourteen years old. At the age of fourteen, I obeyed the gospel. We were having a gospel meeting and I went forward to be baptized. I was surprised to see my mom and dad who were also present at the meeting come forward to be baptized too. I never will forget that night. We came home and, as I laid my head on the pillow, I knew that life would be different now.

The physical abuse was over, as much as I can remember, but the verbal abuse continued. Dad made me feel that he never thought I would amount to anything, that somehow I would embarrass him. I never felt that he cared for what it would do to me, only that I would embarrass him. Later I realized that he didn't mean to be that way. He wanted me to be a good person. Dad died of heart failure when I was nineteen. It is so ironic that I became everything and more than he wanted for me. But *not* because of anything he did, but *in spite* of what he did. Somehow through all of it, I developed a love of the Lord and trust in him. I wanted to be a faithful Christian and obey what the Lord would want me to do.

Results of Abuse
Dad died about a year after I married and left home. We never made peace with what happened between us. I don't remember Dad ever saying

he was sorry. Sometimes the morning after he had been drunk and gone on one of his tirades, he would say he was sorry but when the actions never changed, "I'm sorry" didn't mean anything.

But now Dad was dead. It was over. All of those years of sadness and fear were gone. I was free! Oh, how wrong I was! The abuse left many scars that would take years to heal. And some of the scars are still there.

1. Anger and resentment. Dad was gone but my bitterness was not. Hate was still inside of me. The fact that he was physically gone didn't end my feelings. I asked, "Why me?" I was the victim. I didn't get to chose which family I was born into. Why did he have to be my father? Why didn't someone do something to stop his abuse? Where was my mom? Why didn't she protect me from his abuse?

My mom chose my dad but her choice affected not only her, but every member of the family. Parents do have a responsibility to protect their children from harm, if possible. But, in her defense, I must say that things are different today than they were in the 1950s and 1960s. There were no agencies one could go to for help like there are today. Even if there were, I am sure she would have been too afraid to seek out help. With Daddy, it was all about control and fear. What he said and wanted was all that mattered. I never talked about his abuse to anyone. I guess I also felt that no one could do anything to change our circumstances.

My anger also included the fact that I had been cheated out of my childhood—that time of life when one can be carefree and happy. I carried around in my heart a heaviness that didn't seem to allow this joy. You are young only once in life and you cannot go back and do it over. Maybe that is where my fun-loving spirit comes from—trying to re-capture the *lost* years of my youth.

I also felt anger and resentment when I started to work on these attitudes that were "destroying" my life. If any of you has been in any counseling program, you know that it can be beneficial, but it is also very difficult and down right hard work. Again I felt, "I am the victim. I didn't cause this. Why do I have to face the struggle and do the work that it takes to overcome it?"

2. Low self-esteem. Another area with which I struggled was how I felt about myself. Dad was verbally abusive and made me feel that I would never amount to anything. How I felt about Dad made me feel less about myself too. Paul wrote, "Children, obey your parents in the Lord: for this is right. Honour thy father and mother; (which is the first commandment with promise)" (Eph. 6:1-2). These verses created a conflict in me because I hated my father and I didn't respect him. My conscience hurt me. I knew that I couldn't please God and have these feelings about my dad. I remembered before his death, praying regularly that he would die. I wanted him out of our lives so that he couldn't hurt us anymore. (How I would be devastated if my children felt that way about me.) I don't know if he even knew how I felt about him. But my conscience did eat at me for my attitudes toward my father. How could I ever be what God wanted me to be? How could I be an example of a godly woman?

Later when I was married, Mike started preaching. Now I was a "preacher's wife." I felt very inferior to other Christians. I didn't come from one of those "perfect Christian homes." Now I realize that this is a myth. There are no perfect homes. All families have problems and challenges. I think things have changed now and Christians share their problems enough so that we have the knowledge that others have problems and work to overcome them, the same as we do. We do our children a disservice when we give them an unrealistic view of life and don't teach them that families and marriages have problems.

3. Marital problems. As a result of my unhappiness at home, I jumped prematurely into a marriage at eighteen years old. Not many are prepared for marriage at that age, but especially someone from my background. Looking back, I feel that the providence of God was there to help me find the man that I did. Mike has been a good husband to me in many ways. We had very little going for us when we married, but we both had a deep commitment to the Lord. We believed that marriage was "for a lifetime."

Everyone comes to marriage with baggage, but in my case, my cart was full and running over. I had major issues that I needed to deal with and no one at eighteen years old is prepared and equipped to handled that kind of problem. I brought eighteen years of abuse, anger, hurt, and resentment into our marriage. Now that I was out from under Dad's control, I was no longer afraid to express my pent up feelings. Unfortunately, I took them out on Mike. I hurt the dearest, best person I had in life in the process.

We fought a lot. I felt so frustrated. Many times I knew it was a plea for help. Mike didn't have a clue what I was dealing with. Mike was raised in a good home. He loved and respected his father. With his love for his own father, I can't imagine how Mike must have felt when he heard me say how much I hated my father and wanted him dead.

We were ashamed of our problems. We didn't talk to any Christians in the local church about them. They wouldn't understand. After all, their marriages were all "perfect." I was sure that they didn't fight—not like Mike and me.

Mike was in school in Indianapolis at Christian Theologial Seminary. They had a counseling program there. He decided to take me there in order to get me "fixed." Naturally, in the course of counseling, Mike found he has some things that needed "fixed" as well. We were at our wits end and were so desperate to know what to do. So we went into counseling. No one knew and even now few know.

Counseling was not a magic wand. It took time and it was hard. I resented that I had to work so hard. Remember, I was the "victim." But in the end, counseling is what saved our marriage and I was better for having worked through the things I had to change. Little by little, over several years, things did change for the better.

4. Hurting my daughter. In all the things I suffered from my abuse, I think this one was the worst. Mike and I were married for six years when we decided to have a baby. I wanted children, but I was afraid to have children and didn't because I didn't want to treat them like my father treated me. Children are a blessing from God and I am so thankful to have two of them—a girl and a boy. They have brought so much joy and happiness to my life that I couldn't begin to tell you all of it. Parents, we owe our children the best we can be. There are no "perfect" homes and no "perfect" parents. We all make mistakes. But, if you know you have major problems in your marriage when you are considering having children, work out those problems before bringing a child into an already difficult situation.

Unfortunately, that is not what we did. We had not started counseling when our first child was born. Then I realized the horrible anger my father had with me now I was taking out on her. There was no physical abuse but there was verbal abuse which can be just as destructive. A counselor friend of mine said, "Hurt people hurt people." I saw my father in my relationship with my child. I was devastated. Paul said in Romans 7:19, "For the good that I would I do not: but the evil which I would not, that I do." We all do bad things we never intended to do. We don't always accomplish the good we mean to. I am thankful to say, I did get help and I have a good relationship with my daughter. She is one of the dearest people on earth to me and she has forgiven me, but I still find it hard to forgive myself. I guess at that time, I could understand Daddy a little better.

5. Effect on my brothers. The abuse in our home affected my brothers just like it affected me. My oldest brother, Gary, was killed in an automobile accident when he was twenty-one. After he left home, he was involved in drinking and drugs. My middle brother, Greg, is a recovering alcoholic. He told me that his last memory of Dad was when he beat him so hard that he peed his pants. Greg was baptized in high school but left the church when he left home. My youngest brother, Michael, was two when Dad died. He doesn't have any memory of the abuse. He too drinks. Only one of my brothers obeyed the gospel and none of them is faithful to the Lord at this time. I mention this to emphasize the impact that an abusive home life has on the children.

Getting Past the Past
People who hear of my home life ask me, "How did you end up where you are today?" Here are some things that helped me. I found the following Indian folktake that expresses my thoughts.

The Wolves Within . . .
An old Grandfather said to his grandson, who came to him with anger at a friend who had done him an injustice.

I too, at times, have felt great hate for those who have taken so much, with no sorrow for what they do. But hate wears you down, and does not hurt your enemy. It's like taking poison and wishing your enemy would die. I have struggled with these feelings many times.

It is as if there are two wolves inside me; one is good and does no harm. He lives in harmony with all around him and does not take offense when no offense was intended. He will only fight when it is right to do so, and in the right way.

But . . . the other wolf . . . ah! The littlest thing will send him into a fit

471

of temper. He fights everyone, all of the time, for no reason. He cannot think because his anger and hate are so great. It is helpless anger, for his anger will change nothing.

Sometimes it is hard to live with these two wolves inside me, for both of them try to dominate my spirit.

The boy looked intently into his Grandfather's eyes and asked, "Which one wins, Grandfather?"

The Grandfather smiled and quietly said, "The one I feed."

I had to learn to quit "feeding" my hatred and bitterness to become victorious over them. Here are some things that helped me:

Ask God for help. During my time of deepest depression, I was told to pray and read my Bible and that is all that I needed to deal with my problems. Don't misunderstand me. I truly believe in prayer. I did a lot of praying and felt that God was with me, no matter how dark the place. I did read my Bible. I found great comfort in the following passages:

The righteous cry, and the Lord heareth, and delivereth them out of all their troubles (Ps. 34:17).

God is our refuge and strength, a very present help in trouble (Ps. 46:1).

But the LORD is my defence; and my God is the rock of my refuge (Ps. 94:22).

This last passage means so much to me. There were times in the darkness of depression that it was a comfort to know that God was with me there in the dark with "his arms around me."

Thou tellest my wanderings: put thou my tears into thy bottle: are they not in thy book? (Ps. 56:8).

God knows that we hurt—that we cry—and he is there to comfort us.

I believe that God did answer my prayers. He let me seek out the help I needed. He will help us, but we first must do our part. I had choices in dealing with my problems. I could try to ignore them and go on or deal with them and then go on. I sought out and received professional counseling. I have learned that seeking out professional help is nothing to be ashamed of. If one has heart problems, he goes to a heart specialist. If one is having trouble overcoming problems from her past, why not go to those who have special training to help one overcome those problems? There is no shame in getting help with emotional problems, problems created by the scars of sin. In my case, medication was needed. One needs to work with her doctor to help find what is needed. Some problems can be resolved with the help of a preacher or elder, but some problems need more professional help.

I have heard some preachers say that those who take anti-depressants are manifesting a lack of faith in God. I have reached an age in my life when I do not need someone else's approval to do what I need to do. However, there was a time when I did not have this self-confidence. Medical doctors are making great progress in understanding the chemical interactions in the brain which contribute to depression and they have developed some medicines which provide help to those who are depressed. What they have already learned helped me to attain some normalcy in my life. How tragic that someone speaking on a subject in which he is not trained might deprive others of the help they need!

Seek support from other Christians. Solomon wrote, ". . .in the multitude of counsellors there is safety" (Prov. 24:6). We were fortunate to have found some Christians who encouraged us and supported us while we worked through our problems. Paul wrote, "Bear ye one another's burdens, and so fulfil the law of Christ" (Gal. 6:2). We gained great comfort and counsel from Elwood and Polly Phillips. I felt like they were my spiritual mom and dad and in so many ways I felt like a daughter to them. They gave us much love and support.

Accept God's forgiveness. Paul wrote, "Brethren, I count not myself to have apprehended: but this one thing I do, forgetting those things which are behind, and reaching forth unto those things which are before, Notwithstanding ye have well done, that ye did communicate with my affliction" (Phil. 3:13-14). One cannot live in the past. The past *is* past. If we need to make the effort to work through past problems, we should do so and then we need to put them behind us and press forward.

Give others some slack. I have learned that sometimes one makes harsh judgments on brothers and sisters who are hurting, without understanding how far they have come and what efforts they are making to live righteously.

Jesus said,

> Judge not, that ye be not judged. For with what judgment ye judge, ye shall be judged: and with what measure ye mete, it shall be measured to you again. . . . Or how wilt thou say to thy brother, Let me pull out the mote out of thine eye; and, behold, a beam is in thine own eye? Thou hypocrite, first cast out the beam out of thine own eye; and then shalt thou see clearly to cast out the mote out of thy brother's eye (Matt. 7:1-2, 4-5).

Jesus told the story of the widow's mite (Luke 21:1-4). I wonder how we might have judged this woman, based solely on outward appearances. If we saw her and didn't know her circumstances, would we criticize her for how little she gave? A lot of people are making a great effort to give what they can, and we are so busy criticizing what they are doing or not doing. We overlook the changes we need to make and focus on others. I believe that, if we have a "beam" in our eyes, we *can't* see clearly the circumstances. Who are we to judge another's heart?

When I find myself being too judgmental, I try to remember where I have been and the struggle it was for me to be at services, having a heavy burden on my heart. As Job said about some of his friends, that they were miserable comforters (16:2), some of us may also be miserable comforters. God knew my circumstances and he was patient with me. Are we patient with our brethren? The passage in Matthew 7 say that with what judgment you use on others God will use on you. God will judge you by that same judgment. Some of us need to change our "measuring stick." 2 Corinthians 2:7 says that we ought to forgive and comfort the penitent sinner so he will not be overwhelmed by excessive sorrow. Matthew 18:6 says, "But whoso shall offend one of these little ones which believe in me, it were better for him that a millstone were hanged about his neck, and that he were drowned in the depth of the sea."

Let us comfort and help those who are hurting, not kick them when they are down!

Conclusion

When Mike asked me if I would speak on this subject, at first I said, "Okay!" But as I began to think about what I would say, I tried to back out a number of times. If you were to ask the other speakers whose subject had them dealing with their painful past, I am pretty sure that they would say the same as I do. This has taken me back to places I didn't want to revisit. I feel that I have worked through my past and look to the future. But the pain will never go away and one has to *press on.*

There is a line in one of my favorite movies which I truly believe. It says, "That which does not kill us, makes us stronger!" Although I probably would change my past were I able, I realize that my past is what made me what I am today and who I am today. I think you call that "character." James said, "My brethren, count it all joy when ye fall into divers temptations; Knowing this, that the trying of your faith worketh patience" (1:2-3).

I hope that by telling my story, I can be a help to some of you. Paul wrote, "Blessed be God, even the Father of our Lord Jesus Christ, the Father of mercies, and the God of all comfort; Who comforteth us in all our tribulation, that we may be able to comfort them which are in any trouble, by the comfort wherewith we ourselves are comforted of God" (2 Cor. 1:3-4). Don't feel embarrassed to share your struggles. All of us go through things, but if we can open up, we can help others working through the same problems. And even if you aren't struggling with these kinds of problems, be alert to the possibility that there may be someone sitting near you at services who is.

Now I know why I needed to do this lecture!

(I dedicate this lecture to my daughter, Jenny. Know that I have always loved and cherished you! Thank you for being a good mother to my grand-sons, Corbin and Ian.)